D0850414

SOCIETY
POLITICS
& ECONOMIC
DEVELOPMENT

SOCIETY
POLITICS
& ECONOMIC
DEVELOPMENT

A QUANTITATIVE APPROACH

BY IRMA ADELMAN AND CYNTHIA TAFT MORRIS

THE JOHNS HOPKINS PRESS, BALTIMORE

WILMINGTON COLLEGE Library WILMINGTON N C

Copyright © 1967 by The Johns Hopkins Press
Baltimore, Maryland 21218

Manufactured in the United States of America

Library of Congress Catalog Card Number 67–21582

All Rights Reserved

HC59
.7
.A73

To
Our Mothers
who bore us
and
Our Husbands
who don't

50925

PREFACE

This book constitutes an attempt to bridge the gap between the theory and the practice of economic development by means of a systematic statistical analysis of social, political, and economic characteristics of nations at varying stages of economic development. A rather detailed interpretation of the results of the analysis leads to an interdisciplinary theory of economic development which is both concrete and comprehensive. Many of the specific conclusions will not be unfamiliar to those well versed in economic development problems in a particular country or region. Nevertheless, the major contribution of the present investigation lies in its relatively rigorous demonstration that the applicability of some of the most commonly held generalizations about economic growth varies greatly with the level of socioeconomic development. In addition, the methodology developed here for analyzing the multifaceted nature of the process of economic growth is applicable and appropriate to further interdisciplinary research in this area. We are, of course, well aware that the conclusions reached on the basis of the present factor analyses need further study and confirmation both through more intensive investigation of contemporary developing countries and by careful inquiry into the historical process of economic growth in those countries that are presently the most prosperous. For this purpose a factor analytic investigation of the historical characteristics of economic growth is currently being undertaken by the present authors.

We are grateful to the Office of Program Coordination of the Agency for International Development for financing the initial stage of our research upon which Chapter IV of this book is based. We are also highly indebted to the National Science Foundation for a three-year grant (GS669) to The American University which provided the major support for the research project. Finally, we are greatly appreciative of the Ford Foundation's Faculty Research Fellowship to Irma Adelman which permitted her to devote a large part of her time to the book during 1965–66.

We wish to acknowledge with gratitude the permission of the *Quarterly Journal of Economics* and of *Economic Development and Cultural Change* to include in this book work previously published in these journals.

Our obligations to individual persons are numerous and varied. We are grateful to Hollis Chenery for making possible the original launching of our investigation. At various stages of research and writing we have benefited greatly from comments, criticisms, and helpful suggestions from David Cole, George Dalton, Everett Hagen, Jonathan Hughes, Max Millikan, Joan Nelson, Karl de Schweinitz, and Alan Strout. In addition, we owe a special debt to Frank Adelman whose detailed critical editing of Chapters V through VIII significantly improved their clarity, style, and content. Our thanks are due also to Charlotte Greenfield for her contribution to the basic research during the summer of 1965 and to Garrett Coleman for his good sense, intelligence, and energy in the preparation of the basic data for all the economic indicators and in the interviewing of experts to validate country classifications. A large number of regional and country experts at the Agency for International Development, the Department of State, the International Monetary Fund, and the Department of Agriculture were extremely helpful in the classification of individual countries with respect to the various indicators included in the study, although final responsibility for both the country classifications and the results of the study rests with the authors. For the excellent job of typing the manuscript and tables we are greatly obligated to Ann James, Pauline Jackson, and Margaret Moe. Finally we should like to express our deep gratitude to our respective husbands for their patience and for the encouragement they have given to our work.

Evanston, Illinois   Irma Adelman
Washington, D.C.   Cynthia Taft Morris
April, 1967

TABLE OF CONTENTS

SOCIETY
POLITICS
& ECONOMIC
DEVELOPMENT

CHAPTER I INTRODUCTION

The interdependence of economic growth and sociopolitical change is generally recognized by social scientists. Development economists in particular are aware that key economic functions used in analyzing advanced economies may take quite different forms in less-developed countries for reasons that are largely political, social, and institutional.[1] However, efforts to extend growth analyses to include noneconomic factors are hampered by the absence of empirical knowledge about the manner in which they operate.

The best method for studying the interaction of economic and noneconomic forces in development would be cooperative research by interdisciplinary teams of social scientists. Unfortunately, few noneconomists have shown interest in comparative empirical investigation of the process of economic growth.[2] It may be desirable, therefore, for development

---

[1] See, for example, B. F. Hoselitz, "Noneconomic Factors in Economic Development," *American Economic Review*, Vol. 47 (May, 1957), pp. 28-41; Benjamin Higgins, "An Economist's View," UNESCO, *Social Aspects of Economic Development in Latin America, II* (New York: National Agency for International Publications, 1963), 141–251, esp. 178–82; P. A. Baran, *The Political Economy of Growth* (New York: Monthly Review Press, 1957); and Karl Polanyi, *The Great Transformation* (Boston: Beacon Press, 1957).

[2] There are, of course, excellent analytical and interpretive studies of development by political scientists and sociologists as well as a few studies by anthropologists. See the bibliography of this book for selected references to these works. There have also been a number of empirical investigations into the social and political characteristics of underdeveloped nations. See, for example, Arthur Banks and Robert Textor, *A Cross-Polity Survey* (Cambridge: M.I.T. Press, 1964), and Bruce M. Russett *et al.*, *World Handbook of Political and Social Indicators* (New Haven, Conn.: Yale University Press, 1964). Two recent comparative studies that use the technique of factor analysis to investigate the characteristics of both developed and underdeveloped nations are P. M. Gregg and A. S. Banks, "Dimensions of Political Systems: Factor Analysis of a Cross-Polity Survey," *American Political Science Review*, LIX, No. 3 (1965), 602–14, and R. J. Rummel, "The Dimensionality of Nations Project," in *Comparing Nations,* ed. Richard Merritt and Stein Rokkan (New Haven, Conn.: Yale University Press, 1966).

3

economists to take the initiative in pursuing and stimulating empirical research in this area.

Our analysis is an attempt to gain more precise empirical knowledge about the interdependence of economic and noneconomic aspects of the development process. Such an analysis will serve two purposes. First, it will suggest hypotheses relating noneconomic to economic variables that are both suitable for testing by more intensive analyses and relevant to the central concerns of development economics. Second, it will under-score the need for more exact knowledge about the interactions of the development process and should therefore stimulate interdisciplinary research.

More specifically, we attempt to gain semiquantitative insights into the relationship of various types of social, economic, and political change with the level and pace of economic development. For this purpose, we defined forty-one indicators of sociopolitical and economic organization and development. They included both quantitative variables and indicators of important qualitative characteristics of countries: for example, the size of the traditional agricultural sector, the importance of the indigenous middle class, the political strength of the traditional elite, the extent of urbanization, and the degree of improvement in financial institutions since 1950. Seventy-four underdeveloped countries were classified with regard to each of these indicators, in most instances for the period 1957–62. We then applied the technique of factor analysis to these data in order to derive their systematic underlying associations.

A few words about this technique are in order. Factor analysis was originally developed by psychologists in connection with the study of mental attributes. It is a branch of the analysis of variance that is pri-marily useful in areas of investigation where adequate theoretical models cannot be developed. Like most statistical methods, factor analysis is a technique for simplifying a mass of data and discovering its underlying regularities. In our case, the original explanatory variables are reduced— by a set of predetermined mathematical rules specific to factor analysis —to a smaller number of independent factors (or clusters of variables that the method has shown to be closely related) in terms of which the whole set of variables can be more easily understood and studied. In addition, the system shows the relative importance of each variable to each of the factors developed. Factor analysis, therefore, reduces a com-plex, unclear phenomenon to its basic components and provides insights into the relative importance of the forces that each component represents.

It is a noteworthy property of the method by which the factors are formed that, once the data input into the analysis is specified, the investigator has no additional control over which combinations of variables are amalgamated into factors and how much weight each variable is assigned in each factor. In view of this, factor analysis can serve as an important vehicle for generating hypotheses concerning the structural properties of a process, even when no good theories exist.

This current investigation is the outgrowth of our previously published study of the relationships between per capita income and selected indices of social and political structure.[3] The current extension of the earlier study focuses primarily upon the dynamics of the development process. It represents not only a substantial enlargement in the scope of our investigation, but also provides a much clearer picture of the process by which economic growth may be induced and of the systematic changes in the pattern of interaction between specific economic and noneconomic forces in development.

The investigation makes several contributions. First, it introduces qualitative characteristics of developing countries into a quantitative analysis of economic growth. As a result, the analysis provides a feeling for the quantitative importance of current generalizations about the various economic and noneconomic impediments to the economic performance of low-income countries. In addition, the study yields an indication of the degree to which even the most common "universal" propositions apply to a varying extent at different levels of socioeconomic development. It therefore goes some way toward supplying a link between the theory of economic growth on the one hand, and development policy on the other, by yielding results that both incorporate institutional attributes and differentiate between different classes of underdeveloped countries. None of the particular findings for countries at different levels of development would be surprising to those familiar with the nature of the entire spectrum of developing nations; nevertheless, the results are of interest in the degree to which they bear out or modify conclusions reached by specialists in development policy.

The next two chapters lay the groundwork for the investigation undertaken in the rest of the book. Chapter II describes the choice of economic, social, and political indices that are used in our study. The reasons

[3] Irma Adelman and Cynthia T. Morris, "A Factor Analysis of the Interrelationship between Social and Political Variables and Per Capita Gross National Product," *Quarterly Journal of Economics,* Vol. 79 (November, 1965), pp. 555–78.

for the selection of each of the forty-one variables is discussed and a detailed definitional scheme is presented together with the individual country classifications. Chapter III is devoted to a discussion of the technique of factor analysis. After a summary of the general characteristics of the method, the statistical model is presented and the practical problems arising from its application are discussed. The reader who is not familiar with mathematics should read only the introduction to this chapter and the sections describing the practical problems of the technique. In Chapter IV the findings of our investigation of the long-run relationship between broad levels of economic development, as represented by per capita GNP, and the transformations in social and political institutions and cultural values associated with economic modernization are presented. From this analysis, the results of the long-run study are then used to group the seventy-four underdeveloped countries into subgroups representing three levels of socioeconomic development. Thus, Chapters II through IV prepare the stage for our short-run analyses of economic growth by setting forth the data and technique of analysis and by establishing the principles of sample selection.

Chapters V through VII present our investigations of the growth process in the short run in countries at each of three stages of socioeconomic development: the lowest stage in which economic activity tends to be embedded in traditional social organization and values; the intermediate level in which, although the spread of the market economy has proceeded relatively far, economic growth is still seriously impeded by the uneven pace of social development and the ineffectiveness of government; and the highest of the three levels where sociostructural bottlenecks are no longer significant barriers to economic and political measures aimed at promoting development. In each chapter the presentation of findings and discussion of results is preceded by a brief typology of the countries composing the sample. The broad picture of the development process that emerges is set forth in Chapter VIII. We conclude this final chapter with a discussion of the policy implications of the analysis with regard to development policy and foreign aid strategy from the point of view of both the donor and the recipient nation.

In general, our results reveal an intimate association between the pace of economic progress and noneconomic forces. Our findings also indicate that the nature and importance of the noneconomic "determinants" of economic dynamism tend to vary systematically with the stage of a country's socioeconomic development. At the lowest level, characteristic of sub-Saharan Africa, social forces are typically the most important non-economic influence upon economic activity, with political change, on the whole, exercising a negligible impact. By contrast, at the highest of the three levels studied, it is political forces that are crucial to economic performance, while social influences have little systematic effect. Economic forces are important throughout, but it is only at the highest relative level of development that they assume their full significance. In addition, the nature of the relevant economic forces tends to vary with the stage of development, with the more specialized economic institutions gaining full weight in explaining differences in rates of economic growth only at the highest level of socioeconomic development. Thus, the broad view of development that emerges is one in which social and political transformations and economic modernization interact in patterns that themselves change as countries progress to higher levels of socioeconomic development.

CHAPTER II
SOCIAL, POLITICAL, & ECONOMIC INDICATORS

In this chapter the choice of indicators of social, political, and economic structure is described in some detail and the choice of sample and numerical scoring scheme is discussed. In presenting the selection of indicators, the general procedures followed in classifying countries are summarized and the principles guiding the choice of variables are examined. Then, for each of the forty-one variables included in the study, a brief discussion of the reasons for inclusion and a description of the methods and sources used in classifying countries are presented, followed by a statement of the classification scheme with the letter scores for the individual countries.

THE SAMPLE

In our choice of sample, we sought to include a broad spectrum of countries which, as of 1950, were underdeveloped with respect to social and economic structure. The date 1950 was chosen because our short-run dynamic analysis was concerned with changes that occurred during the period 1950–64.[1] Developed countries were excluded because we wished to focus primarily on the process of transition as countries at low levels of development move from economic stagnation into a stage of self-sustained growth. Initially, therefore, we included all non-European countries that, as of 1950 or thereafter, were in receipt of intergovernmental aid from the United States. While the great majority of these countries had achieved independence by 1962, we did not require that they be independent but only that they be recognized national units.

There were two exclusions of less-developed countries from the sample which should be noted. A few non-European countries receiving United States assistance were dropped from the sample after preliminary data

[1] The study thus includes several countries in which per capita GNP, while low in 1950, had by 1964 become relatively high. These countries, strictly speaking, may no longer be considered underdeveloped.

were collected because the sources of information to which we had access proved inadequate. The major exclusion, and the one most likely to introduce a bias in our results, was that of the less-developed communist countries. The reason for excluding these countries was the overwhelming lack of comparable data, particularly with regard to various aspects of economic structure. It is true that data were also poor for a number of noncommunist countries which we did include in the sample; however, in classifying the latter countries according to their economic, social, and political characteristics, we had access to the judgments of a large number of regional experts. The resources available during our research were not sufficient for us to gather a similar volume of judgment on communist countries.

The seventy-four countries included in our final sample are listed below:[2]

Afghanistan	Indonesia
Algeria	Iran
Argentina	Iraq
Bolivia	Israel
Brazil	Republic of the Ivory Coast
Burma	(Ivory Coast)
Cambodia	Jamaica
Federal Republic of Cameroun	Japan
(Cameroun)	Jordan
Ceylon	Republic of Kenya (Kenya)
Republic of Chad (Chad)	Korea (South Korea)
Chile	Laos
Republic of China (Taiwan)	Lebanon
Colombia	Liberia
Costa Rica	Libya
Cyprus	Malagasy Republic (Malagasy)
Dahomey	Malawi
Dominican Republic	Mexico
Ecuador	Morocco
El Salvador	Nepal
Ethiopia	Republic of Niger (Niger)
Republic of Gabon (Gabon)	Nigeria
Ghana	Nicaragua
Greece	Pakistan
Guatemala	Panama
Republic of Guinea (Guinea)	Paraguay
Honduras	Peru
India	Philippines

[2] The names used in listing countries in the country classification schemes, where different from the official names, are given in parentheses.

Rhodesia	Trinidad
Republic of Senegal (Senegal)	Tunisia
Sierra Leone	Turkey
Somali Republic	Uganda
South Africa	United Arab Republic (U.A.R.)
Sudan	Uruguay
Surinam	Venezuela
Syrian Arab Republic (Syria)	Vietnam (South Vietnam)
Tanganyika	Yemen
Thailand	Zambia

Several decisions regarding the choice of appropriate national units should be noted. On the advice of regional experts, we considered the members of the Federation of Rhodesia and Nyasaland as separate national units, although they were federated for most of the period on which our country classifications were based. Tanganyika rather than Tanzania was used as the appropriate national unit for reasons of data. The year in which Zanzibar and Tanganyika merged to form Tanzania, 1964, followed the period upon which most of our classifications were based; the exceptions are five dynamic variables that were defined for the period 1950 to 1964. Almost all our data, therefore, refer to Tanganyika, not Tanzania. Finally, it should be noted that "Korea" refers to South Korea, and "Vietnam" to South Vietnam.

THE VARIABLES

The variables chosen for our study were of three different types: (1) those for which classification could be based on published statistics; (2) those for which it was necessary to combine statistical and qualitative elements; and (3) those which were purely qualitative in nature. The procedures used in defining indicators and in ranking countries for each of these types will be discussed in turn.

With respect to indicators defined by published statistics, the classification of countries was relatively simple. Four to six categories were established and, where data permitted, gradations within categories were also differentiated. For several indicators, such as the extent of urbanization, the use of categories resulted in the loss of some information regarding countries for which point estimates were available. However, the grouping of data enabled us to classify countries for which we had no point estimates by means of consultation with country experts.

Sometimes more than one statistical series was used to describe a particular feature of society. The variable portraying the extent of mass

11

communication, for instance, is based upon a composite index of newspapers in circulation and radios in use. Another variable in which several statistical characteristics were combined is the degree of cultural and ethnic homogeneity, which is defined in terms of the proportion of the population speaking the same language, the extent of racial homogeneity, and the extent of religious homogeneity.[3]

A second type of indicator included in our study is distinguished by the blending of judgment with statistical data. The indicators of the extent of social mobility and the degree of national integration are examples of noneconomic variables which have both statistical and qualitative elements. In addition, most of the economic indicators are of this type. Our usual procedure with these semiquantitative indicators was to define three or, at the most, four categories in broad qualitative terms and to use statistical data to determine the exact boundaries between categories. With our indicator of the effectiveness of financial institutions, for instance, we established three main categories in terms of an over-all judgment regarding the success of financial institutions in attracting private savings and in providing medium- and long-term credit. We then employed quantitative estimates of time and demand deposits plus money as a percentage of GNP, and data on domestic savings rates to help define the limits of each category. The procedures that we used in obtaining the basic qualitative information and in cross-checking the assignment of each country to a particular category were the same as those to be described for the purely qualitative indicators.

A third type of country characteristic included in this study is the purely judgmental indicator. The majority of our social and political indicators are of this type. A primary requirement for the inclusion of a qualitative variable was that we be able to arrive at category descriptions that were sufficiently precise and inclusive to permit unambiguous classification of most countries. In almost all instances this proved possible; however, as will be discussed later, consultation with country and regional experts was indispensable for completing country classifications with respect to many of these indicators. Since the inclusion of a broad range of qualitative indicators is a distinctive feature of our investigation, we will describe in some detail the procedures used in formulating these indicators and in classifying countries with respect to them.

---

[3] For further details on the variables referred to in this section, see the discussion of the individual indicators below.

The first step in preparing the data for the definition of qualitative indicators was to examine a large number of recent country studies, published and unpublished, and to extract from them the information relevant to the characteristics in which we were interested. We then drew up a preliminary classification scheme for each of the indicators we wished to include. We used a priori reasoning to specify and rank the elements in each definitional scheme, and we determined the number of categories and the category limits in the light of the distribution of country traits and the nature of country data. We then proceeded to assign each country to a particular letter category. When our provisional country classifications were as complete as preliminary data permitted, it became evident that the basic information for a number of variables[4] was sufficiently inadequate to warrant a sizable intake of expert opinion in order that the country classifications be complete and valid. We therefore circulated to about thirty country and regional experts a description of the classification schemes and a list of countries we had not been able to classify. A combination of written answers and interviews was used to obtain their opinions. For the remaining indicators that incorporated qualitative elements, interviews were used primarily as a means of cross-checking preliminary country classifications rather than as a basic data input.

The use of interviews in validating our country classifications requires some comment since interviews were our principal means of resolving doubtful classifications for all of the indicators. Interviewees were presented selected sets of preliminary country classifications with a request for corrections and help with completion.[5] When more than one expert made corrections of an individual country classification which were consistent in direction and degree, we accepted the corrections without further study. Where corrections were consistent with respect to direction but differed somewhat in degree, a rough average of the corrections was

---

[4] The degree of social tension, the extent of political stability, the degree of centralization of political power, the degree of administrative efficiency, and the extent of nationalism and sense of national unity. The last was subsequently redefined, but interview material on selected elements of the original definition remained relevant to the redefinition.

[5] The advantage of presenting experts prepared sets of preliminary classifications for criticism was the great economy in the use of time which the forms facilitated. The majority of the operational country and regional experts whom we consulted would not have had time to complete a detailed questionnaire but were willing and often intrigued to check our judgments on countries with which they were familiar.

calculated. Where corrections showed marked inconsistency and differences, an attempt was made to reformulate the categories in an effort to obtain more consistent classification of individual countries.

Another source used in cross-checking a number of political indicators and several of the social indicators was Arthur Banks's and Robert Textor's *A Cross-Polity Survey*.[6] This study provided us with basic information for four of the final variables (the degree of competitiveness of political parties, the predominant basis of the political party system, the political strength of the military, and the degree of cultural and ethnic homogeneity) and with valuable cross-checks for eight others (the degree of social tension, the degree of modernization of outlook, the strength of democratic institutions, the degree of freedom of political opposition and press, the extent of centralization of political power, the political strength of the traditional elite, the extent of leadership commitment to economic development, and the extent of political stability). Further details on sources used in cross-checking country classifications will be found in the sections on the individual indicators.

THE SCORING

Since the use of factor analysis requires that the variables be specified numerically, the final task in preparing the data was the assignment of scores to the letter classifications. It is obvious, of course, that the choice of a numerical scale for qualitative indicators is arbitrary. The scale we chose was a simple linear one which ranged from 1 to 100. We assigned a score of 90 to the highest letter classification, *A,* and a score of 10 to the lowest letter classification of each characteristic (*C, D, E,* or *F*). We then scored the intermediate letters at equidistant intervals between 10 and 90. Plus and minus classifications were not scored at equidistant intervals but were scored in such a manner that the distance between the plus and minus of different adjacent categories was approximately double the difference between any given letter classification and its plus or minus. The full scoring scheme is presented at the top of the following page.

---

[6] The raw characteristic deck of *A Cross-Polity Survey* became available to us in November, 1963, when our preliminary classification of countries was underway.

A to F	*A to E*	*A to D*	*A to C*
A+ 95	A+ 95	A+ 97	A+ 100
A 90	A 90	A 90	A 90
A− 85	A− 85	A− 83	A− 80
B+ 75	B+ 75	B+ 67	B+ 60
B 70	B 70	B 60	B 50
B− 66	B− 65	B− 54	B− 40
C+ 59	C+ 55	C+ 41	C+ 20
C 55	C 50	C 35	C 10
C− 51	C− 45	C− 29	C− 01
D+ 44	D+ 35	D+ 16	
D 40	D 30	D 10	
D− 36	D− 25	D− 04	
E+ 29	E+ 15		
E 25	E 10		
E− 21	E− 05		
F+ 14			
F 10			
F− 06			

PRINCIPLES GUIDING THE CHOICE OF INDICATORS

Before turning to a detailed consideration of the indicators, a brief explanation of the general principles influencing our choice of variables is appropriate. In making the choice, we were guided by two possibly conflicting principles: those of inclusiveness and parsimony. With respect to the first of these, we strove to represent in our measures the most important aspects of economic, social, and political institutions and performance. Since factor analysis permits the use of a relatively large number of intercorrelated variables, we wished to include a broad selection of indicators that would describe the many facets of low-income countries relevant not only to economic but also to social and political development. More specifically, the social variables were chosen to portray the principal social aspects of urbanization and industrialization; the political indicators were selected to represent leading characteristics of the emergence of modern states; and the economic indices were designed to sum-

15

marize the changes in economic structure and institutions typical of industrialization and economic growth. We found it necessary at an early stage of classifying countries to reject several indicators that appeared desirable a priori, but that could not be formulated with sufficient concreteness to permit unambiguous classifications. The importance of achievement motivation and social attitudes toward economic activity were indicators we were obliged to reject for this reason.

With respect to the second principle influencing our choice of variables, that of parsimony, we strove not to multiply our indices of any particular feature of society but rather to combine within each single classification scheme interrelated aspects of the relevant feature. In the definition of composite indicators, we sought to include closely inter-correlated traits conceptually relevant to the fundamental country characteristic we wished to describe. It should be noted, of course, that in order to avoid ambiguous statistical results an effort was made to include in any single indicator only elements that were closely interrelated. The indicator of the level of effectiveness of tax systems illustrates the application of the principle of parsimony. Three main aspects of tax systems were included in a single index: the ratio of total government revenues to GNP, the ratio of direct tax revenue to total government revenues, and the presence or absence of widespread difficulties in collecting taxes. In general, attempts to introduce into the analysis a large number of narrow indices, no one of which was adequate in itself to characterize any given feature of institutions or performance, tended to yield results that were considerably less amenable to interpretation than results obtained with broad indicators. Thus, the final choice of variables for our investigation covers a broad range of the salient sociopolitical and economic features of developing countries without, however, including a multiplicity of narrow indicators of any particular feature. These variables are listed below in the order in which they will be discussed:

Size of the Traditional Agricultural Sector
Extent of Dualism
Extent of Urbanization
Character of Basic Social Organization
Importance of the Indigenous Middle Class
Extent of Social Mobility
Extent of Literacy
Extent of Mass Communication

Degree of Cultural and Ethnic Homogeneity
Degree of Social Tension
Crude Fertility Rate
Degree of Modernization of Outlook
Degree of National Integration and Sense of National Unity
Extent of Centralization of Political Power
Strength of Democratic Institutions
Degree of Freedom of Political Opposition and Press
Degree of Competitiveness of Political Parties
Predominant Basis of the Political Party System
Strength of the Labor Movement
Political Strength of the Traditional Elite
Political Strength of the Military
Degree of Administrative Efficiency
Extent of Leadership Commitment to Economic Development
Extent of Political Stability
Per Capita GNP in 1961
Rate of Growth of Real per Capita GNP: 1950/51–1963/64
Abundance of Natural Resources
Gross Investment Rate
Level of Modernization of Industry
Change in Degree of Industrialization since 1950
Character of Agricultural Organization
Level of Modernization of Techniques in Agriculture
Degree of Improvement in Agricultural Productivity since 1950
Level of Adequacy of Physical Overhead Capital
Degree of Improvement in Physical Overhead Capital since 1950
Level of Effectiveness of the Tax System
Degree of Improvement in the Tax System since 1950
Level of Effectiveness of Financial Institutions
Degree of Improvement in Financial Institutions since 1950
Rate of Improvement in Human Resources
Structure of Foreign Trade

SOCIOCULTURAL INDICATORS

The interdependence of changes in social organization and values and economic growth has long been recognized by social scientists, although it has undergone relatively little formal investigation. Karl Marx was

17

one of the first to point to changes in social relations as a keystone in the theory of economic development. Since his time, economic historians have frequently underlined the importance of social structure in influencing the pattern of economic change. Familiar examples of their concern with social factors in the growth process are Sombart's analysis of the "spirit of capitalism" as a moving force in the rise of Western industry, Tawney's study of the impact upon economic growth of the Protestant ethic, and recent investigations into the role of social structure in explaining differences in rates of economic growth in the nineteenth century.[7] In addition, development economists almost invariably underline the importance of social transformations in initiating economic growth, although they rarely attempt to incorporate noneconomic influences into their formal theories.[8]

Sociologists and anthropologists interested in the problems of contemporary developing countries consistently stress the close interaction between the sociocultural and economic aspects of change. Hoselitz, for example, studies the process of economic growth in terms of sociological pattern variables summarizing selected types of change which can be described by transformations along a continuum from traditional communally oriented values to individualistic achievement-oriented values. Niel Smelser and others view social and economic development as part of the processes of differentiation and concomitant reintegration of social and economic structure which typically accompany industrialization and urbanization; these concepts, derived in part from the work of Durkheim

[7] See Karl Marx, *Capital, The Communist Manifesto, and Other Writings* (New York: The Modern Library, 1932), pp. 324ff.; Werner Sombart, "Capitalism," *Encyclopaedia of Social Sciences, III* (New York: Macmillan, 1930); R. H. Tawney, *Religion and the Rise of Capitalism* (New York: Harcourt, Brace and Co., 1926); Alexander Gerschenkron, *Economic Backwardness in Historical Perspective* (Cambridge: The Belknap Press, 1962); and John E. Sawyer, "Social Structure and Economic Progress: General Propositions and Some French Examples," *American Economic Review,* Vol. 41 (May, 1951), pp. 321–29.

[8] W. W. Rostow is an exception to this generalization in that his theory of stages in economic development incorporates an analysis of the social prerequisites of economic take-off. See *The Stages of Economic Growth* (New York: Cambridge University Press, 1962). The following are among the many examples of emphasis made by development economists upon noneconomic determinants of growth: Colin Clark, "The Fundamental Problems of Economic Growth," *Weltwirtschaftliches Archives,* Vol. 94 (March, 1965), pp. 1–9; A. O. Hirschman, *The Strategy of Economic Development* (New Haven, Conn.: Yale University Press, 1958), Chapter I; W. A. Lewis, *The Theory of Economic Growth* (London: George Allen and Unwin, 1955), Chapter I; and Gunnar Myrdal, *Economic Theory and Under-Developed Regions* (London: Gerald Duckworth, 1957), Chapter I.

and Parsons, have also been used by Smelser in reinterpreting the social aspects of economic change during the industrial revolution in Great Britain.[9] The work of Clifford Geertz and J. L. Sadie are examples of investigations by anthropologists which serve to emphasize the interdependence of sociocultural and economic change. J. L. Sadie writes, for example, that "the economic condition of the underdeveloped community is fundamentally a function of its socio-cultural customs and institutions, in consequence of which the generation of economic development of a people by themselves is neither more nor less than a socio-psychological process."[10]

In view of the acknowledged importance of the social and cultural aspects of the process of economic development, our study includes a wide range of sociocultural indicators. The following variables were designed to depict broad characteristics of the social structure of developing countries: the indicators of the size of the traditional agricultural sector, the extent of dualism, the character of basic social organization, the importance of an indigenous middle class, and the extent of social mobility. Additional variables were chosen to summarize further aspects of social change commonly associated with industrialization and urbanization; in particular, these were the indicators of the extent of literacy, the extent of mass communication, the degree of cultural and ethnic homogeneity, the degree of social tension, the crude fertility rate, and the degree of modernization of outlook. Finally, a direct index of the extent of urbanization was included.

Size of the Traditional Agricultural Sector

Inherent in the processes of industrialization and economic growth is a major shift of population from the agricultural to the urban industrial sector of the economy. It is typical of low-income countries that large proportions of their populations live in relatively self-contained agricultural communities in which production is primarily for local consumption.

---

[9] See B. F. Hoselitz, *Sociological Aspects of Economic Growth* (New York: The Free Press of Glencoe, 1960), Chapter II; N. J. Smelser, *The Sociology of Economic Life* (Englewood Cliffs, N.J.: Prentice-Hall, 1963), pp. 106ff.; Talcott Parsons, *The Social System* (Glencoe, Ill.: The Free Press, 1951); Emil Durkheim, *The Division of Labor in Society* (Glencoe, Ill.: The Free Press, 1949); and, finally, N. J. Smelser, *Social Change in the Industrial Revolution* (Chicago: University of Chicago Press, 1959).

[10] J. L. Sadie, "The Social Anthropology of Economic Underdevelopment," *Economic Journal*, Vol. 70 (June, 1960), p. 294.

19

These communities farm their land using traditional techniques of production which are largely determined by inherited social values and organization. As has frequently been pointed out, this conventional communal technology is unlikely to undergo significant transformation without the complex socioeconomic changes associated with the expansion of production for the market.[11] The importance to economic growth of expanding agricultural output lies partly in the need to provide increased food supplies to growing urban areas and in the additional market for domestic output created by increases in agricultural cash incomes. In addition, increases in agricultural productivity are required to release to industry the labor required for its expansion.[12] Thus, an essential aspect of the process of industrialization is the transformation of the community-determined production and exchange relationships characteristic of traditional subsistence agriculture into the more specialized and impersonal economic relationships typical of market economies.

The indicator we have chosen to summarize variations in the relative weight of the traditional agricultural sector measures the proportion of the population engaged in self-sufficient subsistence agriculture. It is well known, of course, that employment data, like most data for low-income countries, are poor or nonexistent. In most less-developed countries, until very recently censuses were taken at irregular intervals or not at all. Even where censuses have been taken, their coverage has usually been limited or their results otherwise unreliable. Furthermore, censuses usually do not include the information on different types of agricultural establishments necessary to estimate either employment or residence on farms in the nonmarket sector.

In view of the overwhelming deficiencies of the basic data on the relative size of the nonmonetized agricultural sector, we established four rather broad categories with respect to this indicator. The grouping of countries into relatively few categories enabled us, where data were lacking or inadequate, to use expert opinion in assigning countries to their appropriate category. The use of judgmental information to obtain point estimates would have been considerably less appropriate.

---

[11] See, for example, E. S. Mason in Montague Yudelman, *Africans on the Land* (Cambridge: Harvard University Press, 1964), p. vii.

[12] There are, of course, other reasons as well for the emphasis made by development economists upon the importance of increased agricultural production. See B. F. Johnston and J. W. Mellor, "The Role of Agriculture in Economic Development," *American Economic Review*, Vol. 51 (September, 1961), pp. 566–93.

The classification of individual countries with respect to the relative importance of their traditional agricultural sectors was accomplished in two stages. The first step was to obtain estimates of the proportion of the total population involved in agriculture as of about 1960. The relevant United Nations data covered less than one-third of the countries included in our investigation.[13] Estimates for about twenty-five additional countries were secured by adjusting Yale Data Program statistics on the proportion of the labor force in agriculture[14] and cross-checking the results with recent country studies. For the remaining third of the countries in the sample, principally African ones, we relied primarily upon rough estimates contained in recent country studies, both published and unpublished. The second step in the classification of countries was then to exclude the population engaged primarily in modern commercial agriculture or in indigenous cash-crop agriculture. For this purpose, qualitative information on the relative weight of different types of agriculture was relied upon to a great extent.[15] Statistical information was used, however, for the minority of countries for which it was available; in this connection, several studies made by the International Labour Organization were particularly useful.[16] Our final country classifications are, of course, only broadly indicative of the relative quantitative weight of traditional subsistence agriculture.

Four principal categories of less-developed countries were distinguished with respect to the size of their traditional subsistence sectors as of about 1960.

A. Countries with 80 per cent or more of their population in traditional subsistence agriculture in which the marketing of crops was of relatively minor importance: Afghanistan (−), Cameroun, Chad, Dahomey (+), Ethiopia, Gabon, Guinea, Laos, Liberia (−), Malagasy, Nepal, Niger, Malawi (−), Sudan (−), Tanganyika, Uganda, Yemen.

B. Countries with from 55 to 79 per cent of their population in tradi-

---

[13] See United Nations, *Compendium of Social Statistics: 1963,* Table 8.

[14] Russett *et al., World Handbook of Political and Social Indicators,* Table 50.

[15] Recent country studies were our principal sources of qualitative information. A few interviews were made to resolve doubtful cases.

[16] See in particular, *African Labour Survey* (Geneva, 1958); *Labour Survey of North Africa* (Geneva, 1960); K. C. Doctor and Hans Gallis, "Modern Sector Employment in Asian Countries: Some Empirical Estimates," *International Labour Review,* Vol. 90 (July-December, 1964), pp. 544–67; and by the same authors, "Size and Characteristics of Wage Employment in Africa: Some Statistical Estimates," *International Labour Review,* Vol. 93 (February, 1966), pp. 149–73.

tional subsistence agriculture in which the marketing of crops was of relatively minor importance: Algeria (−), Bolivia, Burma, Cambodia (+), Indonesia, Iran, Iraq, Ivory Coast, Kenya, Libya (+), Morocco, Nigeria, Pakistan, Rhodesia, Senegal, Sierra Leone, Somali Republic, South Korea, South Vietnam, Thailand, Tunisia, Zambia.

C. Countries with from 25 to 54 per cent of their population in traditional subsistence agriculture in which the marketing of crops was of relatively minor importance: Brazil, Ceylon (−), Colombia, Dominican Republic, Ecuador, El Salvador, Ghana, Guatemala (+), Honduras, India (+), Jordan, Mexico, Nicaragua, Panama (+), Paraguay, Peru (+), Philippines, Surinam, Syria, Taiwan, Turkey (+), U.A.R.

D. Countries with less than 25 per cent of their population in traditional subsistence agriculture in which the marketing of crops was of relatively minor importance: Argentina, Chile, Costa Rica, Cyprus, Greece, Israel (−), Jamaica, Japan, Lebanon, South Africa, Trinidad, Uruguay, Venezuela.

Extent of Dualism

One of the most striking characteristics of the socioeconomic structure of many developing nations is that, side by side with a dominant traditional sector in which conventional techniques and communal self-sufficiency prevail, there exists a rapidly growing exchange sector. Technology in the exchange sector tends to be modern where expansion has been largely the result of foreign investment in extractive, plantation, or estate activities; it tends to be traditional where expansion has taken place through shifts of indigenous producers into the small-scale cultivation of cash crops. Partly as a consequence of the limited interaction between the two sectors, varying degrees of dualism affect many facets of life in these countries. In defining dualism some authors emphasize the marked contrast in social organization and cultural style between the traditional subsistence and exchange sectors.[17] Others underline the presence of technological dualism as an outcome of the growth along sharply differing production functions of modern exchange sectors and traditional

[17] The best known example is J. H. Boeke, *Economics and Economic Policy of Dual Societies* (New York: Institute of Pacific Relations, 1953).

sectors.[18] Still others have taken the more eclectic view of dualism as typically involving a wide range of economic and social dichotomies.[19]

It is to be expected that the presence and extent of socioeconomic and technical dualism might have a marked effect on the path of economic growth. Arthur Lewis, among the best-known of those economists who have incorporated the fact of dualism into a model of growth, underlines the importance to the expansion of a modern capitalist sector of surplus labor obtainable from subsistence agriculture in which the marginal product tends toward zero.[20] More recently, Fei and Ranis have viewed growth under economic dualism as the key analytically important stage of development as countries proceed from essentially stagnant agrarian economies toward economic maturity.[21]

In classifying countries with respect to the extent of dualism, we have attempted to rank them on a scale, one pole of which is the largely agrarian society having an extremely small exchange sector and the other pole of which is the incipient stage of economic maturity in which continuous interaction between modern and nonmodern elements in the economic system is a pervasive phenomenon. Intermediate points along the scale are defined by two types of dualistic growth: one type in which a foreign-financed and -directed, technically advanced sector is superimposed upon a predominantly agrarian society; the other in which the growth of an indigenous small-scale cash-crop sector using conventional techniques evolves at the expense of a traditional subsistence sector.[22] The former type is ranked as more highly dualistic than the latter since it involves a more marked cleavage and contrast between the nonmonetized traditional sector and the market sector with respect to socioeconomic structure and technology. In this type of dualistic economy the over-

[18] See R. S. Eckaus, "The Factor-Proportions Problem in Underdeveloped Areas," *American Economic Review,* Vol. 45 (September, 1955), pp. 539–65.

[19] See, for example, W. J. Barbour, *The Economy of British Central Africa* (Stanford: Stanford University Press, 1961), p. 4.

[20] W. A. Lewis, "Economic Development with Unlimited Supplies of Labour," *Manchester School of Economic and Social Studies,* Vol. 22 (May, 1954), pp. 139–91; and by the same author, "Unlimited Labour: Further Notes," *Manchester School of Economic and Social Studies,* Vol. 26 (January, 1958), pp. 1–32.

[21] J. C. H. Fei and Gustav Ranis, "Agrarianism, Dualism and Economic Development," in *The Theory and Design of Economic Development,* ed. Irma Adelman and Erik Thorbecke (Baltimore: The Johns Hopkins Press, 1966), pp. 3–41.

[22] For a useful characterization of these two types of dualistic economic growth see United Nations, Department of Economic Affairs, *Structure and Growth of Selected African Economies* (New York, 1958), pp. 1–5.

whelming preponderance of the economy often remains relatively untouched by the rise of the market sector. The second type of dualistic economy in which an important market sector consists largely of indigenous cash-crop production and related activities is ranked as further removed from an unchanging traditional agrarian society since it tends to alter patterns of activity and incentives within traditional indigenous communal societies more rapidly. The lowest category in the indicator of the extent of dualism includes those overwhelmingly agricultural economies that are not dualistic because the extent of their modern exchange sectors is negligible.

The precise criteria used in classifying countries with respect to the extent of dualism as of about 1960 and the individual classifications are presented below.

A. Countries characterized by some significant modernization of methods of production in almost all sectors of the economy and in which there is no clear-cut sectoral or geographic cleavage between the modern and nonmodern segments of the economy; that is, traditional and modern production methods exist side by side in almost all sectors of the economy: Argentina, Chile, Cyprus, Greece, Israel, Jamaica, Japan (+), Lebanon, South Africa (−), Taiwan, Trinidad, Uruguay.

B. Countries characterized by a moderately definite sectoral or geographic cleavage between (1) an important industrial and/or mining and/or agricultural exchange sector in which modern technology may or may not prevail and (2) a predominantly nonmonetized sector in which traditional hand and animal production methods prevail. Countries in this category differ from those in category C in two respects: (1) a single, geographically distinct, traditional nonmonetized sector is not overwhelmingly predominant; if such a sector exists, it tends to be less important than the exchange sector; (2) these countries have only moderately contrasting socioeconomic organization and styles of life between the exchange sector and the traditional nonmonetized sector. Included in this category and classified B− are a number of countries in which the exchange sector consists of important, large, modern, expatriate or government activities and significant indigenous small-scale commercial enterprises, in which there is also a fairly large and distinct nonmonetized traditional sector: Algeria (−), Brazil, Ceylon, Colombia, Costa Rica, Dominican Republic, Ecuador, El Salvador, Ghana, India, Ivory Coast (−), Jordan, Kenya (−), Mexico, Nicaragua, Nigeria (−), Pakistan,

24

Panama, Paraguay (−), Philippines, Rhodesia, South Korea, Syria, Surinam (−), Thailand, Turkey, U.A.R., Venezuela.

C. Countries in which there is a sharp and pervasive sectoral or geographic cleavage between an important exchange sector and an important traditional nonmonetized sector. These countries are characterized by (1) a sharp contrast between levels of technology, types of economic organization, and social styles of life in the exchange sector and the traditional sector and (2) by the predominance of a traditional nonmonetized sector in which strong traditional patterns of social organization remain relatively untouched by the activities of the exchange sector in spite of significant intermittent labor flows into the exchange sector: Bolivia, Burma, Cameroun (−), Gabon (+), Guatemala (+), Honduras, Indonesia, Iran (+), Iraq (+), Liberia, Libya (+), Morocco (+), Peru (+), Senegal (−), Sierra Leone (−), South Vietnam, Sudan (+), Tanganyika (−), Tunisia (+), Uganda (+), Zambia (+).

D. Countries not characterized by significant dualism by reason of the extremely limited development of their exchange sector combined with the overwhelming predominance of the nonmonetized traditional sector: Afghanistan, Cambodia (+), Chad (−), Dahomey (−), Ethiopia, Guinea, Laos, Malagasy, Malawi, Nepal (−), Niger (−), Somali Republic, Yemen (−).

Extent of Urbanization

The positive association of urbanization with industrialization and economic growth is well known. Cities provide concentrations of population from which industrial labor may be drawn; they also contain a greater variety of skills and resources than do rural areas. Even more important perhaps, urbanization promotes values favorable to entrepreneurship and industrial growth; in particular, cities typically tend to favor a propensity to analyze traditional institutions and to innovate and accept change since, in the relatively impersonal and fragmented setting of urban life, the all-embracing bonds of traditional community systems are difficult to maintain.[23] This, of course, is not to say that urbanization necessarily leads to industrialization; indeed, it is common knowledge that centuries before the industrial revolution cities developed as seats of government,

[23] For discussion of the importance of urbanization to economic growth, see B. F. Hoselitz, "The Role of Cities in the Economic Development of Underdeveloped Countries," in *Sociological Aspects of Economic Growth,* pp. 159–84.

centers of learning, and foci for the expansion of commerce.[24] Neverthe-less, from a contemporary point of view, industrialization cannot proceed far without some degree of urbanization. Some writers hold the view that in actuality urbanization is the first phase in the economic and politi-cal modernization of a nation and that until a country reaches some critical minimum extent of urbanization, substantial extensions of literacy, mass communication, and the associated capacity for industrialization are impossible.[25] Once a certain degree of urbanization is reached, however, the importance of further urbanization to economic growth probably declines. Even countries at low levels of socioeconomic development (with less than 20 per cent of their population in cities) may be over-urbanized in the sense that the flow of the underemployed from the countryside is greater than can be absorbed by the expansion of urban industrial enterprise, at least in the short run. When this occurs, social discontent arising from unemployment, poverty, and dissatisfied aspira-tions may be aggravated by the process of urbanization and as a conse-quence the process of development may be slowed down.[26]

In general, it seems likely that, once some minimum extent of urbaniza-tion is reached, the importance of cities in the process of economic development lies less in their more concentrated provision of human resources than in their role as an agent in fostering those changes in social structure and values that are essential to entrepreneurial activity, occupa-tional mobility, and thus, indirectly, to economic growth.

Our indicator of the extent of urbanization is a straightforward statisti-cal one in which all the data were obtained from a prepublication copy of *Urbanization: Expanding Population and Shrinking World* made avail-able to us through the courtesy of the Urban Land Institute.[27] In fact, it is notable that this indicator is the only one included in our study for which a complete series of recent and comparable data was available. The fol-lowing are categories into which we grouped the countries in our sample with respect to the proportion of the population living in urban areas containing over 20,000 people.

[24] *Ibid.,* p. 163.
[25] See, for example, Daniel Lerner, *The Passing of Traditional Society* (Glencoe, Ill.: The Free Press, 1958), pp. 61ff.
[26] See P. M. Hauser, "The Social, Economic, and Technological Problems of Rapid Urbanization," in *Industrialization and Society,* ed. B. F. Hoselitz and W. E. Moore (Paris: UNESCO-Mouton, 1963), pp. 199–217.
[27] Technical Bulletin No. 43 (Washington, D.C., 1966), Table III.

A. Countries with 30 per cent or more of their total population in urban areas of 20,000 or more inhabitants: Argentina (+), Chile, Colombia, Greece (−), Israel (+), Lebanon, Japan (+), Mexico (−), Philippines, South Africa (−), Surinam, U.A.R., Uruguay (−), Venezuela.

B. Countries with at least 20 but less than 30 per cent of their total population in urban areas of 20,000 or more inhabitants: Bolivia, Brazil, Ecuador (−), Jamaica, Morocco, Nicaragua (−), Panama (+), Peru, Rhodesia, South Korea, Syria (+), Taiwan (+), Turkey.

C. Countries with at least 10 but less than 20 per cent of their total population in urban areas of 20,000 or more inhabitants: Algeria (+), Costa Rica (−), Cyprus (−), Dominican Republic, El Salvador, Ghana (−), Guatemala (−), Honduras (−), India, Indonesia, Iran (+), Iraq (+), Libya (+), Paraguay (+), Senegal, South Vietnam (+), Thailand, Trinidad, Tunisia (+).

D. Countries with at least 5 but less than 10 per cent of their total population in urban areas of 20,000 or more inhabitants: Afghanistan, Burma, Cambodia (+), Ceylon (+), Dahomey (−), Gabon (−), Guinea, Ivory Coast, Jordan, Kenya, Laos, Malagasy, Pakistan, Sierra Leone (−), Sudan (−), Zambia (+).

E. Countries with less than 5 per cent of their total population in urban areas of 20,000 or more inhabitants: Cameroun, Chad, Ethiopia, Liberia, Malawi (−), Nepal, (−), Niger (−), Nigeria (+), Somali Republic (+), Tanganyika, Uganda (−), Yemen (−).

Character of Basic Social Organization

It has often been observed that in the long run economic development has almost invariably been accompanied by significant transformations in the pattern of family kinship relationships.[28] Historically, the characteristic transformation associated with industrialization and urbanization has been from a traditional society in which a multifunctional tribal, clan, or extended family unit dominated all realms of individual decision-making into a society in which the dominant kinship unit was the "conjugal" or nuclear family with its much more restricted area of authority. The economic relevance of the spread of the smaller nuclear family with its

[28] See B. F. Hoselitz, "Social Structure and Economic Growth," in *Sociological Aspects of Economic Growth,* p. 4.

specialized social functions is severalfold. While the extended family, clan, or tribe, by distributing to the group or community the fruits of special individual efforts, tends to diminish incentives for performing risk-taking activities and thus to have an adverse effect upon investment, the small family system facilitates the linking of personal effort and rewards for effort.[29] At the same time that the role of the family becomes more specialized and restricted, other more impersonal mechanisms tend to evolve for the purpose of evaluating individual performance on the basis of merit rather than of status within the extended family, clan, or tribal group.[30] It should also be noted that the conjugal family, in placing a greater burden on individuals for supporting their children, tends to be more conducive to the extension of practices of family limitation which in turn facilitate upward social and economic mobility.[31]

Case studies of traditional social organization suggest that changes in kinship patterns play a permissive rather than causal role in the development process. W. E. Moore, for example, hypothesizes as much as a generational lag between the entry of an individual into a transformed social system and his commitment to modern small-family norms.[32] Other writers suggest that under certain circumstances the joint family may even contribute positively to economic growth by providing an extended means for individual financing of business expansion and by offering a source of social stability in the face of rapid economic change.[33] Nevertheless, the typical long-run association seems to be between greater economic development and the movement toward smaller family units governing purely social relationships.

The indicator we have chosen to measure the extent of breakdown in traditional kinship systems is a purely qualitative one. We divided the countries into three groups according to whether the predominant form of basic social organization as of about 1960 was the immediate family group, the extended family (or clan), or the tribe. Countries were as-

[29] See, for example, J. L. Sadie's study of the South African Bantu in "The Social Anthropology of Economic Underdevelopment," pp. 294–303. See also Manning Nash, "Kinship and Voluntary Associations," in *Labor Commitment and Social Change in Developing Areas,* ed. W. E. Moore and A. S. Feldman (New York: Social Science Research Council, 1960).

[30] See M. F. Millikan and D. L. M. Blackmer (eds.), *The Emerging Nations* (Boston: Little, Brown and Co., 1961), p. 21.

[31] See the discussion below of our indicator of fertility.

[32] Moore and Feldman (eds.), *Labor Commitment and Social Change,* p. 67.

[33] See, for example, Clark Kerr *et al., Industrialism and Industrial Man* (Cambridge: Harvard University Press, 1960), p. 20.

sumed to be situated along a scale, the lower end of which is typified by the predominance of traditional tribal social organization and the higher end of which is characterized by the prevalence of the conjugal family group. A movement from one end of the scale to the other thus represents those transformations of basic social relationships which in the long run typically accompany industrialization and urbanization.

The principal sources of information for this classification were recent country and regional studies. Initially, we attempted to differentiate two categories of countries in which tribal organization prevailed: those in which the influence of the tribe was pervasive and those in which the authority of the tribe had been considerably weakened; however, we could not arrive at sufficiently unambiguous distinctions between the two. In the final formulation of the indicator, therefore, we grouped all countries in which tribal allegiances were widespread into a single category with plus and minus grades to indicate clear cases of particularly strong or weak tribal traditions and organization.

Our definition of the indicator of the character of basic social organization and the country classifications are given below.

A. Countries in which the predominant form of basic social organization is the immediate family group. Countries in this category with important population subgroups that have extended family or clan systems are classified $A-$: Argentina, Bolivia ($-$), Brazil, Burma, Chile, Colombia, Costa Rica, Cyprus, Dominican Republic, Ecuador ($-$), El Salvador ($-$), Greece, Guatemala ($-$), Honduras, Israel, Jamaica ($+$), Japan, Lebanon ($-$), Mexico, Nicaragua, Panama ($-$), Paraguay, Peru ($-$), Surinam ($-$), Trinidad, Turkey, Uruguay, Venezuela.

B. Countries in which the predominant form of basic social organization is the extended family or clan. Countries in this group having important tribal sectors are classified $B-$: Cambodia ($-$), Ceylon, India, Indonesia, Iran ($-$), Iraq ($-$) Laos ($-$), Pakistan, Philippines, South Korea, South Vietnam, Syria, Taiwan, Thailand, U.A.R.

C. Countries in which strong tribal allegiances are widespread. Where these allegiances are very strong throughout the nation, the country is classified $C-$. Where there has been marked weakening of tribal ties in important rural areas as well as in urban areas, the country is classified $C+$. The remaining countries in this category are classified C: Afghanistan ($-$), Algeria ($+$), Cameroun, Chad ($-$), Dahomey, Ethiopia ($-$), Gabon, Ghana ($+$), Guinea ($+$), Ivory Coast, Jordan, Kenya, Liberia ($-$), Libya ($-$), Malawi, Malagasy, Morocco ($+$), Nepal, Niger ($-$),

29

Nigeria (+), Rhodesia, Senegal (+), Sierra Leone, Somali Republic, South Africa (+), Sudan, Tanganyika, Tunisia (+), Uganda (−), Yemen (−), Zambia.

Importance of the Indigenous Middle Class

An aspect of social organization commonly associated with economic growth is the availability of a pool of commercial, entrepreneurial, professional, and technical talents. Generally speaking, these talents tend to be drawn from those occupational groups that are often referred to as the middle class. Historically, in the economic development of Western Europe, the middle classes were a driving force in the growth of business enterprise. Economic historians as different in their approaches as Marx, Sombart, Schumpeter, and Gerschenkron have all pointed to the rising groups of manufacturers, traders, and their associates as the source of the capitalist "spirit" and the entrepreneurial talent that propelled the economies of nineteenth-century Europe forward.[34] It is clear from many country studies that the growth of a robust middle class remains of crucial importance in contemporary low-income nations. However, the specific groups that contribute most to economic development may differ greatly from those that were important in the nineteenth century, and, indeed, the very term "middle class" with its Western "bourgeois" connotation is not very appropriate. In developing countries today, for example, it often happens that salaried government officials, rather than private businessmen, provide the leadership for economic change and innovation. Furthermore, to an even greater extent than in nineteenth-century Europe, a large part of the available talent important for economic growth is often found among expatriate groups in the population. At the same time, current experience with the problems of developing nations suggests that the presence of active indigenous groups in the middle class is considerably more conducive to the initiation of a widespread growth process than is the existence of expatriate groups that characteristically tend to concentrate their efforts within the existing modern sectors. Therefore, in deriving our indicator of the size of the middle class we have ranked the presence of indigenous groups considerably higher than the presence of expatriate elements.

[34] See Marx, *Capital, The Communist Manifesto, and Other Writings*, pp. 324ff.; Sombart, "Capitalism," *Encyclopaedia of Social Sciences, III;* J. A. Schumpeter, *The Theory of Economic Development* (Cambridge: Harvard University Press, 1959), Chapter 2; and Gerschenkron, *Economic Backwardness*, Chapter 3.

Our indicator of the importance of the indigenous middle class as of about 1960 assigns less-developed countries to five principal categories on the basis of (1) statistical estimates of the importance of selected middle-class occupations together with (2) qualitative information concerning the comparative weight of indigenous and expatriate elements in the middle class. As mentioned above, statistical estimates of employment for most low-income countries are extremely poor. United Nations data on the distribution of the active male population by broad occupational groups[35] provided us with information for less than half the countries in our sample. For a few additional countries appropriate estimates were available from recent country studies. These data on the distribution of employment were used to determine whether, as of about 1960, less than 10 per cent, from 10 to 19 per cent, or over 19 per cent of the male labor force was in commerce, banking, insurance, or in technical, professional, managerial, administrative, or clerical employments. For the large number of countries for which no precise employment estimates could be obtained, one of two approaches was taken. First, all countries for which qualitative information[36] indicated the overwhelming predominance of expatriate elements in the middle class were assigned to a special category. Where qualitative information indicated the simultaneous presence of a small, growing indigenous class, the country was given a higher score. The majority of countries for which employment data were lacking was classified by these characteristics. Second, it was assumed that all countries that had less than 20 per cent of their total population outside the agricultural sector[37] also had less than 10 per cent of their active male population employed in the middle-class occupations listed above; this assumption enabled us to complete the classification of almost all of the remaining countries for which employment data were unavailable. A few doubtful cases were resolved by interview.

The following are the precise classification scheme and country scores for the indicator of the importance of the indigenous middle class.

[35] United Nations, *Compendium of Social Statistics: 1963* (New York, 1963), Tables 68 and 69; United Nations, *Demographic Yearbook: 1964* (New York, 1964), Table 10.

[36] The principal sources of qualitative information were recent country studies and, for African countries, G. H. T. Kimble, *Tropical Africa* (New York: Twentieth Century Fund, 1960).

[37] For the sources of this information, see the references listed for the indicator of the size of the traditional agricultural sector.

A. Countries with a relatively important indigenous middle class in which at least 20 per cent of the active male population, as of about 1960, was in commerce, banking, insurance, or in technical, professional, managerial, administrative, or clerical employments. Excluded from this category, however, would be any countries meeting this statistical criterion in which the middle class was dominated by expatriate elements: Argentina (+), Ceylon, Chile, Greece, Israel (+), Japan (+), Lebanon, Mexico, Taiwan, Trinidad, Uruguay, Venezuela.

B. Countries with a significant but fairly small indigenous middle class in which, as of about 1960, at least 10 per cent but not more than 19 per cent of the active male population was in commerce, banking, insurance, or in technical, professional, managerial, administrative, or clerical employments. Excluded from this category, however, are countries meeting this criterion in which the middle class is dominated by expatriate elements: Brazil, Colombia, Costa Rica, Cyprus, Dominican Republic, Ecuador, El Salvador (−), Guatemala, India, Iran (−), Iraq (−), Jamaica, Jordan, Nicaragua (−), Nigeria (−), Pakistan, Panama, Paraguay (−), Peru, Philippines, South Korea, Surinam, Syria, Tunisia, Turkey, U.A.R.

C. Countries in which, as of about 1960, expatriate entrepreneurial, commercial, administrative, and technical groups dominated the middle class but in which a growing, though still small, indigenous middle class also existed: Dahomey (−), Ghana, Ivory Coast, Sudan, Tanganyika, Thailand, Uganda.

D. Countries in which, as of about 1960, expatriate entrepreneurial, commercial, administrative, and technical groups dominated the middle class almost completely; indigenous middle-class groups were negligible. Countries in which an important settled expatriate group comprising over 1 per cent of the population operated in several sectors of the economy are classified D+: Algeria (−), Burma, Cambodia, Cameroun, Chad, Ethiopia, Gabon, Honduras, Indonesia, Kenya, Laos, Liberia, Libya, Malagasy, Malawi, Morocco (+), Niger, Rhodesia (+), Senegal (+), Sierra Leone, Somali Republic, South Africa (+), South Vietnam, Zambia.

E. Countries in which the indigenous middle class is extremely small or negligible and in which there is no important expatriate middle class. All countries for which it is estimated that less than 10 per cent of the active male population, as of about 1960, was in the middle class occupations listed above and in which there was not an important expatriate middle class are included in this category: Afghanistan, Bolivia (+), Guinea, Nepal (−), Yemen.

Extent of Social Mobility

The positive association between social mobility and industrialization has often been emphasized.[38] However, the multiple facets of social mobility and their varying importance to economic growth are not always made clear. There are the attitudinal aspects of mobility: the degree to which individual attainments are met with social recognition and advance; and in particular, the extent to which economic achievements receive positive social approval. Historical studies tend to emphasize the importance to innovation and entrepreneurship of social values that emphasize individual achievement. For example, the comparative slowness of French industrial advance during the nineteenth century has been explained by economic historians as having resulted in part from the relatively rigid patterns of social stratification and social values prevalent at that time.[39] With respect to contemporary developing countries, the manner in which the social values associated with extended kinship systems form a barrier to individual initiative and economic achievement has been well documented.[40] As development occurs, however, increases in specialized activities for the market tend gradually to raise the social value of economic activities.

Closely related to the attitudes affecting social mobility is the extent of opportunity for an individual to advance by means of ability rather than social status. Of course, it is to be expected that the possibilities for vertical mobility will be greater, the larger the number of jobs requiring special proficiency. Furthermore, the expansion of industry normally entrains an increase in employment opportunities and thus in upward

[38] See, for example, B. F. Hoselitz, "Non-Economic Barriers to Economic Development," *Economic Development and Cultural Change,* Vol. 1, No. 1 (1952), pp. 10–11.

[39] Sawyer, "Social Structure and Economic Progress," pp. 327ff.; Alexander Gerschenkron, "Social Attitudes, Entrepreneurship, and Economic Development," in *Economic Backwardness,* gives further bibliographical references on p. 63. See B. F. Hoselitz, "Entrepreneurship and Capital Formation in France and Britain since 1700," National Bureau of Economic Research, *Capital Formation and Economic Growth* (Princeton: Princeton University Press, 1955), for emphasis on other factors, however.

[40] See the references cited in the discussion of our indicator of the character of basic social organization.

mobility. Finally, a significant aspect of social mobility is the extent of opportunity in a society to obtain skills and education; inevitably a narrow educational base limits the scope for individual improvements in status. Thus, the process of industrialization and the increase in opportunities for social mobility interact as countries proceed toward sustained economic development.[41]

In choosing a variable to represent the extent of social mobility we looked for reasonably specific characteristics that would summarize the important aspects of social mobility. One element included in the definition of an index of social mobility was the extent of access to education. The measure of educational opportunity that we used was the ratio of the population five to nineteen years of age enrolled in primary and secondary schools.[42] A second element incorporated in the classification scheme was the extent of opportunity to advance into middle-class occupations (clerical, administrative, technical, managerial, commercial). We measured this aspect of social mobility by the importance of the indigenous middle class.[43] The final element in the definition was the presence or absence of prohibitive cultural or ethnic barriers to upward social mobility. No special category was provided for the few countries having such barriers; rather, for each country with such barriers, the score received on the basis of the other two elements in the scheme was reduced by one letter grade. In our original formulation of the indicator of social mobility we included an index of the openness of access to political leadership presented in *A Cross-Polity Survey;*[44] however, it proved not to be closely related to the other aspects of mobility and resulted in ambiguity in our statistical results.[45]

In the final definitional scheme, three broad categories of social mobility were distinguished.

A. Countries that, as of about 1960, were characterized by considerable social mobility, measured by the standards of less-developed coun-

[41] For a discussion of the various aspects of opportunities for social mobility, see Gino Germani, "The Strategy of Fostering Social Mobility," in UNESCO, *Social Aspects of Economic Development in Latin America, I,* pp. 211–30.

[42] Russett *et al., World Handbook of Political and Social Indicators,* Table 63.

[43] See the discussion of our indicator of the importance of the indigenous middle class for the sources of these data.

[44] Banks and Textor, *A Cross-Polity Survey,* raw characteristic number 45 (political leadership).

[45] For a detailed description of the indicator that included the openness of access to leadership, see our article "A Factor Analysis of the Interrelationship between Social and Political Variables and Per Capita Gross National Product," pp. 558–59.

tries, as indicated by relatively broad access to educational attainments (i.e., a school enrollment ratio of over 40 per cent) and fairly good opportunities to enter middle-class occupations. (Clerical, administrative, technical, commercial, and professional occupations represent at least 10 per cent of the active male population.) In addition, countries in this category are characterized by the absence of prohibitive cultural or ethnic barriers affecting important segments of the population. Countries in which *either* the above middle-class occupations form more than 20 per cent of the active male population or the school enrollment ratio is more than 50 per cent are classified *A*+. Countries in which there is nevertheless a marked degree of social stratification are classified *A*−: Argentina (+), Brazil, Ceylon (−), Chile (−), Colombia, Costa Rica, Cyprus (−), Greece (+), Israel (+), Jamaica, Japan (+), Lebanon, Mexico (−), Philippines (−), South Korea, Surinam, Taiwan, Trinidad, Turkey, Uruguay (+), Venezuela.

B. Countries that, as of about 1960, were characterized by fairly limited social mobility as indicated by school enrollment ratios of less than 40 per cent but more than 25 per cent and by the fact that middle-class occupations formed only 5–10 per cent of the active male population. Also included in this category are a few countries that meet the first two criteria for category A but in which the presence of prohibitive ethnic or cultural barriers affects significant segments of the population: Dominican Republic, Ecuador, El Salvador, Ghana, Iran (−), Iraq (−), Jordan, Nicaragua, Nigeria (−), Panama, Paraguay, Peru, South Africa (−), Syria, Thailand, Tunisia, U.A.R.

C. Countries that, as of about 1960, were characterized by a low degree of social mobility as indicated by very limited access to education (school enrollment ratios of less than 25 per cent) and the existence of little opportunity to enter middle-class occupations. Countries that also had rigid, traditionally determined social castes are classified *C*−. Countries that, generally speaking, had extremely low social mobility but in which either (1) registered school enrollment ratios were nevertheless above 25 per cent or (2) the middle class, while very small, was rapidly growing are classified *C*+. Also included in this category are a few countries that meet the criteria for category B except for the presence of prohibitive cultural or ethnic barriers affecting significant segments of the population: Algeria, Afghanistan (−), Bolivia (+), Burma (+), Cambodia (+), Cameroun, Chad, Dahomey (+), Ethiopia (−), Gabon, Guatemala, Guinea, Honduras (+), India, Indonesia (+), Ivory Coast

35

(+), Kenya (+), Laos, Liberia, Libya (+), Malagasy (+), Malawi (+), Morocco, Nepal (−), Niger, Pakistan (+), Rhodesia, Senegal, Sierra Leone, Somali Republic, South Vietnam, Sudan, Tanganyika (+), Uganda (+), Yemen (−), Zambia (+).

Extent of Literacy

A great deal has been written in recent years about the contribution of education and its by-products to economic growth. Statistical analyses of factors accounting for output increases in selected advanced economies give considerable weight to massive expansions in secondary education as a source of the rise in aggregate productivity.[46] Studies of low-income countries also emphasize the role of education in economic as well as in social development but they stress the importance of primary education and its key product, literacy.[47] It is certainly generally accepted that literacy is an essential economic asset in industrial urban occupations, facilitating the training of unskilled as well as skilled workers. In addition, it is an important modern mechanism for integrating both the social and political structures of a nation. Indeed, it has been maintained that literacy is the basic personal skill underlying the whole process of modernization.[48]

While most students of the subject would agree that literacy is important economically, it is often stressed that the productivity of investment in literacy varies at different stages of development. In particular, the economic gains from increased literacy at very low stages of socioeconomic evolution may level off quickly and may not become very marked

[46] See E. F. Denison, *The Sources of Economic Growth in the United States* (New York: Committee for Economic Development, 1962), and OECD Study Group in the Economics of Education, *The Residual Factor and Economic Growth* (Paris, 1964). A brief summary of studies of this and related types may be found in Frederick Harbison and C. A. Myers, *Education, Manpower and Economic Growth* (New York: McGraw-Hill, 1964), pp. 3ff.

[47] See H. H. Golden, "Literacy and Social Change in Underdeveloped Countries," *Rural Sociology,* Vol. 20 (March, 1955), pp. 1–7; M. J. Herskovits, *The Human Factor in Changing Africa* (New York: Alfred A. Knopf, 1962), Chapter 8; and C. A. Anderson, "The Impact of the Educational System on Technological Change and Modernization," *Industrialization and Society,* ed. Hoselitz and Moore, pp. 266–67. Recently, there has been a tendency for emphasis upon the training of high-level manpower to replace concern with extensions in primary education. See, for instance, Harbison and Myers, *Education, Manpower and Economic Growth,* Chapter 2. See also the various country studies in Frederick Harbison and C. A. Myers (eds.), *Manpower and Education* (New York: McGraw-Hill, 1965).

[48] Lerner, *The Passing of Traditional Society,* p. 64.

again until the society reaches a point at which widespread transformations of social structure facilitate the full use of literacy.

Of course, it would have been desirable to devise a broader and more accurate indicator of the stock of education embodied in the working population than the rate of literacy. However, appropriate data on years of schooling of various segments of the population, for example, are available for only a handful of developing countries. Data on school enrollment ratios are not suitable since they refer only to additions to the stock of education.

Our indicator of the extent of literacy is a purely quantitative one for which the basic source was Russett *et al., World Handbook of Political and Social Indicators.*[49] For a few countries having poor data, however, the judgment of country experts was used to adjust published figures that were clearly overestimates. While the dates of available estimates of literacy vary from country to country, most of them relate to 1958. In view of the large margin of error in many of these estimates, we have checked them where possible with estimates from other sources.

The following is the classification scheme for the indicator of the extent of literacy.

A. Countries in which at least 65 per cent of the adult population is literate. Those in which over 85 per cent is literate are classified $A+$; those in which 75–85 per cent is literate are classified A; and those in which 65–74 per cent is literate are classified $A-$: Argentina (+), Chile, Costa Rica, Greece, Israel (+), Jamaica, Japan (+), Panama (−), Paraguay (−), Philippines, South Korea, Surinam (−), Thailand (−), Trinidad (−), Uruguay (+).

B. Countries in which 35–64 per cent of the adult population is literate. Those in which rates of literacy are 55–64 per cent are classified $B+$; those in which rates of literacy are 45–54 per cent are classified B; and those in which rates of literacy are 35–44 per cent are classified $B-$: Brazil, Burma, Ceylon (+), Colombia (+), Cyprus (+), Dominican Republic (−), Ecuador (+), El Salvador (−), Honduras (−), Lebanon, Mexico, Nicaragua (−), Peru, South Africa (−), Taiwan, Turkey (−), Venezuela (+).

C. Countries in which 16–30 per cent of the adult population is literate. Those in which rates of literacy are 30–34 per cent are classified $C+$; those in which rates of literacy are 23–29 per cent are classified C;

[49] Table 64.

and those in which rates of literacy are 16–22 per cent are classified $C-$:
Algeria $(-)$, Bolivia $(+)$, Cambodia $(-)$, Ghana $(-)$, Guatemala,
India $(-)$, Indonesia $(-)$, Jordan $(-)$, Kenya $(-)$, Malagasy $(+)$,
Rhodesia, South Vietnam $(-)$, Syria, Tunisia $(-)$, Uganda $(-)$,
U.A.R. $(-)$, Zambia.

D. Countries in which less than 16 per cent of the adult population
is literate. Those in which rates of literacy are 11–15 per cent are classified $D+$; those in which rates of literacy are 6–10 per cent are classified
D; and those in which rates of literacy are under 6 per cent are classified $D-$: Afghanistan, Cameroun $(-)$, Chad $(-)$, Dahomey $(+)$,
Ethiopia $(-)$, Gabon, Guinea, Iran $(+)$, Iraq, Ivory Coast, Laos $(+)$,
Liberia, Libya $(+)$, Malawi $(-)$, Morocco $(+)$, Nepal $(-)$, Niger
$(-)$, Nigeria, Pakistan $(+)$, Senegal, Sierra Leone, Somali Republic
$(-)$, Sudan, Tanganyika, Yemen $(-)$.

Extent of Mass Communication

The importance of mass communication to social change, and thus
implicitly to economic development, has been emphasized in recent years
by the rapid expansion of communications research oriented toward the
problems of less-developed countries.[50] As is often pointed out, modern
media systems are an important mechanism both for diffusing thought
patterns and demands for industrial products and for inducing greater
participation in national political systems;[51] it is indeed a fact in advanced
societies that both newspapers and radios are important means for the
articulation of group political interests and thus for the effective working
of participant political systems.

Close relationships between the evolution of mass media and other
indicators of urbanization and industrialization are underlined by statistical analyses. The Yale Political Data Program's *World Handbook of
Political and Social Indicators,* for example, gives the following corre-

---

[50] See, for example, the essays in Lucian W. Pye (ed.), *Communications and
Political Development* (Princeton: Princeton University Press, 1963), as well as
Wilbur Schramm, *Mass Media and National Development* (Stanford: Stanford
University Press, 1964), and Lerner, *The Passing of Traditional Society,*
Chapter 2.

[51] See, for example, Daniel Lerner, "Communication Systems and Social Systems: A Statistical Exploration," *Behavioral Science,* Vol. 2 (October, 1957), p.
267.

lations (based on large samples of developed and less-developed countries) between daily newspaper circulation per 1,000 population and each of the following variables: employment in industry as a percentage of working age population, 0.80; per capita GNP, 0.80; radios per 1,000 population, 0.87; percentage of population over fifteen years of age which is literate, 0.88; and percentage of population in cities of over 20,000, 0.69.[52]

The role of mass communication media in the modernizing process appears to vary systematically with different stages of development according to some recent studies. In a recent study of the Middle East, it is suggested that the modernization of social systems characteristically shows three phases: the first marked by rapid urbanization, the second by a sharp increase in literacy, and the third by greatly expanded media participation.[53] This suggestion is to some extent supported by statistical analyses which indicate that literacy rates and urbanization show greater elasticity than does the use of radios with respect to variations in per capita income in the lowest ranges of per capita GNP, while the reverse is true in the higher ranges of per capita GNP which include less-developed countries.[54]

In selecting an indicator of mass communication we have chosen a composite index based on daily newspaper circulation and number of radio receivers. The former has been given somewhat greater weight since it appears to be the more reliable series.[55] The principal sources for the information used are the United Nations data reported in the *World Handbook of Political and Social Indicators*. The classification of each country depends upon the deciles within which it falls when all countries for which data are available are ranked.[56] The detailed basis for the classification is as follows:

---

[52] Russett *et al.*, *World Handbook of Political and Social Indicators*, p. 272.

[53] Lerner, *The Passing of Traditional Society*, pp. 61–63. His index of media participation is a composite indicator of daily newspaper circulation, number of radio receivers, and cinema seating capacity.

[54] Russett *et al.*, *World Handbook of Political and Social Indicators*, Figure B–1, p. 300.

[55] There is a slight tendency toward understatement in countries reporting radios licensed rather than radios in use. See Russett *et al.*, *World Handbook of Political and Social Indicators*, p. 118.

[56] The data as well as the case deciles are presented in Table 31 (Daily Newspaper Circulation per 1,000 Population) and Table 35 (Radios per 1,000 Population), *ibid*.

Classification	Case Deciles of Newspaper Circulation	Case Deciles of Radios Licensed or in Use
A+	II	II or III
A	II	IV
A	III	III or IV
A−	IV	III or IV or V

Argentina, Chile, Costa Rica (−), Cyprus, Greece, Israel (+), Japan, Lebanon (−), Mexico (−), Panama, Peru (−), South Korea (−), Trinidad (−), Uruguay (+), Venezuela (−).

B+	V	III or IV or V
B	V	VI
B−	VI	V or VI or VII
B−	VII	V

Algeria (−), Bolivia (−), Brazil, Cameroun, Ceylon (−), Colombia (+), Dominican Republic (−), Ecuador, El Salvador (+), Gabon (−), Ghana (−), Guatemala (−), Honduras (−), Iran (−), Jamaica (+), Morocco (−), Nicaragua (+), Paraguay (−), Rhodesia (−), South Africa (+), Surinam (+), Taiwan, Tunisia (−), Turkey (−), U.A.R. (−).

C+	VI	VIII
C+	VII	V or VI or VII
C+	VIII	V
C	VII	VIII
C−	VII	IX
C−	VIII	VII or VIII or IX
C−	IX	VI
C−	X	V

Burma (−), India (−), Indonesia (−), Iraq (−), Jordan (+), Kenya (−), Liberia (−), Libya (+), Malagasy (−), Philippines (+), Senegal (−), South Vietnam (+), Syria (+), Thailand (−), Uganda (−).

D+	VIII	X
D+	IX	VIII or IX or X
D	IX	X
D−	X	IX or X

Afghanistan, Cambodia (+), Chad (−), Dahomey (−), Ethiopia (−), Guinea (−), Ivory Coast (+), Laos (−), Malawi (−), Nepal (−), Niger (−), Nigeria (+), Pakistan (+), Sierra Leone (+), Somali Republic (−), Sudan, Tanganyika, Yemen (−), Zambia (+).

Degree of Cultural and Ethnic Homogeneity

A familiar characteristic of many less-developed countries is the presence of diversity in language, culture, religion, and race. Among countries at the earliest stage of social and economic development, the "primordial attachments" of kinship, race, language, religion, and custom tend to be very strong.[57] The resulting lack of social and economic integration contributes to their difficulties in initiating a process of economic growth. In addition, these primordial attachments characteristically come into severe conflict with the requirements for effective political integration and, in particular, with the need for more generalized commitments to a relatively impersonal nation-wide civil order. Not only does cultural and ethnic heterogeneity tend to hamper the early stages of nation-building and economic growth, but in addition, the initial effects of urbanization and industrialization may be to intensify awareness of religious, racial, and cultural differences and thus to produce social tensions that, in the short run at least, create additional impediments to socioeconomic and political development. In general, therefore, it seems reasonable to conclude that, other things being equal, less-developed countries that are relatively homogeneous with respect to cultural, religious, and ethnic characteristics are less hampered in the achievement of social and political integration and in the initiation of continuous economic growth than more heterogeneous societies.[58]

Historically, unifying cultural and ethnic transformations usually have been extremely slow, taking in some instances several centuries to reach completion. Nevertheless, as countries have become more urbanized and industrialized, the closer agglomerations of the population, the greater occupational and geographic mobility, the greater extent of literacy, and the wider spread of modern communication media have all tended to promote the gradual development of common languages and an associated increase in cultural homogeneity; to a lesser extent they have contributed to increased ethnic and religious homogeneity. Not only does

[57] See Clifford Geertz, "The Integrative Revolution, Primordial Sentiments and Civil Politics in the New States," *Old Societies and New States,* ed. Clifford Geertz (New York: The Free Press of Glencoe, 1963), pp. 109ff.

[58] However, for a contrasting view—that the more integrated society is less likely to adapt to change than the poorly integrated one—see Ralph Linton, "Cultural and Personality Factors Affecting Economic Growth," in *The Progress of Underdeveloped Areas,* ed. B. F. Hoselitz (Chicago: University of Chicago Press, 1952), pp. 87–88.

41

history give evidence of a positive long-term impact of economic growth upon the extent of cultural homogeneity, but the substantial economic advance of the relatively homogeneous societies of the West over the past century also tends to confirm the proposition that cultural homogeneity in turn favors better economic performance.

In defining an indicator of cultural and ethnic homogeneity we combined three country characteristics into a single index: the extent of linguistic, religious, and racial homogeneity. The element receiving the greatest weight, the proportion of the population speaking the dominant language, was chosen to summarize the over-all degree of homogeneity of the culture. The *World Handbook of Political and Social Indicators*[59] provided the basic information on linguistic homogeneity for about two-thirds of the countries in our sample. The remaining countries were classified with the help of Banks's and Textor's *A Cross-Polity Survey*,[60] the *Encyclopaedia Britannica*, and a small number of interviews. The principal sources of data on religious and racial homogeneity were *A Cross-Polity Survey*[61] and the *Encyclopaedia Britannica*. Country studies and interviews were also helpful in completing a number of classifications.

A. Countries in which, generally speaking, over 85 per cent of the population speaks the dominant language and in which over 70 per cent of the population is of the same race. The countries meeting these criteria are divided into two groups. (1) Countries in which over 90 per cent of the population is of the same race and in which the religion is relatively homogeneous are classified *A+*.[62] (2) Countries in which over 90 per cent of the population is of the same race but in which the religion is heterogeneous are classified *A*. Countries in which the religion is homo-

---

[59] Russett *et al.*, Table 39.

[60] Raw characteristic number 18 (linguistic homogeneity). We relied more heavily on the source cited in note 59, however, because we preferred an index of speakers of a dominant language rather than one of speakers to whom the dominant language was their mother tongue.

[61] Raw characteristics number 16 (religious homogeneity) and number 17 (racial homogeneity). Banks's and Textor's estimates of racial composition were not sufficiently gradated for our purpose, so a good deal of supplementary information was necessary. We introduced their index of religious homogeneity with only a few changes and additions.

[62] The definitions of religious homogeneity and religious heterogeneity used in this classification system are those given in *A Cross-Polity Survey;* that is, a country is homogeneous with respect to religion if 80–85 per cent of the population is of the predominant religion and it is heterogeneous if less than 80–85 per cent is of the predominant religion.

geneous but in which the predominant race constitutes only 71–90 per cent of the population are also classified *A*: Argentina (+), Cambodia (+), Chile (+), Costa Rica (+), Greece (+), Honduras (+), Japan, Jordan (+), Lebanon, Libya (+), Nicaragua, Panama, Paraguay, Somali Republic (+), South Korea, South Vietnam, Syria (+), Taiwan, Thailand (+), Tunisia (+), Turkey (+), U.A.R. (+), Uruguay (+), Yemen.

B. Countries in which over 70 per cent of the population speaks the dominant language but in which (1) less than 71 per cent of the population is of the same race, (2) the religion is heterogeneous, or (3) both characteristics (1) and (2) apply. The following tabulation specifies the gradations within this category:

Score	Language	Race	Religion
B+	over 85%	71–90%	homogeneous
B+	over 85%	51–70%	heterogeneous
B	over 85%	51–70%	homogeneous
B	over 85%	under 51%	either
B	71–85%	over 90%	either
B−	71–85%	under 91%	either

Algeria, Brazil (+), Ceylon, Colombia (+), Cyprus, Dominican Republic (+), Ecuador, El Salvador, Gabon, Indonesia, Iraq, Jamaica (+), Malagasy, Mexico, Morocco, Rhodesia, Trinidad, Venezuela (+).

C. Countries in which 51–70 per cent of the population speaks the dominant language. The countries meeting this criterion are divided into three groups. (1) Those in which over 90 per cent of the population is of the same race and in which the religion is homogeneous are classified *C*+. (2) Those in which either (*a*) over 90 per cent of the population is of the same race but the religion is heterogeneous or (*b*) 71–90 per cent of the population is of the same race with no specification about religion, are classified *C*. (3) All countries in which 50–70 per cent of the population speaks the dominant language and in which less than 71 per cent is of the same race are classified *C*−: Afghanistan, Burma (+), Chad (−), Dahomey, Ethiopia, Ghana, Guatemala (−), Iran (+), Israel (+), Laos (−), Malawi, Nepal (−), Pakistan (+), Peru (−), Sudan (−) Surinam (−), Tanganyika.

D. Countries in which less than 51 per cent of the population speaks the dominant language. The countries in this category are divided into two groups. (1) Those in which over 90 per cent of the population is

of the same race and in which the religion is homogeneous are classified
$D+$. (2) All the remaining countries in which less than 51 per cent of
the population speaks the dominant language are classified D: Bolivia,
Cameroun, Guinea, India ($+$), Ivory Coast, Kenya, Liberia, Niger,
Nigeria, Philippines ($+$), Senegal ($+$), Sierra Leone ($+$), South Africa,
Uganda, Zambia.

Degree of Social Tension

The frequent occurrence of serious social tensions and social conflict
in the early stages of industrialization, urbanization, and modernization
has often been noted.[63] In the first place, the breakup of the traditional
kinship and tribal groups that are characteristic of low-income countries
produces tensions, both personal and social, between primary loyalties to
the small community and the new, broader loyalties demanded by the
modern nation-state; tensions of this type have varied manifestations such
as caste conflicts or struggles between central and tribal political authorities. As mentioned in discussing cultural homogeneity, another source of
tension arises because the process of nation-building acts to intensify conflicts within the nation between groups that have different and opposing
bonds of culture, race, custom, or religion.[64] Thus, it is not surprising to
find evidence that at the early stages of industrialization and urbanization
there is an interaction between socioeconomic changes that produce tensions which in turn may slow down further economic development.

There is, however, a contrasting view of the relationship between social
tensions and economic development according to which the strains and
conflicts of change can become important mechanisms for inducing further economic and social transformations. A number of sociologists view
social disturbances and outbreaks as often being intimately related to the
processes of differentiation of socioeconomic structure and of its subsequent reintegration. In their view social tensions may reflect the uneven-

---

[63] See, for example, Hauser, "The Social, Economic, and Technological Problems of Rapid Urbanization," and B. F. Hoselitz, "Main Concepts in the Analysis
of the Social Implications of Technical Change," in *Industrialization and Society,*
ed. Hoselitz and Moore, pp. 211 and 12–13, respectively. See also W. E. Moore,
"The Social Framework of Economic Development," in *Tradition, Values, and
Socio-Economic Development,* ed. Ralph Braibanti and J. J. Spengler (Durham,
N.C.: Duke University Press, 1961), p. 71.

[64] See Geertz, "The Integrative Revolution, Primordial Sentiments and Civil
Politics in the New States."

ness in the pace of differentiation and integration or in turn be initiators of the differentiation process.[65] Smelser, for example, in his analysis of social change in the industrial revolution, sees dissatisfactions and discontent with conventional social and economic roles as the initial cause of the successive differentiations in social and economic structure which accompanied the industrial revolution.[66] According to this view one would expect a positive association, at least in the short run, between social tensions and more rapid economic growth.

A final proposition relating long-run economic growth with fewer social tensions should be noted. It is self-evident that at all stages of socioeconomic evolution the continued presence of extreme social tensions accompanied by widespread and violent outbreaks inevitably hampers economic development because of their adverse effect on risk-taking activities and therefore on investment. Thus, one would anticipate a long-run positive relationship between better economic performance and the absence of extreme and widespread social tensions.

The indicator of the degree of social tension we have chosen for our study is a purely qualitative one, several attributes of which should be specially noted. In the first place, in order to obtain reasonably unambiguous category descriptions, evidence of overt social tensions was of necessity weighed more heavily than evidence of potential underlying tensions. Secondly, for final country classifications we relied greatly upon consultation with about thirty regional experts to whom a statement of category descriptions and preliminary country scores was circulated. Preliminary classifications were based upon recent country studies; a useful cross-check on these was also provided by Banks's and Textor's *A Cross-Polity Survey*.[67] Finally, it should be emphasized that the judgments with respect to the degree of social tension refer only to the period 1957–62, for which we had reasonably adequate interview information; a number of countries would have been scored differently had the time period been extended to 1964 or 1965.

The classification scheme for this indicator distinguishes between three principal categories.

A. Countries that during the period 1957–62 were suffering from

---

[65] N. J. Smelser, "Mechanisms of Change and Adjustment to Change," in *Industrialization and Society*, ed. Hoselitz and Moore, pp. 32–48.

[66] Smelser, *Social Change*, pp. 402ff.

[67] Raw characteristics number 31 (political enculturation) and number 32 (sectionalism).

marked social tensions accompanied by considerable violence and social instability arising from racial, tribal, religious, or cultural tensions: Algeria, Burma, Ceylon, Cyprus, Indonesia, Iran, Iraq, Jordan, Kenya, Laos, Rhodesia, South Africa, South Vietnam ($-$), Zambia.

B. Countries characterized by important social tensions during the period 1957–62, accompanied by some violence or other overt manifestations of tension which were not, however, widespread. These tensions may have arisen from any of the sources mentioned in the definition of category A. Countries experiencing occasional or frequent but very small-scale violence connected with social unrest are classified $B+$: Afghanistan, Argentina, Bolivia ($+$), Cameroun ($+$), Chad, Chile, Colombia ($+$), Dahomey, Dominican Republic, Ecuador ($+$), El Salvador, Ethiopia ($+$), Ghana, Guatemala, Guinea, Honduras, India ($+$), Israel ($-$), Ivory Coast, Lebanon, Liberia ($-$), Libya ($-$), Malagasy, Malawi, Morocco, Nicaragua, Niger, Nigeria, Pakistan ($+$), Panama, Peru ($+$), Senegal, Somali Republic ($+$), South Korea, Sudan ($+$), Syria, Taiwan ($-$), Trinidad ($-$), Uganda, Venezuela ($+$), Yemen.

C. Countries characterized by insignificant social tensions or by moderate social tensions of which there were very few or no overt signs during the period 1957–62: Brazil ($+$), Cambodia ($+$), Costa Rica, Gabon, Greece, Jamaica, Japan ($-$), Mexico ($+$), Nepal, Paraguay, Philippines ($+$), Sierra Leone, Surinam, Tanganyika ($+$), Thailand ($+$), Tunisia ($+$), Turkey, U.A.R., Uruguay.

Crude Fertility Rate

It is generally accepted that patterns of population growth intimately condition a country's success in raising its standard of living. Furthermore, there is considerable evidence that suggests the existence of a systematic tendency for mortality rates and fertility rates to decline as countries progress to higher levels of development. Historically, in Western Europe, for example, economic development was accompanied by dramatic decreases in mortality rates later succeeded by declines in birth rates caused largely by decreases in average family size. Most recent authors agree that this historical decline in rates of fertility resulted from a complex of interrelated social changes which accompanied the process of industrialization and urbanization.[68] Opinions vary, however, regard-

[68] See United Nations, Department of Social Affairs, Population Division, *The Determinants and Consequences of Population Trends* (New York, 1958), p. 77.

46

ing the relative importance of different social forces in accounting for declines in fertility. Some writers emphasize the spread of the market and the concomitant improvement in opportunities for geographic and occupational mobility which tend to create economic advantages for smaller families. Others point particularly to the fact that in an urban setting children become more of a direct burden than in rural areas. Still others, in explaining lower birth rates, stress the attitudinal changes characteristic of industrialization and urbanization—in particular the tendencies toward greater application of rational thought patterns to everyday decisions—which tend to generate preferences for family limitation.[69]

While there are thus good reasons to expect lower fertility to accompany economic development in the long run, the exact nature of the relationship is by no means clear. The response of fertility rates to economic change is often not immediate, typically occurring after a considerable time lag. A possible explanation for the time period required for changes in fertility patterns is that positive values associated with fertility are embedded in long-established and slowly changing customs and institutions;[70] in this regard a contrast may be made between fertility and mortality, the latter being an undesired event in all societies.

Our indicator of fertility is a purely statistical one based upon estimates of crude fertility rates for, in the majority of cases, the period 1955–59. The principal source for these estimates was information collected by the United Nations.[71] As is well known, data on fertility are often unreliable. Wherever possible, therefore, estimates based on sample surveys or demographic analyses of census data were used, even if they were for an earlier or more recent period than 1955–59. Since fertility rates tend to change rather slowly, we felt that differences of a few years in time period were not important. In contrast, differences between informal estimates originating within countries and subsequently published census-based estimates were in some instances very large. For countries

---

[69] For discussion of these forces and the various views regarding them, see *ibid.,* Chapter V; A. J. Coale and E. M. Hoover, *Population Growth and Economic Development in Low-Income Countries* (Princeton: Princeton University Press, 1958); and W. J. Goode, *The Family* (Englewood Cliffs, N.J.: Prentice-Hall, 1964), Chapter 8. See also the paper by the present authors, "A Quantitative Study of Social and Political Determinants of Fertility," *Economic Development and Cultural Change,* Vol. 14 (January, 1966), pp. 129–57.

[70] See W. E. Moore, "Industrialization and Social Change," in *Industrialization and Society,* ed. Hoselitz and Moore, p. 327.

[71] See the *Demographic Yearbook, 1962, 1963,* and *1964.*

for which reliable estimates were not available for any period, several cross-checks were made of data obtained from United Nations sources and country studies. First, the data were checked for consistency with estimates contained in recent country studies of over-all population growth rates, mortality rates, and average life expectancy.[72] Second, they were cross-checked with qualitative information on practices of family limitation. Finally, where possible, they were cross-checked with more reliable estimates for similar neighboring countries.

The less-developed countries in our sample were grouped into the following broad categories according to their crude fertility rates. Unless otherwise noted, plus and minus scores are assigned to countries having fertility rates close to the limits of the category.

A. Countries with crude fertility rates of 50 per 1,000 population or more: Burma (−), Dahomey, Ghana (−), Guinea, Ivory Coast, Nepal (−), Niger, Nigeria (−), Sierra Leone, South Vietnam (−), Zambia.

B. Countries with crude fertility rates of from 40 to 49 per 1,000 population: Afghanistan, Bolivia, Brazil, Cambodia, Cameroun, Chad (+), Colombia, Costa Rica (+), Dominican Republic (−), Ecuador, El Salvador, Guatemala (+), Honduras, Indonesia (−), Iran, Iraq, Jordan (−), Kenya (+), Laos, Liberia, Libya, Malawi, Malagasy, Mexico, Morocco, Nicaragua, Pakistan, Panama (−), Paraguay, Peru, Rhodesia, Senegal, Somali Republic, South Africa (−), South Korea, Sudan (+), Surinam, Syria, Taiwan, Tanganyika, Tunisia (−), Turkey, Uganda, U.A.R. (−), Venezuela, Yemen.

C. Countries with crude fertility rates of from 30 to 39 per 1,000 population: Algeria, Ceylon, Chile, Ethiopia, Gabon (+), India (+), Jamaica (+), Lebanon (+), Philippines (−), Thailand, Trinidad (+).

D. Countries with crude fertility rates of under 30 per 1,000 population. Those in which the fertility rate is from 26 to 29 per 1,000 population are classified D+: Argentina, Cyprus (+), Greece, Israel (+), Japan, Uruguay.

---

[72] For example, if a country had an estimated average life expectancy of 35 years, we assumed that its mortality rate could not be less than 25 per 1,000. Given an estimate for population growth of 3 per cent per annum, it appeared that any estimate of the crude fertility rate of less than 50 per 1,000 could be taken as unreasonable.

Degree of Modernization of Outlook

In discussing indicators of social and cultural change we have on several occasions mentioned the importance to economic growth of the creation of attitudes favorable to change and innovation. Indeed, many social scientists would agree with W. E. Moore that an essential aspect of the transformation of a less-developed society into a developed one is the "transformation of the contents of the minds of the elite who direct and of the men who man" the society and polity.[73] Various authors have attempted to define the essence of that "modernization" of men's outlook which they stress is necessary to social, economic, and political change. One school of thought, stimulated by Max Weber,[74] sees a fundamental spiritual characteristic of advanced societies as being the emphasis upon individual rationality of thought and behavior based upon the belief that man can control his environment. As mentioned above, Hoselitz suggests along these lines that advanced countries can be distinguished from underdeveloped ones in terms of sociological pattern variables that describe socioeconomic development as a movement from ascriptive, particularistic, and diffuse socioeconomic values and structure toward the achievement-oriented, universalistic, and specific relationships and attitudes characteristic of developed societies.[75] Another approach taken by a number of sociologists and political scientists underlines the individual's sense of participation in the sociocultural and political life of his nation as the key mental trait of the citizens of modern societies. To quote Edward Shils,

A modern society is not just a complex of modern institutions. It is a mode of integration of the whole society. It is a mode of relationship between the center and the periphery of the society. Modern society entails the inclusion of the mass of the population into the society in the sense that both elite and mass regard themselves as members of the society and, as such, as of approximately equal dignity. It involves a greater participation by the masses in the values of the society, a more active role in the making of society-wide decisions, and a greater prominence in the consideration of the elite.[76]

[73] "Theory, Ideology, Non-Economic Values, and Politico-Economic Development," in *Tradition, Values and Socio-Economic Development,* ed. Braibanti and Spengler, p. 5.

[74] *Theory of Social and Economic Organization* (Glencoe, Ill.: The Free Press, 1957).

[75] Hoselitz, "Social Structure and Economic Growth," pp. 28ff. The concept of "pattern variables" originates in the work of Talcott Parsons, *The Social System.*

[76] "On the Comparative Study of the New States," in *Old Societies and New States,* ed. Geertz, p. 21.

Daniel Lerner is another student of transitional societies who emphasizes the individual's sense of participation as the essence of the "modern" outlook. In probing the sources of the participant society, he maintains that the essential element in the makeup of the modern man is a "psychic mobility" that enables him to identify with new aspects of his environment and to adapt readily to them.[77]

In developing an index of the degree of modernization of outlook we were obliged to depend on a broad characterization of less-developed countries which was based largely upon judgmental information. Two qualitative elements were combined in the index. First, we divided countries into two broad classes: those in which the outlook of educated urban groups was "significantly" modernized and those in which it was not. Countries were judged to have significant modernization of outlook only if the adoption of Western or modern styles of living had gone considerably farther than external forms and dress, and had entailed the evolution of at least some important modern forms of social and political participation such as voluntary associations. The second element in the index was a judgment of whether programs of political, social, and economic modernization (health programs, economic institution-building) have or have not gained significant support among the urban population and among some of the rural population. The principal sources of information for these judgments were recently published country studies in addition to a small number of interviews with regional experts who were personally familiar with a large number of countries in their region. Valuable cross-checks for our classifications of some of the countries in the sample were provided by Banks's and Textor's *A Cross-Polity Survey*.[78] In our final definition of the indicator of the degree of modernization of outlook as of about 1960, three principal categories of less-developed countries were distinguished.

A. Countries in which the outlook of the urban educated population was significantly modernized, judging by the standards of less-developed countries, and in which programs of political, social, and economic modernization had gained significant support among both the urban and rural populations: Argentina, Brazil, Chile, Costa Rica (−), Cyprus (−), Greece, India, Israel (+), Jamaica, Japan (+), Lebanon, Mexico,

---

[77] *The Passing of Traditional Society*, pp. 48–49.

[78] Raw characteristics number 20 (westernization) and number 23 (political modernization: periodization).

Philippines, Rhodesia, South Africa, Taiwan, Trinidad, Turkey, U.A.R. (−), Uruguay, Venezuela.

B. Countries in which the outlook of the urban educated population was significantly modernized but in which programs of political, social, and economic modernization had gained significant support only among the urban population: Algeria, Bolivia, Ceylon, Colombia (+), Dominican Republic, Ecuador (−), El Salvador (−), Ghana (+), Guatemala, Honduras (−), Ivory Coast (−), Kenya, Nicaragua (+), Nigeria (+), Pakistan, Panama, Paraguay, Peru (−), Surinam, Tunisia (+), Zambia.

C. Countries in which the outlook of the educated urban sector was partially but not significantly modernized and in which programs of modernization, if they existed, had gained relatively little support among either the urban or rural population: Afghanistan, Burma, Cambodia, Cameroun, Chad, Dahomey, Ethiopia, Gabon, Guinea, Indonesia, Iran, Iraq, Jordan, Laos (−), Liberia, Libya, Malagasy, Malawi, Morocco (+), Nepal (−), Niger, Senegal, Sierra Leone, Somali Republic, South Korea (+), South Vietnam, Sudan (+), Syria, Tanganyika, Thailand, Uganda, Yemen (−).

POLITICAL INDICATORS

The interrelationship between the political characteristics of developing nations and economic growth has received considerable attention in recent years.[79] Both the contemporary scene and historical experience provide instances of successful economic development under quite diverse political systems. In Western Europe, for example, successful economic performance has been associated with political democracy and a moderately important government economic role; in contrast, the rapid economic development of the Soviet Union has been achieved with an authoritarian form of government and massive government economic

---

[79] The following references are only a few of the many that might be cited: G. I. Blanksten, "Transference of Social and Political Loyalties," in *Industrialization and Society,* ed. Hoselitz and Moore; Phillips Cutright, "National Political Development: Measurement and Analysis," *American Sociological Review,* Vol. 28 (April, 1963), pp. 253–64; S. M. Lipset, "Some Social Requisites of Democracy: Economic Development and Political Legitimacy," *American Political Science Review,* Vol. 53 (March, 1959), pp. 69–105; Millikan and Blackmer (eds.), *The Emerging Nations;* and A. F. K. Organski, *The Stages of Political Development* (New York: Alfred A. Knopf, 1965). See also G. A. Almond and J. S. Coleman (eds.), *The Politics of the Developing Areas* (Princeton: Princeton University Press, 1960).

activity. Although similar contrasts may be drawn from among less-developed countries, recent investigations of the political systems of developing nations suggest that there may nevertheless be systematic patterns of political change associated with economic development.

While there is general agreement on the importance of the interaction of political influences and economic growth, the literature on the subject is complicated by lack of agreement on the nature of political development. Each approach to political development tends to produce its own distinct view of the political transformations typically accompanying urbanization and industrialization. G. A. Almond, in the well-known volume *The Politics of the Developing Areas*,[80] defines a "modern" political system as one in which specialized political structures (such as political parties or bureaucracies) emerge having functionally distinct regulatory roles which they perform within the political system as a whole.[81] This view of political development implies that structural differentiation of the political system is the characteristic long-run concomitant of economic development. It has received some statistical support in a recent article in the *American Sociological Review* in which, for a sample of seventy-seven developed and underdeveloped countries, an index of the extent of the complexity and specialization of national political institutions was found to be closely correlated with selected measures of social and economic development.[82]

Another approach to political change defines political development as an increase in government efficiency in utilizing the human and material resources of the polity for national goals. According to A. F. K. Organski, *The Stages of Political Development*,[83] the key political transformations accompanying successive stages in economic development relate to the role and efficiency of government. In particular, Organski suggests that the basic social and economic changes characteristic of the early stages of economic growth, such as the decline of traditional agricultural social systems, tend to produce a systematic shift in the primary function of government from the establishment of central political rule to the pro-

[80] "A Functional Approach to Comparative Politics," in *The Politics of the Developing Areas,* ed. Almond and Coleman, pp. 3–64. For a somewhat similar view of political development, see F. W. Riggs, "Bureaucrats and Political Development: A Paradoxical View," in *Bureaucracy and Political Development,* ed. Joseph LaPalombara (Princeton: Princeton University Press, 1963), pp. 122–23.

[81] Almond, "A Functional Approach to Comparative Politics," p. 18.

[82] Cutright, "National Political Development: Measurement and Analysis."

[83] P. 7.

motion of economic modernization. In general, Organski's study under-lines the importance of both increased government efficiency and effec-tive national integration in the process of economic development.

A third and quite different analysis of political change is that of Lucian Pye to whom contemporary development in the political realm consists of a historically unique process of diffusion of a current world culture that comprises a set of secular, rational, humanistic values for political life.[84] These values form part of a world-wide cultural climate that deter-mines the general direction and aims of development for the new states. From Pye's standpoint the fundamental problem of nation-building is that of finding a satisfactory reconciliation between the universalistic dimension of world culture and the parochial expressions of the local culture.[85]

There are many other approaches to political development which stress the variety and significance of the interactions between political and nonpolitical aspects of change.[86] Daniel Lerner, for example, sees political, economic, and social development as closely interrelated aspects of the modernization of society, the final stage of which is the evolution of fully participant democratic institutions.[87] Everett Hagen seeks the source of political and economic modernization in the emergence of a particular type of creative personality.[88] Generally speaking, both of these authors stress attitudinal changes common to both socioeconomic and political development.

Current approaches to the growth of nation-states thus offer a wide variety of hypotheses and propositions that relate political and socio-economic transformations of society. In our choice of political variables, therefore, we have attempted to represent several important spheres of the political life of a developing society. The processes of political inte-gration are characterized by two variables: the indicator of the degree of

[84] L. W. Pye, "Democracy, Modernization and Nation Building," in *Self-Government in Modernizing Nations*, ed. J. R. Pennock (Englewood Cliffs, N.J.: Prentice-Hall, 1964), p. 15.

[85] *Ibid.*, p. 22.

[86] C. C. Moskos, Jr., in a recent bibliography on political sociology (Evanston, Ill.: Northwestern University, 1966 [typescript]), classifies approaches to political development in eleven categories, of which we mention only five here (the systems, economic, cultural, communications, and psychological approaches).

[87] *The Passing of Traditional Society*, Chapter 2.

[88] E. E. Hagen, *On the Theory of Social Change* (Homewood, Ill.: The Dorsey Press, 1962).

centralization of political power and the indicator of the degree of national integration and sense of national unity. Another broad sphere depicted by several variables reflects the evolution of "stable but sensitive political mechanisms for relating the interests and the demands of the society to political power."[89] The variables chosen for this purpose were the strength of democratic institutions, the extent of freedom of political opposition and press, the degree of competitiveness of political parties, the predominant basis of the political party system, and the strength of the labor movement. A third important group of political variables incorporated in our study describes the character and orientation of political administration and leadership. This group is composed of the indicators of the degree of administrative efficiency, the political strength of the traditional elite, the political strength of the military, and the extent of leadership commitment to economic development. Finally, we incorporated in our analysis a measure of the extent of political stability.

Degree of National Integration and Sense of National Unity

An important aspect of the growth of modern nation-states is the process of integrating the political system and of creating a sense of national unity among the population. As mentioned above, the greater the initial cultural and ethnic heterogeneity of a society, the less likely it is that modern integrative mechanisms such as education and mass communication media will be effective in promoting a unified polity and society. In addition, there is a purely political aspect of the lack of integration. In countries where the ties of most of the population are still "primordial," such as those of kin, tribe, and race, the creation of a national government is likely, for a time at least, to result in parallel and nonintegrated structures of authority: that is, on the one hand, a multiplicity of purely local traditional (often tribal) authorities and, on the other hand, a national political structure that lacks grass roots mechanisms for the articulation of local interests. As countries develop and become more integrated economically and socially, it becomes more likely that their formal political institutions will reflect the spread of the more generalized commitments to a nation-state that are characteristic of the advanced countries of the world.[90] Thus, in the long run, economic and social

[89] Millikan and Blackmer (eds.), *The Emerging Nations,* p. 74.
[90] See Blanksten, "Transference of Social and Political Loyalties," pp. 177ff.

development tends to be accompanied by a process of gradual transference of social and political loyalties from traditional communally based sociopolitical organizations to the more aggregated political structures typical of higher levels of development.

In defining a variable to represent the process of national integration, we chose a purely qualitative one. Our first attempt involved the combination of two qualitative elements into a single index: the intensity of the political and economic nationalism of a country's leaders and the pervasiveness among the population of a sense of national unity. A statement of category descriptions together with our preliminary country classifications was circulated to some thirty regional experts with a request for corrections and suggestions. It appeared from their comments that the two elements included in the index were not necessarily associated with each other.[91] As a result, we decided after further study that an indicator measuring both cultural and political aspects of the degree of national integration would be better conceptually than one that included extent of nationalistic feeling or chauvinism of the leadership. In our redefintion we combined statistical information on the proportion of the population speaking a common language[92] with two qualitative aspects of integration: the degree of integration of local political structures with national political institutions and the prevalence among the population of a sense of national identity. The principal sources of qualitative information for this indicator were recent country studies and the interviews referred to above.

In the final classification scheme, less-developed countries were grouped into four broad categories.

A. Countries characterized by a marked degree of national integration as indicated by the overwhelming predominance of a common language and culture and by the reasonably effective integration of central and local political systems. In addition, well-developed senses of national unity prevail in these countries: Argentina, Chile, Colombia, Costa Rica ($-$), Greece, Japan, Mexico, Taiwan, Turkey, U.A.R., Uruguay, Venezuela.

---

[91] For a definition of this index and for results in which it was incorporated, see the study by the present authors, "A Factor Analysis of the Interrelationship between Social and Political Variables and Per Capita Gross National Product," pp. 559ff. We are also grateful to Everett Hagen for his suggestion that we treat the two elements separately.

[92] See the discussion of the degree of cultural and ethnic homogeneity for the sources of this information.

B. Countries characterized by a moderate degree of national integration. In all these countries political systems are fairly well integrated, over 60 per cent of the population speaks the predominant language, and a majority of the population has a well-developed sense of national unity. However, important minorities exist in these countries which do not speak the predominant language and/or do not share in the sense of national identity of the majority: Brazil, Cambodia (−), Ceylon, Dominican Republic, Ecuador (−), El Salvador, Ghana (−), Honduras (−), Indonesia (−), Israel (+), Jamaica, Jordan, Lebanon, Nicaragua (−), Panama, Paraguay (−), South Korea, Syria, Trinidad, Tunisia.

C. Countries characterized by a small degree of national integration in which, however, the majority of the population speaks a common language. In these countries local and central political systems are poorly integrated and the sense of over-all national unity is weak among most of the population: Algeria, Burma, Cameroun, Cyprus, Ethiopia, Gabon, Guatemala, Iran, Iraq, Laos, Libya, Malagasy, Morocco, Nepal (−), Pakistan (+), Peru (+) Philippines (+), Rhodesia, Somali Republic, South Vietnam, Sudan (−), Surinam, Thailand, Yemen (−).

D. Countries characterized by a marked absence of national integration as indicated by the absence of a common language and culture, ineffective integration of local and central political systems, and little or no sense of over-all national unity. In all these countries less than half the population speaks a common language: Afghanistan, Bolivia, Chad, Dahomey, Guinea, India (+), Ivory Coast, Kenya (+), Liberia, Malawi (+), Niger, Nigeria (+), Senegal, Sierra Leone, South Africa, Tanganyika, Uganda, Zambia.

Degree of Centralization of Political Power

The relationship between the degree of centralization of political power and economic performance appears to vary at different levels of socioeconomic evolution. Contemporary developing countries in the lowest income bracket generally have not yet achieved effective national unification on either the economic or the political plane. Indeed, they often suffer from marked discontinuity between central government structures and local traditional tribal authorities.[93] Among countries at this low stage of socioeconomic growth, a movement from very low to

[93] See G. A. Almond in the introductory chapter to *The Politics of the Developing Areas,* ed. Almond and Coleman, p. 58.

56

somewhat higher levels of development is typically accompanied by greater centralization of political power in the sense of the firmer establishment of an effective nation-wide network of government authority.[94] There is also historical evidence that countries which were politically more unified tended to perform better economically. Growth rates in nineteenth-century Germany and Italy, for example, were higher in the decades following unification than during those before.[95]

Among countries that have achieved a fair degree of political integration, however, the relationship between economic performance and the degree of political centralization is not of the same nature. Among Latin American countries, for example, there appears to be a tendency toward greater concentration of political power, more authoritarianism, and weaker traditions of local government than is typically the case in advanced Western democracies.[96] This contrast suggests a positive long-run interrelationship in politically unified nations between greater political decentralization, more effective democracy, and higher standards of living. Even in the Soviet Union the recent trend apparently has been in the direction of more decentralization of decision-making, higher standards of living, and possibly more democracy.[97]

With respect to the short-run situation in the low-income developing world, a number of investigators have pointed to a tendency for leaders promoting economic modernization to favor greater authoritarianism and centralization of government power.[98] As discussed above, at low levels of development the persistence of parochial particularist attachments, the presence of political disunity, the absence of a strong indigenous middle class, and the lack of traditions of civil politics, among other things, help render strong centralized governments more effective in promoting economic development than democratic systems.

[94] Organski makes this point in *The Stages of Political Development,* Chapter II.

[95] Change in the extent of political unification was, of course, only one of a number of influences that accounted for changes in economic performance. For a general discussion of, and data on, growth rates in various countries in the latter half of the nineteenth century, see S. J. Patel, "Rates of Industrial Growth in the Last Century, 1860–1958," *Economic Development and Cultural Change,* Vol. 9 (April, 1961), pp. 316–50.

[96] See, for example, the country studies in M. C. Needler, *Political Systems of Latin America* (Princeton: Van Nostrand, 1964).

[97] See Jan Tinbergen, "Do Communist and Free Economies Show a Converging Pattern?" *Soviet Studies,* Vol. 12 (April, 1961), pp. 333–41.

[98] See, for example, Edward Shils, *Political Development in the New States* (The Hague: Mouton, 1962), p. 67.

Our indicator of the degree of centralization of political power defines four categories of countries, the lowest of which is characterized by marked discontinuity between independent, local, traditional authorities and the central government, and the highest of which is characterized by a highly centralized, relatively unified, authoritarian central governmental structure. Intermediate between these are centralized nonauthoritarian governments and moderately centralized governments tending toward democratic decentralization. In our preliminary definition of this indicator we were doubtful about the rank order of the two categories of relative decentralization: that defined by democratic decentralization and that defined by a cleavage between traditional local political authorities and central, often authoritarian, governments. We finally decided that the latter represented a lesser degree of effective centralization than the former.[99] Thus, the final indicator represents a continuum with respect to degree of centralization. Strictly interpreted, this variable is not intended to represent a movement from more democratic systems to less democratic systems, although it is evident that it may be related to such a movement.

The primary sources of information for this classification were recent country studies and a series of more than thirty consultations with regional and country experts. These were found to be necessary because of the tendency of written published and unpublished reports to characterize almost all governments of less-developed countries as centralized without sufficiently differentiating among them. In our cross-check of country classifications several raw characteristics from Banks's and Textor's *A Cross-Polity Survey* were also consulted.[100]

Below is the precise classification scheme for our indicator of the degree of centralization of political power during the period 1957–62.

A. Countries with highly centralized authoritarian governments in which most major decisions were referred to the central executive, central government control was at least reasonably effective throughout most

[99] We are grateful to Everett Hagen for underlining this difficulty and for suggesting the order of rank which we finally accepted. For results based upon the alternative ordering, see our study "A Factor Analysis of the Interrelationship between Social and Political Variables and Per Capita Gross National Product."

[100] Banks and Textor, *A Cross-Polity Survey*, raw characteristics number 28 (representative character of current regime), number 30 (freedom of group opposition), number 46 (leadership charisma), number 47 (vertical power distribution), and number 48 (horizontal power distribution).

of the country, and regional and local government authorities had relatively little political power. In addition, countries in this category were characterized by considerable repression of opposition by the central government: Afghanistan, Algeria, Cambodia, Dominican Republic, Ethiopia (−), Gabon, Ghana, Guinea, Iran, Iraq, Jordan, Kenya, Liberia, Nepal, Paraguay (−), Rhodesia, Senegal, South Korea (−), Sudan (−), Syria, Taiwan, Thailand, U.A.R.

B. Countries with highly centralized, reasonably effective government control throughout most of the country and weakness of local and regional government institutions. Countries in this category are distinguished from those in category A by the absence of significant measures of repression by the central government: Costa Rica (−), El Salvador, Guatemala (+), Honduras (−), Indonesia, Libya, Morocco, Nicaragua (+), Pakistan, Panama, Peru, Somali Republic, Surinam, Tanganyika, Tunisia (+), Turkey (+).

C. Countries characterized by a movement toward administrative decentralization of political power. Central governments may have continued to be strong, but decentralized national, regional, or local government authorities had, or were gaining, significant political power: Argentina, Bolivia, Brazil, Ceylon, Chile (+), Colombia, Cyprus, Greece, India, Israel, Jamaica, Japan, Lebanon, Malagasy, Malawi, Mexico, Nigeria, Philippines, Sierra Leone, South Africa, Trinidad, Uganda, Uruguay, Venezuela, Zambia.

D. Countries characterized by centralization of government authority without marked repression of opposition, in which, however, central governments did not maintain effective administrative control throughout important parts of the country. Local village or tribal authorities continued to be the key administrative units in many areas: Burma, Cameroun, Chad, Dahomey, Ecuador (+), Ivory Coast, Laos, Niger, South Vietnam, Yemen.

Strength of Democratic Institutions

The interconnection between the extent of democracy and economic performance has been much discussed in recent years. A number of social scientists, dealing primarily with noncommunist countries, maintain that in the long run more effective economic development tends to be accompanied by more democratic systems. J. S. Coleman, for exam-

59

ple, in the summary essay of *The Politics of the Developing Areas*,[101] finds for a sample of forty-six less-developed noncommunist countries a positive correlation between composite rank order on eleven indices of economic development and a three-way classification of countries with respect to the degree of competitiveness of their political systems. The explanation of this association suggested by the Almond-Coleman analysis is that as countries become more developed and differentiated economically their political systems also become more differentiated, moving in the direction of greater articulation of political interests (through voluntary associational groups), greater aggregation of interests (through political parties), and greater explicit political socialization (through the spread of mass communication media).[102] Everett Hagen, in discussing findings similar to those of Coleman, points to the manner in which industrialization, urbanization, and geographic movement "widen horizons and create new ambitions" that are inevitably conducive to political change. He underlines, however, that there is also an opposite flow of causation as the breakdown of traditional sociopolitical forms tends in turn to promote more rapid economic change.[103] A somewhat similar explanation of the positive long-term association between more democratic practices and higher standards of consumption and investment is given by Daniel Lerner. In his view the principal mechanism for social and economic growth is the diffusion, through increases in urbanization, literacy, and mass communication media, of desires and capacities for greater individual participation in both the proceeds of economic growth and in collective decision-making.[104]

While Coleman, Hagen, Lerner, and others[105] thus posit a long-run positive association between economic development and more competi-

[101] J. S. Coleman, "Conclusion: The Political Systems of the Developing Areas," in *The Politics of the Developing Areas*, ed. Almond and Coleman, p. 538. For somewhat similar analyses that reach the same general conclusion, see Lipset, "Some Social Requisites of Democracy," pp. 69–105, and E. E. Hagen, "A Framework for Analyzing Economic and Political Change," in Robert E. Asher *et al., Development of the Emerging Countries* (Washington, D.C.: The Brookings Institution, 1962), pp. 1–38.

[102] See Chapter I of *The Politics of the Developing Areas*, ed. Almond and Coleman, pp. 26ff.

[103] Hagen, "A Framework for Analyzing Economic and Political Change," pp. 10–11.

[104] See Lerner, *The Passing of Traditional Society*, p. 74, for this view.

[105] See, for example, D. E. Apter, *The Politics of Modernization* (Chicago: University of Chicago Press, 1965), pp. 449–50; and Pye, "Democracy, Modernization and Nation Building," p. 24.

tive participant political systems, they do not maintain that such a relationship necessarily holds in the short run or at all levels of development. Indeed, a number of investigators emphasize that in the early stages of economic growth oligarchic governmental structures tend to be more effective in raising growth rates than are democratic systems. Several reasons have been proposed for an association between oligarchic systems and more rapid economic development: among them, leadership desires for more rapid decision-making than is usually feasible in a parliamentary system; the instability of representative institutions in the face of regional, cultural, and political disunity; and the absence of such prerequisites for the functioning of a democracy as literacy and individual motivation toward political participation.[106]

Our indicator of the strength of democratic institutions is primarily qualitative and refers to the period 1957–62. Several qualitative elements and one statistical element were combined in the index: (1) the presence or absence of at least two reasonably effective competitive political parties; (2) the freedom of political parties and other voluntary groups to oppose the government; (3) the stability of the political party system (as indicated by the length of tenure of leaders, for example); and (4) the extent of experience with democratic forms. Data on the percentage of the voting-age population participating in national elections[107] were useful in indicating broad differences in degree of participation by individuals in the political system.

The principal sources of judgmental information for the initial country classifications were recent country studies. Banks's and Textor's *A Cross-Polity Survey* provided us with extensive cross-checks on judgments regarding the competitiveness of political parties and the degree of freedom of political opposition;[108] it also offered substantial information on the stability of party systems.[109] Final cross-checks were made by means of about ten interviews with country experts which were designed to resolve doubtful classifications.

---

[106] For discussion of the reasons for the tendency for oligarchic solutions to problems of economic development to be more effective, see Shils, *Political Development in the New States*, p. 67; and Lloyd A. Fallers, "Equality, Modernity, and Democracy in the New States," in *Old Societies and New States*, ed. Geertz, p. 217.

[107] Russett *et al., World Handbook of Political and Social Indicators*, Table 24.

[108] Banks and Textor, *A Cross-Polity Survey*, raw characteristics number 30 (freedom of group opposition) and number 41 (party system; quantitative).

[109] *Ibid.*, raw characteristic number 43 (stability of party system).

In the classification scheme described below there are two categories of countries in which democratic forms were in operation during the period 1957–62 and two categories in which the practice of democracy was intermittent, limited, or nonexistent during this period.

A. Countries characterized by relatively well-established nation-wide democratic institutions. At least two political parties operated effectively during the entire period 1957–62; political parties were free to oppose the government; and at least 30 per cent of the voting-age population participated in national elections. Countries with over 70 per cent voter participation are classified $A+$, those with 30–40 per cent voter participation are classified $A-$, and the rest are classified A: Chile $(-)$, Colombia $(-)$, Costa Rica, Greece $(+)$, India, Israel $(+)$, Jamaica $(+)$, Japan $(+)$, Lebanon, Philippines, Surinam $(-)$, Uruguay.

B. Countries in which nation-wide democratic parliamentary institutions operated fairly effectively during the period 1957–62, judging by the standards of less-developed countries, but in which the effectiveness of these institutions was restricted by low voter participation, constraints upon opposition parties, instability of the party system, and/or inexperience with democratic forms: Argentina $(+)$, Cyprus $(+)$, Malagasy $(+)$, Mexico, Morocco, Nigeria $(+)$, Rhodesia, South Africa, Trinidad $(+)$, Uganda $(+)$, Venezuela.

C. Countries in which nation-wide democratic parliamentary institutions operated during some part of the period 1957–62 but in which these institutions gave evidence of marked instability or weakness. Included in this category are countries in which parliamentary forms were established or suspended at some time during the period. Countries with only a single effective political party, in which opposition was permitted during part of the period or in which the internal organization of the party was fairly democratic, are classified $C-$: Algeria, Bolivia $(-)$, Brazil $(+)$, Burma, Ceylon, Dahomey $(-)$, Dominican Republic $(-)$, Ecuador, El Salvador, Gabon, Guatemala, Honduras, Kenya, Laos, Malawi, Nicaragua, Pakistan $(-)$, Panama, Peru, Senegal $(-)$, Sierra Leone $(+)$, Somali Republic, Tanganyika $(-)$, Turkey $(+)$, Zambia.

D. Countries in which there was little or no effective practice of nation-wide institutional democracy during the period 1957–62. Countries in which all political parties were banned or ineffective during most or all of the period 1957–62 are classified $D-$: Afghanistan $(-)$, Cambodia, Cameroun, Chad, Ethiopia $(-)$, Ghana, Guinea, Indonesia, Iran, Iraq $(-)$, Ivory Coast, Jordan $(-)$, Liberia, Libya, Nepal $(-)$, Niger,

Paraguay, South Korea, South Vietnam, Sudan, Syria, Taiwan, Thailand, Tunisia, U.A.R., Yemen (−).

Degree of Freedom of Political Opposition and Press

An important aspect of the strength of democratic institutions is the degree of freedom of political opposition and press. Of course, these freedoms may exist prior to the evolution of effective mechanisms for individual participation in a democratic political system; however, once specialized institutions have been created to articulate and aggregate specific group interests in national politics, the presence in the society of reasonable freedom of expression and of political opposition becomes a *sine qua non* of effective democracy.

Since relatively few less-developed countries have extensive freedom of opposition or press, it is useful when defining an indicator to represent them to distinguish among the many countries having some form of restrictions. Therefore, we have assigned relatively high scores to countries in which restrictions on the press and on political opposition are only occasional or fairly limited. Successively lower scores were given to countries having increasingly restrictive government controls. Two further points should be noted about the definition of this indicator. First, the degree of freedom of political opposition was weighed more heavily than the degree of freedom of press since the former was felt to be a better indicator of genuine institutional freedom. Second, the presence or absence of controls over foreign newspapers was excluded from consideration.

As with our over-all measurement of the effectiveness of democratic institutions, the primary source for the preliminary classification of countries was recent country studies. Once again, the indices of freedom of press and freedom of group opposition presented in *A Cross-Polity Survey*[110] gave us a valuable independent cross-check on the judgmental information gathered from other sources. As a result, only a handful of interviews was required to resolve doubtful cases.

The final classification scheme summarizing the degree of freedom of political opposition and press during the period 1957–62 is presented below.

A. Countries in which political parties (other than extremist parties

[110] *Ibid.*, raw characteristics number 13 (freedom of the press) and number 30 (freedom of group opposition).

opposing constitutional forms of government) were free to organize, operate, and oppose the government throughout all or most of the period 1957–62. Countries in which domestic freedom of the press was nevertheless somewhat restricted or intermittent are classified $A-$: Algeria, Argentina $(-)$, Brazil $(-)$, Ceylon, Chile, Colombia, Costa Rica, Cyprus, Greece, Honduras $(-)$, India, Israel, Jamaica, Japan, Lebanon $(-)$, Malagasy, Malawi $(-)$, Morocco, Nigeria, Panama, Peru, Philippines, Sierra Leone, Surinam, Trinidad, Uganda, Uruguay, Venezuela.

B. Countries in which political parties, while generally free to organize, were limited in their political activities and in their freedom to oppose the government during part or all of the 1957–62 period. Countries in which domestic freedom of the press was restricted or intermittent during the period are classified $B-$: Burma $(-)$, Cameroun, Chad, Dominican Republic $(-)$, Ecuador, El Salvador, Gabon $(-)$, Guatemala $(+)$, Kenya, Laos $(-)$, Libya $(-)$, Mexico, Nicaragua $(-)$, Niger $(-)$, Rhodesia $(-)$, Senegal, Somali Republic, South Africa, South Korea $(-)$, Syria $(-)$, Tanganyika, Turkey $(-)$, Zambia.

C. Countries in which political parties were limited to nonpolitical activities or in which political opposition to the government was banned during the period 1957–62. Those in which political opposition was banned and in which domestic freedom of the press was absent are classified $C-$. The remaining countries are classified C: Afghanistan $(-)$, Bolivia, Cambodia, Dahomey $(+)$, Ethiopia $(-)$, Ghana $(-)$, Guinea $(-)$, Indonesia, Iran $(+)$, Iraq, Ivory Coast, Jordan $(-)$, Liberia, Nepal $(-)$, Pakistan $(-)$, Paraguay, South Vietnam, Sudan $(-)$, Taiwan, Thailand, Tunisia, U.A.R. $(-)$, Yemen $(-)$.

Degree of Competitiveness of Political Parties

The presence of competitiveness among political parties is one dimension of an effective democratic system. At the lower end of the scale of political competitiveness, a movement from a pure dictatorship to a system with a national unity party and subsequently to a system with two competing parties clearly represents a movement toward greater democracy. However, while at least two competing parties are necessary for a political system to assure representation of the diverse groups in a society, further multiplication of parties does not necessarily produce a more participant democratic system, even though, strictly speaking, it may lead to an increase in the degree of political competitiveness. With respect to the relationship between competition among parties and economic change, there is evidence (cited above in our discussion of the strength of democratic institutions) of a tendency for countries with no political parties or with only a single party to rank low on indices of the level of economic development as well as on most spectra of political development.

In deriving an index of the competitiveness of parties during the period 1957–62, we differentiated only slightly between countries having two parties and countries having more than two parties operating at a national level.[111] We did differentiate significantly between countries with two or more parties in which there was reasonable expectation of rotation or sharing of government control among parties and those in which there was not. Finally, it should be noted, of course, that classification of a country with respect to the number of political parties sharing or rotating control of the political system is not tantamount to classification according to strength of the democratic system. A country may have two nationally operative political parties, for example, and yet be characterized by extremely low voter participation, significant restrictions on freedom of the press, or marked instability of the party system.

The primary source of information on degree of competitiveness used in classifying individual countries was Banks's and Textor's *A Cross-Polity Survey*, raw characteristic number 41 (party system: quantitative). Recent country studies were consulted as a cross-check on the particular time period used in our definition of the indicator. Where a country had an operative party system during only part of the period 1957–62, classification was made on the basis of the longest consistent subperiod.

A. Countries in which there were two or more reasonably effective political parties, between at least two of which rotation or sharing of government control could reasonably be expected. Countries in which there were more than two national parties are classified A and those in which there were only two are classified $A-$: Algeria, Argentina, Brazil, Burma, Ceylon, Chile, Colombia ($-$), Costa Rica, Cyprus, Ecuador, El Salvador, Guatemala, Honduras ($-$), Israel, Jamaica ($-$), Kenya, Laos, Lebanon, Malawi, Morocco, Nigeria, Panama, Peru, Philippines ($-$), Rhodesia, Sierra Leone ($-$), South Africa, South Korea ($-$), Surinam, Turkey, Uganda, Venezuela, Zambia.

---

[111] In this connection we are grateful to Everett Hagen for his suggestion that we redefine this indicator.

B. Countries in which there were two or more effective political parties without a reasonable expectation that rotation or sharing of government control would occur. Countries in which at least two parties had significant power at the national level but in which one of these was unable to win a majority are classified *B*. Those in which only one party was effective at the national level but in which one or more other parties retained their identity in national elections are classified *B* −: Bolivia (−), Greece (−), India (−), Iran, Japan, Malagasy (−), Mexico (−), Paraguay (−), Senegal (−), Somali Republic (−), South Vietnam (−), Taiwan (−), Trinidad, Uruguay.

C. Countries in which there was only one political party effective at the national level and in which all others had been banned or were adjuncts to the dominant party: Cambodia, Cameroun, Chad, Dahomey, Dominican Republic, Gabon, Ghana, Guinea, Ivory Coast, Liberia, Nicaragua, Niger, Tanganyika, Tunisia, U.A.R.

D. Countries in which there were no political parties effective at the national level: Afghanistan, Ethiopia, Indonesia, Iraq, Jordan, Libya, Nepal, Pakistan, Sudan, Syria, Thailand, Yemen.

Predominant Basis of the Political Party System

The broad contrast between the nature of political parties in advanced democracies and in most underdeveloped countries is well known. Generally speaking, in most economically developed democracies each of several competitive parties tends to represent a fairly wide range of interests having a given class or ideological orientation and to formulate pragmatic programs that combine and articulate these interests. In contrast, most low-income nations have either noncompetitive political systems or competitive systems in which particularistic (ethnic, religious, regional) or highly personalistic parties predominate. Within the range of income represented by most contemporary developing nations, it is not quite so clear how the character of political parties is related to differences in economic performance. With respect to the upper end of the low-income spectrum, specialists in Latin American politics stress the high incidence in Latin America of both personalistic parties and parties having a class or ideological orientation. According to the group approach to political development, as expressed by Blanksten,[112] for example, one would expect countries with parties having the latter more

[112] Blanksten, "Transference of Social and Political Loyalties," pp. 176–77.

aggregative orientation to be more developed economically than countries where narrowly based personalistic parties are common. With respect to the lower end of the economic scale, there appears to be a tendency among newly independent African and Asian countries for a single, dominant, nationalist party to control the political life of the country. A certain number of these countries, however, have multiparty political systems in which particularistic bonds are the preferred basis for the demarcation of parties.[113] Recent historical experience does not provide a clear pattern of progression from single dominant mass-based parties toward parties based on cultural, ethnic, religious, or regional identifications or of progression in the opposite direction. Nevertheless, there are a priori grounds for expecting countries with the more competitive system to be better developed politically and economically. In particular, it would seem that a competitive party system articulating specific particularist interests is more likely to evolve once a minimum level of individual political and economic participation is attained, while the creation of an all-embracing nationalist party initially requires only the presence of a strong common impetus toward independence from colonial rulers.

To summarize the tendencies just discussed, we have defined an indicator of the predominant basis of political party systems in terms of a spectrum, the lower end of which is marked by the absence of parties or by the dominance of a single party with nationalistic appeal and the upper end of which is characterized by articulate aggregative parties having a class or ideological orientation. Thus, progression along the scale involves (1) a movement toward greater articulation of first, primordial particularist interests, then personalistic interests, and finally associational interests (such as those of labor unions and industrialists); and (2) a movement toward greater combination or aggregation of small group interests into larger associations with more rationally formulated pragmatic national programs.

The primary data for the country classifications were taken from *A Cross-Polity Survey*.[114] Two difficulties experienced in classifying countries should be noted. The first was the problem of scaling an essentially typological characteristic; we resolved this difficulty along the lines dis-

---

[113] See, for example, Pye (ed.), *Communications and Political Development,* pp. 59–60.

[114] Raw characteristics number 42 (party system: qualitative) and number 44 (personalismo).

cussed above. A second related difficulty arose with respect to countries having mixed party systems: for example, those having both ideological and personalistic parties or those having both personalistic and particularist parties.[115] The solution to the first problem helped resolve the second problem. Where a country had an approximately equal weight of parties defined by two adjacent categories, a score lying between the two was taken to represent its mixed system. As it happened, almost every ambiguous case could be resolved in this manner. In the remaining cases we were able with the help of expert opinion to make a definite judgment regarding the type of party which predominated. As with the indicator of competitiveness, where a country had an operative political party system during only part of the period 1957–62, classification was made on the basis of the longest subperiod.

The definition of our indicator of the predominant basis of the political party system during the period 1957–62 follows below.

A. Countries with political systems characterized by the predominance of a party or parties having, among other things, significant class or ideological orientation. Countries in which political parties had a mixture of important ideological and personalistic elements are classified $A-$. Excluded from this category are countries in which there is an important exclusively mass-directed or national unity party: Algeria, Argentina, Bolivia $(-)$, Brazil $(-)$, Burma $(-)$, Ceylon, Chile, Colombia, Costa Rica, Greece $(-)$, India, Israel, Jamaica, Japan, Mexico, Morocco, South Korea $(-)$, Turkey, Venezuela.

B. Countries in which political parties in general were highly personalistic rather than doctrinal or nationalistic. Party systems in some of these countries were characterized by extensive political opportunism. Countries in which political parties had a mixture of significant personalistic and religious, cultural, ethnic, or regional elements are classified $B-$: Cambodia $(-)$, Ecuador, El Salvador, Guatemala, Honduras, Iran, Laos, Liberia, Nicaragua, Panama, Peru, Philippines, Taiwan, Uruguay.

C. Countries in which the predominant basis of political parties was the regional, ethnic, cultural, or religious groupings of the population: Cameroun, Chad, Cyprus, Dahomey, Kenya, Lebanon, Malagasy, Malawi, Niger, Nigeria, Rhodesia, Sierra Leone, Somali Republic, South Africa, Surinam, Trinidad, Uganda, Zambia.

D. Countries in which the dominant national unity party did not have

---

[115] Other combinations were rare.

a significant class or ideological orientation: Dominican Republic, Gabon, Ghana, Guinea, Ivory Coast, Paraguay, Senegal, South Vietnam, Tanganyika, Tunisia, U.A.R.

E. Countries in which there were no effective political parties or in which all parties had been banned for more than three years of the period 1957–62: Afghanistan, Ethiopia, Indonesia, Iraq, Jordan, Libya, Nepal, Pakistan, Sudan, Syria, Thailand, Yemen.

Strength of the Labor Movement

A familiar sociopolitical concomitant of the process of industrialization is the growth of trade-union organization. While there have been historical instances of unions of agricultural workers, the creation of durable, stable labor organizations has typically accompanied the growth of industrial enterprise. A number of reasons have been put forth for the association of trade-union growth with industrialization. One contemporary explanation suggests that only fully urbanized industrial workers who have no expectation of returning to their rural homes are likely to become so committed to the urban industrial way of life that their protests and demands will take the form of permanently organized economic and political action.[116] Another view of the positive long-run association between stronger trade unions and higher levels of industrialization and development stresses the importance of labor unions as specialized structures of interest articulation and aggregation which formulate and transmit explicit political demands to other political structures such as political parties and legislatures.[117] According to this view, a salient characteristic of relatively developed economies is that almost all important economic interests are represented by organized groups having a voice in national politics.[118] The presence of unions thus becomes a significant indication of the working of a participant democratic system. In contrast, traditional, predominantly agricultural societies are characterized either by the presence of organized groups representing specific cultural or regional rather than economic interests or by the absence of articulate interest groups at the national level.

There is considerable controversy with respect to the short-run rela-

---

[116] Clark Kerr, "Changing Social Structures," in *Labor Commitment and Social Change in Developing Areas,* ed. Moore and Feldman, pp. 351–52.

[117] See *The Politics of the Developing Areas,* ed. Almond and Coleman, p. 36.

[118] Blanksten, "Transference of Social and Political Loyalties," p. 176.

69

tionship between unions and economic growth. One view, held by Dunlop and De Schweinitz, for example, is that because trade unions favor consumption they tend to reduce (or prevent an increase in) the proportion of resources going into investment and thus to retard the rate of economic growth. Other points of view emphasize the positive effects of unions as modernizing influences and agents of social welfare.[119]

The derivation of an index of the strength of the labor movement was complicated by the absence of data on trade-union memberships for most of the countries in our sample. The indicator chosen was a primarily qualitative composite that combined several aspects of labor-union strength: the extent of their political power, their freedom from political restrictions, their independence of government influence, and the extent of their popular support. Finally, within each category a lower score was given to countries having a very small industrial labor force from which unions could potentially draw their membership.

In classifying individual countries with respect to the strength of their labor movements during the period 1957–62, recent studies of labor movements in less-developed countries were the principal source of information. Particularly useful were several collections of articles, two edited by Walter Galenson and one by E. M. Kassalow. Recent volumes by Troncoso and Burnett and by Millen were also very helpful.[120] Preliminary judgments based on these data were cross-checked by several interviews with regional experts which were directed at assigning doubtful cases to specific categories.

A. Countries in which labor movements were relatively well-established and active and had considerable popular support (judging by the standards of less-developed countries), considerable independent political power, and significant freedom to oppose the government. The labor organizations in these countries, though substantially independent, were usually allied with one or more political parties. Countries in which, as

[119] For a review of this controversy, see Adolf Sturmthal, "Unions and Economic Development," *Economic Development and Cultural Change*, Vol. 8 (January, 1960), pp. 199–205.

[120] See Walter Galenson (ed.), *Labor and Economic Development* (New York: John Wiley & Sons, 1959); Walter Galenson (ed.), *Labor in Developing Economies* (Berkeley: University of California Press, 1962); E. M. Kassalow (ed.), *National Labor Movements in the Postwar World* (Evanston, Ill.: Northwestern University Press, 1963); M. P. Troncoso and B. G. Burnett, *The Rise of the Latin American Labor Movement* (New York: Bookman Associates, 1960); and B. H. Millen, *The Political Role of Labor in Developing Countries* (Washington, D.C.: The Brookings Institution, 1963).

of about 1960, the industrial labor force was 30 per cent of or less than the total nonagricultural labor force are classified $A-$: Argentina, Bolivia $(-)$, Ceylon, Chile, Costa Rica, Indonesia, Israel $(+)$, Japan, Jamaica, Mexico, Morocco $(-)$, Trinidad $(+)$, Uruguay, Venezuela.

B. Countries with fairly well-established independent labor movements that had moderate political power but that in most instances were limited in their freedom to oppose the government. In a number of these countries political parties dominated the labor movement; however, excluded from this category are countries in which the labor movement was controlled by a single political party that dominated the nation. Countries that had a very small industrial labor force are classified $B-$: Brazil, Cameroun $(-)$, Colombia, Cyprus, Dahomey $(-)$, El Salvador, Guatemala $(-)$, Greece, Honduras, India $(+)$, Kenya $(-)$, Lebanon, Liberia $(-)$, Malagasy $(-)$, Malawi, Nigeria, Philippines, Rhodesia, Senegal $(-)$, Sierra Leone $(-)$, South Africa, Surinam, Tunisia, Uganda $(-)$, Zambia.

C. Countries in which a fairly well-established labor movement was either government sponsored or seriously restricted in its activities by the government. This category includes countries in which a single political party dominated the labor movement. Countries that had a very small industrial labor force are classified $C-$: Algeria $(-)$, Dominican Republic, Ghana $(-)$, Guinea $(-)$, Nicaragua, Peru, Sudan $(-)$, Tanganyika $(-)$, Turkey, U.A.R.

D. Countries in which the labor movement was negligible or in effect proscribed. Countries with a very small independent labor movement that had negligible political influence are classified $D+$. Countries in which labor organization was banned completely are classified $D-$. The remaining countries are classified D: Afghanistan $(-)$, Burma, Cambodia, Chad $(+)$, Ecuador $(+)$, Ethiopia $(-)$, Gabon, Iran $(+)$, Iraq, Ivory Coast $(+)$, Jordan, Laos, Libya $(+)$, Nepal, Niger, Pakistan, Panama $(+)$, Paraguay $(+)$, Somali Republic $(+)$, South Korea $(+)$, South Vietnam, Syria, Taiwan, Thailand $(-)$, Yemen $(-)$.

Political Strength of the Traditional Elite

The emergence of a political leadership committed to economic modernization is generally agreed to be essential to the socioeconomic transformation that a traditional society must undergo for an effective take-off into self-sustained growth. At very low levels of development

71

the breakup of the social and political control exercised by traditional land-owning elites or other tradition-oriented bureaucratic, military, or religious elites is important for the initiation of economic growth for at least two interrelated reasons. First, control of the wealth of a country by a traditional elite tends to result in spending by wealth-owners for services, luxury goods, land, and other real estate rather than for the expansion of business enterprise. Second, tradition-oriented actions and ideologies tend to be dominated by ascriptive particularistic norms that often conflict with the requirements for economic modernization and technological change.[121] Thus, the extent of the social and political influence of the traditional elite is an aspect of the social structure of low-income countries which is very relevant to a study of economic development.

In classifying less-developed countries with respect to the role of the traditional elite, we grouped them into three broad categories according to the political strength of their tradition-oriented elites during the period 1957–62. We interpreted the traditional elites to include both traditional land-holding elites and bureaucratic, religious, or military elites who favored the preservation of traditional political, social, and economic organization, institutions, and values. Qualitative information from recent country studies was the principal source used in the preliminary classification of individual countries. Also very useful were Edwin Lieuwen's *Arms and Politics in Latin America,*[122] Manfred Halpern's *The Politics of Social Change in the Middle East and North Africa,*[123] and Banks's and Textor's *A Cross-Polity Survey.*[124] Once preliminary country scores were assigned, we consulted twelve regional experts for clarification of doubtful classifications. These consultations made it evident that our preliminary category descriptions did not provide for countries that were under colonial rule during part of the 1957–62 period or for countries in which the role of traditional national elites changed significantly during that period. To deal with the former group we introduced a distinction between tradition-oriented and modernizing colonial elites; to deal with the latter we assigned a special score to countries in which the power of the traditional elite showed a marked decline during the period.

[121] See B. F. Hoselitz, "Tradition and Economic Growth," in *Tradition, Values, and Socio-Economic Development,* ed. Braibanti and Spengler, pp. 83–113.

[122] (Rev. ed.; New York: Frederick A. Praeger, 1961).

[123] (Princeton: Princeton University Press, 1963).

[124] Raw characteristics number 45 (political leadership) and number 53 (character of bureaucracy).

The classification scheme for the indicator of political strength of the traditional elite during the period 1957–62 groups countries into three principal categories.

A. Countries in which traditional land-owning and/or other tradition-oriented national elites were politically dominant during the greater part of the period 1957–62. Any country in which a feudal type landed aristocracy was in complete control is classified *A*+. Countries in which no important landed aristocracies existed but in which the controlling elites nevertheless exhibited clearly traditional attitudes are classified *A*−. The remaining countries are classified *A*: Afghanistan (+), Algeria (−), Cambodia (−), Ecuador, El Salvador, Ethiopia (+), Guatemala, Honduras (−), Iran, Laos (−), Liberia (−), Libya (−), Nepal, Nicaragua, Panama, Paraguay, Peru, Rhodesia (−), South Vietnam (−), Thailand (−), Yemen.

B. Countries in which tradition-oriented national or colonial elites had moderate political influence during an important part of the period 1957–62. In many of these countries, commercial and industrial groups, modernizing military leaders, or modernizing bureaucrats exercised growing political power during the period. Countries in which the latter groups were or became more influential than the traditional elites during the period are classified *B*−: Argentina (−), Brazil (−), Ceylon (−), Chile, Colombia. Dahomey (−), Ivory Coast (−), Jordan, Nigeria (−), Morocco (+), Pakistan (−), Philippines (−), Senegal (+), Sierra Leone (−), South Africa, South Korea (−), Tanganyika (−), Uganda (−), Uruguay (−), Zambia (−).

C. Countries in which tradition-oriented elites had little or no political power during most of the period 1957–62. This category includes countries in which modernizing colonial regimes were succeeded by modernizing national governments during the period. Countries in which traditional elites were excluded from political activity either by legislation or by force during most of the period are classified *C*−: Bolivia (−), Burma, Cameroun, Chad, Costa Rica, Cyprus, Dominican Republic, Gabon, Ghana (−), Greece, Guinea (−), India, Indonesia (−), Iraq, Israel, Jamaica, Japan, Kenya, Lebanon, Malawi, Malagasy, Mexico (−), Niger, Somali Republic, Sudan (+), Surinam, Syria, Taiwan (−), Trinidad, Tunisia, Turkey (−), U.A.R. (−), Venezuela.

Political Strength of the Military

Although the incidence of military intervention in civilian politics is quite high in developing countries, relatively few studies have been made of the relationship between military institutions and economic or political development. Until recently a view commonly held was that militarism is inherently antipathetic to both the evolution of democracy and to broadly based economic growth. In the past few years, however, a number of political scientists have undertaken the study of armies in underdeveloped countries as potentially modern political structures capable of acting as effective modernizing agents. As Lucian Pye pointed out at a 1959 conference on the role of the military in underdeveloped countries, the members of the army of a low-income nation may be more receptive of Western technology and organization and more divorced from traditional patterns of action than are civil bureaucracies.[125] In addition, armies often provide training in specialized modern skills and offer a vehicle for the creation of a generalized sense of national identity. Finally, they can provide a channel for upward social mobility. Indeed, Manfred Halpern takes the position that in the Middle East and North Africa armies have been agents of change and reform.[126] In considering the military in sub-Saharan Africa, Coleman and Brice also emphasize the modernizing influence of the army in increasing literacy among recruits and in training them in modern skills and health practices.[127] In contrast, however, Edwin Lieuwen, in examining a wide range of countries in Latin America, concludes that although there have been noted exceptions, armies have tended to be a conservative force operating in the civil politics of Latin America.[128] Historically, armies have played both positive and negative roles in the modernization process, in general proving themselves better at the establishment of an orderly and stable framework for growth than at continuous administration of a political system.[129]

[125] L. W. Pye, "Armies in the Process of Political Modernization," in *The Role of the Military in Underdeveloped Countries,* ed. J. J. Johnson (Princeton: Princeton University Press, 1962), pp. 73ff; see also Millikan and Blackmer (eds.), *The Emerging Nations,* pp. 31–34.

[126] Manfred Halpern, "Middle Eastern Armies and the New Middle Class," in *The Role of the Military in Underdeveloped Countries,* ed. Johnson, p. 279.

[127] J. S. Coleman and Belmont Brice, Jr., "The Role of the Military in Sub-Saharan Africa," *ibid.,* pp. 394ff.

[128] *Arms and Politics in Latin America,* p. 155.

[129] See Millikan and Blackmer (eds.), *The Emerging Nations,* pp. 31–37.

While opinions of the relationship between the military and economic development thus vary, it is clear that the political strength of the military is relevant to a study of the process of economic growth. In defining an indicator to represent variations in the role of the military we grouped less-developed countries into three broad categories determined respectively by a marked, moderate, or negligible military influence in the political arena. For our preliminary classification of the individual countries the primary sources were recent country studies together with, for Latin American countries, Edwin Lieuwen's *Arms and Politics in Latin America*.[130] When Banks's and Textor's *A Cross-Polity Survey*[131] became available to us it also proved extremely useful since its definition of the military's political participation was very similar to ours. Finally, various essays in *The Role of the Military in Underdeveloped Countries*[132] offered us a cross-check on a number of our classifications.

The classification scheme for our indicator of the political strength of the military during the period 1957–62 is presented below.

A. Countries in which the military was in direct political control during some part of the period 1957–62. Those in which the military was in direct control during the entire period are classified $A+$. Those in which the military controlled the civilian government for only one or two years of the period are classified $A-$. The remaining countries are classified A: Algeria $(-)$, Argentina $(-)$, Burma, Dominican Republic, El Salvador, Guatemala $(-)$, Honduras $(-)$, Nicaragua, Pakistan, Paraguay $(+)$, Peru $(-)$, South Korea $(-)$, Sudan, Syria, Thailand, Turkey $(-)$, U.A.R., Yemen $(-)$.

B. Countries in which the military was an important political influence but was not in direct political control during most of the period 1957–62. Those in which the tie between the military and the civilian government was very close are classified $B+$. Those in which military influence was significant during less than the entire period 1957–62 are classified $B-$. The remaining countries are classified B: Afghanistan $(+)$, Brazil $(+)$, Cambodia, Ecuador, Ethiopia $(+)$, Ghana $(-)$, Indonesia $(+)$, Iran, Iraq $(+)$, Jordan $(+)$, Kenya $(-)$, Laos $(+)$, Lebanon $(+)$, Nepal, Rhodesia, Senegal, South Africa, South Vietnam $(+)$, Taiwan, Venezuela $(+)$.

---

[130] *Ibid.*
[131] Raw characteristic number 54 (political participation by the military).
[132] J. J. Johnson (ed.).

C. Countries in which the military had little or no political influence during the period 1957–62: Bolivia, Cameroun, Ceylon, Chad (+), Chile, Colombia, Costa Rica, Cyprus, Dahomey, Gabon, Greece, Guinea, India, Israel, Ivory Coast, Jamaica, Japan, Liberia, Libya, Malagasy, Malawi, Mexico, Morocco, Niger, Nigeria, Panama, Philippines, Sierra Leone, Somali Republic, Surinam, Tanganyika, Trinidad, Tunisia, Uganda, Uruguay, Zambia.

Degree of Administrative Efficiency

The contributions that an effective bureaucracy can make to economic development have frequently been noted by social scientists. Rationally organized administrative services can help establish and strengthen the legal and public service facilities necessary for steady growth; they can help create financial institutions and tax instruments favorable to the expansion of private economic activity, or they can take direct responsibility for initiating development projects and plans.[133]

In line with Max Weber's classical formulation of bureaucracy, modernization of bureaucratic administration may be said to involve the creation of such attributes within the bureaucracy as "hierarchy, responsibility, rationality, achievement orientation, specialization and differentation, discipline, professionalization."[134] In a recent analysis of bureaucracy and economic performance, Hoselitz emphasizes the interrelationship between the processes of economic and administrative modernization. He points out that in traditional societies, recruitment to bureaucracies tends to exhibit the same strong admixture of ascription as does recruitment in fundamental social institutions; thus, practices that constitute corruption or nepotism by Western standards may actually be "the generalization of commonly accepted principles of recruitment and selection for occupational roles to a special institution—the administrative services."[135] In contrast, recruitment in more advanced societies is based, at least in principle, on achievement criteria. As countries evolve toward "modernity," both economic organization and government administration tend to be subject to the same process of structural

---

[133] See J. J. Spengler, "Bureaucracy and Economic Development," in *Bureaucracy and Political Development*, ed. LaPalombara, pp. 225–26.

[134] "An Overview of Bureaucracy and Political Development," in *Bureaucracy and Political Development*, ed. LaPalombara, p. 10.

[135] B. F. Hoselitz, "Levels of Economic Performance and Bureaucratic Structures," in *Bureaucracy and Political Development*, ed. LaPalombara, p. 176.

differentiation; with respect to administration this means that administrative functions become specialized within specific institutions charged with the fulfillment of designated national goals.[136]

The indicator of administrative efficiency chosen for our study was a qualitative one in which interviews with regional and country experts were an important source of information in classifying individual countries. Another main source of information was recent country studies. The classifications were cross-checked with Banks's and Textor's *A Cross-Polity Survey*, raw characteristic number 53 (character of bureaucracy).

Several criteria were used in grouping countries into three broad categories of degree of efficiency of the public administration: in particular, the degree of permanence and training of administrators (an indirect measure of whether recruitment is based upon qualifications for the job); the extent to which corruption, inefficiency, and incompetence seriously hamper government functioning; and the extent to which instability of policy at higher levels of administration promotes inefficiency. Classification of individual countries was based upon judgments regarding the period 1957–62. In the event of marked changes during the period, greater weight was given to the more recent years.

A special comment on the reliability of this indicator is required. It is obvious that personal judgments regarding the over-all efficiency of the complex organs and processes composing a country's administrative system will be highly subjective. For this reason we were prepared to omit an indicator of administrative efficiency in the event that expert opinion turned out to be conflicting and inconsistent. In practice, however, we obtained a reasonably good consensus from the experts consulted on a ranking into broad groups of the countries with which they were familiar. Nevertheless, it should be noted that, due to the broad nature of the judgments required, the element of subjectivity in this indicator may be somewhat greater than in the other qualitative indicators incorporated in our study.

The classification scheme for the indicator of the extent of administrative efficiency follows.

A. Countries in which public administration was reasonably efficient. These countries had relatively well-trained civil services and did not suffer from instability of policy at higher administrative levels. Corruption was not widespread. Finally, bureaucratic inefficiency was not as

[136] *Ibid.,* p. 197.

marked as in most less-developed countries: Chile (−), Colombia (−), Costa Rica (−), Greece, India, Israel, Jamaica, Japan (+), Kenya, Malawi (−), Mexico (−), South Africa, Taiwan (−), Tanganyika, Trinidad (−), Tunisia (−), Turkey (−), Uganda, U.A.R. (−), Uruguay, Venezuela (−), Zambia (−).

B. Countries in which public administration was marked by considerable bureaucratic inefficiency but in which there was, nevertheless, a permanent body of administrators. Corruption may have been common, and there may have been moderate instability of policy at higher levels of administration, but these phenomena did not operate to the point where they seriously interfered with government functioning: Algeria, Argentina (+), Brazil (−), Burma (−), Cameroun (−), Ceylon, Cyprus, Dahomey (−), El Salvador, Gabon, Ghana (+), Ivory Coast (−), Lebanon, Malagasy, Morocco, Nicaragua (−), Nigeria (+), Pakistan (−), Panama, Peru (−), Philippines (+), Rhodesia, Senegal, Sierra Leone (−), South Korea (−), South Vietnam (−), Sudan (+), Surinam (+), Syria, Thailand (−).

C. Countries in which public administration was characterized by extreme bureaucratic inefficiency and/or widespread corruption and/or serious instability of policy at higher administrative levels. Countries in which all three of these phenomena prevailed are classified C−: Afghanistan, Bolivia, Cambodia, Chad, Dominican Republic, Ecuador, Ethiopia (+), Guatemala, Guinea, Honduras, Indonesia, Iran (+), Iraq, Jordan, Laos (−), Liberia (+), Libya, Nepal (−), Niger, Paraguay, Somali Republic, Yemen (−).

Extent of Leadership Commitment to Economic Development

It is almost a truism to point out that the extent of commitment of the political leadership of a country to economic development is a significant determinant of its success in raising the country's standard of living. This is particularly true of contemporary low-income countries in which sociostructural, cultural, and attitudinal barriers to development are sufficiently strong to render unlikely a pattern of economic growth based primarily on individual enterprise. More specifically, many developing nations today suffer from marked imbalances in their economies and a variety of bottlenecks that seriously impede production and distribution. Given the weakness of their private sectors, they are unlikely to move forward economically without effective action on the part of their governmental leadership.[137]

The difficulty in defining an indicator of the extent of leadership commitment to economic development is the familar one of establishing criteria applicable to the broad range of countries included in the sample. Formal national planning is often important and has been given such widespread emphasis that a large number of less-developed countries are now attempting to provide themselves with an over-all integrated national plan.[138] In practice, of course, the actual extent of formal planning ranges from occasional projects explicitly designed to raise the rate of economic growth to comprehensive planning based on formal planning models.

The existence and effectiveness of central plans and planning agencies in themselves, however, are not an adequate indication of a government's commitment to development since the activities of a variety of government organs may, taken together, represent more intense leadership efforts to promote growth than do explicit plans and planning groups. The appropriate concept for judging leadership commitment appears rather to be the extent and nature of activities that promote development by what has been called the "central guidance cluster." This guidance cluster would normally include a variety of government or even semiprivate agencies such as the head of the central bank, the financial minister, the head of the budget office, or government cabinet members and others who participate in the central decisions that guide the economy.[139] It is the attitudes of these leadership groups and the extent of their willingness to make purposive attempts to achieve institutional change which are relevant to an evaluation of leadership commitment to economic development.

In defining an indicator of leadership commitment to development during the period 1957–62, we have differentiated three broad categories on the basis of the following judgments: (1) whether the heads of government and semiofficial national agencies (such as ministries of finance, planning agencies, and privately owned central banks) involved

[137] For a discussion of these problems, see Albert Waterston, *Development Planning: Lessons of Experience* (Baltimore: The Johns Hopkins Press, 1966), Chapter 1.

[138] Myrdal, *Economic Theory and Under-Developed Regions*, p. 79.

[139] Peter Wiles makes these points in his review of Jan Tinbergen's *Central Planning* (New Haven, Conn.: Yale University Press, 1964), *American Economic Review*, Vol. 55 (September, 1965), p. 910.

in direct or indirect central guidance of the economy typically make concerted efforts to promote the economic growth of the country; (2) whether or not this planning effort includes purposive attempts to alter institutional arrangements that clearly block the achievement of development goals; and (3) whether or not there is a national plan and a planning group functioning within the government which is charged full time with executing the plan. The details of the classification scheme and the individual country classifications follow.

A. Countries in which government leadership exhibited sustained and reasonably effective commitment to economic development (during the period 1957–62) as indicated by the concerted efforts of leaders in government and other semiofficial agencies involved in central guidance of the economy to promote economic growth, and purposive attempts by the government leadership to alter institutional arrangements unfavorable to growth. In addition, most countries in this category practiced some form of reasonably effective development planning: Ghana (−), Greece (−), India, Israel (+), Jamaica, Japan, Mexico, Pakistan (−), South Africa, Trinidad, Tunisia (−), U.A.R., Venezuela.

B. Countries in which some government leaders evidenced a definite commitment to economic development (during the period 1957–62) as indicated by the practice of some form of national development planning. However, it was typical of the countries in this category that the activities of agencies involved in central guidance of the economy were poorly coordinated and that government attempts to alter institutional arrangements unfavorable to economic growth were infrequent or poorly sustained: Afghanistan, Algeria (−), Argentina (−), Bolivia (−), Brazil, Burma (−), Cambodia (−), Cameroun, Chad (−), Chile, Colombia (+), Dahomey (−), Gabon (+), Guinea, Indonesia, Iran (−), Ivory Coast, Jordan (−) Kenya (−), Malagasy (−), Niger, Nigeria (+), Peru, Philippines (−), Senegal, Sierra Leone (−), Somali Republic, Sudan, Surinam, Taiwan, Tanganyika, Thailand, Turkey, Uganda (−).

C. Countries in which there was little or no evidence of leadership commitment to economic development (during the period 1957–62) as indicated by the absence of development plans and government planning groups. In addition, concerted efforts by agencies not formally engaged in planning to promote economic growth were lacking: Ceylon, Costa Rica, Cyprus, Dominican Republic, Ecuador, El Salvador, Ethiopia, Guatemala, Honduras, Iraq, Laos, Lebanon, Liberia, Libya, Malawi,

Morocco, Nepal, Nicaragua, Panama, Paraguay, Rhodesia, South Korea, South Vietnam, Syria, Uruguay, Yemen, Zambia.

Extent of Political Stability

The importance of political stability to sustained economic growth is almost self-evident. Since the expansion of both industrial enterprise and physical infrastructure rely heavily upon fixed capital formation, returns on which may involve considerable time lags, reasonable assurance regarding the stability of the general political framework is necessary to induce investment and innovation in these areas. This is not to say that transfers of political power may not occur without disrupting economic processes; it means rather that the impact of changes in legislation, administration, and political procedures should be sufficiently foreseeable to permit long-term commitment of resources.[140]

While there is a consensus regarding the importance of political stability to continuous economic development, it is often stressed that the processes of economic, social, and political modernization tend in themselves to create conditions of political instability in low-income nations which, if serious, may in turn hamper the development of these nations. In the early stages of the transformation of a traditional society, increasing awareness of the possibility of change and improvement creates dissatisfactions and discontents that may lead to political ferment if economic advances are not large enough to permit realization of the rising aspirations of the population.[141] Another source of political instability in these societies is the presence of acute tensions between diverse ethnic, cultural, or religious groups which are often brought into conflict by the establishment of an independent national government encompassing a variety of such groups.[142] Furthermore, the absence of stable interest groups, other than those representing traditional ties of race and tribe, for the articulation of the changing needs of the populace can result in discontinuity between central political mechanisms and the mass of the people; it can also result in a tendency for these mechanisms to be used for the solution of private personal problems rather than for the resolu-

[140] This point is made by Moore, "The Social Framework of Economic Development," pp. 68–69.
[141] See Hagen, "A Framework for Analyzing Economic and Political Change," p. 37. However, as mentioned below, Hagen emphasizes that economic growth may provide opportunities to discontented groups which tend to reduce instability.
[142] See the discussion above of sources of social tension in developing countries.

81

tion of general social problems.[143] Thus, political instability may to some extent be considered an expected concomitant of the early process of transition to a modern society.

Nevertheless, as nations advance farther in the direction of socioeconomic and political modernization, there are a number of reasons to expect a net positive relationship between political stability and economic growth to emerge or become stronger. As already suggested, long-term investment and thus continuous growth require reasonable stability of the political framework. In addition, as Everett Hagen has pointed out, substantial expansion in new economic opportunities may lessen potential political and social disturbances by providing an outlet for the energies of discontented groups.[144] Moreover, socioeconomic and political development eventually tends to reduce serious imbalances in the society, thereby reducing instability associated with unevenness in the pace of modernization.[145] Finally, the evolution of effective political structures for administration and planning and of effective political mechanisms for articulating the needs of various interest groups also tends to reduce political tensions and conflict to some degree.[146]

Several aspects of political stability were combined in deriving an overall stability index: (1) the extent of internal security throughout the country; (2) the extent of continuity in form of government; and (3) the extent of consensus about the prevailing form of government. In estimating the extent of internal security throughout the country, we used evidence on actual rather than potential violence. We combined data on deaths from domestic group violence per one million population (1950–62), available for forty-four of the countries of our sample in the *World Handbook of Political and Social Indicators*,[147] with qualitative information from recent country studies on the extent and frequency of group violence. In our evaluation of countries with respect to continuity in form of government, we did not interpret a single reasonably peaceful change in form of government at the time of, or within a few years of, independence as evidence of political instability. Nor were frequent changes in the political leaders of a parliamentary system considered indicative of political instability unless they were accompanied by marked

---

[143] Millikan and Blackmer (eds.), *The Emerging Nations*, pp. 70–71.
[144] Hagen, "A Framework for Analyzing Economic and Political Change," p. 37.
[145] Halpern, *The Politics of Social Change*, p. 360.
[146] Millikan and Blackmer (eds.), *The Emerging Nations*, p. 71.
[147] Russett *et al.*, Table 29.

alterations in, or uncertainty about, legislation or administrative procedures. The primary evidence of significant lack of continuity in form of government which we used in classifying individual countries was the frequency and importance of military and other radical coups. Recent country and regional studies were the principal sources of information used on the incidence and violence of coups. The final element in our index, extent of consensus about the form of government, information on which also came from country studies, was used mainly to differentiate between reasonably stable polities and those characterized by moderate political instability. Of necessity, overt manifestations of lack of consensus, such as intense political antagonisms or significant communist subversion, were used rather than judgments regarding unexpressed lack of consensus.

Once our preliminary country classifications were prepared, interviews with country experts were very helpful in resolving doubtful cases. In addition, we cross-checked our classifications with two of the indicators in Banks's and Textor's *A Cross-Polity Survey*: governmental stability and stability of party system.[148]

The classification scheme for our indicator of the extent of political stability during the period 1950–63, follows below. It should be noted that this is the only one of our sociocultural or political indicators for which the time period considered is longer than five years.[149]

A. Countries characterized by reasonable political stability (during the period 1950–63), judging by the standards of less-developed countries, as indicated by relatively effective internal security, considerable continuity in form of government, and the absence of overt indications of lack of consensus about the prevailing political system. Included in this category are countries in which a single change in form of government was achieved quite peacefully at the time of, or within a few years of, the country's independence: Afghanistan, Chile, Costa Rica, Gabon, Ghana, Greece, Guinea, India, Israel, Ivory Coast, Jamaica, Japan (+), Liberia, Libya, Malagasy, Mexico, Nicaragua, Nigeria, Philippines, Sierra Leone, Surinam, Taiwan, Trinidad, Tunisia, U.A.R. (−), Uruguay.

B. Countries characterized by moderate political instability without

---

[148] Raw characteristics number 27 and number 43.

[149] The indicator of political stability used in our article "A Factor Analysis of the Interrelationship between Social and Political Variables and Per Capita Gross National Product," pp. 555–78, was a three-way classification based on the period 1957–62 only.

much domestic violence. Included in this category are countries in which there have been important nonviolent changes in form of government (other than peaceful ones associated with independence), marked internal political antagonisms, and/or significant communist subversion without much violence. Also included here are countries in which there has been sporadic and relatively insignificant violence that did not threaten the internal security of the country: Argentina, Cambodia (+), Cameroun, Chad, Colombia, El Salvador, Ethiopia (+), Morocco, Nepal, Niger, Pakistan, Paraguay, Peru, Somali Republic, South Africa, Sudan, Tanganyika (+), Thailand (+), Turkey, Uganda (+).

C. Countries characterized by moderate political instability and significant domestic violence. Included in this category are (1) countries with considerable continuity in form of government combined with sporadic but important domestic violence that did not, however, threaten the internal security of the country for more than a brief period; and (2) countries in which one or two coups accompanied by limited violence were followed and/or preceded by considerable periods of moderate political stability. Countries in which there was extensive short-lived violence followed and/or preceded by considerable periods of moderate stability are classified C−: Brazil (+), Bolivia, Ceylon (−), Cyprus (−), Dahomey, Ecuador, Iran, Jordan, Kenya (−), Lebanon (+), Malawi, Panama, Senegal, South Korea (−), Venezuela (+), Yemen.

D. Countries characterized by considerable political instability during an important part of the period 1950–63 as indicated by violent coups, violent domestic outbreaks, and/or insurrections. Most of these countries had relatively high rates of death from domestic violence. Countries in which insurrections were widespread or of long duration, resulting in the continued absence of effective government control over the country, are classified D−: Algeria (−), Burma (+), Dominican Republic, Guatemala, Honduras, Indonesia, Iraq, Laos (−), Rhodesia, South Vietnam (−), Syria, Zambia.

ECONOMIC INDICATORS

Since the economic characteristics of developing countries are traditionally the primary domain that economists explore in investigating the phenomenon of economic development, little justification for the inclusion of economic indicators in our study is required. Indeed, one may view all the noneconomic attributes of nations discussed above as influential in economic development primarily through their impact upon the supplies and uses of the conventional factors or "agents" of production: resources, capital, and labor.

In choosing economic indicators for our investigation, we have attempted to include not only indicators of the abundance of natural resources and capital but also a variety of variables representing major characteristics of economic structure and institutions as of about 1961. Per capita GNP in 1961 and rates of change in per capita GNP from 1950/51 to 1963/64 have been selected as the dependent variables for, respectively, our long-run and short-run studies of economic performance. The indicators of the level of modernization of techniques depict important structural and technological characteristics of both industry and agriculture while measurement of the level of adequacy of physical overhead capital gives an indication of the current extent of the basic economic facilities necessary for a sustained growth effort. A direct measurement of the structure of foreign trade describes selected characteristics of the export sector. To represent the degree of development of economic institutions, we have included two further variables, the level of effectiveness of the tax system and the level of effectiveness of financial institutions. Finally, a number of dynamic indicators have been incorporated which summarize recent changes in economic structure and institutions; these are the change in the degree of industrialization, improvements in agricultural productivity, physical overhead capital, the tax system, and financial organization, and the rate of improvement in human resources.

Per Capita GNP in 1961—Rate of Growth of Per Capita GNP:
1950/51–1963/64

Current estimates of national income per capita are deficient in several respects as measures of intercountry differences in levels of economic welfare[150] or of variations among countries in success in raising economic welfare. In the first place, comparisons based on national income per capita are often misleading because national income estimates generally fail to include nonmarketed output and services which vary greatly in importance from country to country. In addition, comparisons may be distorted both by differences among countries in the distribution of

---

[150] See I. M. D. Little, *A Critique of Welfare Economics* (2nd ed.; Oxford: The Clarendon Press, 1957), p. 6.

income and in patterns of consumer preferences. These distortions may be particularly large for predominantly subsistence economies in which a large proportion of the value of marketed output originates in a rapidly expanding foreign extractive sector.[151] A further difficulty arises when estimates made in local currencies are translated into common units of measurement. The use of foreign exchange rates for this purpose is often unsatisfactory because exchange rates fail to reflect the prices of domestically consumed goods that do not enter into foreign trade. This source of distortion is likely to become particularly important when countries at widely varied levels of development are compared.[152]

If we define economic performance as the extent of success in increasing not economic welfare but rather the ability to produce goods and services, then the national income or product may be viewed as a measure of the differences in productive capacity. While this interpretation of economic performance avoids the problems associated with differences among countries in income distributions and tastes, it introduces the equally difficult problem of comparing aggregate products associated with different compositions of output and produced by different techniques.[153]

In spite of these well-known deficiencies of per capita GNP as a measure of economic performance, we have chosen it as the dependent variable for our study for several reasons. It is, first of all, the dependent variable to which most contemporary writers give attention because, in spite of its inadequacies, it seems in practice to be a reasonably reliable guide to broad differences in productive capacity and levels of economic welfare. Then too, estimates of per capita GNP are available for a large

[151] For discussion of the deficiencies of national income as a measure of differences among countries in levels and rates of change in economic welfare, see E. E. Hagen, "Some Facts about Income Levels and Economic Growth," *Review of Economics and Statistics,* Vol. 42 (February, 1960), pp. 62–67, and D. C. Paige *et al.,* "Economic Growth: The Last Hundred Years," *National Institute Economic Review,* July, 1961, Appendix II, pp. 42–49. For references to the theoretical literature on the conceptual difficulties involved in measuring gains in welfare, see Little, *A Critique of Welfare Economics,* Chapters 6 and 7.

[152] It has been suggested that there is a systematic tendency for the use of foreign exchange rates to undervalue a low-income country's output by a greater degree, the greater the disparity in per capita income between the two countries being compared. See Hagen, "Some Facts About Income Levels and Economic Growth," p. 67.

[153] For discussion of the difficulties associated with the use of national income as a measure of total productive capacity and changes in productive capacity, see G. W. Nutter, "On Measuring Economic Growth," *Journal of Political Economy,* Vol. 65 (February, 1957), pp. 51–63.

number of countries. Finally, a more satisfactory practical alternative is unavailable for countries in which data are in general extremely poor.

For our study of long-run economic performance we obtained almost all the estimates of per capita GNP in 1961 presented in Table II–1 from a single source. For countries that lacked national income accounts, these estimates represent expert guesses based on knowledge of both the particular country and countries having similar levels and structures of production. It should be noted that no adjustments have been made to correct distortions arising from the use of official exchange rates since the price data necessary for this purpose were inadequate or entirely lacking.

For the study of short-run economic performance we chose as our dependent variable the rate of growth of real per capita GNP in constant prices between 1950/51 and 1963/64. It is obvious, of course, that estimates of changes in per capita GNP suffer from many of the same deficiencies as point estimates for a single year. In making comparisons among countries, the comparison of rates of change obviates the problem of conversion into common units through the use of foreign exchange rates. At the same time, however, the problems arising from differences in the distribution of income and in the structure of production are complicated by changes within as well as among countries. The most serious problem arises for countries in which a very small modern sector has expanded rapidly since 1950 while the subsistence agricultural sector of the country has remained largely stagnant. While we made no adjustment for many countries of which this was true, we did make an adjustment for a few extreme cases. Four African countries in which, as of 1960, 90 per cent of the population had been negligibly affected by the growth process were classified in a special category just above the category defined by very small growth rates of per capita GNP, even though monetary growth rates alone would have put them in a higher category.

The classification scheme for rates of growth of per capita GNP during the period 1950/51–1963/64 follows below. Unless otherwise noted, plus and minus classifications are assigned to countries close to category limits. Data for classifying countries with respect to this indicator were considerably less accurate than data for point estimates for 1961. Reasonably reliable estimates for the entire period were available for only 29 of the countries in our sample. The remaining countries were classified in the following manner. First, countries for which estimates were available for less than the full time period were classified by means of a

Library

87

TABLE II–1: Per Capita GNP in 1961

Country	Per Capita GNP	Country	Per Capita GNP
Afghanistan...................	70	Laos.........................	60
Algeria.......................	281	Lebanon......................	411
Argentina.....................	379	Liberia.......................	159
Bolivia.......................	113	Libya........................	204
Brazil........................	186	Malagasy Republic.............	75
Burma........................	58	Malawi......................	40
Cambodia.....................	101	Mexico.......................	313
Federal Republic of Cameroun....	86	Morocco.....................	150
Ceylon.......................	137	Nepal........................	53
Republic of Chad..............	40	Republic of Niger..............	40
Chile.........................	453	Nigeria.......................	82
Republic of China (Taiwan)......	145	Nicaragua.....................	213
Colombia.....................	283	Pakistan......................	79
Costa Rica....................	344	Panama.......................	416
Cyprus.......................	416	Paraguay......................	130
Dahomey.....................	40	Peru.........................	181
Dominican Republic...........	218	Philippines....................	117
Ecuador......................	182	Rhodesia.....................	215
El Salvador...................	220	Republic of Senegal............	175
Ethiopia......................	44	Sierra Leone..................	70
Republic of Gabon.............	200	Somali Republic................	40
Ghana.......................	199	South Africa...................	427
Greece.......................	431	Sudan........................	94
Guatemala....................	175	Surinam......................	310
Republic of Guinea............	60	Syrian Arab Republic...........	152
Honduras.....................	207	Tanganyika...................	59
India........................	80	Thailand......................	97
Indonesia....................	83	Trinidad......................	594
Iran.........................	211	Tunisia.......................	161
Iraq.........................	194	Turkey.......................	193
Israel........................	814	Uganda.......................	68
Republic of Ivory Coast.........	184	United Arab Republic..........	120
Jamaica......................	436	Uruguay......................	450
Japan........................	502	Venezuela....................	692
Jordan.......................	184	Vietnam (South Vietnam)........	89
Republic of Kenya.............	80	Yemen.......................	90
Korea (South Korea)...........	73	Zambia.......................	170

Source: Agency for International Development, Statistics and Reports Division, "84 Underdeveloped Countries—Two Thirds World Population Grouped According to Estimated Annual Per Capita Income (U.S. Dollar Equivalent), 1961" (Washington, D.C., April, 1963).

combination of the available quantitative data and qualitative information on trends in standards of living over the years for which data were not available. Since we were attempting to place countries within broad categories rather than to obtain point estimates, most countries of this kind could be classified with reasonable certainty. Second, a number of countries for which no data existed, for the most part low-income African countries, were classified on the basis of purely qualitative indications. Since most of these have been relatively stagnant economically but at the same time have sufficient land per capita to permit the expansion of subsistence agriculture to feed the growing population, they could be classified with reasonable certainty in the category of no substantial change in per capita GNP during the relevant time period.

A. Countries with average annual growth rates in real per capita GNP of 3 per cent or more during the period 1950/51–1963/64. Countries with average annual growth rates of 5 per cent or more are classified *A +*. Excluded from this category are countries in which, as of about 1960, over 90 per cent of the population was in the traditional subsistence sector where per capita income had not changed significantly since 1950: Greece (+), Iraq, Israel (+), Jamaica, Japan (+), Jordan (+), Libya, Nicaragua (−), South Africa (−), Taiwan, Thailand, Trinidad.

B. Countries with average annual growth rates in real per capita GNP of from 2.0 to 2.9 per cent during the period 1950/51–1963/64. Excluded from this category are countries in which, as of about 1960, over 90 per cent of the population was in the traditional subsistence sector where per capita GNP had not changed significantly since 1950: Algeria (−), Brazil, Burma, Cyprus, El Salvador, Ghana, Iran, Lebanon (−), Mexico, Peru (+), Philippines (−), Rhodesia (−), South Korea (−), Turkey (−), U.A.R. (−), Venezuela (+), Zambia.

C. Countries with average annual growth rates in real per capita GNP of from 1.0 to 1.9 per cent during the period 1950/51–1963/64. Excluded from this category are countries in which, as of about 1960, over 90 per cent of the population was in the traditional subsistence sector where per capita GNP had not changed significantly since 1950: Chile, Colombia, Costa Rica, Ecuador, Guatemala, Honduras, India (+), Ivory Coast (+), Kenya, Nigeria, Pakistan (−), Panama, Sudan, Tunisia (+).

D. Countries in which average annual growth rates in real per capita GNP of 1 per cent or more were reported but in which, as of about

89

1960, over 90 per cent of the population was in the traditional subsistence sector where per capita income had not changed significantly since 1950. Of these countries, those reporting average annual growth rates of 3 per cent or more are classified $D+$, those reporting growth rates of from 2.0 to 2.9 per cent are classified D, and those reporting growth rates of from 1.0 to 1.9 per cent are classified $D-$: Ethiopia, Gabon ($+$), Liberia, Tanganyika.

E. Countries with average annual growth rates in real per capita GNP of from 0.0 to 0.9 per cent during the period 1950/51–1963/64: Afghanistan, Argentina, Cambodia, Cameroun, Ceylon, Dominican Republic, Laos, Malagasy, Nepal, Paraguay, Senegal, Sierra Leone, Somali Republic, South Vietnam, Surinam, Syria, Uganda, Uruguay.

F. Countries in which negative average annual rates of change in per capita GNP occurred during the period 1950/51–1963/64: Bolivia, Chad, Dahomey, Guinea, Indonesia, Malawi, Morocco, Niger, Yemen.

Abundance of Natural Resources

The relationship between the abundance of natural resources and economic growth has long been of interest to economists. Indeed, classical economics was called the "dismal science" because of its basic premise that within countries, the increasing scarcity of natural resources relative to population would eventually lead to decreasing returns to economic activity.[154] While neoclassical economists tended to de-emphasize the impact upon output of exogenous changes in population and resources,[155] the expansion in scope of interest in economic development in recent years has led again to an emphasis upon the positive role of natural resources in the process of economic growth. A number of contemporary growth models, for example, incorporate the presence of "surplus" re-

[154] For a detailed discussion of the views of the classical economists on the relationship between natural resources and standards of living, see Edwin Cannan, *A History of the Theories of Production and Distribution from 1776 to 1848* (3rd ed.; London: Staples Press, 1917), Chapter 5. John Stuart Mill gives a more optimistic view than did earlier writers of the possibility that technological progress may successfully offset diminishing returns in agriculture and mining; see his *Principles of Political Economy*, ed. W. J. Ashley (rev. ed.; London: Longman's Green, 1909), Book I, Chapter 12.

[155] See, for example, J. E. Meade, *A Neo-Classical Theory of Economic Growth* (New York: Oxford University Press, 1961), Chapter 1, and R. M. Solow, "A Contribution to the Theory of Economic Growth," *Quarterly Journal of Economics,* Vol. 70 (February, 1956), pp. 65–94.

sources (i.e., those for which alternative domestic uses do not currently exist) and analyze the manner in which their exploitation contributes to the expansion of trade and income.[156] Other studies point to historical evidence that greater abundance of mineral resources has consistently tended to attract larger amounts of foreign investment.[157] Still others both underline the important degree to which a country's resource endowment can be increased through scientific exploration and the application of technology and emphasize the extent of substitutability among resources as well as between resources and other inputs in the growth process.[158] Finally, there is a considerable and growing body of literature on the role of agricultural resources in the development process.[159]

The selection of a composite indicator to represent natural resource abundance is difficult because any choice requires judgment regarding the nature and extent of substitutability among different classes of resources. The alternative solution of using a narrow indicator is conceptually unsatisfactory since there is no a priori reason to expect the abundance of any single type of resource, taken alone, to be systematically associated with economic performance. In deriving a composite index of resource abundance, therefore, we defined abundance primarily in terms of three broad classes of resources: agricultural land, fuel, and mineral resources other than fuel. It is generally agreed that an abundance of each of these types of resources can contribute significantly to economic growth, particularly at very low income levels. Agricultural land is crucial for the feeding of the population and as a source of agricultural exports; indigenous fuel supplies are critical to the development of industry and transportation; while mineral resources provide a major

[156] See R. E. Caves, " 'Vent For Surplus' Models of Trade and Growth," in R. E. Baldwin *et al., Trade, Growth and the Balance of Payments* (Chicago: Rand McNally, 1965), pp. 95–115, for discussion of models of this type and references to the literature relating to them.

[157] See, for example, Joseph Grunwald, "Resource Aspects of Latin-American Economic Development," in *Natural Resources and International Development,* ed. Marion Clawson (Baltimore: The Johns Hopkins Press, 1964), pp. 307–26.

[158] For a statistical study of the United States which underlines the manner in which substitutability among resources and technological advance may more than offset any tendency toward diminishing returns, see H. J. Barnett and Chandler Morse, *Scarcity and Growth: The Economics of Natural Resource Availability* (Baltimore: The Johns Hopkins Press, 1963), Chapter 11.

[159] For references to this literature, see B. F. Johnston and J. W. Mellor, "The Role of Agriculture in Economic Development," and J. W. Mellor, "The Process of Agricultural Development in Low-Income Countries," *Journal of Farm Economics,* Vol. 44 (August, 1962), pp. 700–16.

attraction for foreign investment. Only when countries have developed a sufficient export base to finance substantial imports of the resources that they lack can one expect the importance of an abundance of natural resources to decline.

In summary, our final definition of natural resource abundance was based on general judgments regarding the abundance and variety of fuel and nonfuel mineral resources together with data on the amount of agricultural land available per capita. The latter statistic was obtained for most countries from either the production yearbooks of the Food and Agricultural Organization or from individual country studies. "Agricultural land" in this connection includes arable land and land under tree crops together with permanent meadows and pastures. It should be noted, of course, that estimates of the number of acres of agricultural land per capita are not only subject to considerable error due to the lack of accurate surveys in most low-income countries but, even when accurate, are merely a rough guide to agricultural resources because of wide variations in the quality of land both within and among countries. Our principal sources for information on fuel and mineral resources were country studies together with the *World Mark Encyclopaedia of the Nations: Americas,* the *Oxford Regional Economic Atlas: The Middle East and North Africa,* and the *Oxford Economic Atlas of the World.*

The classification scheme and country scores for this indicator are stated below.

A. Countries with an over-all abundance and wide variety of known natural resources as indicated in most instances by more than three acres of agricultural land per capita and the presence of important fuel, nonfuel mineral, and forest resources. Also included in this category and classified *A* — are a few countries with generally abundant resources but with only from one to three acres of agricultural land per capita and/or with significant deficiencies in either known nonfuel mineral or forest resources (but not in both). Excluded from this category are all countries that are without important known fuel resources or that have less than one acre of agricultural land per capita: Algeria (−), Argentina, Bolivia (−), Brazil (+), Chile, Iran (−), Mexico, Morocco (−), Peru, Rhodesia (−), South Africa (−), Turkey, Venezuela (+).

B. Countries with either (1) relatively abundant agricultural resources (one acre or more of agricultural land per capita) together with a marked deficiency in all fuel resources or significant deficiencies in both known nonfuel mineral and forest resources or (2) limited agricultural resources (less than one acre of agricultural land per capita) together with an overall abundance of known forest, fuel, and nonfuel mineral resources. In order to meet criterion (1), a country must have some important nonagricultural resources in addition to relatively abundant agricultural resources: Afghanistan (−), Burma, Cameroun, Colombia (+), Costa Rica (−), Cyprus (−), Ecuador (−), Gabon (−), Ghana, Greece, Guinea, Honduras, Indonesia, Iraq (+), Liberia, Libya, Malagasy (−), Nicaragua, Nigeria (+), Panama, Sierra Leone, Syria (−), Tanganyika, Trinidad, Tunisia, Zambia.

C. Countries with either (1) limited agricultural resources (less than one acre of agricultural land per capita) together with some important known fuel, nonfuel mineral, or forest resources (but not an over-all abundance of these resources) or (2) relatively abundant agricultural resources (one acre or more of agricultural land per capita) together with the absence of any significant known nonagricultural resources. Excluded from this category, however, are countries meeting criterion (2) in which agricultural resources consist overwhelmingly of meadows and pastureland: Cambodia, Ceylon (−), Dominican Republic, El Salvador, Ethiopia (−), Guatemala (+), India, Israel, Ivory Coast (+), Jamaica (+), Japan (+), Jordan, Kenya (+), Malawi, Nepal (−), Paraguay (+), Philippines (+), Senegal (+), South Korea (+), South Vietnam (−), Sudan, Surinam (−), Thailand, Uganda, U.A.R., Uruguay (+), Yemen.

D. Countries with either (1) limited agricultural resources (less than one acre per capita) together with no significant known fuel and nonfuel mineral resources and no accessible exploitable forests or (2) one acre or more of agricultural land per capita consisting overwhelmingly of meadows and pastureland together with no significant known nonagricultural resources: Chad, Dahomey, Laos (+), Lebanon, Niger, Pakistan, Somali Republic, Taiwan (+).

Gross Investment Rate

If one were to choose a single influence upon the pace of economic growth which, over the years, has received the most attention from economists it would probably be the supply of capital. The classical economists gave it close attention, and, when problems of economic growth again took the stage in the twentieth century, capital scarcity was for a time considered to be the crucial bottleneck in the development process. In post-Keynesian growth models of the Harrod-Domar type,

93

for example, the proportion of output devoted to new capital formation has been a key determinant of the rate of economic growth.[160] Other well-known growth models in which capital supply has played a central role are those of W. A. Lewis and W. W. Rostow.[161]

Although capital formation continues to be stressed as an important element in economic development, there has been a marked shift in emphasis in recent years toward other influences on development such as improvements in technology, the supply of entrepreneurship, and the wide variety of noneconomic influences that underlie the supplies of production factors.[162] Furthermore, economists are once again stressing the long-familiar proposition that efficiency in the allocation and use of capital is at least as important as the size of the total investment fund.[163]

In defining an indicator of capital formation, we established six categories for grouping countries with respect to the average ratio of gross investment to gross national product for the period 1957–62. Data for classifying individual countries were obtained from the United Nations and the Agency for International Development.[164] For a number of countries that do not have national income accounts the estimates obtained refer to a single year rather than to the entire period; for these estimates, we sought some confirmation from expert opinion and cross-checked them with Rosenstein-Rodan's estimates for 1961.[165]

The deficiencies in the data on investment rates when making intercountry comparisons are well known. Among other things, the relative prices of consumer goods and investment goods differ greatly from country to country, thus distorting comparisons of the importance of investment. There are also variations in the extent to which countries incorporate nonmarket economic activity, particularly within the sub-

[160] For a survey of capital stock adjustment theories of economic growth, see H. J. Bruton, "Contemporary Theorizing on Economic Growth," in *Theories of Economic Growth,* ed. B. F. Hoselitz (New York: The Free Press of Glencoe, 1960), Chapter 7.

[161] Lewis, "Economic Development with Unlimited Supplies of Labour"; W. W. Rostow, "The Take-Off into Self-Sustained Growth," *Economic Journal,* Vol. 66 (March, 1956), pp. 25–48.

[162] See the sections above on social and political indicators for references to the rapidly growing literature on noneconomic influences upon economic development.

[163] See, for example, the essays in Jan Tinbergen *et al., Investment Criteria and Economic Growth* (New York: Asia Publishing House, 1961).

[164] The United Nations, *Yearbook of National Accounts Statistics: 1964,* country tables; and AID, various internal documents.

[165] P. N. Rosenstein-Rodan, "International Aid for Underdeveloped Countries," *Review of Economics and Statistics,* Vol. 43 (May, 1961), Table 3-*A*, pp. 127ff.

94

sistence sector, in their estimates of national investment and product; as a result of the omitted items, investment rates for some countries may appear excessively low.[166] When, in addition, a comparison involves a highly dualistic economy in which a rapidly expanding foreign extractive sector exists side by side with a large subsistence sector, the ratio of measured investment to national product may take an extreme value reflecting modern sector activity almost exclusively. To handle this last problem we established a special category for a small number of countries in which measured investment originated to an overwhelming extent in a single foreign-financed extractive sector. We attempted no other adjustments of the data, however, since the requisite information for making adjustments was pervasively inadequate.

The classification scheme for the indicator of gross investment rates during the period 1957–62 follows below.

A. Countries in which gross investment rates were 23 per cent or more. Countries in which the overwhelming proportion of investment originated in a single foreign-financed extractive sector are excluded, however: Israel, Jamaica, Japan, Trinidad, Venezuela.

B. Countries in which gross investment rates were from 18.0 to 22.9 per cent. Countries in which the overwhelming proportion of investment originated in a single foreign-financed extractive sector are excluded: Argentina, Colombia, Costa Rica, Peru, Taiwan, Tunisia.

C. Countries in which gross investment rates were from 16.0 to 17.9 per cent. Also included in this category and classified $C-$ are countries that had gross investment rates of 16 per cent or more in which the overwhelming proportion of investment originated in a single foreign-financed extractive sector: Algeria, Brazil, Burma, Ceylon, Cyprus, Ecuador, Ghana, Greece, Iran $(-)$, Iraq $(-)$, Lebanon, Liberia $(-)$, Libya $(-)$, Mexico, Nicaragua, Panama, Rhodesia, South Africa, Surinam, Syria, Zambia $(-)$.

D. Countries in which gross investment rates were from 14.0 to 15.9 per cent: Afghanistan, Bolivia, Cambodia, India, Kenya, Nigeria, South Korea, Tanganyika, Thailand, Turkey, U.A.R., Uganda, Uruguay.

E. Countries in which gross investment rates were from 12.0 to 13.9 per cent: Chad, Chile, Dahomey, El Salvador, Gabon, Guatemala,

---

[166] For evidence of the marked understatement of both rural savings and rural investment in the national accounts of India, for example, see K. N. Raj, "The Marginal Rate of Savings in the Indian Economy," *Oxford Economic Papers*, n.s., Vol. 14 (February, 1962), pp. 36–50.

Guinea, Honduras, Ivory Coast, Jordan, Niger, Pakistan, Paraguay, Philippines, Senegal.

F. Countries in which gross investment rates were 11 per cent or less: Cameroun, Dominican Republic, Ethiopia, Indonesia, Laos, Malagasy, Malawi, Morocco, Nepal, Sierra Leone, Somali Republic, South Vietnam, Sudan, Yemen.

Level of Modernization of Industry—Change in Degree of Industrialization since 1950

The close association between industrialization and rising living standards is one of the most familiar facts of economic development. Statistical analyses, for example, consistently yield marked positive correlations between per capita GNP and the proportion of both employment and national product originating in the industrial sector.[167] There are many reasons for this association between greater industrialization and rising incomes. Among the most important are the change in composition of consumer demand in favor of nonfood products, the shift in comparative advantage in favor of domestic production as domestic markets and levels of skill and technology increase, and the growth of intermediate demand for industrial products as consumer goods industries expand.[168] While some degree of industrialization is usually considered an inevitable concomitant of economic development, there is considerable controversy over the extent to which industrialization is desirable; some economists maintain that specialization in primary rather than industrial products contributes most to growth in countries with abundant natural endowments, while others stress that industrialization brings indirect benefits, such as the enlargement of opportunities for individual advancement and the emergence of an environment conducive to change and innovation, that almost invariably facilitate economic development.[169]

[167] See, for example, H. B. Chenery, "Patterns of Industrial Growth," *American Economic Review,* Vol. 50 (September, 1960), pp. 624–54, esp. the references cited on pp. 653–54. See also Simon Kuznets, "Quantitative Aspects of the Economic Growth of Nations, II: Industrial Distribution of National Product and Labor Force," *Economic Development and Cultural Change,* Vol. 5 (July, 1957), Supplement, pp. 3–111.

[168] See the references cited in note 167.

[169] For the former view, see Jacob Viner, *International Trade and Economic Development* (Glencoe, Ill.: The Free Press, 1952), Chapter 3; for a summary statement of the latter view, see Bruton, "Contemporary Theorizing on Economic Growth," pp. 262ff.

One of the most striking characteristics of the process of industrialization, both historically and in present-day developing countries, is the increased application of modern production methods.[170] In the typical country at the lowest level of development, industry tends to be primarily handicraft, with the exception, in some countries, of modern methods used in a foreign extractive sector. As the country grows economically, domestic consumer goods industries using small power-driven machines tend to be established first. At a somewhat later stage of development, when managerial and labor skills become relatively abundant, the typical developing country finally turns to production of the variety of intermediate goods required for the further expansion of industry.[171]

To measure the relationship between industrialization and economic growth, we have developed two variables: first, a composite indicator of the extent of modernization of production techniques in industry as of about 1961, and second, an index of the change in the over-all degree of industrialization since 1950. The indicator of the level of modernization of industry is composed of three principal elements: (1) a rough quantitative estimate of the relative importance of indigenous modern power-driven industrial activities compared with that of traditional handicraft production (these estimates were based primarily on judgments from recent country studies and were cross-checked with data on installed capacity of electrical energy per capita[172]), (2) the degree of modernity of machinery and organization in the modern industrial sector as indicated by the incidence of the most up-to-date large-scale and/or otherwise relatively efficient production methods: and (3) the diversity and range of goods produced in the modern industrial sector. Qualitative in-

[170] For an extensive description and analysis of the application of more modern methods to industrial production in the eighteenth and nineteenth centuries, see David S. Landes, "Technological Change and Development in Western Europe, 1750–1914," in *The Cambridge Economic History of Europe. Volume VI: The Industrial Revolutions and After, Part I,* ed. H. J. Habakkuk and M. Postan (Cambridge, England: The University Press, 1966), pp. 274–601.

[171] For a discussion of the role of technology in the economic growth of contemporary underdeveloped countries, see R. S. Eckaus, "Technological Change in the Less-Developed Areas," in Asher *et al., Development of the Emerging Countries,* pp. 120–52.

[172] The primary source of data on installed capacity of electrical energy in 1961 was the United Nations, *Statistical Yearbook: 1963,* Table 131. Population estimates for 1961 were taken from Russett *et al., World Handbook of Political and Social Indicators,* Table 1.

formation for both (2) and (3) was taken from recent country studies. Doubtful cases were resolved by interviews.

The classification scheme for the level of modernization of industry (as of about 1961) groups countries into the four broad categories described below.

A. Countries with industrial sectors that, as of about 1961, were producing a wide variety of domestic consumer and/or export goods and at least some intermediate goods by means of power-driven factory production methods. In addition, these countries had several industries in which the most modern large-scale or otherwise relatively efficient production methods were applied. Finally, all countries had at least 80 kilowatt-hours per capita installed electrical capacity. While handicraft industry and domestic putting-out systems were still significant in the production of domestic consumer goods in many of these countries, they were less important than factory production for a considerable variety of consumer goods: Argentina (−), Brazil, Chile, Costa Rica (−), Cyprus (−), Greece (−), Israel, Jamaica (−), Japan (+), Mexico, Rhodesia (−), South Africa, Taiwan, Trinidad (−), Uruguay, Venezuela.

B. Countries with industrial sectors that, as of about 1961, were producing a fair variety of consumer and/or export goods by means of power-driven factory production methods and that had several industries in which the most modern large-scale or otherwise relatively efficient production methods were applied to some extent. These countries, however, are differentiated from those in category A by the fact that handicraft industry and/or the domestic putting-out system were relatively more important in the production of domestic consumer goods, taken as a whole, than were modern methods of production. Finally, almost all the countries in this category had from 25 to 80 kilowatt-hours per capita installed electrical capacity. Countries in which the majority but by no means all of the modern production units were in the foreign-financed and managed sector are classified $B-$: Algeria (−), Bolivia (−), Colombia, Iran (−), Iraq (−), Morocco (−), Peru, Philippines (+), South Korea (+), Syria, Tunisia (−), Turkey.

C. Countries with industrial sectors in which, as of about 1961, a limited number of domestic consumer and/or export goods were produced by means of small-scale, power-driven factory production methods and in which the most modern large-scale or otherwise relatively efficient production methods, if they existed, were generally confined to production that was foreign-financed and managed. Countries that had a very limited number of the most modern large-scale or otherwise relatively efficient domestically financed production units are classified *C*+. In addition, these countries were characterized by the overwhelming predominance in consumer goods production of handicraft industry and/or the domestic putting-out system. Finally, with only a few exceptions, countries in this category had less than 25 kilowatt-hours per capita of installed electrical capacity: Burma (−), Cambodia (−), Ceylon, Dominican Republic, Ecuador, El Salvador (+), Gabon, Ghana, Guatemala, Honduras, India (+), Indonesia (−), Ivory Coast (−), Jordan (+), Kenya (−), Lebanon, Liberia (+), Libya, Malawi (−), Nicaragua (+), Nigeria, Pakistan, Panama, Paraguay (−), Senegal (−), Sierra Leone (−), South Vietnam (−), Sudan (−), Surinam (−), Thailand (−), Uganda (−), U.A.R. (+), Zambia.

D. Countries in which industrial development as of about 1961 was very slight and was characterized by handicraft industry and/or the domestic putting-out system. Small-scale factory production was either nonexistent or contributed a negligible proportion of the output of domestic consumer and export goods. The most modern large-scale or otherwise relatively efficient production methods in most instances did not exist; countries that had a single modern foreign-financed large-scale plant are classified *D*+. Finally, in almost all these countries there were less than 10 kilowatt-hours per capita installed electrical capacity: Afghanistan, Cameroun (+), Chad, Dahomey, Ethiopia, Guinea, Laos, Malagasy, Nepal, Niger, Somali Republic, Tanganyika, Yemen.

Our index of the over-all change in the degree of industrialization since 1950 is a composite of three statistical elements: (1) the average annual rate of change in constant prices in industrial output (mining, manufacturing, electricity, and water) for the period 1950–63; (2) the change since 1950 in the proportion of gross domestic product originating in industry; and (3) the change since 1950 in the proportion of the total male labor force employed in industry. The first of the three elements, the average percentage increase in the total absolute size of the industrial sector, was the primary one by which countries were grouped into three broad categories. Data on changes in industrial output for about half the countries in the sample are available in the United Nations, *Yearbook of National Accounts Statistics: 1964*.[173] The majority of the remaining

[173] Table *4B*, pp. 373ff.

countries were classified with respect to this attribute on the basis of judgmental information. The second and third elements in the index, the changes in the relative importance of industrial employment and output, were used to judge the change in the proportionate weight of the industrial sector. Data on the percentage of the active male labor force in industry are from the United Nations, *Compendium of Social Statistics: 1963*,[174] the United Nations, *Demographic Yearbook: 1964*,[175] and in a few instances, the International Labour Organization, *International Labour Yearbook: 1964*. Data on the proportion of gross domestic product originating in industry are primarily from the United Nations, *Yearbook of National Accounts Statistics: 1964*.[176] Data on both labor force and output in industry were supplemented by qualitative judgments regarding trends since 1950 because statistical estimates were either unsatisfactory or entirely lacking for about one-third of the countries in our sample. In fact, one reason for including three measures of the change in degree of industrialization was that data were not sufficient to validate the use of any single measure.

The final classification scheme for our indicator of the change in degree of industrialization since 1950 is stated below.

A. Countries that have demonstrated a marked change in the degree of industrialization since 1950, as indicated by an average annual rate of increase in constant prices in industrial output of over 7.5 per cent during a substantial part of the period 1950–63. In addition, these countries have shown some increase in the proportion of GDP originating in industry, with the great majority showing an increase of from 4 to 10 percentage points. Practically all those for which data are available also showed a rise in the proportion of the total male labor force employed in industry: Brazil, Burma, Ceylon, Greece, Iran, Jamaica, Japan, Nicaragua (−), Nigeria, Pakistan, Peru, Philippines, South Africa, South Korea, Sudan, Syria, Taiwan, Thailand, Turkey, U.A.R., Venezuela.

B. Countries that have demonstrated a moderate increase in the degree of industrialization since 1950 as indicated by an average annual rate of increase in constant prices in industrial output of from 3.0 to 7.5 per cent during a substantial part of the period 1950–63. Some but not all of these countries have also experienced a moderate increase of a few percentage points in the proportion of GDP originating in industry

[174] Table 69, pp. 396ff; included in "industry" were SITC categories *1–5*.
[175] Table 9.
[176] Table 3, pp. 364ff.

and/or the proportion of the total male labor force employed in industry. Also included in this category are several countries for which estimates of rates of change in industrial output are not available but in which either (1) data on industrial employment and/or output show an increase in the relative weight of industry or (2) qualitative information indicates a moderate increase in the relative importance of industry: Argentina, Cambodia, Chile, Colombia, Costa Rica, Cyprus, Ecuador, El Salvador, Guatemala, Honduras, India, Iraq, Israel, Jordan, Lebanon, Libya, Mexico, Morocco, Panama, Paraguay, Surinam, Trinidad, Tunisia, Uganda, Uruguay.

C. Countries in which there has been either no marked change or an actual decline in the degree of industrialization. Countries in which average rates of increase in real industrial output were less than 3 per cent for a substantial part of the period 1950–63 and in which there was no significant change in the relative weight of industrial employment or output are classified *C*. A number of countries for which no statistical data are available are also classified *C* on the basis of qualitative information indicating that there has been no significant change in the degree of industrialization. Countries for which available data and/or qualitative information indicate that there has been a decline in the relative importance of the industrial sector since 1950 are classified *C*−: Afghanistan, Algeria (−), Bolivia, Cameroun, Chad (−), Dahomey, Dominican Republic, Ethiopia, Gabon (−), Ghana, Guinea, Indonesia (−), Ivory Coast, Kenya, Laos, Liberia, Malagasy, Malawi, Nepal, Niger, Rhodesia, Senegal, Sierra Leone, Somali Republic, South Vietnam, Tanganyika (−), Yemen, Zambia.

Character of Agricultural Organization

An important concomitant to successful industrialization, particularly in countries at low-income levels, is the modernization of the agricultural sector. One aspect of agricultural progress which helps determine the extent of over-all economic advancement is the pattern of ownership and management of agricultural land. In this context a great deal has been written about the need of many underdeveloped nations for reform of land tenure systems.[177] One reason for expecting a direct connection

[177] See, for example, Mellor, "The Process of Agricultural Development in Low-Income Countries," p. 704; and Doreen Warriner, *Land Reform and Development in the Middle East* (2nd ed.; New York: Oxford University Press, 1962), pp. 6–7.

between agrarian structure and agricultural output is that under the traditional tenancy systems characteristic of many low-income countries the proceeds of production increases do not go primarily to those who farm the land and therefore do not provide sufficient incentives for innovating activity. In addition, however, there is another aspect of agricultural organization, closely related to ownership patterns, which is also important to economic growth; that is, variations in the size of farming units. In particular, the prevalence of individual holdings too small to be economically viable is likely to retard economic development even where individual ownership-management is common.

In view of the acknowledged importance of the character of agricultural organization, we included in our analysis a composite indicator of ownership-management patterns and of the economic viability and orientation of the agricultural sector as of about 1960. In classifying individual countries a large number of recent country studies was consulted in addition to a number of regional studies having data on the distribution of types of ownership and tenancy.[178] To resolve doubtful cases we consulted a small number of country experts.

In determining and ranking the elements incorporated in the indicator of agricultural organization, we viewed the various types of agrarian structure as if located along a scale, one end of which is represented by the traditional subsistence economy in which cash production is insignificant and the other end of which is depicted by commercial agriculture in which owner-operated farms are sufficiently large to be economically viable. Intermediate on the scale are large owner-absentee commercial farms or plantations. The ranking of different types of agricultural organization along this scale does not imply that individual countries move through all the stages represented on the continuum; rather, the ranking is indicative of the respective capacities of different agrarian structures for productivity increases and expanded output. At the lower end of the scale the essential processes involved in advances in agricultural organization are associated with the expansion of cash-crop production for the market. At the upper end of the scale, where commercialization of agriculture has proceeded quite far, a positive change in agrarian structure

---

[178] Particularly useful were U.S., Department of Agriculture, Economic Research Service, *Changes in Agriculture in 26 Developing Nations, 1948 to 1963* (Washington, D.C.: U.S. Government Printing Office, 1965); and J. P. Powelson, *Latin America—Today's Economic and Social Revolution* (New York: McGraw-Hill, 1964).

102

is represented by the breakup of large owner-absentee farming units and the establishment of economically viable owner-operated forms of organization which facilitate the linking of efforts to increase productivity with rewards for innovation and improvement.

The precise classification scheme for the indicator of the character of agricultural organization as of about 1960 and the individual country scores are summarized below.

A. Countries characterized by the predominance of commercial owner-operated farms that are sufficiently large to be economically viable. Countries in which the remaining part of the agricultural land consists primarily of commercial farms too small to be economically viable and/or subsistence farms (tenant or owner-operated) on which the marketing of surpluses is incidental are classified $A-$; all the other countries are classified A. Excluded from this category are all countries in which, as of about 1960, 55 per cent or more of the population was in a traditional subsistence sector in which cash-cropping was insignificant: Costa Rica $(-)$, Ghana $(-)$, Greece $(-)$, Israel, Jamaica $(-)$, Japan, Lebanon $(-)$, Mexico $(-)$, South Africa $(-)$, Taiwan $(-)$, Trinidad $(-)$, Turkey $(-)$.

B. Countries characterized by the predominance of large owner-absentee commercial farms or plantations in which the absentee owners are either expatriate or indigenous. Countries in which the remaining part of the agricultural land is farmed primarily by small, economically viable commercial owner-operated enterprises are classified $B+$. Those in which the remaining part of the agricultural land is farmed primarily by small subsistence units (owner-operated or tenant) in which marketing of crops is unimportant or in which the size of the unit is too small to be economically viable are classified $B-$. All other countries are classified B. Excluded from this category are all countries in which, as of about 1960, over 55 per cent of the population was in a traditional nonmonetized sector: Argentina $(+)$, Brazil $(-)$, Chile $(+)$, Colombia $(-)$, El Salvador $(-)$, Nicaragua $(-)$, Peru $(-)$, Syria $(-)$, Uruguay, Venezuela $(-)$.

C. Countries characterized by the predominance of small owner-operated subsistence farms in which the marketing of surpluses is of incidental importance or in which the size of the farming unit is too small to be economically viable. Countries in which the remaining part of the agricultural land consists primarily of commercial owner-operated farms (indigenous or expatriate) that are large enough to be economically viable are classified $C+$. Those in which the remaining part of the agricultural land is farmed primarily by owner-absentee commercial enterprises or plantations are classified C; also classified C are those in which the remaining part of the land is farmed by a combination of these two types. Finally, countries in which the remaining part of the agricultural land consists primarily of small subsistence tenant farms or communally owned farmland in which cash-cropping is insignificant are classified $C-$: Afghanistan ($-$), Algeria ($+$), Bolivia, Burma, Cambodia ($+$), Cameroun ($-$), Ceylon ($+$), Cyprus ($+$), Dahomey ($-$), Dominican Republic ($+$), Ecuador, Guatemala ($+$), Guinea, Honduras, India, Indonesia, Iraq, Ivory Coast ($+$), Jordan ($+$), Laos ($-$), Libya ($-$), Malagasy, Nigeria ($+$), Pakistan ($-$), Panama ($+$), Paraguay ($+$), Philippines ($+$), Rhodesia ($+$), Senegal ($+$), Sierra Leone ($+$), South Korea ($+$), Sudan ($+$), Surinam ($+$), Thailand ($+$), Tunisia ($+$), Uganda, U.A.R. ($+$), Zambia ($+$).

D. Countries characterized by the predominance of communally owned agricultural lands and/or small subsistence tenant-operated farms in which the marketing of crops is unimportant. Countries in which the remaining part of the agricultural sector consists primarily of commercial owner-operated farms (indigenous or expatriate) that are large enough to be economically viable are classified $D+$. Countries in which the entire agricultural sector consists almost exclusively of communally owned lands are classified $D-$. The remaining countries are classified D: Chad, Ethiopia, Gabon, Iran ($+$), Kenya ($+$), Liberia ($+$), Malawi ($+$), Morocco ($+$), Nepal, Niger ($-$), Somali Republic, South Vietnam ($+$), Tanganyika ($+$), Yemen.

Level of Modernization of Techniques in Agriculture—Degree of Improvement in Agricultural Productivity since 1950

The importance of the agricultural sector to economic development as a source of supply of both labor and food to growing urban industrial areas has received a good deal of attention in recent analyses of economic growth.[179] For example, a number of economists, stimulated by W. A. Lewis,[180] have incorporated increases in productivity in the agricultural

[179] See the references cited in the discussion of natural resource abundance, note 159 above.

[180] Lewis, "Economic Development with Unlimited Supplies of Labour," and "Unlimited Labour: Further Notes."

104

sector as an essential element in their models of national economic growth.[181] Without improved organization of existing factors and increased application of new techniques in agriculture, supplies of agricultural products are frequently not adequate to meet the increased demand for them which typically accompanies urbanization and industrialization. The resultant rise in agricultural prices, by shifting the terms of trade against industry, can seriously impede the growth of industrial production. In addition, since the process of economic growth for the average underdeveloped country involves a major shift of employment from agriculture to industry, the increased food requirements of the growing population must typically be produced by a relatively smaller agricultural work force. Thus, in general, one would expect to find that countries that are more industrialized and urbanized have higher levels of productivity in their agricultural sectors than do countries at lower levels of economic development.

Our indicator of the level of modernization of techniques in agriculture is a composite variable based upon (1) judgments regarding the extent of use of mechanical power, fertilizer, and other modern techniques in agriculture cross-checked by quantitative data (where available and appropriate) on the use of tractors and fertilizer and (2) qualitative and quantitative information regarding the relative weights of traditional and modern agriculture. Since data on employment and product in the traditional and modern agricultural sectors are generally unavailable,[182] we used estimates of the traditional subsistence sector together with qualitative information on the modern agricultural sector to obtain a rough indication of the prevalence of modern techniques. Statistical data on the use of tractors and the use of chemical fertilizers as of about 1961 were drawn primarily from the Food and Agricultural Organization, *Production Yearbook: 1963.*[183] Qualitative information for prelimi-

[181] For example, Gustav Ranis and J. C. H. Fei, "A Theory of Economic Development," *American Economic Review,* Vol. 51 (September, 1961), pp. 533–65; and B. F. Johnston and S. T. Nielsen, "Agriculture and Structural Transformation in a Developing Economy," *Economic Development and Cultural Change,* Vol. 14 (April, 1966), pp. 279–301.

[182] Estimates of wage employment in the modern sector are available for some countries in the recent studies of the International Labour Organization referred to in note 16 of this chapter.

[183] The relevant tables were 100, 101, 102, 103, and 104. Estimates of total agricultural population were from Table 4A. For countries having no direct data on total agricultural population, we used data on total population contained in Russett *et al., World Handbook of Political and Social Indicators,* Table 1, together with

nary classifications was taken from a large number of recent country studies. Since we found, however, that preliminary data in a number of instances did not provide us with consistent country scores, we consulted regional and country experts to resolve the doubtful classifications.

The classification scheme presented below groups countries with respect to the level of modernization of techniques in the agricultural sector as of about 1961.

A. Countries in which the agricultural sector was characterized by the moderate use of mechanical power and other modern techniques that were not, however, applied exclusively to the production of a single crop. This moderate use of modern methods by these countries was indicated (where appropriate) by the use of more than 1 tractor per 1,000 agricultural population, the use of more than 5 kg of chemical fertilizer (nitrogen, phosphate, potash) per 1,000 agricultural population, and/or significant use of improved pastures, modern breeding practices, and/or modern irrigation systems: Argentina ($-$), Chile ($-$), Cyprus ($-$), Greece ($-$), Israel ($+$), Jamaica ($-$), Japan ($+$), Lebanon ($-$), South Africa ($-$), Taiwan, Trinidad ($-$), Uruguay ($-$), Venezuela ($-$).

B. Countries that had (1) a relatively important monetized agricultural sector in which there was some significant use of modern techniques (mechanical power, fertilizer, better breeding practices, improved pastures, where appropriate) in addition to (2) a fairly important nonmonetized traditional subsistence sector that in most instances had absorbed more than 25 but less than 55 per cent of the total population as of about 1960). Countries in which the monetized sector was only weakly modernized as indicated by the limited use of primarily small-scale modern techniques are classified $B-$. Excluded from this category are countries in which more than 55 per cent of the total population was in the traditional subsistence agricultural sector as of about 1960: Algeria, Brazil, Ceylon, Colombia, Costa Rica, Dominican Republic ($-$), Ecuador ($-$), El Salvador ($-$), Honduras ($-$), Jordan ($-$), Mexico, Nicaragua, Peru, Philippines ($-$), Surinam, Syria ($-$), Turkey ($-$), U.A.R. ($-$).

C. Countries that had the same characteristics as those in category B except that their monetized agricultural sectors involved relatively fewer

---

estimates of the proportion of the population in the agricultural sector; for the sources of the latter estimates, see the discussion of our indicator of the relative weight of the traditional subsistence sector.

people than did their traditional sectors. In these countries more than 55 per cent of the total population was in the traditional subsistence sector as of about 1960. Countries in which the monetized sector was only weakly modernized as indicated by the limited use of primarily small-scale modern techniques are classified *C−*: Burma (−), Cambodia, Cameroun, Ghana, Guatemala, India, Indonesia, Iran (−), Iraq (−), Kenya (+), Malagasy, Morocco (+), Nigeria (−), Pakistan, Panama (+), Paraguay (−) Rhodesia (+), Sierra Leone (−), Somali Republic, South Korea (−), South Vietnam, Sudan, Tanganyika, Thailand, Tunisia (+), Uganda, Zambia.

D. Countries that were characterized by the almost exclusive use of traditional agricultural methods. In these countries there was no significant use of mechanical power, chemical fertilizers, or other modern agricultural techniques: Afghanistan, Bolivia (+), Chad, Dahomey, Ethiopia, Gabon, Guinea, Ivory Coast, Laos, Liberia, Libya, Malawi, Nepal, Niger, Senegal, Yemen.

In defining an indicator of the degree of improvement in agricultural productivity since 1950 we again combined qualitative and quantitative elements. An increase in agricultural productivity was defined as an increase in total agricultural output greater than could be accounted for by additional inputs of the same quality as those prevailing in 1950. We examined statistical series relating to the increased use of tractors and chemical fertilizers but found them unreliable as an indicator of changed techniques for a sufficient number of countries, apparently because of changes in the coverage of the data; therefore, we did not use them systematically to determine boundaries between categories. We relied primarily on qualitative judgments contained in recent country studies and on interviews when grouping countries into four categories with respect to the extent of such improvements as the more extensive use of mechanical power or chemical fertilizers, more modern irrigation systems, better crop rotation, improvement of pastures, and more scientific breeding. It should be noted that we did not consider the fact of increased agricultural output since 1950 in itself to be indicative of improved techniques since in a number of countries, including many African ones, agricultural output has increased significantly through the expansion of the area of cultivation by means of existing techniques.

The following is the classification scheme for our indicator of the degree of improvement in agricultural productivity between 1950 and 1963.

107

A. Countries in which there has been marked improvement in agricultural productivity since 1950, as indicated (where appropriate) by marked increases in the use of chemical fertilizers or mechanical power, the completion of important modern irrigation systems, or marked extensions in the use of other modern agricultural techniques. In addition, these countries generally have experienced substantially greater over-all growth rates of agricultural output than increases in population: Costa Rica (−), El Salvador, Greece, Israel, Japan, Jordan (−), Mexico, Nicaragua (−), Philippines (−), South Africa, Sudan, Syria (−), Taiwan.

B. Countries in which there have been moderate improvements in agricultural productivity since 1950. Among these countries are a number in which cultivatable land has been expanded through the application of modern irrigation methods or multicropping techniques: Brazil (+), Cambodia (−), Ceylon, Colombia, Ghana, India, Iran, Ivory Coast (−), Jamaica, Kenya, Lebanon, Nigeria, Pakistan (−), Panama, Peru, Senegal (−), South Korea (+), Tanganyika (−), Thailand (+), Trinidad, Turkey, Uganda (−), U.A.R., Venezuela.

C. Countries in which there has been no significant improvement in agricultural productivity since 1950. Included in this category are some countries in which substantial increases in total agricultural output have occurred but in which the increases in output are largely due to additional inputs of the same quality as those generally prevailing in 1950: Afghanistan, Argentina (+), Bolivia (−), Burma, Cameroun (+), Chad, Chile (+), Cyprus, Dahomey, Ecuador, Ethiopia, Gabon, Guatemala, Honduras, Indonesia, Iraq, Laos (−), Liberia (−), Libya, Malagasy, Malawi, Morocco (−), Nepal, Niger, Paraguay (−), Rhodesia, Sierra Leone, Somali Republic, South Vietnam, Surinam, Tunisia (−), Zambia.

D. Countries in which agricultural output in about 1963, compared to agricultural output in 1950, had remained static or had declined because of a reduction in land under cultivation and/or a decline in the average quality of other inputs: Algeria, Dominican Republic, Guinea, Uruguay, Yemen.

Level of Adequacy of Physical Overhead Capital—Degree of Improvement in Physical Overhead Capital since 1950

Physical overhead capital, particularly in the form of transportation and power networks, is crucial to the development of low-income countries. Power supplies are necessary for the creation of a modern industrial sector, and transportation is essential both to the spread of production for the market and to the expansion of consumer demand for the products of industry and agriculture. Furthermore, investment in both transportation and power tends to be subject to marked pecuniary external economies which, particularly at the lowest level of development, greatly facilitate direct investments in other fields. Finally, the services of neither transportation nor power can as a rule be imported; thus, international trade cannot significantly reduce the size of the investment in physical overhead capital necessary to create national markets and a steadily expanding industrial sector. It is for these reasons that investment in transportation and power plays a central role in theories of the "big push," controversies over balanced or unbalanced growth, and discussions of the role of external economies in the growth process.[184]

To describe the extent of physical overhead capital in less-developed countries, we have defined both an indicator of the adequacy of physical overhead capital as of about 1961 and an indicator of improvements in physical overhead capital since 1950. Although statistics on transportation and power are better than most data on low-income economies, we found that the only generally useful series for measuring level of adequacy of overhead capital was that of kilowatt-hours per capita installed electrical capacity;[185] this served as a rough guide to intercountry differences in the extent of power installations and tended to be confirmed by qualitative information. In contrast, data on mileage of roads, for example, however deflated, proved unreliable as a measure of adequacy of transportation networks because of the extent of substitutability between various means of transportation and the wide intercountry differences in geography. Therefore, in classifying individual countries we relied heavily upon qualitative judgments contained in recent country studies on the

[184] See, for example, P. N. Rosenstein-Rodan, "Notes on the Theory of the 'Big Push,' " together with the comments of Celso Furtado and Ragnar Nurkse in the International Economic Association's *Economic Development for Latin America*, ed. H. S. Ellis and H. C. Wallich (New York: St. Martin's Press, 1963), Chapter 3; the selections on "Growth—Balanced or Unbalanced?" in G. M. Meier, *Leading Issues in Development Economics* (New York: Oxford University Press, 1964), pp. 250–66, and the references cited on pp. 283–84; and Tibor Scitovsky, "Two Concepts of External Economies," *Journal of Political Economy*, Vol. 62 (April, 1954), pp. 143–51.

[185] The source for data on electrical capacity was the United Nations, *Statistical Yearbook: 1963,* Table 131. Population figures for adjusting to a per capita basis were from Russett *et al., World Handbook of Political and Social Indicators,* Table 1.

general adequacy of internal transportation systems (land, water, air, as appropriate) in meeting current requirements for raising economic growth rates. Preliminary classifications that appeared doubtful were resolved through a small number of interviews with country and regional experts.

The seventy-four less-developed countries in our sample were grouped into four broad categories with respect to the adequacy of their physical overhead capital as of about 1961.

A. Countries in which internal transportation systems (including roads, rails, and waterways) and power networks were reasonably effective in meeting current requirements for more rapid economic development. Feeder roads to agricultural regions formed a reasonably adequate network for the marketing of agricultural products, and intercity connections were fully established. For inclusion in this category it was not required, however, that a country's transportation facilities have been in particularly good condition; it was required only that they have been more or less serviceable. With respect to power facilities, countries in this category had power networks which were, generally speaking, adequate to their current needs as indicated in part by the fact that almost all of them had installed electrical capacity of more than 90 kilowatt-hours per capita: Argentina, Chile, Costa Rica (−), Cyprus, Greece, Israel, Jamaica, Japan, Lebanon, Mexico, South Africa, Taiwan, Trinidad, Uruguay (−), Venezuela.

B. Countries in which internal transportation systems and power networks, while generally adequate for the current needs of economic development, suffered fairly marked deficiencies in limited parts of their systems which were to some extent hindering their further development. For example, some of these countries lacked feeder roads to agriculture in significant sections of the country; others were suffering from power breakdowns due to inadequate installations. Excluded from this category are countries in which the major geographical portion of the country was suffering from lack of both transportation and power facilities. Most of the countries in this category had from 25 to 90 kilowatt-hours per capita installed electrical capacity: Algeria, Brazil (−), Ceylon, Colombia, Dominican Republic, El Salvador, Jordan, Morocco, Nicaragua (−), Panama (+), Peru (−), Philippines, Rhodesia, Syria, Tunisia, Turkey, U.A.R.

C. Countries in which internal transportation and power systems, while serving the commercialized sector of the economy without major deficiencies and bottlenecks, failed to provide a network of continuous services over a major, if not predominant, geographical portion of the country. In particular, widespread lack of feeder roads to agriculture hindered the current development efforts of many of these countries while in others, lack of power installations hindered the development of industry in important sections of the country. Most of the countries in this category had between 10 and 25 kilowatt-hours per capita of installed electrical capacity: Bolivia, Burma, Cambodia, Cameroun, Ecuador, Gabon, Ghana, Guatemala, India, Indonesia, Iran, Iraq, Ivory Coast (−), Kenya, Libya, Nigeria, Pakistan, Senegal, South Korea, South Vietnam, Surinam, Thailand, Uganda, Zambia.

D. Countries in which transportation and power systems were pervasively inadequate throughout the overwhelming portion of the country and in which this inadequacy constituted a major bottleneck to further economic development. Most of these countries had less than 10 kilowatt-hours per capita of installed electrical capacity and in addition, many of them had less than 200 miles of paved roads in the entire country: Afghanistan, Chad, Dahomey (+), Ethiopia, Guinea, Honduras (+), Laos, Liberia, Malagasy, Malawi, Nepal, Niger, Paraguay (+), Sierra Leone, Somali Republic, Sudan, Tanganyika, Yemen.

In choosing an indicator of the degree of improvement in physical overhead capital since 1950, we constructed a composite indicator of transportation improvements in which data on average annual rates of change in miles of paved roads (1957–64)[186] and data on net ton-kilometers of goods transported by railway (1948–63)[187] were used to define category boundaries. The data on roads for 1957–64 were supplemented by qualitative information on the construction of roads between 1950 and 1957 obtained from recent country studies. It did not prove

[186] Statistics on miles of paved roads in 1957 and 1964 for almost every country in our sample were provided through the courtesy of the International Road Federation, Washington, D.C. Coverage for earlier years was not sufficient for us to carry the quantitative comparison back farther than 1957. We did not include unpaved roads because examination of the data showed wide variations in the coverage of the relevant data both within and among countries.

[187] The source for data on net ton-kilometers carried by railway is the United Nations, *Statistical Yearbook: 1963*, Table 145. For some countries, data are based on a shorter time period. This series is not, of course, a direct measure of improvements in railways laid or in the amount of railway stock since, within limits, net ton-kilometers carried can vary by reason of changes in utilization alone. On the average, however, over a number of years one would expect railway capacity and ton-kilometers carried to show similar proportionate changes.

possible to broaden the indicator by using estimated rates of change in installed electrical capacity since 1950 primarily because, among the lower-income countries in the sample, the construction of one or two large electricity plants serving a small area often yielded disproportionately high percentage increases in total electrical capacity due to the extremely small base from which these countries started. In addition, since population estimates for the early 1950's were lacking for many of the countries in our sample, it was not possible to compute these rates of change on a per capita basis. The use of criteria based on the assumption of substitutability between road and railway construction gave us country classifications that were more consistent with judgmental information and expert opinion regarding the expansion of physical overhead capital than we obtained by using only a single statistical series.

The definition of our indicator of improvement in physical overhead capital since 1950 and the relevant country classifications are summarized below.

A. Countries that have shown significant improvement in physical overhead capital since 1950. Classified $A+$ are countries that have shown either (1) an average annual rate of increase in miles of paved roads (1957–64) of 15 per cent or more or (2) an annual rate of increase in miles of paved roads of 10 per cent or more plus an average annual rate of increase of net ton-kilometers carried by rail of 10 per cent or more. Classified $A-$ are countries that have shown either (1) an average annual rate of increase in miles of paved roads of 10 per cent or more (1957–64) or (2) an average annual rate of increase in miles of paved roads of more than 7 per cent plus an average annual rate of increase of net ton-kilometers carried by rail of more than 7 per cent. All countries that by 1964 had less than 500 miles of paved roads are excluded from this category: Afghanistan (+), Argentina (−), Brazil (+), India (−), Iran (+), Iraq (+), Israel (−), Japan (−), Kenya (+), Libya (+), Nicaragua (−), Nigeria (+), Rhodesia (+), South Africa (−), South Korea (+), Taiwan (−), Thailand (−), Trinidad (−), Turkey (+), Uganda (−), Venezuela (−).

B. Countries that have shown moderate improvement in physical overhead capital as indicated by either (1) an average annual rate of increase in miles of paved roads of 5 per cent or more (1957–64) or (2) an average annual rate of increase in net ton-kilometers carried by rail of 10 per cent or more. In addition, countries that meet the criteria for category A but that by 1964 had less than 500 miles of paved roads are in-

112

cluded. Also included are a few countries in which moderate improvements in physical overhead capital took place prior to 1957 but not thereafter: Burma, Cameroun, Chile, Colombia, Cyprus, Dahomey, Ecuador, El Salvador (+), Ghana, Greece (+), Ivory Coast, Jordan, Laos, Liberia, Malagasy, Mexico (−), Morocco, Panama, Paraguay (+), Philippines, Senegal, Sierra Leone, Somali Republic (+), South Vietnam, Sudan, Syria, Tanganyika, U.A.R.

C. Countries that have shown relatively little improvement in physical overhead capital as indicated by an average annual rate of change in miles of paved roads of less than 5 per cent (1957–64) and an average annual rate of change in net ton-kilometers carried by rail of less than 10 per cent: Algeria, Bolivia, Cambodia (+), Ceylon, Chad, Costa Rica (+), Dominican Republic, Ethiopia, Gabon, Guatemala, Guinea, Honduras, Indonesia, Jamaica, Lebanon, Malawi, Nepal, Niger, Pakistan, Peru, Surinam, Tunisia, Uruguay, Yemen, Zambia.

Level of Effectiveness of the Tax System—
Degree of Improvement in the Tax System since 1950

The contributions that an effective tax system can make to the economic growth of underdeveloped countries are varied. Taxation above all enables governments to secure control over resources that they can then use to finance the basic investments in physical and social overhead capital necessary to successful development. Taxes are also a major instrument for making the distribution of income more equitable or for altering it in order to promote private savings. Furthermore, taxation is a principal means for avoiding inflation by absorbing the excess of personal incomes over the supply of consumption goods which is typically created by the development process.[188]

Preliminary experimentation with measures of the effectiveness of tax systems confirmed the view held by a number of development specialists that no single quantitative measure, such as the ratio of direct tax to total tax revenue, is sufficient for differentiating among the tax systems of less-

[188] For discussion of the contributions of taxation to economic development, see U. K. Hicks, *Development Finance: Planning and Control* (New York: Oxford University Press, 1965), pp. 67ff.; and the chapters by Nicholas Kaldor and V. L. Urquidi in Organization of American States, *Fiscal Policy for Economic Growth in Latin America* (Baltimore: The Johns Hopkins Press, 1965).

developed countries.[189] One reason is that countries at low levels of development with inefficient tax administrations may do better to raise additional revenues by improving their collection of existing taxes than by introducing more modern tax instruments which require fairly high levels of administrative capacity. Other countries that are tapping a foreign extractive sector through direct taxation may do better for the future stability of tax revenues to shift their emphasis away from direct income taxes toward broader-based indirect taxes suitable to their limited capacity to administer taxation. For these and related reasons we have chosen a multicriteria indicator of the level of effectiveness of tax systems. The ratio of total domestic government revenue to GNP was selected as a broad over-all measure of success in raising revenue. The ratio of direct tax revenue to total government revenue was a second element incorporated in the indicator; however, special treatment was given countries in which a single foreign extractive sector provided almost all direct tax revenue. These two statistical elements were combined with qualitative judgments regarding the breadth of the tax base and the efficiency of tax collections.

The sources for the statistical data on tax systems were for the most part publications of the International Monetary Fund and the United Nations.[190] Where available, data on local government revenue were included in the estimates. Qualitative information came from recent country studies and was cross-checked by means of about a dozen interviews with regional and country experts.

The final classification scheme for the indicator of the level of effectiveness of tax systems, as of about 1960, divides countries into four groups as presented below.

[189] See, for example, Richard Goode, "Reconstruction of Foreign Tax Systems," in the *Proceedings of the Forty-fourth Annual Conference of the National Tax Association, 1951* (Sacramento, Calif., 1952).

[190] More specifically, the sources were the United Nations, *Yearbook of National Accounts Statistics: 1964*, country tables; United Nations, *Statistical Yearbook: 1963*, Table 181; United Nations, ECAFE, "Design of Fiscal Policy for Increasing Government Saving," *Economic Bulletin for Asia and the Far East*, Vol. 13 (December, 1962), Table 7; U Tun Wai, "Taxation Problems and Policies of Underdeveloped Countries," *IMF Staff Papers*, Vol. 9 (November, 1962), pp. 428–48; and A. Abdel-Rahmen, "The Revenue Structure of the CFA Countries," *IMF Staff Papers*, Vol. 12 (March, 1965), pp. 73–118. Also useful in classifying Latin American countries was R. Desai, "Fiscal Capacity of Developing Economies," in Organization of American States, *Fiscal Policy for Economic Growth in Latin America*, Chapter 2, Table 2.

114

A. Countries that had a moderately effective tax system as indicated in most instances by (1) a ratio of government domestic revenue to GNP of at least 15 per cent and (2) a ratio of direct tax revenue to total government domestic revenue of at least 20 per cent. These countries generally were characterized also by the absence of widespread difficulties in either direct or indirect tax collections. Countries in which the direct tax base was relatively broad are classified $A+$: Algeria ($-$), Argentina ($-$), Brazil, Burma ($-$), Ceylon, Chile, Greece, Israel ($+$), Jamaica, Japan ($+$), Panama, South Africa ($+$), South Korea, Trinidad, Venezuela.

B. Countries that had tax systems of limited effectiveness as indicated in most instances by (1) a ratio of government domestic revenue to GNP of at least 15 per cent and (2) a ratio of direct tax revenue to total government domestic revenue of at least 10 per cent. These countries generally were characterized also by the absence of widespread difficulties in the collection of indirect taxes but often experienced considerable difficulty in collecting direct taxes. Excluded, however, are countries in which revenues derived almost exclusively from a foreign-owned extractive sector and in which tax institutions were rudimentary. Also included in this category and classified $B-$ are a few countries with a less than 10 per cent direct tax/government domestic revenue ratio but with a significantly higher than 15 per cent government domestic revenue/GNP ratio: Cambodia, Colombia ($+$), Cyprus, Ecuador, Ghana ($+$), Kenya, Lebanon, Mexico ($+$), Nigeria ($+$), Peru ($+$), Rhodesia, Syria, Taiwan ($+$), Thailand ($-$), Tunisia, U.A.R. ($+$).

C. Countries that had relatively ineffective tax systems as indicated in most instances by (1) a ratio of government domestic revenue to GNP of 10–14 per cent and (2) a ratio of direct tax revenue to total government domestic revenue of less than 10 per cent. The tax systems of these countries generally were characterized also by an extremely narrow tax base and/or widespread difficulties in the collection of taxes. Also included are a few countries in which the direct tax/government domestic revenue ratio was 10 per cent or more but in which the principal form of direct tax was a traditional land tax. Excluded from this category are countries in which tax revenues derived almost exclusively from a foreign-owned extractive sector and in which tax institutions were rudimentary: Cameroun ($-$), Costa Rica ($+$), Dahomey, Dominican Republic, El Salvador, Gabon ($-$), Guatemala, Guinea, Honduras, India ($+$), Indonesia ($-$), Ivory Coast ($+$), Jordan ($-$), Malagasy ($-$), Morocco,

Nicaragua (−), Pakistan (+), Paraguay (−), Philippines (+), Senegal, Sierra Leone, South Vietnam, Sudan (−), Surinam, Tanganyika, Turkey (+), Uganda (+), Uruguay.

D. Countries that had pervasively inadequate tax systems as indicated by a ratio of government domestic revenue to GNP of less than 10 per cent and/or by heavy dependence upon a foreign-owned extractive sector for taxes combined with rudimentary tax institutions: Afghanistan, Bolivia, Chad, Ethiopia, Iran, Iraq (+), Laos, Liberia (+), Libya (+), Malawi, Nepal, Niger, Somali Republic, Yemen, Zambia (+).

To represent the change in the effectiveness of tax systems since 1950, we used a composite variable composed primarily of three statistical elements. The change in the ratio of government domestic revenue to GNP was chosen as one broad measure of the change in over-all success in raising revenue. A second measure of the extent of over-all improvement was the average annual rate of increase in real government domestic revenue. This second measure proved necessary to evaluate countries experiencing rapid rates of growth of GNP during the years since 1950; in some of these, stability in the ratio of domestic revenue to GNP has been maintained only through considerable improvement in the coverage and flexibility of their tax systems. The average annual rates of change in total money government domestic revenue were deflated where possible by using the implicit GNP deflater calculated from United Nations sources.[191] The third statistical element in our index of improvement in tax systems was the change in the ratio of direct tax to total government domestic revenue, a common indicator of changes in the structure of tax systems.[192] Since the relevant data for estimating the above measures were lacking for many countries in our sample, qualitative information from recent country studies and interviews with country and regional experts were used where necessary to classify individual countries. The sources used were in general the same as those referred to above in our discussion of the level of effectiveness of tax systems.

The classification scheme for our indicator of the degree of improve-

---

[191] United Nations, *Yearbook of National Accounts Statistics: 1964.*

[192] It should be noted that for all these statistical series, individual country classifications were often based upon varying subperiods within the 1950–64 period. These subperiods were generally of from eight to ten years. The variations provided one of the reasons for obtaining qualitative cross-checks for the classifications.

116

ment in the tax systems of underdeveloped countries since 1950 is stated below.

A. Countries that have shown a marked improvement in their tax systems since 1950 as indicated by qualitative judgments and by success in meeting one of the following three criteria: (1) an average annual rate of increase in real government domestic revenue of more than 10 per cent; (2) an increase in the ratio of government domestic revenue to GNP of more than 5 percentage points combined with an average annual rate of increase in real government domestic revenue of more than 5 per cent; or (3) an increase in the ratio of government domestic revenue to GNP of more than 10 percentage points. Countries in which marked improvement has occurred only since 1961 are excluded: India (−), Israel, Lebanon, Peru (−), South Korea (−), Syria, Thailand (−), Tunisia (−), Turkey (−), U.A.R. (−).

B. Countries that have shown a moderate improvement in their tax systems since 1950 as indicated by qualitative judgments and in most instances by both an average annual rate of increase in government domestic revenue of more than 5 per cent and an increase in the ratio of government domestic revenue to GNP of more than 2 percentage points. In addition, almost all the countries in this category meet one of the following criteria: (1) an increase in the ratio of direct tax to government domestic revenue of more than 5 percentage points; or (2) a marked improvement in the collection of indirect taxes. Countries excluded from category A because marked improvement had occurred only since 1961 are included here: Brazil (−), Burma (+), Cambodia (+), Cameroun, Ceylon (+), Chile (+), Colombia (+), Cyprus, Dominican Republic, Ecuador, Gabon, Greece (+), Honduras, Iran, Iraq, Ivory Coast, Jamaica (+), Japan, Jordan (+), Kenya, Mexico, Morocco, Nigeria (+), Pakistan, Panama (−), Philippines, Sudan, Taiwan (+), Trinidad (−), Venezuela (−).

C. Countries that have shown limited improvement in their tax systems since 1950 as indicated by qualitative information or statistical measures that give evidence of at least one of the following: (1) success in increasing government domestic revenue at least enough to meet rising government expenditures; (2) moderate improvements in the collection of indirect taxes; or (3) a moderate increase in the ratio of direct tax to total government domestic revenue. This group includes: Argentina (+), Bolivia, Chad, Dahomey (−), El Salvador, Ghana, Liberia, Libya (+),

Malagasy, Nepal, Niger, Senegal, Sierra Leone, Somali Republic, South Africa (+), South Vietnam, Uganda.

D.   Countries that have shown no significant improvement in their tax systems since 1950 as indicated by available statistical information and by qualitative judgments. Included in this category and classified D− are countries in which statistical measures and/or qualitative information suggest that there has been a deterioration in the effectiveness of their tax systems since 1950: Afghanistan, Algeria, Costa Rica (+), Ethiopia, Guatemala (−), Guinea, Indonesia (−), Laos (−), Malawi, Nicaragua, Rhodesia (+), Paraguay, Surinam, Tanganyika (+), Uruguay, Yemen, Zambia.

Level of Effectiveness of Financial Institutions— Degree of Improvement in Financial Institutions since 1950

A fundamental aspect of the economic performance of a developing country is its success in increasing the proportion of total domestic resources available for investment or, in other words, the extent to which it raises its rate of domestic savings. It is equally important, however, that the available internal savings be effectively channeled into productive investment. In the execution of both these functions, financial institutions (central banks; commercial, savings, and specialized development banks; and, where they exist, developed monetary exchanges) can play an important role.[193] At very low levels of income the volume of voluntary domestic savings entering the banking system tends to be extremely low and lending tends to flow mainly to commercial enterprises, foreign trade, or the modern expatriate sector. At the same time, within the predominant traditional portion of the economy, savings by producers tend to be directly invested and long-term investment to be financed through local

[193] For discussion of the functions of financial institutions in promoting economic development, with special reference to contemporary underdeveloped countries, see Edward Nevin, *Capital Funds in Underdeveloped Countries: The Role of Financial Institutions* (New York: St. Martin's Press, 1961), Chapter 4; and Hicks, *Development Finance,* pp. 51ff. Other general treatments of domestic financing of economic development are E. M. Bernstein, "Financing Economic Growth in Underdeveloped Economies" in W. W. Heller *et al., Savings in the Modern Economy* (Minneapolis: University of Minnesota Press, 1953), Chapter 16; and United Nations, Department of Economic Affairs, *Domestic Financing of Economic Development* (New York, 1950).

118

unorganized money markets.[194] Countries at higher income levels generally have financial institutions that are more effective both in attracting savings and in financing medium- and long-term investment. While financial institutions thus provide an important mechanism for facilitating both savings and investment, nevertheless, their positive influence upon economic development in the short run may vary greatly according to whether other social, political, and economic conditions are favorable to economic growth.

We have chosen two indicators to represent, respectively, the long-run level and the short-run improvement in the effectiveness of financial institutions. In each case, we have sought to construct a composite variable that combined the success of financial intermediaries in attracting private savings with the extent to which they provided medium- and long-term credit to the major sectors of the economy. Our preference for fairly broad indicators was reinforced by the fact that the use of single statistical measures earlier in our research had not been fruitful. Our indicator of the level of financial institutions as of about 1961 includes two statistical measures of the flow of internal savings through a country's financial system: the gross domestic savings rate and the ratio of the sum of time and demand deposits plus money to GNP. A third element in the index is a judgmental classification based on the extent of the flow of capital from the banking system into medium- and long-term investment in industry and agriculture. The principal sources of the statistical data were publications of the United Nations and the International Monetary Fund,[195] while the judgmental information was taken primarily from recent country studies. Preliminary classifications were then cross-checked in

[194] See, for example, U Tun Wai, "Interest Rates Outside the Organized Money Markets of Underdeveloped Countries," *IMF Staff Papers,* Vol. 6 (November, 1957), pp. 80–142.

[195] Sources for estimates of average gross domestic savings rates for the period 1957–62, were the United Nations, *Yearbook of National Accounts Statistics: 1964,* country tables; United Nations, Conference on Trade and Development, *Economic Growth and External Debt—An Analytical Framework* (March, 1964), Table 9 titled "Some Indicators of Economic Growth"; and recent country studies. The sources for data on the volume of time and demand deposits and money were the International Monetary Fund, *International Financial Statistics* (October, 1965), country tables, and the *Supplement to International Financial Statistics: 1965/66;* for these data, an average was taken for the years 1957–62. GNP estimates came from the same IMF sources; the United Nations, *Yearbook of National Accounts Statistics: 1964;* and recent country studies. Where possible, an average of GNP estimates for the 1957–62 period was taken, but for some countries only a point estimate for 1960 or 1961 was available.

about a dozen interviews with country and regional experts. The final classification scheme and the accompanying country scores follow below.

A. Countries in which financial institutions are at least moderately effective in attracting private savings and in which these institutions provide a fairly adequate supply of medium- and long-term credit to both industry and agriculture. All countries that in recent years have had *both* ratios of time and demand deposits plus money/GNP of more than 30 per cent *and* gross domestic savings rates of more than 13 per cent are included in this category; in addition, a number of countries are included which meet only one of these statistical criteria but which nevertheless are judged to have relatively effective financial institutions: Argentina (−), Brazil (−), Greece, Israel (+), Jamaica, Japan (+), Lebanon (−), Mexico (−) South Africa, Trinidad (−), Venezuela.

B. Countries in which local financial institutions (including those that are foreign owned or directed) are able to attract a small but not insignificant volume of indigenous private savings. In these countries the financial institutions provide at least some medium- and long-term credit for both the industrial and agricultural sectors, although the total amount is small. Included in this category and classified *B−* are countries in which voluntary private savings are negligible but in which the government is able to obtain a flow of compulsory savings, at least part of which is used by government-controlled financial intermediaries to provide medium- and long-term credit to industry and agriculture. Also classified *B−* are countries in which an overwhelming part of voluntary private savings leave the country. All countries in the *B* category, as of about 1960, had either gross domestic savings rates of more than 9 per cent or ratios of time and demand deposits plus money/GNP of more than 15 per cent: Algeria (−), Burma (−), Ceylon, Chile (−), Colombia (+), Costa Rica (+), Cyprus (−), Ecuador (−), El Salvador, Ghana, India (+), Iran, Iraq, Ivory Coast (−), Jordan (−), Kenya, Morocco (−), Nicaragua, Nigeria (−), Pakistan, Panama (−), Peru (+), Philippines (+), Rhodesia (+), Senegal (−), South Korea (−), South Vietnam (−), Sudan (−), Surinam (−), Syria, Taiwan (+), Thailand (+), Tunisia, Turkey, Uganda (−), U.A.R., Uruguay (+).

C. Countries in which local financial institutions (including those that are foreign owned or directed) attract a negligible volume of indigenous private savings and in which the funds for financing medium- and long-term investment in the technologically advanced sectors of the economy stem almost completely from foreign capital inflow. In all these countries investment in the agricultural sector (except in the technologically advanced portion) is either self-financed or financed through unorganized money markets. All countries that have both a gross domestic savings rate of less than 9 per cent and a ratio of time and demand deposits plus money/GNP of less than 15 per cent are included. In addition, a number of countries are included that meet only one of these statistical criteria but that are nevertheless judged to have very inadequate financial institutions; for example, countries that have no branches of their institutions outside the capital city are included here: Afghanistan, Bolivia, Cambodia (+), Cameroun (−), Chad, Dahomey, Dominican Republic (+), Ethiopia (−), Gabon, Guatemala, Guinea, Honduras (+), Indonesia (−), Laos (−), Liberia, Libya (+), Malagasy (−), Malawi (−), Nepal (−), Niger, Paraguay (−), Sierra Leone, Somali Republic, Tanganyika (+), Yemen (−), Zambia (+).

In choosing a variable to represent the improvement in financial institutions, we sought to classify countries on the basis of statistical measures of the extent of increase since 1950 in both the volume of private saving through the banking system and the volume of lending by banks to the private sector. To measure changes in institutional effectiveness in attracting savings, we computed the percentage point change in the ratio of the volume of time and demand deposits to GNP for the period 1950/51–1962/63.[196] As a rough measure of changes in the extent of institutional lending to private persons and businesses, we calculated the approximate increase in the real value of private domestic liabilities to the banking system during the same period.[197] For those countries for which data for computing these two measures were unavailable, we examined several series of data which were partially indicative of the activities of their financial systems and classified the countries on the basis of the predominant *direction* of movement in recent years in the several series.[198] The series used were the changes in the volume of time deposits, demand de-

---

[196] For a number of countries this had to be based on data covering a shorter subperiod.

[197] There is, of course, no appropriate price index for deflating data on private domestic liabilities to the banking system or any other financial data. To obtain a rough approximation of real changes, we have used, wherever data permits, the implicit GNP deflator computed from real and money estimates of average rates of change in GNP which were taken from the United Nations, *Yearbook of National Accounts Statistics: 1964*. Once again, for a number of countries, data refer to a shorter subperiod than 1950/51–1962/63.

[198] We are grateful to Dr. Richard Goode for his suggestions along these lines.

121

posits, foreign assets held by the banking system, and domestic government and private liabilities to the banking system. Data for all these series were drawn primarily from the publications of the International Monetary Fund.[199]

The definitional scheme for our indicator of the improvement in effectiveness of financial institutions since 1950 follows below.

A. Countries that have demonstrated a marked improvement in the effectiveness of their financial institutions as indicated by qualitative information on saving and lending activities and, in most instances, by either (1) an increase of more than 5 percentage points in the ratio of time and demand deposits to GNP or (2) a more than five-fold increase in the real value of private domestic liabilities to the banking system. Also included in this category are some countries for which data to compute (1) and (2) were insufficient but in which there has been a marked increase in the real value of *both* the sum of private and government liabilities to the banking system and the volume of time and demand deposits: Ceylon (−), Cyprus (−), Greece, Guatemala (−), Honduras (−), India (−), Iran (−), Israel, Japan (+), Jordan (−), Nicaragua (−), Pakistan (−), Peru (−), Philippines (−), Rhodesia (−), South Africa, South Korea, Sudan (−), Syria (−), Taiwan (+), Thailand (−), Trinidad (−), Turkey (−), Venezuela.

B. Countries that have demonstrated a moderate improvement in the effectiveness of their financial institutions as indicated by qualitative information on saving and lending activities and, for those countries for which the relevant data are available, by either (1) an increase of 2–4 percentage points in the ratio of time and demand deposits to GNP or (2) a twofold to fourfold increase in the real value of private domestic liabilities to the banking system. Also included in this category are countries for which data were insufficient to compute (1) or (2) but in which there has been a positive (but not marked) increase in the real value of the sum of both private domestic and government liabilities to the banking system, the volume of time and demand deposits, and total foreign assets held by the banking system: Bolivia (−), Brazil, Burma, Cambodia (−), Cameroun (−), Chile (−), Colombia, Costa Rica, Dominican Republic, Ecuador, El Salvador, Iraq (−), Ivory Coast (−),

[199] See the references in note 195 of this chapter. It should be noted that private and government liabilities to the banking system are listed in the country tables under "domestic credit" as "claims by banks on the private and government sectors."

Jamaica, Lebanon, Libya (−), Mexico, Morocco (−), Nigeria, Panama, South Vietnam (−), Tanganyika (−), Tunisia (−), U.A.R. C. Countries that have shown no significant improvement in the effectiveness of their financial institutions as indicated by qualitative information on saving and lending activities and, for countries for which the relevant data are available, by either (1) a negligible increase or a decrease in the ratio of the sum of demand and time deposits to GNP or (2) a negligible increase or a decrease in the real value of private domestic liabilities to the banking system. Also included in this category are countries for which data were insufficient to compute (1) or (2) but in which there has been both a decrease in the real value of foreign assets held by the banking system and a decrease in the real value of the liabilities of domestic government to the banking system, the volume of time deposits and/or the volume of demand deposits: Afghanistan (+), Algeria, Argentina, Chad (−), Dahomey, Ethiopia (+), Gabon (+), Ghana, Guinea (−), Indonesia, Kenya, Laos (−), Liberia, Malagasy (+), Malawi (−), Nepal, Niger (−), Paraguay (+), Senegal, Sierra Leone, Somali Republic, Surinam, Uganda, Uruguay, Yemen, Zambia (+).

Rate of Improvement in Human Resources

The contribution of education to economic performance has received a good deal of attention in recent years. As discussed above in the section on our indicator of the extent of literacy, education tends both to improve the quality of the labor force and to promote sociopolitical integration and modernization.[200] Not unexpectedly, a number of recent cross-sectional studies of economic performance have yielded consistent evidence of a positive association between levels of economic development and the rate of additions to the stock of education (measured by school enrollment ratios).[201] However, intercountry analyses have paid less attention to the interaction of short-term economic performance and in-

[200] See the references cited in the section above on our indicator of the extent of literacy.

[201] See, for example, the United Nations, *Report on the World Social Situation, with Special Reference to the Problem of Balanced Social and Economic Development* (New York, 1961); Harbison and Myers, *Education, Manpower and Economic Growth;* and Walter Galenson and Graham Pyatt, *The Quality of Labour and Economic Development in Certain Countries* (Geneva: International Labour Office, 1964).

creases in educational levels.[202] It is not to be expected, of course, that the education of primary-school children would significantly affect economic growth in the short run. On the other hand, both secondary and higher-level education might be expected to improve the quality of the labor force over a period as short as a decade and thus to contribute positively to short-run economic performance.

As a measure of the rate of improvement in human resources, we have incorporated in our analysis Harbison's and Myers' composite index of levels of human resource development. However, we interpret this index to refer to the rate of improvement in human resources since it is a weighted average of secondary and higher-level enrollment ratios rather than an average of the related stocks of education. This index is composed of two elements: enrollment at the second level of education as a percentage of the age group fifteen to nineteen and enrollment at the third level of education as a percentage of the appropriate age group, with the latter being given five times the weight of the former.[203] Since this composite index was calculated by Harbison and Myers for only about two-thirds of the countries in our sample, we extended it to the remaining countries in the following manner. First of all, we established four broad categories defined in terms of the Harbison and Myers index. We then obtained, for about 1961, estimates of total enrollment at the second and third levels from the recent UNESCO surveys of education.[204] To obtain estimates of the ratio of enrollment to the total population of the appropriate age group for countries where population data were inadequate, we used rough approximations based on surveys of similar countries whenever possible; we were able to classify some countries in the lowest category without an estimate of the appropriate enrollment ratios because of the extremely low level of total enrollment.[205] We were not

[202] Galenson and Pyatt, in the study referred to in note 201, include as one of their indicators of the change in the quality of labor the change in various school-enrollment ratios since 1950; they find some indication of a positive relationship between accelerated additions to educational stock and more rapid rates of growth of per capita GNP over the period.

[203] Harbison and Myers, *Education, Manpower and Economic Growth,* Chapter 3.

[204] UNESCO, *World Survey of Education* (New York, 1961–66), III and IV, country tables.

[205] Estimates of total population for 1961 are from Russett *et al., World Handbook of Political and Social Indicators,* Table 1. The United Nations demographic yearbooks were used to obtain the breakdown of population by age group where available.

able to make adjustments for length of schooling similar to those made by Harbison and Myers, but we considered these to be less important for the broad approximations necessary for our four-way classification than they would have been for point estimates.

The final classification scheme is defined in terms of the Harbison and Myers index described on pages 31–32 of their book, *Education, Manpower and Economic Growth*, and refers generally to the year 1961.

A. Countries that showed significant rates of increase in their stock of human resources as indicated by a Harbison composite index number of 40.0 or higher. An *A*− rating is given to countries that have an index number of between 40.0 and 45.0. An *A*+ rating is given to those countries that have an index number higher than 75.0: Argentina (+), Chile, Costa Rica, Cyprus, Greece, Israel (+), Japan (+), Panama, Philippines (+), South Africa (−), South Korea, Syria, Taiwan, U.A.R. (−), Uruguay, Venezuela.

B. Countries that showed moderate rates of increase in their stock of human resources as indicated by Harbison composite index numbers of between 20.0 and 39.9. A *B*− rating is given to countries that have an index number of between 20.0 and 25.0. A *B*+ rating is given to countries that have an index number of between 35.0 and 39.9: Brazil (−), Ceylon, Colombia (−), Ecuador (−), Ghana (−), India (+), Iraq, Jamaica, Jordan (+), Lebanon (−), Mexico, Pakistan, Paraguay (−), Peru, Surinam (+), Thailand (+), Trinidad, Turkey.

C. Countries that were making slight to moderate additions to their stock of human resources as indicated by a Harbison composite index number of between 6.0 and 19.9. A *C*− rating is given to countries that have an index number of between 6.0 and 8.0. A *C*+ rating is given to countries that have an index number of between 15.0 and 19.9: Algeria, Bolivia, Burma, Cambodia (−), Cameroun (−), Dominican Republic, El Salvador (+), Gabon (−), Guatemala, Honduras, Indonesia, Iran (+), Libya, Malagasy (−), Morocco, Nicaragua, Nepal (−), South Vietnam, Sudan (−), Tunisia (+).

D. Countries that were making relatively few improvements in their stock of human resources as indicated by a Harbison composite index number of less than 6.0. A *D*− rating is given to countries that have an index number of less than 2.0. A *D*+ rating is given to countries that have an index number of between 4.0 and 5.9: Afghanistan (−), Chad (−), Dahomey, Ethiopia (−), Guinea, Ivory Coast, Kenya (+), Laos,

Liberia (+), Malawi (−), Niger (−), Nigeria (+), Rhodesia, Senegal (+), Sierra Leone (+), Somali Republic (−), Tanganyika, Uganda (+), Yemen (−), Zambia.

Structure of Foreign Trade

The contribution of international trade to economic growth is a subject of considerable interest to development economists because of the importance of the foreign trade sector in many, if not most, contemporary developing countries. The nineteenth-century classical and modern neo-classical views have been that international specialization and trade tend to have a significant positive influence on the standard of living of the trading countries.[206] In addition to positive views of trade and growth based on a static theory of comparative advantage, there have been a number of studies of the dynamic interaction between the growth of trade and changes in income.[207] These "export-based" growth theories underline the positive multiplier effects of an expanding export sector but at the same time emphasize that these beneficial effects depend on the extent to which the proceeds from export sales are distributed throughout the entire economy.[208] Indeed, several economists have argued that, in general, it has been the foreign investors in the export sector and the advanced trading nations rather than the underdeveloped countries that have gained from international trade.[209] Others have suggested that trade has in fact tended to increase significantly the degree of inequality in income among countries.[210]

[206] For a recent statement of this view, see, among others, Gottfried Haberler, *International Trade and Economic Development* (Cairo: National Bank of Egypt, Fiftieth Anniversary Commemoration Lectures, 1959), reprinted with omissions in Theodore Morgan, G. W. Betz, and N. K. Choudhry (eds.), *Readings in Economic Development* (Belmont, Calif.: Wadsworth Publishing Co., 1963), pp. 240–49.

[207] For a discussion for these models, see R. E. Caves, *Trade and Economic Structure* (Cambridge: Harvard University Press, 1963), Chapter 9.

[208] Douglass C. North emphasizes this point in *The Economic Growth of the United States, 1790–1860* (Englewood Cliffs, N.J.: Prentice-Hall, 1961), Chapter 1. See also R. E. Baldwin, "Patterns of Development in Newly Settled Regions," *Manchester School of Economic and Social Studies,* Vol. 24 (May, 1956), pp. 161–79; and Meier, *Leading Issues in Development Economics,* pp. 371–76.

[209] For a summary of this literature, see G. M. Meier, *International Trade and Development* (New York: Harper and Row, 1963), Chapter 7.

[210] See Myrdal, *Economic Theory and Under-Developed Regions,* Chapter 5.

There are other reasons for the increasing emphasis in recent years upon the disadvantages of dependence by an underdeveloped economy upon export trade. First, there have been marked fluctuations in the proceeds from most exports typically produced by less-developed countries. These have affected most adversely countries dependent on sales from only one or two major crops or products for export proceeds. Secondly, there is evidence of relatively low long-run elasticities of demand for many primary products, particularly foodstuffs, produced by underdeveloped countries. Thirdly, the failure of many low-income countries to alter their structures of production in response to unfavorable export markets and thus their slowness in diversifying their export economies tend to accentuate the unfavorable consequences of instability of export proceeds and low elasticities of demand for products.[211]

Our indicator of the structure of trade of underdeveloped countries is a purely statistical composite measure of (1) the extent to which developing countries have shifted from the exporting of primary products and raw materials to the increased exporting of processed and manufactured commodities and (2) the extent to which these countries have diversified their exports. To represent the first of these aspects of trade structure, we used the percentage of total exports accounted for by manufactured goods (SITC categories 3 to 8[212]) in 1961. The degree of diversification in trade structure was measured by the percentage of total exports accounted for by the four leading exports and the two leading exports, respectively, of each country. Data were obtained for almost all countries from the United Nations, *Yearbook of International Trade Statistics* for 1962 and 1963 (country tables); recent country studies were used to complete data for only a handful of countries.

The classification scheme and country scores for the indicator of the structure of trade as of 1961 follows below.

A. Countries in which manufactured commodities accounted for more than 20 per cent of total exports. Countries that showed significant diversification of exports as indicated by the fact that their four leading ex-

---

[211] See the United Nations, *Instability in Export Markets of Underdeveloped Countries* (New York, 1952); A. C. Harberger, "Some Evidence on the International Price Mechanism," *Journal of Political Economy,* Vol. 65 (December, 1957), pp. 506–21; and the chapters by Gottfried Haberler ("Terms of Trade and Economic Development") and T. W. Schultz ("Economic Prospects of Primary Products") in *Economic Development for Latin America,* ed. Ellis and Wallich.

[212] We exclude, however, raw and uncut diamonds.

ports accounted for less than 40 per cent of total exports are classified *A*+. Countries in which the four leading exports accounted for more than 70 per cent of total exports are classified *A*−. Chile (−), India, Israel, Japan (+), Lebanon (+), Mexico, Peru (−), Pakistan, Rhodesia (−), South Africa (+), Taiwan (+), Zambia (−).

B. Countries in which manufactured commodities accounted for between 10 and 20 per cent of total exports. Countries that, in addition, showed moderate diversification of exports as indicated by the fact that their two leading exports accounted for less than 40 per cent of total exports are classified *B*+. Countries in which the two leading exports accounted for more than 70 per cent of total exports are classified *B*−: Afghanistan, Algeria, Cameroun, Gabon (−), Greece, Kenya (+), South Korea (+), Syria, Tunisia (+), Uganda (−), U.A.R. (−).

C. Countries in which (1) manufactured commodities accounted for less than 10 per cent of total exports and (2) less than 75 per cent of total exports came from the four leading commodities. Countries that showed moderate diversification of exports as indicated by the fact that their two leading exports accounted for less than 50 per cent of total exports are classified *C*+: Argentina (+), Brazil, Cyprus (+), Dominican Republic, Ethiopia, Honduras, Jordan, Malagasy (+), Morocco (+), Nicaragua, Nigeria (+), Paraguay (+), Philippines (+), Tanganyika (+), Thailand, Turkey (+), Uruguay.

D. Countries in which (1) manufactured commodities accounted for less than 10 per cent of total exports; (2) more than 75 per cent of total exports came from the four leading commodities; and (3) the two leading commodities made up less than 75 per cent of total exports: Bolivia, Burma (−), Cambodia (−), Dahomey (+), Ghana (−), Guinea, Indonesia (+), Iran (−), Ivory Coast, Jamaica (+), Libya (−), Malawi, Nepal, Sudan, Yemen.

E. Countries in which (1) manufactured commodities accounted for less than 10 per cent of total exports and (2) extreme concentration of exports existed as indicated by the fact that the two leading commodities accounted for more than 75 per cent of total exports: Ceylon, Chad, Colombia, Costa Rica (+), Ecuador (+), El Salvador (+), Guatemala (+), Iraq (−), Laos, Liberia, Niger (+), Panama (−), Senegal (+), Sierra Leone, Somali Republic (+), South Vietnam, Surinam, Trinidad (+), Venezuela.

SUMMARY

The forty-one indicators defined in this chapter represent a wide range of social, political, and economic characteristics of underdeveloped countries. They summarize both leading aspects of the social and economic transformations commonly associated with urbanization and industrialization and important political attributes of the growth of modern nation-states. In the selection of variables the inclusion of numerous narrow measures of socioeconomic and political structure was avoided; rather, an effort was made to choose fairly broad indicators of those features of developing societies most likely to influence economic performance. The variables included do not, of course, cover all facets of underdeveloped countries which a priori appear significant in the process of economic development. For example, important motivational attributes such as the degree of social approval of economic activity and the extent of achievement motivation are excluded since they could not be defined with sufficient concreteness to permit reliable classification of individual countries. In addition, a number of relevant economic characteristics are not represented by reason of the inadequacy and unreliability of available data; examples are the extent of the economic role of the government and the distribution of investment expenditures. Finally, it should be noted that several variables were dropped at an early stage in the investigation because their substantive contribution to an explanation of economic growth rates appeared negligible. Among these were the recency of independence, the level of health of the population, and the structure of the labor force. The final choice of indicators for the current factor analyses, in spite of inevitable limitations, covers a broad spectrum of both the noneconomic and economic attributes of low-income nations most likely to determine the extent of the success of these nations in improving economic performance.

CHAPTER **III** THE TECHNIQUE OF ANALYSIS

The technique used in this paper, factor analysis, was developed originally by psychologists in connection with the determination of mental factors from scores on various psychological tests. The primary purpose of factor analysis is to reduce the original number of explanatory variables to a smaller number of independent factors in terms of which the whole set of variables can be understood. Factor analysis thus provides us with a simpler, more compact explanation of the regularities apparent in the empirical results.

The technique of factor analysis shares certain characteristics with both nonquantitative comparative studies and statistical regression analyses. In essence, it is equivalent to a systematic application of comparative studies which simultaneously tests a large number of *ceteris paribus* propositions.

As in regression analysis, factor analysis breaks down the original variance of a variable into variance components associated with the variation of a set of other quantities. In regression analysis, the variable whose variations are decomposed in this manner is known as the dependent variable, and the variables that account for different portions of its variation are the independent variables. In factor analysis, all variables are dependent and independent in turn. Thus, by contrast with regression analysis, which is a study of dependence, factor analysis is a study of mutual interdependence.[1]

Another point that distinguishes factor analysis from regression analysis is that in factor analysis the final explanatory variables are not observable magnitudes. They are, rather, groupings of the original variables into a number of clusters known as "factors." Each cluster consists of a linear combination of the initial variables included in the study. More specifically, each factor is an eigenvector of the correlation matrix among

[1] This point is made by M. G. Kendall, "Factor Analysis as a Statistical Technique," *Journal of the Royal Statistical Society, Series B,* **61.**

the original variables.[2] The mathematical principles by which each cluster or "factor" is formed from the observable variables are as follows: (1) Those variables that are most clearly intercorrelated are combined within a single factor. (2) The variables allocated to a given factor are those that are most nearly independent of the variables allocated to the other factors. (3) The factors are derived in a manner that maximizes the percentage of the total variance attributable to each successive factor (given the inclusion of the preceding factors). (4) The factors are independent (uncorrelated with each other).[3]

As pointed out above, it is the purpose of factor analysis to represent each variable as a linear combination of several underlying factors. Two types of factors are distinguished: common factors, which are required to explain the intercorrelations among the variables, and unique factors, which account for that portion of the variation of a variable which cannot be attributed to the correlation of the variable with other variables in the set. It is assumed that each variable can be expressed as a linear composite of the m common factors, a unique factor, and a random error. Factor analysis, therefore, can be interpreted as a regression of the observed variables on the unobserved common factors and on a specific factor.

A major aim of factor analysis is to determine the coefficients that relate the observed variables to the common factors.[4] These coefficients, which are referred to as factor loadings, play the same role in factor analysis as do regression coefficients in correlation analysis. Since the squared factor loadings represent the relative contribution of each factor to the total standardized variance of a variable,[5] the sum for each variable of its squared factor loadings (known as the "communality") indicates the extent to which the common factors account for the total unit variance of the variable. Thus, the role of the communality in factor analysis is analogous to the role of the coefficient of multiple determination, R^2, in regression analysis.

The merit of factor analysis lies in its power to simplify statistical data arising from complex and comparatively unexplored areas of scientific

[2] See H. H. Harman, *Modern Factor Analysis* (Chicago: University of Chicago Press, 1960), Chapter VII.

[3] One can also drop this last restriction, but its inclusion is obviously preferable a priori.

[4] The contribution of the unique factor can be evaluated as a residual.

[5] See the section on the statistical model in this chapter.

endeavor. In the more advanced fields of scientific inquiry the task of simplification is carried out in two steps. First, a theoretical statistical model, which the data may be presumed to obey, is formulated. The data are then analyzed in light of the model and checked against it. However, the theory of the dynamics of social and political development is not sufficiently well specified to permit the formulation of reasonable a priori models against which the empirical results could be tested. Under such circumstances it becomes desirable to make only very general specifications and to try to use the data as a guide in the formulation of hypotheses concerning the relative importance of different sources of variation. It is the latter approach that underlies the use of factor analysis. As pointed out by Thurstone,[6] who pioneered in the use of factor analysis in psychology:

Factor analysis has its principal usefulness at the border line of science. It is naturally superseded by rational formulations in terms of the science involved. Factor analysis is useful, especially in those domains where basic and fruitful concepts are essentially lacking and where crucial experiments have been difficult to conceive. The new methods have a humble role. They enable us to make only the crudest first map of a new domain. But if we have scientific intuition and sufficient ingenuity, the rough factorial map of a new domain will enable us to proceed beyond the exploratory factorial stage to the more direct forms of psychological experimentation in the laboratory.

The next few sections of this chapter are technical discussions of the statistical bases of factor analysis. The reader who is not familiar with mathematics may omit these sections and continue with the discussion of the various practical considerations of importance in the application of the technique.

THE STATISTICAL MODEL

To state the method more specifically, let x_i be the ith variable and x_{ij} be the value assumed by the ith variable on the jth observation. In our study, the variables are the social and political indicators; the observations are the various underdeveloped countries included in our sample. A particular x_{ij} thus represents the score assigned to the jth country on the ith social or political characteristic.

As pointed out above, it is the purpose of factor analysis to represent

[6] L. L. Thurstone, *Multiple Factor Analysis* (Chicago: University of Chicago Press, 1961), p. 56.

133

each variable x_i ($i = 1, \ldots, n$) as a linear combination of several underlying factors. Two types of factors are distinguished: common factors, which are necessary to explain the intercorrelations among the variables, and unique factors, which account for that portion of the variation of a variable which cannot be attributed to the correlation of the variable with other variables in the set. If we denote the cth common factor as F_c and the n unique factors as U_i, the basic postulate of factor analysis is that

$$x_i = a_{i1} F_1 + \cdots + a_{im} F_m + b_i U_i + c_i E_i, \qquad (1)$$

where E_i is a random error term. In other words, it is assumed that each variable x_i can be expressed as a linear composite of the m common factors, a unique factor, and a random error. Factor analysis can thus be interpreted as a regression of the observed x_i on the unobserved common factors F_c and on a specific factor. A major purpose of factor analysis is to determine the coefficients $a_{i1}, \ldots, a_{im}$ of the common factors.[7]

It is apparent from equation (1) that the system as it stands is underdetermined inasmuch as it contains more parameters than observations, regardless of the number of observations taken. It is therefore necessary to introduce additional postulates in order to evaluate the a_{ic}. It is usual to assume in this connection that: (1) the unique factors are uncorrelated with the common factors and with the error terms; (2) the common factors are uncorrelated with the errors; (3) the common factors, the unique factors, and the errors are independent among themselves; and (4) x_i, F_c, U_i, and E_i have unit variances.

While the raw data of a factor analysis are the values of the statistical variables x_{ij}, it is customary to reduce these data to a set of correlation coefficients among the observed variables before the factor analysis is undertaken. In view of assumptions 1–4 above, the correlation between any two variables x_i and x_k ($i, k = 1, 2, \ldots, n$) can be written as

$$r_{ik} = a_{i1} a_{k1} \neq a_{i2} a_{k2} \neq \cdots \neq a_{im} a_{km} \qquad (2)$$

for $i \neq k$ and as

$$r_{ii}^2 = a_{i1}^2 \neq a_{i2}^2 \neq \cdots \neq a_{im}^2 \neq b_i^2 \neq c_i^2 \qquad (3)$$

for $i = k$.

[7] The contribution of the unique factor can then be evaluated as a residual.

In (3), a_{ic}^2 represents the contribution of the factor F_c to the total standardized variance of x_i, b_i^2 indicates the role of the unique factor, and c_i^2 denotes the contribution of the error term. Psychologists refer to

$$h_i^2 = a_{i1}^2 \neq \cdots \neq \cdots \neq a_{im}^2 \qquad (4)$$

as the "communality" of the variable x_i. The communality of a variable indicates the extent to which the common factors account for the total unit variance of the variable. The communality in factor analysis is thus analagous to the value of the coefficient of multiple determination, R^2, in regression analysis. The "uniqueness" of the variable is expressed as $(b_i^2 \neq c_i^2)$[8]; it represents the extent to which the common factors fail to account for the variance of x_i.

As pointed out in the introductory discussion, the basic purpose of factor analysis is to derive a simpler representation of the apparent interactions among the original variables in the study. In other words, its aim is to represent the x_{ij} by a number of common factors m smaller than the number n of original variables x_i. Geometrically, this is equivalent to finding the coordinates of an m-dimensional subspace of the original n-dimensional space through which to express the points representing the N sample countries. The method used in this study to extract factor patterns is based upon taking the principal axes of the n-dimensional ellipsoids, which are the loci of the clusters of points of uniform frequency density, as reference axes for the new m-dimensional space.

Algebraically, the complexity of the factor pattern (i.e., the number of factors, m, included in the model) is equal to the rank of the matrix of observed values $X = (x_{ij})$ $(i = 1, \ldots, n; j = 1, \ldots, N)$. However, since the rank of the matrix of observed values is equal to the rank of the correlation matrix, the factor pattern can also be found from the correlation matrix

$$R = (r_{ik}) \qquad (i, k = 1, \ldots, n).$$

When the correlation matrix contains ones in the diagonal, its rank is usually n and the variables are then describable in terms of not less than n factors. Since it is desired to express the n variables in terms of less than n common factors, a factor pattern of the requisite form can be obtained by substituting a correlation matrix R^* for correlation matrix R with the communalities h_i^2 replacing the $r_{ii} = 1$ on the diagonal. That is,

---

[8] Here b_i^2 is known as the "specificity" of x_i and c_i^2 as the "unreliability" of x_i.

$$R^* = \begin{bmatrix} h_1^2 \, r_{12} \, r_{13} \, \cdots \, r_{1n} \\ r_{21} \, h_2^2 \, r_{23} \, \cdots \, r_{2n} \\ r_{31} \, r_{32} \, h_3^2 \, \cdots \, r_{3n} \\ \cdot \qquad\qquad \cdot \\ \cdot \qquad\qquad \cdot \\ \cdot \qquad\qquad \cdot \\ r_{a1} \cdots\cdots\cdots h_n^2 \end{bmatrix}, \tag{5}$$

and the rank of R^* is generally less than n.

The factor pattern to be determined may now be represented by

$$X_i^* = a_{i1} F_1 + \cdots + a_{ip} F_p + \cdots + a_{im} F_m + c_i E_i \; (i = 1, \ldots, n) \tag{6}$$

with the unique factor omitted. The asterisk in (6) indicates that the value of the ith variable is that estimated from its factor pattern rather than the actual value. Successive factors are extracted in order of decreasing contribution to the total communality.

Estimation of the Factor Pattern [9]

To select the first factor coefficients, a_{i1}, we let

$$X^* = \begin{bmatrix} X_1^* \\ \cdot \\ \cdot \\ \cdot \\ \cdot \\ \cdot \\ \cdot \\ X_n^* \end{bmatrix} \qquad a_1 = \begin{bmatrix} a_{i1} \\ \cdot \\ \cdot \\ \cdot \\ \cdot \\ \cdot \\ \cdot \\ a_{n1} \end{bmatrix}.$$

[9] The exposition in this section is adapted from the discussion of principal components given in T. W. Anderson, *An Introduction to Multivariate Statistical Analysis* (New York: John Wiley & Sons, 1958), Chapter 11, and T. Klock and R. Bannink, "Principal Component Analysis Applied to Business Test Data," *Statistica Neerlandica*, Vol. 16 (1962), pp. 64–65. Several other techniques of factor estimation have been developed. These are discussed in detail in Harman, *Modern Factor Analysis*, Chapters 7–11.

The first factor, F_1, is defined as the normalized [10] linear combination of X_i^* which accounts for the maximal variance. Thus, we write

$$F_1 = a_1' \cdot X^* . \qquad (7)$$

The variance of F_1, which is σ_{F1}, is

$$\sigma_{F1}^2 = E(F_1 F_1') = E(a_1' \cdot X^*) \ (a_1' \cdot X^*)' = a_1' E(X^* X^{*\prime}) a_1 . \qquad (8)$$

Since it is desirable for the correlations reproduced from factor equation (6) to represent the observed correlation matrix R^*, we require that

$$E(X^* X^{*\prime}) = R^* . \qquad (9)$$

(Recall that the variables x_i are in standard form.) The variance of F_1 then becomes

$$\sigma_{F1}^2 = a_1' R^* a_1 . \qquad (10)$$

This quantity must be maximized subject to the normalization constraint that

$$a_1' = a_1 = 1 . \qquad (11)$$

Using the method of Lagrange multipliers, the function to be maximized may be written as

$$V = a_1' R^* a_1 - \lambda(a_1' a_1 - 1) \qquad (12)$$

where λ is the Lagrange multiplier. The vector of partial derivatives of V with respect to the elements of a_1 is

$$\frac{\delta V}{\delta a_1} = 2 R^* a_1 - 2 \lambda a_1 . \qquad (13)$$

Setting (13) equal to zero leads to the equations

$$R^* a_1 = \lambda a_1 \qquad (14)$$

or

$$(R^* - \lambda I) a_1 = 0 , \qquad (15)$$

which implies that

$$[R^* - \lambda I] = 0 . \qquad (16)$$

---

[10] The weights of the X_i^* have the unit sum of squares.

The problem of finding the elements of a thus reduces to that of determining the characteristic roots and associated characteristic vectors of R^*. In view of (11), the substitution of (14) for (10) yields

$$\sigma^2_{F_1} = a_1' \, R^* \, a_1 = a_1' \, \lambda \, a_1 = \lambda . \tag{17}$$

To maximize the variance accounted for by the first factor we must therefore set λ_1, the characteristic root corresponding to the first factor F_1, equal to the maximal characteristic root of R^*. Equation (15), with λ_1 replacing λ, can then be solved for the components of a_1.

To obtain the second factor, F_2, we proceed in a similar manner except that the maximization is now subject to an additional constraint: We require that the second factor, F_2, be uncorrelated with the first. That is,

$$0 = E \, (F_2 \, F_1) = E(a_2' \, X^*) \quad (a_2' \, X^*)^1 = E(a_2' \, X^* \, X^{*\prime} \, a_1')$$
$$= a_2' \, E(X^* \, X^{*\prime}) \, a_1 = a_2 \, R^* \, a_1 = a_2 \, \lambda_1 \, a_1 = \lambda_1 \, a_2' \, a_1 . \tag{18}$$

Since $\lambda \neq 0$, (18) implies that

$$a_2' \, a_1 = 0 . \tag{19}$$

To obtain F_2 we must therefore maximize

$$Q = a_2' \, R^* \, a_2 - \lambda \, (a_2' \, a_2 - 1) - \mu \, a_2' \, R^* \, a_1 \tag{20}$$

Where λ and μ are Lagrange multipliers. Taking partials as before, the result is

$$\frac{\delta Q}{\delta a_2} = 2 \, R^* \, a_2 - 2 \, \lambda \, a_2 - 2 \, \mu \, R^* \, a_1 \tag{21}$$

or

$$R^* \, a_2 - \lambda \, a_2 - \mu \, R^* \, a_1 = 0 .$$

If we premultiply (22) by a_1'. we get

$$a_1' \, R^* \, a_2 - \lambda \, a_1' \, a_2 - \mu \, a_1' \, R^* \, a_1 = 0 . \tag{23}$$

But the first two terms on the left-hand side of (23) are zero according to (18) and (19).[11] Therefore, (23) implies that

$$\mu \, a_1' \, R^* \, a_1 = \mu \, \lambda_1 = 0 . \tag{24}$$

---

[11] From (18) we have $a_2' \, R^* \, a_1 = 0$, if we take the transpose $a_1' \, R^{*\prime} \, a_2 = 0$. Since R^* is symetric, $R^{*\prime} = R^*$ and therefore $a_1' \, R^* \, a_2 = 0$. Similarly, the transposition of $a_2' \, a_1 = 0$ yields $a_1' \, a_2 = 0$.

Since $\lambda_1 \neq 0$, (24) states that $\mu = 0$. If we substitute (24) for (22), the conditions to be solved to obtain the components of a_2 become

$$(R^* - \lambda I) a_2 = 0 . \tag{25}$$

It is thus apparent that if a_2 is the characteristic vector associated with the second largest characteristic root of R^*, the components of F_2 will satisfy all our constraints.[12] To find the cth factor, one merely extracts the cth largest characteristic root of R^* and finds its associated characteristic vector. The components of this characteristic vector will be the coefficients a_{ic} ($i = 1, \ldots, n$) or F_c.

One important question that arises in practical applications of factor analysis is that of determining the appropriate number of factors to be extracted. Unfortunately, no multiple decision procedure for which an adequate statistical theory exists, even asymptotically, has been developed for this purpose. At best a sequence of tests could be applied. Thus, one might test the hypothesis that $m = m_0$ against the alternative that $m > m_0$; should this hypothesis be rejected, one could then test the hypothesis that $m = m_0 + 1$ against the alternative that $m > m_0 + 1$, etc. However, even if the significance level of each of these tests were known separately, the probabilities associated with the entire sequence of tests would not emerge. This is a computationally difficult procedure. Ad hoc rules, therefore, are frequently used to determine m. The rules used in our computations will be discussed below.

Up to now the discussion has proceeded as if the communalities h_i^2 were known a priori. Since this is not the case, iterative procedures are employed to estimate the h_i^2. Initial values of the communalities are approximated and the a_{ic} are estimated by the technique described above. The values of the communalities derived from the calculated a_{ic} are then compared with the initial estimates. If the agreement is reasonable, the calculated a_{ic} are used as final values. Otherwise, the calculation is repeated, using the communalities derived in the first interaction as new initial estimates. This process is repeated until satisfactory agreement between the calculated communalities and the communalities resulting from the previous iteration is obtained. While no proof of the convergence of this procedure exists, it always appears to converge in practice.

---

[12] This procedure is also equivalent to finding the maximal of first factor residuals, R_1^*. This matrix may be defined as $R_1^* = R^* - a_1 a_1'$; it consists of the residual correlations with the contribution of the first factor removed. For proof of this statement see Harman, *Modern Factor Analysis*, pp. 158–159.

Rotation of Factor Matrix

The factor structure that corresponds to any correlation matrix R^* is not unique. Any linear combination (rotation) of the factor structure also satisfies our condition ([9]) that $E(X^* X^{*\prime}) = R^*$. Thus, the derivation of the previous section assumed that

$$X^* = A F + \mu , \qquad (26)$$

where X^*, F, and μ had the same meaning as before and A is the $(n \times m)$ matrix of factor loadings. Instead of (26), however, we may assume that

$$X^* = BF + \mu , \qquad (27)$$

where, for a nonsingular $(m \times m)$ matrix T, $B = AT$ and $F = Tf$. Then (27) becomes

$$X^* = A T T^{-1} F + \mu = A F + \mu , \qquad (28)$$

and

$$
\begin{aligned}
E (X^* X^{*\prime}) &= E (Bf + \mu) (B f + \mu)' \\
&= E (B f f' B') + E \mu \mu' \\
&= E [A T T^{-1} F F' (T^{-1} - 1)' T' A'] + E \mu \mu' \quad (29) \\
&= E (A F F' A') + E \mu \mu' = R^* .
\end{aligned}
$$

We are therefore unable to distinguish in our observations between postulate (26) and postulate (27). That is, any nonsingular rotation of our original factor solution is also an admissible factor structure. This indeterminacy may be resolved by requiring that the factor structure offer as simple a description of the underlying regularities in the data as possible. Of course, the criterion of simplicity chosen is to some extent arbitrary. The method used in our computations to derive a simpler factor structure, the varimax technique, emphasizes the simplification of the description of the factors in terms of the original variables. It is obvious that a factor would be most readily interpretable if the loadings of each of the variables in that factor were either zero or unity. Such a description would also maximize the variance of the loadings of the variable for each factor. The simplicity of a factor p, S_p, is therefore defined as the normalized variance of its squared loadings. That is,

$$S_p = \frac{1}{n} \sum_{i=1}^{n} \left(\frac{b_{ip}^2}{h_i^2} \right)^2 - \frac{1}{n^2} \left(\sum_{i=1}^{n} \frac{b_{ip}^2}{h_i^2} \right)^2, \qquad (30)$$

where
$$p = 1, \ldots, m.$$

In equation (30), b_{ip} is the factor loading of the ith variable in the pth factor after rotation and h_i^2 is the communality of the ith variable. If the criterion for maximum simplicity of a complete factor matrix is taken to be the sum of the simplicities of the individual factors, the function to be maximized for the varimax rotation becomes

$$V = \frac{1}{n} \sum_{p=1}^{m} \sum_{i=1}^{n} \left(\frac{b_{ip}}{h_i} \right)^4 - \sum_{p=1}^{n} \left(\sum_{i=1}^{n} b_{ip}^2 / h_i^2 \right)^2. \tag{31}$$

Factors are rotated two at a time for all possible pairs of factors. For any given rotation, that angle of rotation is chosen which makes the maximal contribution to V.

The normalized rotated loadings for a particular pair of factors, p and q, and a given angle of rotation, φ, in the plane of the factors p and q are stated

$$\left(\frac{b_{ip}}{h_i} \ \frac{b_{iq}}{h_i} \right) = \left(\frac{a_{ip}}{h_i} \ \frac{a_{iq}}{h_i} \right) \left(\begin{matrix} \cos \varphi & - \sin \varphi \\ \sin \varphi & \cos \varphi \end{matrix} \right). \tag{32}$$

The angle of rotation φ is found by substituting (32) into (31) and maximizing (31) with respect to φ. This procedure leads to the following conditions on the angle of rotation:

$$\tan 4\,\varphi = \frac{2 \sum_{i=1}^{n} u_i V_i - \frac{2}{n} \sum_{i=1}^{n} u_i \cdot \sum_{i=1}^{n} V_i}{\sum_{i=1}^{n} (u_i^2 - V_i^2) - \frac{1}{n} \left(\sum_{i=1}^{n} u_i \right)^2 \left(\sum_{i=1}^{n} V_i \right)^2} \tag{33}$$

where
$$u_i = \frac{a_{ip}^2 - a_{iq}^2}{h_i^2}$$

and
$$V_i = \frac{2 a_{ip} a_{iq} \cdot}{h_i^2}$$

Equation (33) can be solved for φ and the rotated factors can then be derived from the known a_{ip} by using the relations within (32).

It should be noted that the varimax technique of factor rotation possesses the important property of leading to a factorial description that is invariant under changes in the composition of the sample of variables used to characterize each factor. Hence it permits the drawing of inferences about varimax factors in the universe from varimax factors derived from the analysis of a particular sample of social and political indicators.

Factor Scores

It is often interesting to find the value of the common factors for each particular observation in the sample.[13] These factor values, which are called factor scores, represent estimates of the values assumed by each of the unobserved common factors for each of the j observations in the sample. Thus, factor scores can be used to rank the members of the sample with respect to each of the c common characteristics. We shall denote these scores as F_{cj} ($c = 1, \ldots, m; j = 1, \ldots, N$).

Factor scores can be derived from the original observations by the method of least squares. We assume for the cth factor that

$$F_c = B_c X^*, \tag{34}$$

where F_c is the value of the cth factor score, B_c is the $(1 \times n)$ row vector of the unknown regression coefficients of the cth factor upon the n variables x_i, and X^* is an $(n \times 1)$ column vector of the x_i, as before. To estimate the B_c by least squares, we first write an equation analogous to (34) to obtain the value of the cth factor score for each of the original N observations:

$$\overline{F}_c = B_c \cdot X ; \tag{35}$$

F_c is now a $(1 \times N)$ vector of factor scores and X is the $(n \times N)$ matrix of the values of x_{ij}. Then $\widehat{B}_c$, the least squares estimate of B_c, can be derived by postmultiplying (35) by $X' (XX')^{-1}$:

$$F_c X' (XX')^{-1} = B_c . \tag{36}$$

This estimated value of $\widehat{B}_c$ can be substituted for (35) to yield a least squares estimate of $\overline{F}_c$:

$$\widehat{F}_c = \overline{F}_c X' (XX')^{-1} X . \tag{37}$$

[13] The derivation follows Harman, *Modern Factor Analysis*, pp. 338–42.

Of course, an equation analogous to (37) can be written for each of the c factor scores. Therefore, (37) in a more general form reads

$$\hat{F} = \bar{F} \, X' \, (XX')^{-1} \, X, \tag{38}$$

where F is the $(m \times N)$ matrix of factor scores whose typical element is F_{cj}, and where F is also $(m \times N)$. In (38) everything but F is known.

To derive factor scores consistent with our previously estimated matrix of factor loadings A, we define F by means of an equation analogous to (26):

$$X = A\bar{F}. \tag{39}$$

From (39) it follows that

$$\bar{F} \, X' = \bar{F} \, \bar{F}' \, A' = A', \tag{40}$$

since $(\bar{F} \, \bar{F}') = I$ according to our assumption (made in the derivation of A) that the factors are orthonormal.[14] For estimation purposes (38) can now be written as

$$\hat{F} = A' \, (XX')^{-1} \, X = A' \, (R)^{-1} \, X, \tag{41}$$

where R is the original correlation matrix.

PRACTICAL CONSIDERATIONS

The Choice of Variables

Factor analysis is sensitive to the nature of the variables included in a study. Consequently, an important safeguard against spurious results is to carry out the analysis omitting various subsets of the original set of variables. In each factor analysis made in the course of our investigation, therefore, several classes of variables were omitted in order to compare the results. More specifically, the process of national development was investigated including, alternately, social and political variables only, purely economic variables, and finally, social, political, and economic variables taken together. To the extent that the important forces that emerge from each of the factor analyses for a given sample represent different manifestations of the same underlying processes, the likelihood is increased that purely random associations have been avoided.

Since any variable must associate in some factor, it is possible that when the number of variables is increased and the number of factors held

[14] Uncorrelated and normalized so that $F_c \cdot F_l = 0$ and $F_c \cdot F_c' = 1$ $(l \neq c)$.

the same, some of the factor loadings will be reduced. As is apparent from our statistical discussion, the principle of extracting factors ensures that the fraction of additional variance explained by each succeeding extracted factor is maximized with respect to the combined variance of all variables included in the analysis. In the process of maximizing the proportion of over-all variance explained by each additional factor, the communality for any given variable may be reduced as additional variables are included. This effect is particularly strong when a variable is incorporated whose simple correlation with all other variables is weak and when the number of factors is not expanded. Of course, this consideration influences both the choice of variables and the choice of number of factors.

To minimize the adverse effects upon our results of including essentially irrelevant variables, we excluded from each factor analysis any variable whose highest simple correlation coefficient was not statistically significant at the 1 per cent level. In earlier experiments based on these data, we found that variables which did not meet this significance criterion tended to behave in a truly random fashion. When several variables of this nature were incorporated into the analysis, they tended to coalesce in a single, meaningless "random factor." When only a single variable of this type was included in an analysis, it usually associated rather weakly with some particular factor and tended to shift its association from factor to factor in successive, very similar preliminary runs.

It might seem surprising that problems caused by the inclusion of almost irrelevant variables should arise in analyses in which the choice of variables is guided by a body of commonly held, a priori theoretical propositions. This merely reflects the fact that changes in the relevance of political, economic, and social forces which take place as development proceeds are not generally incorporated into models of the development process. Development models usually assign to particular forces their average importance for all underdeveloped economies, whereas, in point of fact, particular forces may be important at some stages of development and essentially irrelevant at others.

In order to further reduce the likelihood of random associations, variables whose highest loading in a given rotated factor matrix was below 0.45 were omitted from that particular study.[15] Such low maximal loadings result from either of two sources. They may occur because the vari-

[15] A typical maximal loading in a rotated factor matrix is higher than 0.65.

ables have little affinity with any of the factors in a particular study yet are forced by the statistical technique to associate with some given factor. They also arise when a variable is closely associated with more than one factor. In the latter case, the variable is inherently composed of the forces represented in more than one factor; an attempt to allocate it to a single factor by rotation is apt to impose an inappropriate statistical specification upon the analysis. Therefore, the inclusion of a variable that in this respect does not meet the requirements imposed by the statistical model may vitiate the entire set of results. In either case, the interpretation of the factor analysis is likely to be more meaningful if variables with low highest loadings are omitted from the analysis. Therefore, we applied the low maximal loading criterion throughout all of our analyses, even where the factor associations appeared reasonable.

The Choice of Number of Factors

The technique of factor analysis is sensitive not only to the choice of variables but also to the number of factors extracted. The relative weight of each factor and the grouping of variables into factors are both affected, to varying degrees, by the more or less arbitrary choice of number of factors. Furthermore, as might be expected, the over-all communality is a monotonically increasing function of the number of factors extracted and is therefore dependent upon the number of factors rotated. Consequently, it is important to ensure that the qualitative interpretation of the analysis does not hinge upon the arbitrary decision made with respect to the number of factors. Consistent criteria for determining the number of factors to be rotated must also be employed.

In selecting the number of factors to be rotated in our studies, a combination of two criteria was used: (1) that the proportion of over-all variance explained by the factors included in the rotated factor matrix be no less than 65 per cent,[16] and (2) providing the criterion of 65 per cent of the over-all variance is met, that any factor accounting for less than 10 per cent of the over-all variance not be retained. Criteria of this nature have been employed by psychologists using factor analysis, and their use is recommended by Harman in his standard work on the subject.[17] The actual limits that we chose were based in part on our experi-

---

[16] For runs with less than twenty variables this criterion was dropped to 60 per cent.

[17] Harman, *Modern Factor Analysis*, p. 363.

145

ence with trial runs. It should be noted that the criteria we have applied tend to impose more stringent requirements for the retention of factors than is usual in practical applications of factor analysis. Early runs indicated that, with our particular kind of data and our unusually small samples, factors accounting for less than 10 per cent, once the 65 per cent criterion was met, were apt to consist of meaningless groupings of variables. Since our primary purpose in writing this book was to use the analyses to suggest hypotheses concerning the forces that underlie the growth process, as represented by the grouping of variables into common factors, it was felt that it would be desirable to impose relatively stringent requirements for the inclusion of factors in order to guard against "nonsense factors." These restraints were applied even though the extraction of a larger number of factors would have improved the over-all statistical fit of the factor pattern to the original data.

The choice of number of factors that was made on the above bases was cross-checked for each run by means of two additional tests. First of all, each factor analysis was reviewed to make sure that adding one more factor would not affect the qualitative interpretation of our results. Secondly, for each factor analysis a random variable was added to the variables included in the study.[18] This random variable was permitted to associate with any of $(m + 1)$ factors, where m was the number of factors selected for rotation by our previous criteria. It was then required that any factor extracted after the factor with which the random variable associates be dropped. The number of factors suggested by this test was always consistent with the number suggested by our previous criteria; the random variable almost always associated with the $(m + 1)$th factor.

As pointed out earlier, statistical significance tests for deciding whether to extract additional factors have been derived for large samples by Lawley and Bartlett. These tests, which are in essence χ^2 (Chi Square) tests based upon the difference between the actual correlation matrix and the correlation matrix that is reproduced from the factor pattern, apply only to large and moderate-sized samples. The Lawley χ^2 statistic[19] was nevertheless computed for all of our factor analyses. In general, this test indicated that a considerably larger number of factors than is presented in our final tables should have been used to explain adequately the over-all

[18] We are indebted to Donald T. Campbell for suggesting this test.
[19] See Harman, *Modern Factor Analysis*, pp. 371–80.

146

pattern of covariance of all the variables in the study. There are several reasons for our decision to disregard this large-sample test. First of all, the test is not applicable to small samples since only the asymptotic sampling distribution is known.

In addition, strictly speaking, the test applies only to factors extracted by the method of maximum likelihood. Finally, this significance test at best provides us with an indication of the purely statistical reliability of the extra factors. A factor that, statistically speaking, might contribute significantly to the fit of the factor pattern, might not have economic significance if the associations that it represents arise from a few accidental events that are specific at most to two or three countries; the weight of these accidental associations in the correlation matrix is of course greater, the smaller the sample. Thus, the likelihood of a divergence between statistical significance and true significance, although inherently unquantifiable, is considerably greater in very small samples than in a large sample, even when a statistical test is equally appropriate to both. In view of all of these considerations, the results of the χ^2 test were ignored.

Choice of Numerical Scale

Many of the variables used in our study are not measurable in the sense that there is no "natural" numerical scale on which they can be represented. Since the use of factor analysis requires that the variables be specified numerically, the choice of a scale for representing country rankings with respect to different features of economic, social, and political institutions involves another arbitrary decision that has to be made before the factor analysis technique can be applied. We chose a simple linear scale for our study. It is obvious, of course, that the choice of a numerical scale for qualitative indicators is an open one. However, the use of an arbitrary scale does not appear to seriously invalidate the results. For, inasmuch as the raw material of factor analysis consists of the correlation matrix among social and political characteristics and inasmuch as correlation coefficients are unaffected by linear changes in scale, the results are invariant with respect to linear transformations of the scale used.

Several nonlinear changes in scale were tried (such as a log transformation and the use of reciprocals), but it was found that the results of these transformations either yielded similar results, made less sense, or varied more with changes in sample size than did the simple linear scale chosen.

THE INTERPRETATION OF FACTOR ANALYSIS

It should be emphasized that, like all multivariate analyses, factor analysis is a study of mutual association rather than a study of causality. The decomposition of the original set of variables into smaller subsets of factors partitions the totality of variables into essentially independent subgroups. In this sense the analysis can be used to infer the extent of independence of a given variable from a given set of forces within a single factor. However, the association found may arise in more than one way. Causality may run from any subset of variables within the factor to any other nonoverlapping subset in the same factor; or the association may arise from some common cause (or causes) omitted from explicit consideration in the factor analysis. Thus, like correlation analyses, factor analyses can provide only information concerning the extent of mutual interdependence. Additional information not contained in the statistical analysis must be used to infer the existence and direction of causality.

CHAPTER **IV** THE LONG-RUN ANALYSIS

An attempt is made in this chapter to gain semiquantitative insights into the long-run interaction of various types of social and political change with the level of economic development. For this purpose, the techniques of factor analysis discussed in Chapter III are applied to per capita income and to the indices representing the social and political structure of seventy-four underdeveloped countries in the period 1957–62 which were described in Chapter II. Purely economic variables (other than average income) have been omitted in this chapter in order to analyze the nature of the interdependence between broad levels of economic development and the transformation of sociopolitical institutions and cultural values associated with industrialization and urbanization. Economic variables will, of course, be introduced in later chapters.

The use of cross-section analysis to obtain insight into the essentially historical phenomenon of long-run development, while common, does require justification. One may view cross-country results as representations of patterns of change typical of individual countries at a given point in time when access to technology and opportunities for trade are, at least in principle, common to all. Historically, however, the process of development occurs in an environment of concurrent change in all aspects relevant to national development. In order to interpret cross-sectional analyses as indications of historical transformations one must therefore conceive of successive points along the statistical fit as successive levels of socio-economic-political development achieved by a typical underdeveloped country in the process of structural change. More specifically, corresponding to each country is a point in n-dimensional space which is determined by a set of n attributes related to the country's stage of social, political, and economic development. The factor analysis fitted to these points in the m-dimensional space of common factors yields a representation of the average relationship among the several factors for the countries in the sample. Since we interpret consecutive points along the factor analysis fit to represent consecutive

149

stages of development, we treat the fit as a representation of the historical path that would be traversed by an average country undergoing socioeconomic and political transformation. If one asked how long it would take, on the average, for a nation to pass from one point on the fit near an actual country to the point on the fit nearest the next more advanced country, one would find that at rates of change typical of these countries in the past it would have taken a long time indeed. For this reason the relationships that emerge from the present factor analysis are interpreted as having primarily long-run validity.

The results of the analysis show that a remarkably high percentage of intercountry variations in the levels of economic development (70 per cent) is associated with differences in noneconomic characteristics. Thus it would appear that it is just as reasonable to look at underdevelopment as a social and political phenomenon as it is to analyze it in terms of intercountry differences in economic structure. That is not to say, of course, that economic forces do not play a significant role in accounting for cross-country variations in dynamic economic performance, especially once the take-off stage has been reached. Nor should the relationships found be interpreted in a causal sense. As indicated in Chapter III, the results of the factor analysis neither demonstrate that economic growth is caused by sociopolitical transformations nor indicate that variations in development levels determine patterns of social and political change. Rather, they suggest the existence of a systematic pattern of interaction among mutually interdependent economic, social, and political forces, all of which combine to generate a unified complex of change in the style of life of a community.

THE FACTOR ANALYSIS:
RESULTS AND INTERPRETATION

The results of the factor analysis are summarized in the matrix of common factor coefficients presented in Table IV–1. Each entry a_{ij} of the matrix shows the importance of the influence of factor j upon sociopolitical indicator i.[1] More specifically, the entries or "factor loadings" indicate the net correlation between each factor and the observed variables.

The interpretation of factor loadings may be made more easily in terms of the squares of the entries in the factor matrix. Each $(a_{ij})^2$

[1] See Chapter III.

150

TABLE IV-1: Rotated Factor Matrix for Per Capita GNP Together with Twenty-four Social and Political Variables [a] (Seventy-four Less-Developed Countries)

Political and Social Indicators	Rotated Factor Loadings				h_i^2
	F_1	F_2	F_3	F_4	(R^2)
Per Capita GNP in 1961	−.73	.31	−.26	−.03	.699
Size of the Traditional Agricultural Sector	**.89**	−.21	.17	−.08	.869
Extent of Dualism	**−.84**	.14	−.30	.04	.824
Extent of Urbanization	**−.84**	.13	−.12	.02	.741
Character of Basic Social Organization	**−.83**	.24	.10	.03	.761
Importance of the Indigenous Middle Class	**−.82**	.14	−.23	−.08	.755
Extent of Social Mobility	**−.86**	.21	−.18	−.18	.848
Extent of Literacy	**−.86**	.32	.03	−.11	.845
Extent of Mass Communication	**−.88**	.28	−.06	−.02	.858
Degree of Cultural and Ethnic Homogeneity	**−.66**	−.30	.34	−.21	.680
Degree of National Integration and Sense of National Unity	**−.87**	−.07	.01	−.18	.792
Crude Fertility Rate	**.63**	−.14	.05	.18	.448
Degree of Modernization of Outlook	**−.75**	.31	−.39	−.03	.805
Strength of Democratic Institutions	−.48	**.72**	−.26	−.19	.857
Degree of Freedom of Political Opposition and Press	−.33	**.82**	−.02	−.10	.802
Degree of Competitiveness of Political Parties	−.32	**.79**	.08	.25	.801
Predominant Basis of the Political Party System	−.43	**.70**	.04	.01	.681
Strength of the Labor Movement	−.38	**.63**	−.36	−.05	.678
Political Strength of the Military	−.26	**−.58**	.36	.41	.706
Extent of Centralization of Political Power	−.07	**−.65**	.08	−.02	.432
Political Strength of the Traditional Elite	.08	−.07	**.73**	.05	.543
Extent of Leadership Commitment to Economic Development	−.14	−.02	**−.80**	−.21	.699
Degree of Administrative Efficiency	−.39	.37	**−.59**	−.16	.663
Degree of Social Tension	.22	.02	.02	**.87**	.816
Extent of Political Stability	−.07	.05	−.39	**−.82**	.821

[a] Bold figures indicate the factor to which each variable is assigned. Variables omitted because of insignificant correlations: none. Variables omitted because of low high loadings: none. Percentage of over-all variance explained by factors: 73.7. Percentage of variance explained by last factor included: 5.0.

represents the proportion of the total unit variance of variable i which is explained by factor j, after allowing for the contributions of the other factors. If the first row of the table is examined, it can be seen that 53

151

per cent of intercountry variations in per capita GNP are explained by Factor I, an additional 10 per cent by Factor II, and another 7 per cent by Factor III; the net contribution of Factor IV is only 3 per cent.[2]

The right-hand column of the table gives the sum of the squared factor loadings, or the "communality" of each variable. The communality indicates the proportion of the total unit variance explained by all the common factors taken together and is thus analogous to R^2 in regression analysis. The communality of per capita GNP, for example, is:

$$(-0.73)^2 + (0.31)^2 + (0.26)^2 + (-0.03)^2 = 0.699$$

That is to say, 70 per cent of intercountry variations in per capita GNP are associated with the four common factors that are extracted from the twenty-four sociopolitical variables incorporated in our analysis. This is a striking result which might not be expected from an analysis that excludes explicit indicators of economic structure from its explanatory variables.

The matrix of factor loadings, in addition to indicating the weight of each factor in explaining the observed variables, provides the basis for grouping the variables into common factors. Each variable may reasonably be assigned to that factor with which it shows the closest linear relationship, i.e., that factor in which it has the highest loading. Where loadings of a variable in two factors are very close, the variable has been assigned to the one with which it is judged to have the closest affinity.[3] Table IV–1 lists first the indicators that have their highest loading in Factor I, then those with highest loadings in Factors II, III, and IV successively. Bold figures indicate the loading in that factor to which each indicator is assigned.

[2] In view of the relatively large size of the sample for the factor analysis in Table IV–1, the first criterion for selecting the number of factors was the requirement that the proportion of over-all variance explained by the factors included in the rotated factor matrix be no less than 70 per cent rather than 65 per cent (the latter being the criterion given in Chapter III for the small-sample studies in Chapters V–VII). Thus, the second requirement for factor selection applied here is that, providing the criterion of 70 per cent of the over-all variance is met, any factor accounting for less than 10 per cent of the over-all variance not be retained. It should be noted that, due to errors in rounding, the sum of the squares of the entries in each row of Table IV–1 (and all subsequent tables) may be slightly different from the communality given for each row in the last column of the table.

[3] This is accepted procedure for combining variables into common factor groups. See, for example, Robert Ferber and P. J. Verdoorn, *Research Methods in Economics and Business* (New York: Macmillan, 1962), p. 105. Unfortunately, no tests for the significance of differences in factor loadings exist; however, it is evident that small differences in loadings cannot be considered significant.

Once variables are assigned to common factors, the factors need to be "identified" by giving a reasonable explanation of the underlying forces that they may be interpreted to represent. To quote Thurstone, who pioneered the use of factor analysis in psychology: "The derived variables are of scientific interest only in so far as they represent processes or parameters that involve the fundamental concepts of the science involved."[4] We shall, therefore, proceed to identify the factors that are specified in the results of our statistical analysis.

The First Factor

The characteristics having their highest loadings in Factor I are size of traditional sector, extent of dualism, degree of urbanization, character of basic social organization, size of the indigenous middle class, extent of social mobility, extent of literacy, extent of mass communication, degree of cultural homogeneity, degree of national integration, crude fertility rate, and degree of modernization of outlook.

More specifically, Factor I may be interpreted to represent the processes of change in attitudes and institutions associated with the breakdown of traditional social organization. Social change may be viewed as taking place through the mechanism of differentiation and of integration of social structure.[5] Differentiation involves "the establishment of more specialized and autonomous social units";[6] integration is the process that coordinates and fuses the interactions of specialized social entities.[7]

Five variables with high loadings in this factor depict the process of social differentiation: the character of the basic social organization groups countries according to the degree of differentiation of nuclear family (the parent-children unit) from extended kinship, village, and tribal complexes; the size of the traditional sector measures the extent to which self-sufficient family-community economic units have broken up; the strength of an indigenous middle class indicates the importance of a specialized group whose economic activities are removed from

[4] *Multiple Factor Analysis,* p. 61.
[5] See Smelser, "Mechanisms of Change and Adjustment to Change," pp. 32ff.
[6] *Ibid.,* p. 33.
[7] Emil Durkheim has pointed out with special emphasis that the increasing division of labor and growing social heterogeneity which accompany industrialization require the creation of new mechanisms for integrating societies. *The Division of Labor,* p. 41.

153

traditional socioeconomic contexts; and the extent of social mobility represents an important concomitant of the breakdown of premodern social structures, that is, the process whereby individual movement between social classes, types of community, and occupations becomes freer and facilitates the adaptation of skills to the requirements of economic change. A fifth variable, the extent of dualism, depicts the transformation of a largely agrarian society into one in which specialized modern social and economic structures typically develop alongside of, but are sharply divided from, the predominant traditional organization; in such a society, as growth proceeds, a continuous interaction between modern and traditional elements performing specialized roles eventually evolves throughout the economy.

The process of social integration is also portrayed by several variables. Improvements in mass communication media, increases in literacy, the growth of linguistic homogeneity, and the process of national integration may all be viewed as part of the evolution of modern mechanisms that tend to weld together relatively diversified social units.

The association of urbanization with Factor I is not unexpected since the growth of cities typically promotes both the specialization of economic activites and the spread of integrative agents such as communication and education. All these modernizing influences, together with the related increases in opportunities for geographic, economic, and social mobility, gradually tend to alter prevailing attitudes in favor of family limitation; thus, we find them associated with declining fertility rates in Factor I.

The final variable within Factor I, degree of modernization, summarizes fundamental changes in sociocultural attitudes which typically accompany urbanization and industrialization. It is an over-all indicator of the extent to which attachments to traditionalism and traditional society have lost their strength.

None of the associations evident in Factor I is surprising. Thus we find that (1) size of the traditional agricultural sector and crude fertility rate are negatively related to per capita GNP; (2) less specialized kinship forms—the tribe, the clan, and the extended family—tend to be found in countries with low per capita income; (3) level of education, extent of mass communication, degree of linguistic homogeneity, and degree of national integration are positively correlated with average GNP; and (4) strength of an indigenous middle class and extent of modernization of outlook vary directly with per capita income.

154

The finding that levels of economic development are closely associated with the degree of specialization and integration of social structure is a familiar one.[8] The rationalization and specialization of economic roles reflected in the decline of traditional social organization, the increase in mobility, and the rise of the middle class are essential concomitants to the creation of an institutional framework favorable to economic change. At the same time, improvements in communication and education, increased urbanization, and modernization of outlook both promote the integration of specialized social units and contribute to an increase in receptivity to technical and organizational innovations which is essential to successful economic performance. In general, therefore, Factor I expresses the strong interaction between economic development and degree of rationalization of social behavior, values, and institutions.

The Second Factor

The sociopolitical indicators with their highest loadings in Factor II are strength of democratic institutions, freedom of political opposition and press, degree of competitiveness of political parties, predominant basis of the political party system, strength of the labor movement, political strength of the military, and degree of centralization of political power. These are all indicators that describe variations in political systems among countries.

In particular, the pattern of associations incorporated in Factor II is strongly suggestive of broad historical and contemporary differences between the political organization of the countries of Western Europe and the North Atlantic and those of the rest of the world. An increase in this factor may be interpreted to represent a movement along a scale that ranges from centralized authoritarian political forms to specialized political mechanisms capable of representing the varied group interests of a society and of aggregating these interests through participant national political organs. Such an interpretation is consistent with the particular juxtaposition of characteristics subsumed in the factor. Thus, a positive change in Factor II is composed of (1) increases in the effectiveness of democratic institutions, freedom of political opposition and press, competitiveness of political parties, and strength of the labor

---

[8] See, for example, Moore, "Industrialization and Social Change," pp. 229–368.

movement; (2) a movement from political parties emphasizing consid-erations of national unity toward those stressing ideological platforms; and (3) decreases in the strength of the military and in the extent of centralization. Historically, the rise of representative parliamentary in-stitutions typically has been accompanied by the strengthening of labor movements, the weakening of the political strength of the military, and the decentralization of political power. This factor, therefore, may be interpreted to represent the extent of development of participant politi-cal systems.

The coefficients resulting from the factor analysis indicate that the configuration of political traits typically associated with participant poli-tical systems is associated to some extent with higher average income. Thus, the variable representing the basis of the political party system shows that there exists a tendency for high-income nations to have ideologically based or personalistic multiparty systems rather than mass-directed one-party systems. Similarly, countries with high incomes often tend to have well-established labor movements and politically weak military groups. Finally, greater decentralization of political power tends to accompany higher income per capita.

The presence of a systematic association between political systems and income per person is neither direct evidence that the evolution of more participant forms of democracy brings about more rapid economic growth nor direct support for the thesis that higher levels of economic development tend to produce more democratic systems. While either theory may be correct, no analysis of covariance (such as correlation study or factor analysis) can rigorously demonstrate which, if any, of the above hypotheses is valid. Indeed, in the present instance, it ap-pears more plausible to us to ascribe the positive association between Factor II and per capita GNP to the existence of common forces that underlie both the transformations of social institutions, which typically accompany economic development, and the changes in political struc-ture characteristic of the evolution of modern political systems. More specifically, the increased functional specialization and the evolution of new mechanisms for integrating society, both of which are familiar con-comitants of economic development, appear to be as basic to the evolu-tion of modern representative political structures[9] as they are to the

[9] In this connection Coleman writes: "The most general characteristic of [a *modern political system*] is the relatively high degree of differentiation, explicitness,

social changes characterizing industrialization. In addition, fundamental to the processes of both socioeconomic and political change is a transformation of basic attitudes affecting the habits, beliefs, and emotions of the individual members of society. It is this transformation of individual outlook which tends to generate not only the receptivity to technical change, enterprise, and initiative, which are crucial to economic growth, but also the acceptance of the breakdown of ascriptive traditional norms which is essential to the creation of political institutions that can incorporate continuing social and political change. We therefore favor a more eclectic, general equilibrium point of view. We shall return again to this question in Chapter VII in our discussion of dynamic results for underdeveloped countries at a relatively high level of socioeconomic development.

The Third Factor

Factor III (which accounts for 7 per cent of total unit variance) is based upon three sociopolitical characteristics: strength of the traditional elite, degree of leadership commitment to economic development, and degree of administrative efficiency. The character of leadership provides the common bond for these indicators.

At one end of the scale are leaders motivated by a strong attachment to the preservation of traditional society. At the other end of the scale are leaders committed to industrialization and to national direction of economic development. A movement along the scale thus implies a decline in the power of traditional elites and a rise in the strength of "industrializing elites."[10]

The signs of the loadings in Factor III indicate a tendency for countries characterized by more efficient industrializing leaders and a weakening of the power of traditional elites to have higher average incomes. This positive association of leadership characteristics and income levels is not unexpected. It is well known, for example, that the breakup of control of the agricultural surplus by traditional landed elites is essential

---

and functional distinctiveness of political and governmental structures, each of which tends to perform, for the political system as a whole, a regulatory role for the respective political and authoritative functions," "The Political Systems of the Developing Areas," p. 532.

[10] The concept of an industrializing elite is discussed in Kerr *et al.*, *Industrialism and Industrial Man,* Chapter 2.

if agricultural productivity is to be increased. The significance for economic growth of the willingness and ability of governments to direct or attract this surplus and other resources into modern sectors is also frequently emphasized.[11] Finally, it is a familiar proposition that more rationalized and less personalistic government administrative structures tend to evolve as countries develop economically and politically.

The relatively small proportion of intercountry differences in per capita GNP associated with the variables summarized by Factor III is surprising. It arises in part because, while per capita GNP is an indicator of the broad stage of economic development, the leadership characteristics are defined only with respect to the period 1957–62 rather than in terms of the country's entire historical experience. As we shall see later, the leadership variables used in this study are of greater relative importance in an explanation of recent short-term economic performance, especially among countries in which the major socioeconomic bottlenecks to growth have been overcome.

The Fourth Factor

An examination of Factor IV shows a negligible association between per capita GNP and social and political stability. This result undoubtedly arises in part from the different time periods reflected in the indicator of development levels and in the stability variables. While per capita GNP is a rough index of a country's long-run achievement in developing its economy, the degrees of social and political stability, as defined in this study, refer only to the period since 1950. Another explanation of the lack of a significant relationship between this factor and income per capita is that two opposing forces are at work relating growth and stability. On the one hand, the breakdown of traditional social and political structures commonly accompanying the industrialization-urbanization process tends frequently to aggravate internal discontent and tensions, thereby creating a negative association between stability and changes in average income. On the other hand, acute and widespread uncertainty clearly tends to retard economic development. This necessity for reasonable social and political stability arises from the well-known interdependence of sociopolitical environment and incen-

[11] See, for example, Johnston and Mellor, "The Role of Agriculture in Economic Development," pp. 571–81.

158

tives to save and invest: the prevalence of tension and instability greatly increases the desire to hoard; an atmosphere of uncertainty tends to promote investment in real estate and commercial activities that show a quick return rather than in productive capital projects that require longer periods of gestation; frequent changes in political leadership may have detrimental economic effects upon personal savings decisions and business investment activity; and finally, to attract foreign investment in the expansion of productive capacity requires that foreign entrepreneurs be assured of reasonably stable and secure domestic social and political conditions. For all these reasons, grave political instability and serious social tensions hamper the growth process, thus producing a long-run tendency for stability and growth to be positively interrelated.

REGIONAL DIFFERENCES IN THE RELATIONSHIP BETWEEN PER CAPITA GNP AND SOCIOPOLITICAL INFLUENCES

One of the tests of the validity of a relationship is the consistency with which it appears in subsamples of the larger population analyzed. Tables IV–2, IV–3, and IV–4 present the rotated factor matrices for per capita GNP together with series of social and political variables for three regions: Africa (Table IV–2), the Near East and Far East (Table IV–3), and Latin America (Table IV–4).[12] It can be seen immediately that the over-all communality for per capita GNP in the three subsample ranges from 67 to 75 per cent. To obtain a degree of "explanation" of variance in the small samples, which is as good as that found in the large sample, is a finding which tends to support the reliability of the full sample results.

In all three regional samples, the grouping of variables into (1) a factor representing the social aspects of industrialization, and (2) a factor (or factors) representing the development of specialized representative institutions is broadly similar. The principal differences in the small-sample results lie, on the one hand, in variations in the relative weight of the political factors as distinct from the social factors and, on the other hand, in the grouping into factors of the leadership and stability variables. These differences and the reasons for them will be discussed in detail below.

[12] Since the principal purpose of the regional-sample analyses in Tables IV–2, IV–3, and IV–4 was to provide a cross-check on the full-sample results of Table IV–1, the same number of factors was extracted in these three analyses as was obtained in the full-sample analysis.

TABLE IV–2: Rotated Factor Matrix for Per Capita GNP Together with Twenty-four Social and Political Variables [a] (Twenty-seven African Countries)

Political and Social Indicators	Rotated Factor Loadings				h_i^2
	F_1	F_2	F_3	F_4	(R^2)
Per Capita GNP in 1961	−.81	−.01	.20	.25	.754
Size of the Traditional Agricultural Sector	**.85**	−.10	−.01	−.04	.733
Extent of Dualism	**−.88**	.09	.02	.08	.781
Extent of Urbanization	**−.75**	.11	.17	.35	.724
Character of Basic Social Organization	**−.63**	.18	−.23	.10	.491
Extent of Social Mobility	**−.64** [b]	.04	−.67	−.02	.854
Extent of Literacy	**−.75**	.31	.05	.07	.665
Extent of Mass Communication	**−.64**	.20	−.02	.54	.739
Degree of Modernization of Outlook	**−.91**	.09	.04	−.05	.834
Degree of Administrative Efficiency	**−.56**	.40	−.21	−.14	.537
Strength of Democratic Institutions	−.25	**.83**	.01	.02	.750
Degree of Freedom of Political Opposition and Press	.13	**.88**	.02	.07	.803
Degree of Competitiveness of Political Parties	−.37	**.83**	.19	−.20	.900
Predominant Basis of the Political Party System	−.05	**.74**	.26	−.02	.614
Strength of the Labor Movement	−.33	**.71**	−.08	−.09	.631
Degree of Social Tension	−.48	.11	**.64**	−.27	.732
Extent of Political Stability	.22	−.28	**−.67**	.17	.601
Political Strength of the Military	−.46	−.33	**.54**	.10	.623
Political Strength of the Traditional Elite	−.12	.04	**.62**	.24	.457
Extent of Leadership Commitment to Economic Development	−.45	−.23	**−.62**	−.08	.649
Importance of the Indigenous Middle Class	−.33	−.01	**−.62**	−.02	.495
Degree of Cultural and Ethnic Homogeneity	.04	.00	−.09	**.84**	.714
Degree of National Integration and Sense of National Unity	−.23	−.17	−.19	**.79**	.741
Extent of Centralization of Political Power	−.27	−.28	.31	**.48**	.485
Crude Fertility Rate	.06	−.05	−.33	**−.72**	.637

[a] Bold figures indicate the factor to which each variable is assigned. Variables omitted because of insignificant correlations: none. Variables omitted because of low high loadings: none. Percentage of over-all variance explained by factors: 67.8. Percentage of variance explained by last factor included: 8.6.

[b] A variable having loadings on two factors which are not significantly different is assigned to that factor to which it is judged to have the closest affinity.

TABLE IV–3: Rotated Factor Matrix for Per Capita GNP Together with Twenty-four Social and Political Variables [a] (Twenty-six Near Eastern and Far Eastern Countries)

Political and Social Indicators	Rotated Factor Loadings				h_i^2
	F_1	F_2	F_3	F_4	(R^2)
Per Capita GNP in 1961	−.58	−.55	−.12	−.09	.672
Size of the Traditional Agricultural Sector	**.82**	.47	.13	.15	.941
Extent of Dualism	**−.87**	−.35	−.18	−.12	.924
Extent of Urbanization	**−.76**	−.14	−.33	−.19	.742
Character of Basic Social Organization	**−.65**	−.19	−.07	−.57	.782
Importance of the Indigenous Middle Class	**−.83**	−.33	−.15	−.13	.838
Extent of Social Mobility	**−.87**	−.20	−.15	−.25	.880
Extent of Literacy	**−.63**	−.24	−.22	−.44	.689
Extent of Mass Communication	**−.84**	−.31	−.04	−.26	.879
Degree of National Integration and Sense of National Unity	**−.81**	.21	−.33	−.06	.814
Degree of Cultural and Ethnic Homogeneity	**−.63**	.49	−.01	.27	.706
Degree of Modernization of Outlook	**−.58**	−.42	−.51	−.34	.891
Political Strength of the Traditional Elite	**.71**	.17	.06	.19	.579
Degree of Administrative Efficiency	**−.63**	−.24	−.53	−.37	.883
Strength of Democratic Institutions	−.33	**−.65**	−.30	−.51	.892
Degree of Freedom of Political Opposition and Press	−.37	**−.65**	−.04	−.60	.921
Strength of the Labor Movement	−.38	**−.69**	−.12	−.28	.717
Political Strength of the Military	.08	**.82**	.13	.28	.784
Crude Fertility Rate	.49	**.72**	.25	.10	.839
Extent of Leadership Commitment to Economic Development	−.18	−.28	**−.76**	.04	.683
Extent of Political Stability	−.09	−.27	**−.92**	.02	.933
Degree of Social Tension	.20	−.15	**.84**	−.01	.772
Predominant Basis of the Political Party System	−.30	−.16	−.23	**−.81**	.830
Degree of Competitiveness of Political Parties	−.30	−.15	.10	**−.88**	.895
Extent of Centralization of Political Power	−.10	.34	−.20	**.69**	.632

[a] Bold figures indicate the factor to which each variable is assigned. Variables omitted because of insignificant correlations: none. Variables omitted because of low high loadings: none. Percentage of over-all variance explained by factors: 80.5. Percentage of variance explained by last factor included: 5.2.

TABLE IV-4: Rotated Factor Matrix for Per Capita Income Together with Twenty-four Social and Political Variables [a] (Twenty-one Latin American Countries)

Political and Social Indicators	Rotated Factor Loadings				h_i^2
	F_1	F_2	F_3	F_4	(R^2)
Per Capita GNP in 1961	−.58	.44	−.32	.22	.675
Size of the Traditional Agricultural Sector	.90	−.27	.07	−.03	.882
Extent of Dualism	−.77	.24	−.11	.39	.809
Character of Basic Social Organization	−.67	.40	.41	.11	.794
Importance of the Indigenous Middle Class	−.66	.09	−.30	.31	.632
Extent of Social Mobility	−.56	.41	−.26	.54	.841
Extent of Literacy	−.62 [b]	.00	−.28	.62	.840
Extent of Mass Communication	−.57	.16	−.55	.33	.757
Degree of Cultural and Ethnic Homogeneity	−.84	−.24	.04	.01	.759
Degree of National Integration and Sense of National Unity	−.83	.21	−.22	.05	.779
Crude Fertility Rate	.66	−.11	.14	−.23	.518
Degree of Modernization of Outlook	−.64	.64	−.02	.25	.883
Strength of Democratic Institutions	−.38	.53	−.36	.51	.820
Predominant Basis of the Political Party System	−.15	.62	−.50	−.27	.725
Extent of Centralization of Political Power	.12	−.67	.47	.09	.686
Strength of the Labor Movement	−.33	.79	−.06	.16	.766
Political Strength of the Military	−.07	−.57	.33	−.53	.722
Extent of Leadership Commitment to Economic Development	−.07	.80	−.13	.16	.686
Degree of Administrative Efficiency	−.52	.52	−.37	.48	.896
Political Strength of the Traditional Elite	.02	−.79	−.21	−.37	.803
Degree of Freedom of Political Opposition and Press	−.37	.22	−.68	.21	.692
Degree of Competitiveness of Political Parties	.00	.00	−.81	−.13	.670
Extent of Urbanization	−.20	.36	−.51	.25	.492
Degree of Social Tension	.15	−.07	−.26	−.75	.657
Extent of Political Stability	−.33	.26	−.09	.72	.704

[a] Bold figures indicate the factor to which each variable is assigned. Variables omitted because of insignificant correlations: none. Variables omitted because of low high loadings: none. Percentage of over-all variance explained by factors: 74.0. Percentage of variance explained by last factor included: 6.2.

[b] A variable having loadings on two factors which are not significantly different is assigned to that factor to which it is judged to have the closest affinity.

Africa

The results of the factor analysis for Africa parallel in important respects those for the entire sample. The grouping of variables into two of the four factors is very similar and the directions of the relationships to per capita income are the same within three of the factors. The interpretation of the forces that Factors I and II represent, which was made in analyzing the full sample, appears to hold for this subsample without significant qualification; however, a few of the social and political variables that had their highest loadings in Factors I and II in the full sample analysis associate with Factor III (representing the character of social and political stability) and Factor IV (depicting the extent of sociopolitical integration) in the African results, thus giving distinctive regional characteristics to the results for this subsample.

A principal distinguishing feature of the African results is the very large percentage of intercountry variations in levels of development explained by Factor I alone. In this region, intercountry differences in social structure and in degrees of modernization of education, communication, and outlook account for as much as two-thirds of cross-country variations in per capita GNP. The explanation for this striking weight of social influences lies in the concentration in Africa of countries that are characterized by the predominance of preliterate communities. As emphasized by Gerschenkron and others, an essential prerequisite for the initiation of a process of economic growth is a social transformation characterized by the breakdown of traditionalism, the spread of literacy, increased communication, and greater receptivity to modern ideas and techniques. The results of the regional analysis underscore the fact that most African nations are still at a stage of development in which traditional social structures create critical barriers to growth.

The degree of "explanation" offered by Factor II is negligible. The quantitatively insignificant association between the political characteristics summarized in this factor and per capita income is probably due to the fact that most African countries have not yet established the basic social prerequisites for the evolution of participant political institutions; literacy rates and receptivity to change, for example, are still extremely low, and attitudes toward political life as yet are strongly conditioned by the relatively static norms of traditional social organization.

The character of the stability-leadership factor (Factor III) is yet

163

another distinctive feature of the African results. In this factor (which adds 4 per cent to the "explanation" of per capita GNP) higher per capita GNP levels are accompanied by more serious social tensions, greater political instability, stronger military influences, a stronger traditional elite, less commitment to economic development, and a weaker indigenous middle class. The negative association of short-run social and political stability with income levels in Africa probably arises in part because of the tensions and unrest created by the early stages of economic change during which traditional social structures and customs are being undermined and transformed. In addition, however, recent independence and improved communications have, in many of these nations, brought into closer contact diverse sectional, ethnic, and religious interests, thereby producing a tendency toward greater social and political conflict.[13] The inclusion in the stability factor of several leadership indicators having the opposite relationship to average income of that found in the full sample (commitment to development, traditional elite, and strength of the military) can also be explained by the relatively small distance that many African countries have progressed in the process of social, economic, and political change; the limited extent of social change that has taken place tends to render national development policies considerably less effective than those at higher levels of development. Thus reflected in this factor is a tendency, though indeed a weak one, for tradition-oriented leaderships supported by the military, rather than by more broadly based middle class elements, to achieve higher income levels than leaderships with the opposite characteristics.

A final, specifically regional feature of the African results is the configuration of relationships depicted in Factor IV in which more cultural and ethnic homogeneity, a greater degree of national integration, more political centralization, and lower fertility rates contribute between 6 and 7 per cent additional "explanation" to the pattern of intercountry differences in per capita GNP. The association of this subset of social and political variables with higher average income emphasizes the urgent need for countries at very low levels of development to attain a minimal degree of social and political integration in order that they can be mobilized for effective economic development. It should be noted in

---

[13] If the time period during which our indicators of stability were defined extended to the present, it is likely that the negative relationship between stability and growth in Africa would be even stronger.

this connection that in the definitional scheme of the extent of centralization, a positive movement at the lower end of the scale is a movement toward greater integration of local traditional government units into the national political system. The grouping of fertility in this factor is not unexpected in view of the well-known tendency for fertility to decline with the breakdown of traditional social structures and the concomitant rise of modern mechanisms of social, cultural, and political integration.

Near East and Far East

The results of the factor analysis for the Near East and Far East also resemble the results for the seventy-four country sample. As before, Factor I is the most important factor associated with differences in development levels. The incorporation in this factor of the strength of the traditional elite, which is negatively associated with per capita GNP, is a perfectly logical one since it reflects a long-run tendency for the influence of tradition-oriented leaders to lessen with the decline of traditional social organization. The inclusion of extent of administrative efficiency in this factor rather than in the leadership-stability factor may be viewed as a reflection of the close association between greater rationalization of administrative procedures and the processes of social modernization.

In the results for the Near and Far East, Factor II contains three of the indicators of the strength of participant political systems contained in the same factor of the full sample; it also includes the political strength of the military and crude fertility rates. The association in this factor of declines in fertility with rises in participant political institutions is probably due to the fact that common changes in personal values and attitudes underlie both transformations. In comparison to the full sample, and even more so to the African subsample, however, Factor II accounts for almost one-third of intercountry variations in per capita GNP. This result reinforces the point made above, that only when countries have proceeded relatively far in the breakdown of traditional social and economic tribal organization can they acquire the capacity for evolving representative forms of national political organization.

Factor III in this sample groups together the indicators of social and political stability with leadership commitment to economic development. Associated with higher per capita income levels are more commitment to development, less social tension, and more stability of the political system. This particular pattern of associations is a reasonable one in view of the well-known long-run tendency for more stability and greater government commitment to economic modernization to promote economic growth. The reason that these relationships between leadership and stability appear only in this sample may be that several higher-income countries in which social and political stability and fairly effective leadership date back a considerable number of years are concentrated in this subgroup.

Factor IV includes a subset of political characteristics that, in the full sample results, associated with the other aspects of the evolution of participant political institutions: the extent of centralization of political power, the predominant basis of the political party system, and the degree of competitiveness of political parties. While the direction of the relationships with per capita GNP is, strictly speaking, the same as in the full sample, it should be noted that the weight of these relationships in explaining per capita income in the Near East and Far East is negligible.

Latin America

The results of the factor analysis for Latin America also display a typically regional pattern while showing marked similarities to those for the full sample. No important differences emerge in the composition of Factor I, but this factor is of less absolute importance here than in the full sample or the other regional results; undoubtedly, because Latin American countries, generally speaking, have reached higher levels of socioeconomic development than most countries in the other two subsamples, basic social transformations have become less important to continued economic progress. As for political influences in this set of results, they assume a distinctly regional guise.

In Latin America, two significant factors represent the evolution of participant political institutions. The first of these includes not only the effectiveness of democratic institutions, strength of the labor movement, basis of the political party system, strength of the military, and centralization of political power, as in the full sample, but also three indicators of leadership characteristics: the degree of administrative efficiency, the extent of leadership commitment to economic development, and the strength of the traditional elite. This factor accounts for close to 20 per cent of cross-country variations in average income.

166

The second of the factors representing the nature of political systems, which alone explains some 10 per cent of the total unit variance of income per capita, is composed of two indicators of the degree of articulation of political party systems (freedom of political opposition and press and degree of competitiveness of political parties) and the indicator of degree of urbanization. The assignment of these two political variables to a separate and significant factor emphasizes the fact that they represent two of the more sophisticated forms of political articulation. The inclusion of urbanization in this factor is entirely consistent with the familiar tendency for effective political articulation of special interests to proceed further in an urban environment than in a rural setting. The important positive association of GNP levels with this factor undoubtedly results from the close relationship between degree of political articulation and degree of urbanization and industrialization. To quote an expert on Latin American political development: "It is typical of Latin America that, with the exception of the landowners and the church, few interests arising in the rural areas are capable of making themselves heard in national politics. In the cities, however, interest groups form more readily and give voice to the demands of urbanized sectors of the population. Similarly, new interests find organized expression in consequence of the processes of restratification, secularization, and commercialization."[14]

Factor IV, in which less social tension and more political stability are positively associated with higher per capita GNP, has slightly more weight on average income than in the full sample or the Near and Far East sample (5 per cent). As discussed above, this is the relationship that one would expect to find in the long run; it may appear somewhat stronger among countries at the Latin American level of development because the counteracting tensions and instability arising from short-run sociopolitical and economic change are somewhat less than among countries at lower levels of development.

THREE LEVELS OF SOCIOECONOMIC DEVELOPMENT

The results of the full sample analysis of the interaction of income per capita with the social and political characteristics of underdeveloped countries can also be used to derive insights into a question that has

[14] G. I. Blanksten, "The Politics of Latin America," in *The Politics of the Developing Areas*, ed. Almond and Coleman, p. 477.

been much discussed in recent literature: the problem of measuring and comparing different levels of development.[15] For reasons that are familiar, per capita GNP is an inadequate indicator of differences in the extent of development. For example, estimates of national income fail to include the economic activities of nonmonetized sectors; they are subject to distortions created by the use of exchange rates and by variations among countries in relative prices; and they conceal large differences from country to country in the distribution of income and the composition of output. Alternative composite measurements of development, such as simple or weighted averages of several social and economic indices, all suffer from the arbitrary choice that governs the selection and weighting of the elements included. One solution to this difficulty is to make use of the factor scores for individual countries which result from the full factor analysis presented in this chapter.[16] These scores rank countries with respect to each of the several broad characteristics represented by the factors that emerge from the analysis. As pointed out in Chapter III, in deriving factor scores on a particular factor, the weight assigned to each characteristic is proportional to the factor loading of the attribute in that factor. The use of factor scores therefore automatically provides a criterion for the selection and weighting of various country attributes in the construction of a composite index of economic development. Much of the arbitrariness inherent in index number construction is thereby removed. The first factor in the results of the full sample, which combines per capita GNP and twelve measures of social change, represents a configuration of country attributes that is consistent with our intuitive understanding of the broad meaning of development and accounts for $(0.72)^2$ or over 50 per cent of intercountry variations in income per capita. We have therefore used the country scores for this factor to rank the seventy-four countries in the sample with respect to their level of socioeconomic development. This ranking was then employed to obtain three samples of countries representative of three successive stages of development.

Initial examination of our results suggested that the inclusion of the indicators of degree of cultural and ethnic homogeneity and degree of national integration in the factor analysis used to group countries into subsamples was not appropriate. Since these characteristics change con-

---

[15] See the references given in the discussion of per capita GNP in Chapter II.
[16] See Chapter III for a discussion and definition of factor scores.

siderably more slowly than the other characteristics in this factor, the time series interpretation of cross-sectional results for these two indicators necessarily applies to a much longer time span than is the case for other indicators of socioeconomic development. When these two indicators are included, the scores of a number of countries on the factor representing socioeconomic development shift significantly because of cultural and linguistic characteristics that have remained essentially unchanged for several hundred years or more.[17] For these reasons, the analysis from which factor scores were taken excluded degree of cultural homogeneity and degree of national integration. In all other respects, however, the factor analysis used for composing samples was identical to that presented in Table IV–1.[18] The categorizing of countries by their factor scores therefore divides them into groups, each of which consists of countries at a more or less similar stage of socioeconomic modernization.

As is apparent from Table IV–5, in which the countries are listed in order of increasing factor scores, the group of countries with the lowest factor scores consists of societies that are primarily tribal and that are characterized by a preponderant nonmarket sector. The intermediate group is made up of countries in which the typical kinship structure is the extended family and in which the exchange sector of the economy is generally much larger than it is in the lowest group. The highest group includes only countries that, although still underdeveloped in the late 1950's, are relatively advanced with respect to both social and economic development.

It will also be noted from Table IV–5 that the grouping of countries based upon per capita GNP would be significantly different from the grouping derived from factor scores. The loading of per capita GNP on Factor I, 0.73, indicates that there is only a simple correlation of 0.73 between per capita GNP and country scores for the complex of characteristics represented by that factor. When per capita GNP is used to compile samples, countries as strikingly different with respect to basic social and

---

[17] For example, the inclusion of degree of cultural and ethnic homogeneity and degree of national integration results in a marked upward shift in scores on Factor I of Near Eastern countries, such as the United Arab Republic and Syria, in which relative homogeneity of language and culture has existed for centuries; it results in a sharp decline in scores for Latin American countries in which the presence of large Indian sectors dates from the nineteenth century.

[18] The difference in the loading of per capita GNP on Factor I is negligible when cultural homogeneity and national integration are omitted.

169

TABLE IV–5: Grouping of Countries by Factor Scores on Factor Representing Level of Socioeconomic Development [a]

	Lowest Group			Intermediate Group			Highest Group		
	Country	Factor Score	Per Cap GNP 1961 ($)	Country	Factor Score	Per Cap GNP 1961 ($)	Country	Factor Score	Per Cap GNP 1961 ($)
	Afghanistan	-1.02	70	Algeria	.18	281	Argentina	1.91	379
	Cambodia	-.55	101	Bolivia	-.35	113	Brazil	.79	186
	Cameroun	-1.34	86	Burma	-.41	58	Chile	1.39	453
	Chad	-1.70	40	Ceylon	.35	137	Colombia	.66	283
	Dahomey	-1.54	40	Ecuador	.54	182	Costa Rica	.78	344
	Ethiopia	-.99	44	Ghana	-.01	199	Cyprus	1.08	416
	Gabon	-.83	200	Guatemala	.35	175	Dominican Rep.	.81	218
	Guinea	-1.47	60	Honduras	.26	207	El Salvador	.71	220
	Ivory Coast	-.98	184	India	-.28	80	Greece	1.47	431
	Kenya	-.53	80	Indonesia	-.40	83	Israel	1.77	814
	Laos	-1.06	60	Iran	.09	211	Jamaica	1.06	436
	Liberia	-1.01	159	Iraq	-.03	194	Japan	1.63	502
	Libya	-.68	204	Jordan	.16	184	Lebanon	1.44	411
	Malagasy	-1.31	75	Pakistan	-.08	79	Mexico	.75	313
	Malawi	-1.57	40	Philippines	.56	117	Nicaragua	.88	213
	Morocco	-.57	150	Rhodesia	.14	215	Panama	.84	416
	Nepal	-1.36	53	South Africa	.62	427	Paraguay	.97	130
	Niger	-1.86	40	Surinam	.54	310	Peru	.68	181
	Nigeria	-.91	82	Syria	.57	152	South Korea	.85	73
	Senegal	-.52	175	Thailand	.50	97	Taiwan	1.05	145
	Sierra Leone	-1.39	70	Tunisia	-.18	161	Trinidad	1.15	594
	Somali Republic	-1.35	40				Turkey	.88	193
	South Vietnam	-.49	89				U.A.R.	.73	120
	Sudan	-.64	94				Uruguay	1.59	450
	Tanganyika	-1.22	59				Venezuela	1.37	692
	Uganda	-1.22	68						
	Yemen	-1.35	90						
	Zambia	-.89	170						

[a] See text for details.

170

economic characteristics as Gabon, Algeria, and Colombia are grouped together. While considerable variety of course remains within samples when countries are assigned by factor scores, the extent of homogeneity with respect to level of social and economic development is greatly increased. Furthermore, the grouping of countries by scores on a factor representing varied aspects of socioeconomic structure is considerably more consistent with the meaning of development, as the term is commonly understood, that is, as an entire complex of interrelated social and economic changes.

SUMMARY AND CONCLUSIONS

In this chapter the nature of the systematic relationship between income per capita and various indicators of social and political structure was explored. In particular, an association was derived between per capita GNP and two aspects of sociopolitical change: the sociocultural concomitants of the industrialization-urbanization process (Factor I) and the evolution of participant political institutions (Factor II). The relationship expressed in Factor I indicates a strong tendency for levels of economic development to be positively correlated with the extent of functional differentiation and integration of diverse social units. A similarly significant positive association is evident in Factor II between income levels and the degree of articulation and integration of political systems. In contrast, a rather weak relationship appears between broad levels of development and indicators summarizing the character of leadership and the degree of social and political stability in the past decade (Factors III and IV).

The results of the regional studies support the findings of the over-all analysis. In addition, they indicate that the role of the social aspects of the industrialization-urbanization process is overwhelmingly important for low income economies in which the absorptive capacity is sharply limited by the inhibiting nature of the social structure. As the barriers to industrialization imposed by the social institutions become weaker, the importance of the forces summarized in Factor I tends to decline. However, even among countries at higher stages of development, the social variables remain the most important element associated with intercountry differences in per capita GNP.

Another feature of the regional analyses is the systematic pattern of variation in the significance of the factor representing the development

171

of representative political systems. At the early stages, Factor II is of negligible importance; it assumes increasing relevance as social institutions become more adaptable to the requirements of economic growth. This association between more democratic and better articulated and integrated political systems, on the one hand, and levels of economic development, on the other, probably arises because both the ability to generate sustained economic growth and the evolution of more sophisticated political institutions require fundamental changes in mentality characteristic of the spread of rational thought patterns. The participant style of life tends to generate a capacity to adapt existing insitutional frameworks to continual economic and social change. This malleability of social structure is essential both to successful entrepreneurial activity and to effective political modernization.

In interpreting the results of this chapter, it is important to bear in mind that, as pointed out in Chapter III, the relationships found between levels of economic development and differences in social and political structure are neither caused nor causal. Rather they reflect the interaction of an organic system of institutional and behavioral change which underlies the process of economic development. As emphasized earlier by one of the authors, "The phenomenon of underdevelopment must be understood . . . in the context of the entire complex of interrelationships that characterize the economic and social life of the community."[19]

The degree of intimate interrelationship found in this analysis between the economic and noneconomic concomitants of a country's historical evolution is rather surprising. It lends support to the views long held by development economists that, in the last analysis, the purely economic performance of a community is strongly conditioned by the social and political setting in which economic activity takes place and that the less developed a nation is, the less powerful is economic policy alone in inducing economic development. It would appear that the splitting off of *homo economicus* into a separate analytic entity, a common procedure since Adam Smith in theorizing about growth in advanced economies, is much less suited to countries that have not yet made the transition to self-sustained economic growth.

[19] Irma Adelman, *Theories of Economic Growth and Development* (Stanford, Calif.: Stanford University Press, 1961), p. 145.

172

CHAPTER V

THE SHORT-RUN ANALYSIS: COUNTRIES AT THE LOWEST LEVEL OF SOCIOECONOMIC DEVELOPMENT

Our insights into the relationships involved in the process of economic, social, and political modernization can be enriched by supplementing the implicitly historical analysis of the previous chapter with an analogous systematic examination of short-run dynamic growth processes in low-income countries during the past fifteen years. Because the more rapid pace of change characteristic of developing nations in recent years can be expected to continue, if not to accelerate, our short-run analysis may also have increased relevance for development policy in countries intent on purposive modernization.

This chapter and the next two are therefore devoted to an examination of the nature of dynamic short-run interactions of economic, social, and political change. Our procedure is to apply the technique of factor analysis to a study of the relationships between the rate of growth of per capita GNP from 1950/51 to 1963/64 and selected indicators of social and political structure, such as those in Chapter IV, as well as various indices of economic institutions and performance. These latter variables include measures of industrialization, technological achievement, and effectiveness of tax and financial systems as well as dynamic indicators of recent changes in economic structure and institutions. The associations found between the rate of growth of per capita GNP and the various factor groupings are used to gain insights into those aspects of economic, social, and political change which are significant at various stages of socioeconomic development.

In the three succeeding chapters, we shall analyze these patterns of interactions for each of three groups of countries representing successive levels of social and economic modernization. The reason for proceeding in this manner is that, as indicated earlier, our investigation of the course of development in the long run suggests that as countries move to higher levels of development there are systematic differences in the relationships between different classes of influences. The procedure we adopt here permits us to understand to some extent the relative significance of economic, social, and political forces in explaining the growth process at various stages of development. As will be recalled from Chapter IV, the division of the seventy-four countries in our full sample into three groups was based on individual country scores for the factor representing the level of social and economic development.

In each of the three studies that follow, the presentation begins with a description of the typical sociopolitical and economic characteristics of countries at the relevant stage of development. These sample typologies serve as background for the interpretation of the results of the factor analyses which is presented in the second portion of each chapter. In the course of the interpretive discussion, we examine in some detail the patterns of interaction operative at each level of development. For this purpose we utilize the results of four separate factor analyses for each group of countries; each of these analyses, while treating development implicitly as a socio-politico-economic process, explicitly includes a separate combination of the three broad disciplines. The four analyses are:

1. a purely economic approach in which the relevant social and political phenomena are reflected indirectly through economic variables that have roots both inside and outside the economic sphere, as well as through the groupings of variables into factors;

2. a purely sociopolitical treatment in which the relevant economic forces appear indirectly in an analogous manner;

3. a socioeconomic analysis; and, finally,

4. an explicit study of an interrelated complex of social, political, and economic patterns.

As pointed out in Chapter III, since the technique of factor analysis is rather sensitive to the nature of the variables included, our approach provides a systematic cross-check on the reliability of the results. As also indicated in Chapter III, to the extent that the factors which emerge from the grouping of variables when the analysis is conducted from the several points of view represent different aspects of the same underlying processes of change and have approximately the same relative significance, the robustness[1] and validity of the statistical results tend to be confirmed.

The final section of each chapter is devoted to a comparison of the

---

[1] Statistically speaking, estimates are "robust" when they are relatively insensitive to differences in the statistical specifications of the model.

short-run and long-run results for that group of countries. For this purpose, long-run analyses that are comparable to the "combined" short-run analyses in terms of the variables included and the sample's make-up are presented. In this connection it should be noted that the long-run analyses given in Tables IV–2, IV–3, and IV–4 of Chapter IV differ from those presented here and in the following two chapters in that they do not include economic variables and are based on a regional rather than a strictly socioeconomic classification of countries.

With respect to our interpretation of the results of the factor analyses presented below, a general methodological point must be made. From a purely statistical point of view, as indicated in Chapter III, the relationships among the several sets of variables in the factor analysis cannot be interpreted in a causal manner. Nevertheless, it is logically permissible to bring a priori knowledge to bear upon the interpretation of the statistical results. Since the present three chapters are devoted to an investigation of the interaction between short-term rates of change in average income and, for the most part, indicators of socioeconomic and political structure, the use of a causal interpretation with causality running from structural characteristics to short-term change would appear to be justified. It is difficult to see how, in the short run at least, causality could run in the opposite direction. Furthermore, it seems unlikely that the patterns of relationships observed in these three chapters could arise from the existence of a common cause (or causes) that is neither explicitly included in the analysis nor so all-inclusive as to be devoid of operational meaning. After all, the list of phenomena represented by the included variables is so extensive that, in general, only extremely broad attitudinal characteristics of nations (such as national spirit or ethos) are not reflected explicitly to some degree in the indicators. We shall therefore use a causal interpretation whenever it appears justified.

We now turn to a study of the interaction of social, economic, and political influences for a group of twenty-eight countries at the lowest level of development. We first provide a bird's-eye view of the nature of the social, economic, and political landscape characteristic of this level of socioeconomic development. In describing the attributes of a typical country it must of course be remembered that there are great variations in the extent to which common characteristics apply to any given nation in the sample. There nevertheless appears to be sufficient uniformity among them and sufficient differences between them and the countries at the next socioeconomic level to justify providing a separate typology.

175

This typology will be helpful in interpreting the results of the statistical analyses presented later in the chapter. It will also help in understanding the differences between the results obtained for this sample and those derived for nations at higher levels of development.

TYPOLOGY OF COUNTRIES AT THE LOWEST LEVEL OF SOCIOECONOMIC DEVELOPMENT

The countries included in this sample are those whose scores on the factor representing level of socioeconomic development are below 0.45.[2] They are, for the most part, African nations south of the Sahara, but a small number of countries in Southeast Asia and the Far East is also included. The complete list reads as follows: Afghanistan, Cambodia, Cameroun, Chad, Dahomey, Ethiopia, Gabon, Guinea, Ivory Coast, Kenya, Laos, Liberia, Libya, Malagasy, Malawi, Morocco, Nepal, Niger, Nigeria, Senegal, Sierra Leone, Somali Republic, South Vietnam, Sudan, Tanganyika, Uganda, Yemen, and Zambia.

A typical country in this group is characterized by the occupation of an overwhelming proportion of its population in traditional subsistence agriculture where production takes place in largely self-contained units and the marketing of surpluses is of only incidental economic importance. Such a country also has a small but growing market economy characterized by either cash-crop peasant agriculture or foreign-owned modern plantation or extractive activites. Often there are significant differences in levels of social and cultural attainment as well as in levels of technology between the market and nonmarket sectors.

Throughout the traditional agrarian and pastoral sectors where typically more than 80 per cent of the population lives, economic, social, and political relationships are largely confined to closely integrated village or kinship groups. Tribal allegiances are extremely important since tribal organization binds a sizable number of villages into larger ethnic, religious, and political complexes. These tribal ties derive strength from their convergent religious, political, and economic character, for it is the tribe that provides the religious bond of primordial belief in a common ancestor—the seat of political leadership and the ultimate authority concerning rights to land. At the same time, the cooperative village group continues to dominate people's daily existence and to provide the focus

[2] See Chapter IV, Table IV–5.

for traditional social and economic activity as well as to constitute the principal administrative unit. These small-scale preindustrial communities are almost completely independent of the nation-state economically and politically and have an internal system of organization based on face-to-face relationships and structure in terms of kinship roles and institutions. Only the most tenuous ties link them with the national polity.

In the traditional sociocultural setting typical of the nonmarket sector of these countries, economic activity tends to be a subsidiary expression of predominantly communal relationships.[3] The principles governing economic activity are not separate from those regulating over-all social behavior. On the contrary, the economic system of tribal societies tends to be embedded in social relations whereas the social relations of advanced economies tend to be embedded in the economic system. For example, barter and exchange are usually expressions of long-term reciprocity relations implying trust and confidence rather than bilateral transactions in which articles of value are exchanged.[4] Since production for market exchange is merely a marginal source of livelihood for the traditional sector, the price mechanism does not serve an important function. It tends neither to stimulate improvements in productive efficiency nor to reallocate factors of production among various economic activities. Economic specialization of tasks occurs almost exclusively as a differentiation of age, sex, and kinship status rather than as a rational method for exploiting market opportunities.

The allocation of factors of production in the traditional economy is largely determined by social custom and does not involve a separate economic calculus. The demand for and the supply of labor are governed by conventional traditional practices rather than by market considerations such as wages. Rights to property are vested communally and are acquired by a prescribed system based on status and lineage within the kinship group; in particular, rights to cultivate land cannot be purchased by payment of rent. For these reasons, capital invested in the various combinations of labor and land cannot readily flow from one branch of production to another as it must if the market mechanism is to perform its regulatory function. As a result, techniques of production do not change in response to market forces and therefore they tend to be quite primitive and static.

[3] See George Dalton, "Traditional Production in Primitive African Economies," *Quarterly Journal of Economics,* Vol. 76 (August, 1962), pp. 360–78.
[4] Polanyi, *The Great Transformation,* p. 61.

177

The sociocultural climate of the countries in this group is character-ized by marked cultural, ethnic, and religious differences among the various tribal complexes, as illustrated by the fact that typically less than 60 per cent of the population speaks the same language. The lack of economic, social, and political integration in these nations persists not only because of the diversity of tribal allegiances but also because of the self-sufficient nature of technology, the prevailing illiteracy of the population, and the absence of mass communication media. In all but six countries, more than 85 per cent of the adult population is illiter-ate; in most instances newspaper circulation is below 10 per 1,000 pop-ulation, while radio licenses are less than 50 per 1,000 population. The lack of transportation facilities within the rural sector and the prevailing inadequacy of connections between the countryside and urban centers, as well as the physical ruggedness of jungle or mountain terrains, are also important contributors to the persistence of a diversity of small-scale local cultures.

As a result of both the geographic and psychic isolation of the typical small community in these countries and the strength of traditional so-cial organization, there is little belief in the modern idea that man by his own action can alter his environment and fate. Attitudes toward birth, health, and death have in most instances remained those instilled by inherited wisdom and convention. Birth rates are rarely under 40 per 1,000 and are in a number of countries over 50 per 1,000. Modern medical practices have made little headway; generally there is only one physician per 10,000 population, and infant mortality rates are often over 150 per 1,000. In addition, the populations of more than four-fifths of the countries in the sample suffer from malnutrition or poorly balanced diets and from significant incidence of tropical, infectious, and parasitic food- and water-carried diseases. While death rates are gener-ally declining, the decline is primarily the result of nationally organized environmental measures to eradicate diseases, such as malaria, rather than the outcome of local adoption of modern standards of sanitation and hygiene. In general, man's outlook in these small rural communities is strongly traditional and programs of modernization have hardly begun to affect the attitudes of the majority of the populace.

Adjacent to the traditional sector, there exists in all countries of this sample a small cash economy which is generally oriented toward pro-duction for export markets. In the countries of West Africa and British East Africa the cash economy has for the most part developed as a supplement to subsistence farming through the expansion of indigenous small holdings in which production of rubber, cocoa, coffee, etc., for export is increased by means of conventional techniques and familial labor. In other countries, such as Libya and several countries of Central Africa, the origin of the market sector has been the foreign development of export-oriented plantations, farming estates, or extractive industries; the use of hired migrant labor from the traditional sector and the application of modern technology characterize these commercial ventures.

The extent of influence of the commercial sector upon traditional social organization varies with the nature of the market sector. Where successful indigenous cash-cropping has evolved, the impact upon customary attitudes and practices tends to be greatest, and the modernizing influence upon communal and tribal relationships the most marked.[5] On the other hand, where large-scale foreign development has occurred in an essentially independent enclave, the economic and social dichotomy between the market-oriented and traditional sectors is considerably greater. The migrant laborers, even while involved in the modern sector, maintain a close attachment to the villages in which their kin reside and to which they intend to return, with the result that they do not act as agents of modernization within their traditional setting.

The urban centers of the countries in this group generally involve less than 10 per cent of the population. Their major economic activities are the commercial and banking services associated with foreign trade, some limited small-scale industry oriented toward the domestic market, and the performance of the bureaucratic functions which nation-states in the modern world require. Modern industry plays only a small part in the economy of these towns. In about half of the countries in the group, industry is primarily of the artisan handicraft type; in the rest, while a limited number of technologically modern industries have evolved, these are usually characterized by small-scale production for domestic consumption. The traditional agricultural economy is still important in the life of these urban communities since many town dwellers continue to engage in subsistence farming and regard their traditional rights to land in the tribal sector as their only source of material security. Furthermore, the majority of the indigenous urban population has recently emigrated from the village and a considerable number of these migrants intend to return to their rural homes.

[5] Aidan Southall (ed.), *Social Change in Modern Africa* (London: Oxford University Press, 1961), p. 4.

179

Even though the primary social and cultural ties of the indigenous urban population remain those of the village and tribe, the towns are nevertheless major centers of change. New types of social relationships are formed there; the distinctive characteristic of these relationships is that they are often based on common economic status, place of work, or other mutual interests rather than on ethnic or familial ties. The formation of these new social relationships arises in part because in the towns, economic activity originates largely in response to market stimuli and therefore tends to be differentiated from the kinship system. In addition, the all-embracing social bonds of traditional community systems are less easily maintained in an urban setting in which key members of the kinship group may be absent. These new relationships are more fluid and subject to change than their rural counterparts and they constitute a vehicle for the generation of attitudes and aspirations that to some extent transcend particularistic tribal loyalties. A further characteristic of towns which accounts for their modernizing influence is the concentration of mass communication media and educational facilities, both of which are important instruments for disseminating new ideas. Finally, the towns provide employment for the small number who have been educated in the West and who seek the wider national roles made available by independence.[6]

It is the small educated middle class that is the driving force behind the modernizing influences exerted by the towns. The middle class, which typically consists of less than 5 per cent of the population, is the focal point of political life and of economic modernization efforts. Its composition reflects the absence of those occupations characteristic of large-scale industry; government employees, clerical workers, and those associated with the commercial life of the country form an unusually large proportion of its membership. In those towns where an important part of economic activity is related to the export of cash crops, the indigenous educated component of the middle class tends to be considerably more significant than in the mining towns of more recent origin. In the latter towns, entrepreneurial and commercial roles are performed almost exclusively by expatriates and as a result, the indigenous population is relegated almost completely to unskilled and semiskilled occupations.

[6] For discussion of the role of towns in the process of change in newly independent nations, see Lucy Mair, *New Nations* (Chicago: University of Chicago Press, 1963), Chapter 5.

180

Social mobility, in the sense of opportunity to enter a growing middle class, is of necessity limited at this level of development by both the extremely small size of the middle class and the very narrow base of the educational system. A typical country in this group has less than 15 per cent of its school-age population in school. At the same time, social mobility, in the sense of the absence of purely social barriers to mobility, does exist in most of these countries since their societies tend to be quite egalitarian with respect to a man's class origins.[7] This is true partly because there are no important differences between the traditional culture of the villages and the culture of the sociopolitical elites, although there may be great differences in education.[8]

Politically, the nations in this group tend to adopt autocratic solutions to the problems of rapid change. As of about 1960, significant freedom of political opposition and press existed in only a handful of the countries in this group. Almost half of them had only one national unity political party with all other parties banned, or no political parties at all. Furthermore, in the remaining countries, while no significant restrictions were placed upon political organization, only about half a dozen of them had two or more reasonably effective political parties in operation. These parties tended to be based on ethnic or religious groupings rather than on class or ideology. The choice of authoritarian types of central government in this group of countries stems at least in part from the need to devise political forms that facilitate the political integration of diverse, heterogeneous, and atomistic traditional units. The great need for political integration is emphasized by the fact that in some of these countries the adoption of Western-type parliamentary machineries at the time of independence led to struggles for national power among different tribal, regional, and religious groups. In several instances these power contests were so sharp that they posed serious threats to the stability of the new national polities. As a result, parliamentary forms were soon replaced by strong executive governments.[9]

---

[7] Exceptions are countries such as Afghanistan, Nepal, and Ethiopia in which traditional social heirarchies include a ruling hereditary aristocracy to which access is closed.

[8] See L. A. Fallers, "Social Stratification and Economic Processes," in *Economic Transition in Africa,* ed. M. J. Herskovits and Mitchell Harwitz (Evanston, Ill.: Northwestern University Press, 1964), pp. 113–30.

[9] See St. Clare Drake, "Democracy on Trial in Africa," in the Annals of the American Academy of Political and Social Science, *Africa in Motion,* July, 1964, pp. 118–19.

An additional factor contributing to the tendency toward authoritarian solutions to problems of political integration is the general ideological orientation of the elite. The recent colonial experience of most of the countries in this group has made their leaders more desirous of political and economic equality with other nations than of internal freedom and democracy. Faced with a scarcity of experienced indigenous entrepreneurs and businessmen and with the lack of a sizable indigenous private industrial base, the leaders, in their intense desire for rapid economic modernization, have tended to resort to central government dictation of economic development efforts.

The use of the government as a vehicle for carrying out nationalist aspirations for rapid modernization and industrialization is, of course, severely impeded by the inadequacy of the government apparatus. Another significant obstacle to government efforts to act as a modernizing agent stems from the tensions and instability created by the process of nation-building. As efforts at political integration proceed, heterogeneous regional and ethnic groups are brought into rivalry with each other; the outcome is increased racial and cultural tensions on the one hand, and, on the other hand, increased tensions between the majority, which remains attached to traditional small-scale societies, and the minority, whose primary attachments are to the nation as a whole. The result is that in all the countries in this group there have been at least occasional outbreaks of violence between tribes, between regions, or between modernizing elites and traditional authorities.

In all the countries in this group, economic institutions are at a very rudimentary stage of development. Financial institutions are of course limited to the cash economy; with few exceptions, they attract a negligible volume of voluntary indigenous private savings. Investment in the traditional sector is almost entirely self-financed or financed through unorganized money markets. Investment in the technologically advanced sector, where it exists, is financed almost completely by private foreign or expatriate capital. One should note, however, that in a small number of countries characterized by peasant cash-crop agriculture, government-controlled financial intermediaries obtain a significant flow of compulsory savings, at least part of which they channel into medium- and long-term credit to industry and agriculture.

Tax institutions tend to be quite underdeveloped, as indicated by ratios of tax revenue to GNP, which are generally less than 12 per cent, and/or by heavy dependence upon a single foreign-owned mineral sec-

182

tor for taxes. Physical overhead capital is in the majority of cases still grossly and pervasively inadequate. At best, transportation and power facilities suffice to satisfy limited current needs in only those geographic regions in which the market sector is relatively advanced. Even in economies with well-served market sectors, however, the inadequacy of the infrastructure still constitutes a major economic bottleneck to further growth.

In view of the social, political, and economic characteristics of the countries in this group, it is hardly surprising that their investment and growth rates have been quantitatively small. In over half the countries, the ratio of net investment to national income for the 1957–62 period was less than 10 per cent, the rate specified by Lewis as the minimum required for the initiation of sustained economic growth.[10] Annual rates of growth in per capita GNP for the great majority of the countries in this group were less than 1.0 per cent per capita during the thirteen-year period 1950/51–1963/64. The remaining countries were of two types. In some, the increase in monetary income per capita was due largely to the income created in a dynamic foreign-owned mineral sector and did not involve significant rises in the average income of the indigenous population; several of these countries registered monetary growth rates of 3 per cent or more. In others, particularly a few countries of East and West Africa, growth rates were between 1 and 2 per cent per capita; in these countries the expansion of peasant cash-crop agriculture has initiated a more widespread improvement in standards of living which presages the possibility of a cumulative growth process.

Even though quantitative evidence suggests that little growth has taken place in the majority of these countries, this fact should not be interpreted to indicate that they are entirely static. Significant changes are taking place in the social and political lives of the people. The expansion of mass communication, education, and transportation is widening the range of individual experience for a growing number of the populace. More and more families are turning to cash-crop production, thereby extending their involvement in the larger society. Urban centers are growing and flows of labor from agriculture into the cities have increased. Finally, efforts on the part of leaders to create a national iden-

---

[10] Lewis, *The Theory of Economic Growth,* Chapter 5. A ratio of net investment to national income of 10 per cent is equivalent to a ratio of gross investment to GNP of about 13 per cent on the assumption that for countries in this group, net investment is approximately three-fourths of gross investment.

tity and to increase the sense of national unity have to some extent been successful in changing the small-group outlook of the indigenous population.

As for economic institutions and physical overhead capital, almost all these countries have experienced some improvements in the past fifteen years. Transportation and power networks have expanded considerably and tax collections have in most instances increased. Monetization of the economy is proceeding rapidly in practically all the countries in this group; however, in most cases this has not been translated into significant expansion of central financial institutions. Almost one-third of the countries have experienced improvements in agricultural productivity through the use of better tools and knowledge; in most of the remaining countries agricultural production has kept pace with population growth as a result of the cultivation of additional lands with existing techniques. While the social, political, and economic transformations taking place in these countries are quite striking, it should be noted that their quantitative impact upon growth rates and levels of over-all development is as yet small.

In summary, a typical country at this stage of socioeconomic development is characterized by a predominant tribal subsistence sector in which economic activity is embedded in social structure, social organization is in small-scale atomistic communities, and the national polity is virtually an unknown concept. Bordering upon the subsistence sector is an expanding market sector from which all social, economic, and political change emanates.

THE RESULTS

We turn now to a study of the interrelationships among the social, political, and economic forces which influence the growth process at the lowest level of development. Several important conclusions emerge from the statistical analysis for countries at this level of development (see Tables V–1—V–4). First of all, it is evident from these tables that the development process of underdeveloped countries in this group cannot be understood without reference to both social and economic phenomena. As the reader will note in the combined (socioeconomic and political) factor analysis (Table V–1), there is no sharp separation between indices of social structure and those of economic organization. This outcome reflects the fact that once the forces leading to economic

184

TABLE V–1: Rotated Factor Matrix for Change in Per Capita GNP (1950/51–1963/64) Together with Thirty-five Political, Social, and Economic Variables ᵃ (Low Sample)

Political, Social, and Economic Indicators	Rotated Factor Loadings					h_i^2 (R²)
	F_1	F_2	F_3	F_4	F_5	
Rate of Growth of Real Per Capita GNP: 1950/51–1963/64	.41	−.27	.18	−.03	−.65	.699
Importance of the Indigenous Middle Class	.76	.36	−.10	−.03	−.15	.744
Extent of Social Mobility	.57	.50	−.03	−.04	−.28	.662
Level of Effectiveness of Financial Institutions	.71	.12	.23	−.28	−.31	.744
Level of Effectiveness of the Tax System	.71	.33	.24	.01	−.12	.691
Level of Modernization of Techniques in Agriculture	.46	.44	.35	−.21	.02	.568
Character of Agricultural Organization	.51	.11	.10	−.04	−.25	.347
Degree of Improvement in Financial Institutions since 1950	.73	−.28	.33	.11	−.16	.764
Degree of Improvement in the Tax System since 1950	.68	.15	.43	.33	.03	.777
Change in Degree of Industrialization since 1950	.67	−.01	.27	.04	−.06	.532
Degree of Improvement in Agricultural Productivity since 1950	.89	−.03	−.07	−.04	−.08	.809
Strength of Democratic Institutions	.21	.83	.11	−.06	−.08	.758
Degree of Freedom of Political Opposition and Press	.10	.87	.07	.10	−.04	.791
Predominant Basis of the Political Party System	−.03	.76	.17	−.16	.12	.654
Degree of Competitiveness of Political Parties	.10	.82	.04	−.43	−.12	.889
Strength of the Labor Movement	.13	.77	.12	−.04	−.33	.730
Political Strength of the Traditional Elite	−.25	−.57	.33	−.24	−.10	.561
Political Strength of the Military	.11	−.67	.07	−.42	.28	.732
Degree of Administrative Efficiency	.42	.54	.06	−.18	−.42	.682
Degree of National Integration and Sense of National Unity	.04	.21	.68	−.03	.48	.740
Degree of Cultural and Ethnic Homogeneity	−.12	−.26	.56	−.02	.41	.564
Extent of Urbanization	.11	.02	.70	−.29	−.14	.603

TABLE V-1 (Continued)

Political, Social, and Economic Indicators	Rotated Factor Loadings					h_i^2 (R^2)
	F_1	F_2	F_3	F_4	F_5	
Extent of Mass Communication	.08	.27	**.75**	.18	−.26	.739
Rate of Improvement in Human Resources	.26	.01	**.85**	.14	.03	.818
Level of Modernization of Industry	.27	.28	**.59**	−.03	−.46	.710
Level of Adequacy of Physical Overhead Capital	.31	.29	**.68**	−.13	−.33	.768
Extent of Political Stability	.12	−.04	.02	**.87**	−.19	.816
Degree of Social Tension	.05	.06	−.11	**−.80**	−.12	.678
Extent of Leadership Commitment to Economic Development	.56	.16	−.33	**.47** [b]	.09	.672
Extent of Literacy	.19	.30	.37	**−.45**	−.19	.502
Character of Basic Social Organization	.22	.07	.45	**−.49**	.40	.659
Extent of Dualism	.59	.17	.34	−.04	**−.60**	.866
Structure of Foreign Trade	.12	.22	.06	.00	**−.55**	.371
Abundance of Natural Resources	.03	.23	.47	.30	**−.61**	.738
Gross Investment Rate	.15	−.02	−.05	.03	**−.71**	.532
Degree of Modernization of Outlook	.55	.24	−.08	−.23	**−.57**	.743

[a] Bold figures indicate the factor to which each variable is assigned. Variable omitted because of insignificant correlations: extent of centralization of political power. Variables omitted because of low high loadings: size of the traditional agricultural sector, degree of improvement in physical overhead capital since 1950, and crude fertility rate. Percentage of over-all variance explained by factors: 68.5. Percentage of variance explained by last factor included: 6.5.

[b] A variable having loadings on two factors which are not significantly different is assigned to that factor to which it is judged to have the closest affinity.

186

TABLE V–2: Rotated Factor Matrix for Change in Per Capita GNP (1950/51–1963/64) Together with Twenty-three Political and Social Variables [a] (Low Sample)

Political and Social Indicators	Rotated Factor Loadings				h_i^2
	F_1	F_2	F_3	F_4	(R^2)
Rate of Growth of Real Per Capita GNP: 1950/51–1963/64............	−.23	.11	−.85	.05	.790
Strength of Democratic Institutions....	**.86**	−.05	−.19	.08	.792
Degree of Freedom of Political Opposition and Press...................	**.90**	.09	−.09	.07	.827
Predominant Basis of the Political Party System....................	**.77**	−.26	.11	.05	.678
Degree of Competitiveness of Political Parties........................	**.80**	−.45	−.19	−.13	.896
Strength of the Labor Movement......	**.78**	−.05	−.22	−.15	.684
Political Strength of the Traditional Elite	**−.54**	−.29	.02	.33	.479
Political Strength of the Military......	**−.66**	−.40	.09	.10	.620
Degree of Administrative Efficiency....	**.56**	−.01	−.50	−.23	.612
Extent of Political Stability...........	.01	**.86**	−.12	.15	.779
Degree of Social Tension.............	.02	**−.68**	−.18	−.29	.583
Extent of Leadership Commitment to Economic Development...........	.17	**.54**	−.19	−.21	.397
Extent of Literacy..................	.32	**−.47**	−.38	.24	.524
Character of Basic Social Organization.	.09	**−.63**	−.07	.29	.499
Size of the Traditional Agricultural Sector.........................	−.13	.35	**.66**	−.15	.591
Extent of Dualism..................	.22	.05	**−.90**	.04	.857
Importance of the Indigenous Middle Class.........................	.44	.14	**−.57**	−.19	.574
Extent of Social Mobility............	.55	.04	**−.57**	−.16	.659
Degree of Modernization of Outlook...	.22	−.12	**−.78**	−.38	.830
Degree of National Integration and Sense of National Unity............	−.16	−.18	.07	**.80**	.705
Degree of Cultural and Ethnic Homogeneity....................	−.22	−.15	.10	**.77**	.669
Extent of Urbanization..............	.05	−.43	−.41	**.47**	.575
Extent of Mass Communication.......	.31	.04	−.39	**.61**	.623
Crude Fertility Rate................	.04	−.21	−.15	**−.57**	.395

[a] Bold figures indicate the factor to which each variable is assigned. Variable omitted because of insignificant correlations: extent of centralization of political power. Variables omitted because of low high loadings: none. Percentage of over-all variance explained by factors: 65.1. Percentage of variance explained by last factor included: 9.7.

TABLE V-3: Rotated Factor Matrix for Change in Per Capita GNP (1950/51–1963/64) Together with Seventeen Economic Variables [a] (Low Sample)

Economic Indicators	Rotated Factor Loadings			h_i^2
	F_1	F_2	F_3	(R^2)
Rate of Growth of Real Per Capita GNP: 1950/51–1963/64	.43	.65	−.10	.626
Level of Effectiveness of Financial Institutions...	**.68**	.25	−.43	.708
Level of Effectiveness of the Tax System	**.58**	.17	−.46	.583
Character of Agricultural Organization	**.52**	.32	−.12	.381
Degree of Improvement in Financial Institutions since 1950	**.69**	.08	−.34	.592
Degree of Improvement in the Tax System since 1950	**.59**	−.11	−.60	.714
Change in Degree of Industrialization since 1950	**.69**	.05	−.28	.560
Degree of Improvement in Physical Overhead Capital since 1950	**.52**	.46	−.08	.494
Degree of Improvement in Agricultural Productivity since 1950	**.90**	.06	−.05	.817
Extent of Dualism	.51	**.53** [b]	−.56	.845
Structure of Foreign Trade	−.04	**.57**	−.25	.387
Abundance of Natural Resources	−.08	**.57**	−.59	.679
Gross Investment Rate	.16	**.81**	.07	.692
Size of the Traditional Agricultural Sector	−.36	−.25	**.49**	.435
Level of Modernization of Industry	.22	.34	**−.74**	.713
Level of Adequacy of Physical Overhead Capital	.19	.27	**−.82**	.783
Level of Modernization of Techniques in Agriculture	.38	.04	**−.53**	.431
Rate of Improvement in Human Resources	.22	−.11	**−.74**	.616

[a] Bold figures indicate the factor to which each variable is assigned. Variables omitted because of insignificant correlations: none. Variables omitted because of low high loadings: none. Percentage of over-all variance explained by factors: 61.4. Percentage of variance explained by last factor included: 8.6.

[b] A variable having loadings on two factors which are not significantly different is assigned to that factor to which it is judged to have the closest affinity.

development have been set in motion, economic and social progress tend to go hand in hand. However, while there is no clear delineation between economic processes and their social counterparts, a detailed study of the statistical results suggests, as we shall see below, that economic forces exogenous to the subsistence sector play a leading role in the initiation of the transition from stagnation to some modicum of dynamic activity.

The second important conclusion that can be inferred from the factor analysis is that the significant dynamic processes at this level of development are the growth of the market sector and the increasing dualism of

TABLE V-4: Rotated Factor Matrix for Change in Per Capita GNP (1950/51-1963/64) Together with Twenty-five Social and Economic Variables [a] (Low Sample)

Social and Economic Indicators	Rotated Factor Loadings				h_i^2 (R^2)
	F_1	F_2	F_3	F_4	
Rate of Growth of Real Per Capita GNP: 1950/51-1963/64	−.44	−.09	−.53	−.07	.488
Degree of Modernization of Outlook...	**−.53**	−.51	−.37	−.28	.764
Importance of the Indigenous Middle Class	**−.82**	−.25	−.07	−.06	.737
Extent of Social Mobility	**−.59**	−.38	−.16	−.28	.600
Level of Effectiveness of Financial Institutions	**−.64**	−.20	−.19	−.52	.759
Level of Effectiveness of the Tax System	**−.63**	−.14	−.13	−.48	.667
Level of Modernization of Techniques in Agriculture	**−.46**	.15	−.17	−.40	.427
Degree of Improvement in Financial Institutions since 1950	**−.73**	.22	−.16	−.12	.625
Degree of Improvement in the Tax System since 1950	**−.70**	.27	−.18	−.23	.653
Change in Degree of Industrialization since 1950	**−.75**	.16	−.08	−.10	.601
Degree of Improvement in Agricultural Productivity since 1950	**−.88**	−.07	−.03	.05	.776
Degree of National Integration and Sense of National Unity	−.10	**.90**	.10	−.14	.840
Degree of Cultural and Ethnic Homogeneity	.10	**.69**	.19	−.23	.578
Rate of Improvement in Human Resources	−.28	**.63**	−.27	−.45	.757
Crude Fertility Rate	−.06	**−.60**	.30	−.36	.589
Extent of Dualism	−.61	−.13	**−.59** [b]	−.38	.876
Structure of Foreign Trade	−.12	−.08	**−.72**	.07	.552
Abundance of Natural Resources	−.05	.03	**−.75**	−.28	.651
Gross Investment Rate	−.14	−.45	**−.53**	−.10	.503
Extent of Mass Communication	−.11	.46	**−.64**	−.38	.779
Extent of Urbanization	−.01	.23	−.16	**−.82**	.757
Character of Basic Social Organization	−.11	.24	.40	**−.70**	.717
Extent of Literacy	−.11	−.02	−.21	**−.60**	.410
Size of the Traditional Agricultural Sector	.30	.12	.12	**.72**	.640
Level of Modernization of Industry	−.34	.06	−.52	**−.52**	.659
Level of Adequacy of Physical Overhead Capital	−.32	.20	−.51	**−.62**	.783

[a] Bold figures indicate the factor to which each variable is assigned. Variable omitted because of insignificant correlations: degree of social tension. Variables omitted because of low high loadings: degree of improvement in physical overhead capital since 1950 and character of agricultural organization. Percentage of over-all variance explained by factors: 66.1. Percentage of variance explained by last factor included: 7.5.

[b] A variable having loadings on two factors which are not significantly different is assigned to that factor to which it is judged to have the closest affinity.

189

the economy brought about by the development of a distinct modern sector alongside the traditional subsistence sector. Both the social and economic aspects of these processes are evident in the factor analyses. Thus, in the sociopolitical results (Table V–2) the dominant factor (Factor III) represents the primarily social transformations involved in these processes, while in the economic analysis (Table V–3) the important factors reflect those economic changes that provide the motivations and opportunities necessary to stimulate the social transformations.

A third conclusion suggested by our results is that the primary impediments to economic growth for countries at this lowest level of socioeconomic development reside in the inhibiting character of the social structure within which economic life tends to be embedded. This conclusion is suggested by the extent to which the social concomitants of the growth of the modern sector, in and of themselves, account for differences in economic performance. (In the sociopolitical analysis, Table V–2, they "explain" 72 per cent of intercountry variations in rates of growth of per capita GNP.) Finally, we must note that political forces exert but a weak quantitative influence upon the rate of development of economies at this level. This can be seen from the fact that the most important political variables, which appear in the factors representing the strength of participant political institutions and the nature of political leadership in both the combined and the sociopolitical analyses, account for less than 10 per cent of intercountry variations in growth rates. In the next few sections we shall examine these conclusions in greater detail.

The Important Social Processes

Inherent in both the growth of the market system and the expansion of the modern sector are two social processes represented in Factor III of Table V–2. The first of these is a process of differentiation of economic activity from the social life of the community through which the rules that govern economic activity within the society tend to become separate from those which underlie the social organization. One aspect of this process of differentiation is the breakdown of the sway of traditional organizational structure and the accompanying increased separation of economic behavior from its conventional social context. This aspect shows up in the dominant explanatory factor of the sociopolitical

190

results as a direct relationship between decreases in the size of the traditional sector and faster economic growth.[11] Another aspect of differentiation is reflected in this same factor by the positive association of the extent of dualism. This indicator represents the transformation of a predominantly agrarian society into one in which a modern industrial, plantation, or estate sector with its own specialized socioeconomic structure and institutions evolves side by side with the traditional subsistence sector.[12] Finally, the growth of an urban class of entrepreneurs, businessmen, and bureaucrats performing specialized economic functions outside the context of traditional kinship relationships and the concomitant increase in opportunities for social mobility are further indicators of the process of differentiation of the economic from the social roles within the society.

The corollary social process associated with the growth of the modern sector and the expansion of the market system is the process of social integration through which the members of small-scale traditional communities are integrated into the larger national economy and society. The attitudinal aspects of the integration process are reflected in part in the dominant factor of Table V–2 by the indicator of the degree of modernization of outlook. The integrative force of the rise of the market economy is depicted in this same factor by the negative relationship between the size of the traditional nonmonetized sector and economic growth rates.[13] These dynamic processes of differentiation and integration are the crucial social concomitants of the growth of market-oriented economic activity and are particularly important in the early phases of

[11] The relevance of some of the differentiation aspects of the growth of market economies has been pointed out in a Western historical context by Karl Polanyi, who writes in *The Great Transformation:* "A self-regulating market demands nothing less than the institutional separation of society into an economic and political sphere. Such a dichotomy is, in effect, merely the restatement, from the point of view of society as a whole, of the existence of a self-regulating market" (p. 71).

[12] It should be noted that the indicator of the extent of dualism is scored in such a manner that at the lower end of the scale a positive change represents the increase in dualism which occurs as the expansion of a distinct modern sector imposes itself upon a predominantly agrarian society. At the upper end of the scale, as will be seen in subsequent chapters, a positive change with respect to this indicator consists of reduced dichotomies between the traditional and the modern as elements of both eventually become intermingled throughout the society.

[13] See Ragnar Nurkse, *Problems of Capital Formation in Underdeveloped Countries* (New York: Oxford University Press, 1953), Chapter 1. As indicated above, this variable also reflects the process of differentiation.

economic development. Together they account for more than 70 per cent of intercountry differences in growth performance at this lowest level of socioeconomic development. The fact that such a large proportion of the variance is related to those differences in social structure characteristic of the expansion of the market economy and the growth of a distinct modern sector serves to emphasize the importance of transforming social organization in a manner that can permit substantial increases in the extent to which economic considerations govern economic behavior.

The critical importance of enlarging the sphere within which economic considerations govern economic behavior in countries at the lowest level of socioeconomic development is perhaps not surprising. After all, most textbooks in elementary economics start out by underlining the role of economic principles of exchange and production in determining the choice of output, the apportionment of output among consumers, the allocation of factors of production among competing uses, the distribution of income, and the rate of capital accumulation in the economy. In fact, economic principles of exchange and production play such a basic role in the functioning of most advanced societies that Western economists tend to take their existence for granted and often devote their efforts to the analysis of ways in which the functioning of the economic system can be improved in the interest of community welfare and to the examination of areas in which economic criteria must, for various reasons, be supplemented or even supplanted by other allocative principles.

Let us consider in more detail the importance of enlarging the area of activity in which economic motivations predominate. First of all, in order for a modern extractive, plantation, or estate sector to develop in a country at the lowest level of socioeconomic development, it is evident that the force of economic incentives must increase, not only among the foreign or expatriate elements, but also in the indigenous traditional society. In particular, a continuous supply of labor to the modern sector can only be assured over a period of years if members of traditional small communities begin to view their labor as exchangeable for economic gain. This change in outlook, to be effective, requires a considerable social transformation within the tribal subsistence society.

To appreciate the extent of the transformations required to enable economic motivations and market-oriented behavior to develop within

192

the indigenous economy, let us look at the operation of a society in which the application of economic criteria to production and exchange is either completely absent or else has only marginal significance. In traditional tribal societies, long-established social customs and norms tend to govern both the production and exchange of goods. With respect to the latter, as has been pointed out by Bohannan and Dalton,[14] practically all the movement of material goods and services in such societies is governed by the three social principles of reciprocity, redistribution, and conversion. The principle of reciprocity dictates recurrent mutual gift exchanges based on kinship obligations. The principle of redistribution specifies more or less periodic, socially obligatory transfers of goods and services (such as the payment of tithes to a priest) for reallocation among the members of the society. The principle of conversion is used in institutionalized situations (such as in the application of inheritance laws among some tribes) or in emergency situations (such as famines and externally forced levies) to cover the conveyance of goods and services by a method of transfer different from that which customarily governs their exchange.

Since all three principles of exchange are clearly social in character, it is evident that the bulk of goods and services in societies in which markets have, at most, a peripheral influence are transferred in accordance with social, not economic, rules. Moreover, it is characteristic of these nonmarket principles of exchange that (1) the terms of trade are not determined in accordance with demand and supply but rather are regulated by tradition; (2) they have a social and generally a moral content, as well as an economic function; (3) participation in these exchanges rarely extends outside a particular kinship and lineage group; (4) different rules of exchange usually govern the transfer of different kinds of goods and services (e.g., luxury versus subsistence products); and, finally, (5) markets for factors of production are nonexistent.

As one might infer from this very abbreviated description, the economic life of a society in which market principles play only a minor role is inherently static and fragmented. The prevalence of traditional barter ratios, reinforced by the ethical and social content of the exchange process and by the absence of factor markets, tends to insulate the

---

[14] Paul Bohannan and George Dalton (eds.), *Markets in Africa* (Evanston, Ill.: Northwestern University Press, 1962), pp. 1–28.

system from both exogenous shocks and internal change.[15] The almost exclusive limitation of the bulk of exchanges in these noncommercialized economies to the kinship groups, and the separation of transactions into different "multicentric" spheres of activity which results from the fact that different transaction principles generally apply to different classes of goods and services, combine to generate fragmentation and isolation among the several realms of exchange. Furthermore, the absence of factor markets tends to preclude positive responses to new technological opportunities in agricultural production. It is therefore not hard to see how the limited extent of market-oriented behavior hampers the development of an economy characterized by a very large nonmarket sector. For such a society only the transformation to an exchange economy dominated by market considerations offers even the possibility of a certain amount of dynamism and economic integration.

The discussion of the preceding paragraphs explains why our factor analyses for the nations in this group indicate so close a relationship between success in raising economic growth rates in the short run and those social changes that are necessary in transforming the traditional subsistence sector into a commercialized arm of society.

The crucial role of social forces in economic growth at this level of development has also been stressed by social anthropologists concerned with economic development. For example, J. L. Sadie points out that sociocultural organization and sociocultural patterns are fundamental determinants of the economic condition of countries at this stage of development. In his words, "economic development of an underdeveloped people by themselves is not compatible with the maintenance of their traditional customs and mores. A break with the latter is a pre-requisite to economic progress. What is needed is a revolution in the totality of social, cultural and religious institutions and habits, and thus in their psychological attitude, their philosophy and way of life."[16]

---

[15] The long-term persistence of these barter ratios, incidentally, suggests that they very likely represent equilibrium ratios (in the economic sense of satisfying the usual marginal conditions), not because they have evolved in response to economic forces, but because they have undoubtedly conditioned the values of the society to conform with the traditional rates of exchange.

[16] Sadie, "The Social Anthropology of Economic Underdevelopment," p. 302.

The Economic Forces

The incentives for the social transformations of the subsistence sector which are necessary for economic growth at this level of development are provided by economic forces. More specifically, the economic mechanism by which social transformations are induced is the expansion of the modern sector. This expansion proceeds in a dualistic manner by means of the creation of a modern export-oriented extractive, plantation, or estate sector. The significant economic forces inherent in this dualistic expansion are illustrated in Factor II of the economic analysis (Table V–3), Factor III of the socioeconomic results (Table V–4), and Factor V of the combined analysis (Table V–1), and they account for over 40 per cent of variations among countries in economic growth rates in the combined and economic analyses. In all three sets of results the factor representing the important economic forces combines the extent of dualism, the structure of foreign trade, the abundance of natural resources and the gross investment rate. The inclusion of the extent of dualism reflects the key role of the expansion of the modern sector in providing economic stimuli to social change within the subsistence sector. The export-orientation of the modern sector which is typical of countries at this level is indicated by the inclusion of the indicator of the structure of foreign trade, which, at the lower end of the scale, represents the great concentration of exports characteristic of the early stages of growth of the modern sector. The incorporation of natural resource abundance depicts the extent to which the growth of the modern sector at this level is based upon the exploitation of natural endowments, particularly agricultural and extractive resources. The unimportance of manufacturing production in modern sector growth at this level is indicated in the economic results by the association of the indicator of industrial modernization with a factor that contributes little to the explanation of economic growth rates (Factor III, Table V–3). Finally, the growth of the modern sector is of course limited by the extent to which investment can take place. The critical role of this constraint is reflected in the inclusion in the important economic factor (Factor II of the economic analysis) of the gross investment rate.

As one might expect, for countries at the lowest level of economic development the strongly inhibiting nature of the traditional social structure and of the associated value system militates against the ability of changes in economic institutions (other than those that affect directly the everyday lives of the members of the society) to generate further change and to lead to economic growth. In particular, we find that none of our indicators of improvements in economic institutions and techniques (changes in tax systems, improvements in financial institutions, increased modernization of industry and of agriculture, and improvement in human resources) contributes to the explanation of intercountry differences in economic growth at this stage. Nor does the level of development of financial and tax institutions appear to be relevant. The unimportance of all of these forces is indicated by the fact that their complete omission from both the economic analysis of Table V–3 and the combined analysis of Table V–1 does not reduce the proportion of the variance in rates of growth of per capita GNP explained by the analysis.[17]

That this imposing array of economic variables makes such a small contribution to explaining over-all economic performance for countries at this low level of development is due in part to the fact that only relatively small differences in the extent of improvements in these aspects of economic performance characterize the countries in this group. Before these more advanced economic forces can move significantly and have much impact, the socioeconomic processes involved in the rise of a modern sector and the expansion of the market economy must lead to a higher level of socioeconomic development than that which exists today in even the most developed countries of this group. The social and economic transformations that stimulate the growth of market-oriented behavior thus constitute prerequisites for the implementation of improvements in economic institutions which will in turn affect the pace of economic growth in the short run.

The Unimportant Social Forces

For countries at this lowest level of development, the extent of purely sociocultural integration and cohesiveness appears to be a relatively

[17] Indeed, the omission of all these indicators from the economic and the combined analyses raises the communality of rates of change in average income from 63 per cent to 73 per cent for the economic analysis and from 70 per cent to 75 per cent for the combined analysis. These increases suggest that the omitted indicators were forced, in the analyses of Tables V–1 and V–3, to associate in factors with which they are not closely related. The possibility that the inclusion of additional variables will reduce some communalities is discussed in Chapter III.

unimportant determinant of economic growth, as can be seen from the results given in Tables V–1 and V–2, in each of which the factor containing measures of the extent of national integration, cultural and ethnic homogeneity, mass communication, and urbanization (Factor III, Table V–1; Factor IV, Table V–2; Factors II and IV, Table V–4) has a negligible weight. This is not surprising on an a priori basis. Clearly, before the social and economic structure of these atomistic societies has been sufficiently transformed so that a minimal amount of contact and interdependence among fragmented kinship and lineage groups can be established, it is unlikely that the absence of national integration and the presence of sociocultural heterogeneity per se will operate as a significant barrier to development. Furthermore, because of the strength of the divisive social forces at this level, there exist only relatively small differences among these countries in the extent of breakdown of tribal allegiance and the degree of ethnic and cultural homogeneity.

The Political Forces

The nature of the political approach to nation-building has only a small effect upon the rate of economic growth for countries at this low level of development. Factor II of Table V–1 and Factor I of Table V–2, which represent these political influences, account for only 5–7 per cent of the intercountry differences in the rate of growth of per capita GNP for these societies. Among the forces that are associated in this factor with better economic performance are more centralized political systems, less effective democratic institutions, greater restrictions on freedom of the press, and more severe limitations on the activities of the political opposition. There is also some tendency for the more rapidly developing of these countries to be controlled by a single national unity party and to possess only very weak voluntary associations such as labor unions. In addition, at this level, those nations characterized by traditionalist leaderships—in particular, those with more control by traditional elites, greater strength of the military, and less rationalization of bureaucratic structures—tend to some extent to have higher rates of growth. Thus, the analysis suggests that there is a weak but positive relationship between more autocratic, less representative forms of government and more rapid growth rates within this group of countries.

197

The direction of these associations is due, by and large, to the fact that at a low level of socioeconomic development the conditions necessary for the establishment of democratic institutions are almost entirely absent. Illiteracy, poverty, and the predominantly animistic character of the established communal religions all combine to hinder the development of individuality and personal independent status within the polity. Furthermore, the particularism and traditionalism typical of small-scale tribal communities pose strong barriers to the development of a sense of national identity and unity. As a result, wherever political mobilization for economic and social modernization does occur, it generally takes the form either of an autocracy buttressed by traditional concepts of legitimacy or of an autocracy characterized by a charismatic leader brought to prominence in the struggle for independence. These systems of political mobilization, as discussed above, tend to emphasize the strengthening of the national image vis-à-vis other nations rather than the promotion of the internal development of participant political systems. The leaders of these systems, who are usually strongly desirous of industrialization and economic development, typically seek more rapid solutions than would be feasible under representative government and, in addition, are often antagonistic toward colonially instituted parliamentary systems. Thus, the tendency for less democratic systems to accompany higher rates of economic growth is to an important extent a reflection of the positive association between more effective systems of political mobilization and better economic performance; at this low level, where the essential conditions for institutions based on widespread participation are generally absent, the more effective political systems tend to be those in which the centralization of political power has advanced farthest. However, the weakness of the association implies that the effectiveness of measures for political mobilization in overcoming the bottlenecks to growth posed by the strength of traditional social organization is quite limited.

Actually, there appears to be little correlation between the form of government and the extent of leadership commitment to economic development at this level, as indicated by the fact that the variable representing leadership commitment, in both the sociopolitical and the combined results, associates with a factor different from the factor describing the strength of representative political institutions. In the sociopolitical results it is the factor depicting the extent of social and political

198

stability that includes leadership commitment to development (Factor II, Table V–2). In this factor, higher literacy rates and weaker tribal organizations are combined with increased social and political instability and less effectiveness of political leadership in the economic realm. These associations are indicative of the social and political constraints that reduce the effectiveness of governmental actions at this level of development. The relative unimportance of differences in the extent of political mobilization for development in explaining intercountry variations in short-term economic growth is evident in the negligible explanation (less than 1 per cent) of rates of growth of per capita GNP offered by the factor incorporating this force (Factor IV, Table V–1). Of course, this does not mean that a national mobilization effort much greater than is typically permitted by the divisive forces characteristic of countries at this level would have insignificant results. Ghana, for example, which a decade and a half ago would have belonged in the low group has developed over a relatively short period to the level of the intermediate group by means of an extent of political mobilization considerably greater than that which typifies the countries in the low group.

Comparison with Long-Run Results

The results of a long-run analysis of economic development for the low group of nations is given in Table V–5. In this analysis the same variables are included as those listed in the combined short-run analysis, with the exception that per capita GNP (as of 1961) replaces the short-term rate of growth in real per capita GNP as the "dependent" variable. A comparison of Table V–5 with Table V–1 reveals no obvious inconsistencies. Indeed, it appears that the same factors that govern economic growth in the short run tend to exercise a similar degree of influence in the long run for countries at this level of development. More specifically, the low level of long-run economic development reflected in low per capita GNP and the currently low short-term rates of improvement in per capita GNP are both largely accounted for by the extent to which traditional social organization and norms still govern economic activity. Thus, at this lowest level of development, the major problems facing nations that seek short-term economic improvements still appear to be long-run in character.

TABLE V-5: Rotated Factor Matrix for Per Capita GNP in 1961 Together with Thirty-five Political, Social, and Economic Variables [a] (Low Sample)

Political, Social, and Economic Indicators	Rotated Factor Loadings					h_i^2 (R^2)
	F_1	F_2	F_3	F_4	F_5	
Per Capita GNP in 1961	.12	.16	−.85	.07	.07	.782
Importance of the Indigenous Middle Class	.76	−.35	.00	.00	.18	.734
Extent of Social Mobility	.58	−.51	−.12	−.03	.21	.656
Degree of Modernization of Outlook	.58	−.22	−.27	−.23	.46	.724
Level of Effectiveness of Financial Institutions	.73	−.08	−.37	−.30	.11	.774
Level of Effectiveness of the Tax System	.73	−.33	−.23	−.02	−.04	.690
Level of Modernization of Techniques in Agriculture	.49	−.48	−.15	−.22	−.26	.609
Character of Agricultural Organization	.52	−.10	−.23	−.04	.14	.356
Degree of Improvement in Financial Institutions since 1950	.74	.27	−.32	.10	−.16	.756
Degree of Improvement in the Tax System since 1950	.67	−.16	−.32	.31	−.31	.768
Change in Degree of Industrialization since 1950	.69	−.01	−.18	.03	−.17	.537
Degree of Improvement in Agricultural Productivity since 1950	.90	.03	.05	−.01	.06	.819
Strength of Democratic Institutions	.22	.84	−.12	−.06	.02	.768
Degree of Freedom of Political Opposition and Press	.09	.89	−.08	.10	.01	.811
Predominant Basis of the Political Party System	−.05	.76	−.09	−.17	−.13	.630
Degree of Competitiveness of Political Parties	.10	.82	−.10	−.43	.12	.888
Strength of the Labor Movement	.15	.74	−.31	−.05	.25	.733
Strength of the Traditional Elite	−.22	.56	−.28	−.27	−.16	.540
Political Strength of the Military	.12	.66	.19	−.43	−.29	.752
Degree of Administrative Efficiency	.46	.52	−.18	−.17	.37	.680

					h^2
Extent of Dualism	.62	−.15	**−.64**	−.06	.22	.867
Extent of Mass Communication	.10	−.27	**−.75**	.13	−.28	.747
Extent of Urbanization	.13	−.01	**−.64**	−.33	−.32	.630
Level of Modernization of Industry	.30	−.25	**−.77**	−.07	.00	.750
Structure of Foreign Trade	.18	−.22	**−.34**[b]	−.02	.33	.299
Abundance of Natural Resources	.08	−.22	**−.74**	.25	.15	.694
Level of Adequacy of Physical Overhead Capital	.33	−.28	**−.73**	−.18	−.16	.788
Extent of Political Stability	.12	.05	−.17	**.87**	.10	.807
Degree of Social Tension	.07	−.06	.06	**−.79**	.16	.670
Extent of Leadership Commitment to Economic Development	.54	−.13	.26	**.50**[c]	.16	.651
Extent of Literacy	.22	−.32	−.34	**−.46**	−.12	.459
Degree of National Integration and Sense of National Unity	.02	.13	−.14	−.05	**−.87**	.797
Degree of Cultural and Ethnic Homogeneity	−.14	.20	−.13	−.04	**−.73**	.607
Rate of Improvement in Human Resources	.27	−.05	−.59	.10	**−.61**	.816
Character of Basic Social Organization	.20	−.10	−.06	−.51	**−.56**	.621
Gross Investment Rate	.19	.06	−.42	.02	**.54**	.502

[a] Bold figures indicate the factor to which each variable is assigned. Variable omitted because of insignificant correlations: extent of centralization of political power. Variables omitted because of low high loadings: degree of improvement in physical overhead capital since 1950, size of the traditional agricultural sector, and crude fertility rate. Percentage of over-all variance explained by factors: 68.7. Percentage of variance explained by last factor included: 6.8. No exclusions for low high loadings have been made in this analysis other than those made in the parallel short-run analysis (Table V–1). See text for explanation.

[b] No exclusions for low high loadings have been made in this analysis other than those made in the parallel short-run analysis (Table V–1). See text for explanation.

[c] A variable having loadings on two factors which are not significantly different is assigned to that factor to which it is judged to have the closest affinity.

SUMMARY

The analysis in this chapter makes it clear that at the lowest end of the socioeconomic scale the nature of the growth process requires both economic and social transformations. It is apparent that for this group of countries the extent to which the sway of tribal society has been reduced and the degree to which the modernization of social structure has proceeded are important determinants of the rate of improvement of purely economic performance. These social transformations are required for the enlargement of the sphere within which economic activity operates independently of traditional social organization. It is also apparent that the economic process by which growth is induced involves the dualistic development of a modern, foreign-trade-oriented sector based on the exploitation of natural resource endowments. This economic process provides both the opportunities and the incentives for the social changes that are essential for the initiation of economic growth at this level of development. The successful diffusion of the market economy and the continuous expansion of a technologically advanced sector entail significant transformations of social structure because of two concurrent phenomena. First, within the traditional agricultural economy, the spread of production for the market inevitably involves a decline in the sway of tribal society over economic actions. Secondly, the expansion of a distinct modern sector augments the importance of market transactions within a traditional society by increasing wage payments to members of indigenous villages as well as by increasing their cash purchases of consumer goods. Therefore, it is the appearance and growth of opportunities for the exchange of goods and for the sale of labor which stimulate the requisite social transformations rather than social changes internal to the traditional society. Political forces do not exert a particularly strong systematic effect on rates of economic growth, even though there is a slight tendency for authoritarian governments to be more effective economically.

CHAPTER VI

THE SHORT-RUN ANALYSIS: COUNTRIES AT THE INTERMEDIATE LEVEL OF SOCIOECONOMIC DEVELOPMENT

We now turn to an examination of the forces influencing the process of growth in countries at the intermediate level of development. To set the stage, we begin as before by presenting a description of the characteristic attributes of the countries in the sample. We then discuss the results of the factor analyses for countries in the intermediate group.

TYPOLOGY OF COUNTRIES AT THE INTERMEDIATE LEVEL OF DEVELOPMENT

The countries of this group are characterized by great geographical and physical diversity as well as a marked heterogeneity of history and culture. Unlike the lowest and highest groups, this sample cannot be defined by a single region. It includes countries that for the most part lie along a broad horizontal span from Gibraltar to the Pacific, but, in addition, it encompasses several Latin American countries. The sample is composed of six countries of the Middle Eastern and Mediterranean areas (Algeria, Tunisia, Iran, Iraq, Syria, and Jordan), seven South Asian and Far Eastern countries (Ceylon, India, Pakistan, Burma, Thailand, Indonesia, and the Philippines), the five lowest-level Latin American countries (Bolivia, Guatemala, Ecuador, Honduras, Surinam), as well as Ghana, Rhodesia, and South Africa from Africa south of the Sahara.

Despite geographic, historical, and cultural heterogeneity, the countries in this group have one outstanding characteristic in common. They are without exception transitional societies in which the process of social, economic, and political modernization has proceeded far enough to profoundly disturb or even completely shatter traditional customs and institutions without, however, proceeding far enough to set them on the path of continuous and effective development.

Transformation and change permeate all societies within this group. Even though there remain pockets where ways of life are little changed

203

from those prevailing a thousand years ago, the behavior patterns of the majority of the people have been profoundly affected by the rapid expansion of urban areas, industrialization, the growing commercialization of agriculture, and increasing exposure to modern technology. In addition, the attitudes, outlook, and aspirations of the populace are rapidly being transformed by the spread of mass communication media and contact with Western ideas. These transformations have weakened traditional social organization and have resulted in increases in social tensions and marked political instability.

Both the pace and extent of social and economic modernization are significantly greater than in countries at the lowest level of development. In addition, as will be discussed below, there are striking qualitative differences between the two groups, particularly in the social realm. With respect to the quantitative extent of modernization, the commercialization of economic activity has proceeded to the point where typically, important segments of the agricultural population participate significantly in the market economy. As of about 1960 a representative country in the intermediate sample had only about 50 per cent of its population in the traditional nonmonetized agricultural sector (the corresponding figure for the lowest sample was close to 80 per cent). Urbanization and the growth of the middle class have also advanced farther among countries in this group. By about 1960 practically all the intermediate-level countries had more than 10 per cent of their population in cities of over 20,000 inhabitants; at the lowest level, only four countries had achieved this degree of urbanization. Similarly, over half the countries in the intermediate group had more than 10 per cent of their indigenous population in middle class occupations and professions whereas indigenous middle classes were either very small or essentially nonexistent in the lowest group.

Indices of extent of exposure to modern instruments of cultural change, political socialization, and national integration also reflect the greater dynamism and extent of change which characterize the countries in the intermediate group when compared with the countries in the lowest group. A substantial majority of intermediate-level countries has achieved literacy rates of at least 20 per cent, school enrollment ratios of at least 30 per cent, and newspaper circulation of at least 15 per 1,000. The corresponding statistics for countries at the lowest level are 6 per cent, 10 per cent, and 2 per 1,000, respectively.

Purely economic transformations have also progressed noticeably further in most intermediate-level countries than in those at the lowest level, although the contrast is less striking than for changes in the social realm. Industrial sectors are larger; the proportion of gross domestic product originating in industry, as of about 1960, is typically close to 10 per cent compared with only about 7 per cent for the lowest sample. Almost half of the countries have tax systems and financial institutions of some limited effectiveness, in contrast with the rudimentary institutions typical of countries at the lowest level. Physical overhead capital, while still generally insufficient for current needs, is no longer as pervasively inadequate as at the lowest level. Finally, the average gross investment rate for the present group is at least 14 per cent, while for the lowest group it is still below that cited by W. A. Lewis and others as the critical minimum for the initiation of a sustained growth process.[1]

Clearly then, the quantitative impact of the forces of urbanization, industrialization, and modernization of ideas and institutions is greater among countries in the present group than among those at the lowest level of development. However, the contrast is even greater than quantitative comparisons suggest. The qualitative differences in the social realm are particularly striking. It will be recalled that, at the lowest level, traditional tribal authority and religion retained overwhelming influence throughout the countryside. In contrast, among most countries at the intermediate level, the extended family and clan are the primary kinship units.[2] In addition, key social linkages provided by traditional figures of authority, such as the Islamic caliph and the traditional hereditary ruler, are fast disappearing. Thus, among countries at the intermediate level, social structure no longer exercises as overpowering an influence upon the daily lives of the majority of the people as it does in countries at the lowest stage of development.

A crucial qualitative dimension of the differences in social structure and norms between the intermediate and lowest groups of countries lies

[1] Lewis, *The Theory of Economic Growth,* Chapter V. The critical minimum cited by Lewis is a ratio of net investment to national income of 10 per cent. As indicated in the previous chapter, this is equivalent to a ratio of gross investment to gross national product of about 13 per cent based on the assumption that for the countries in the group, net investment is approximately three-fourths of gross investment.

[2] While the extended family system is not, of course, an advance over tribal organization in any normative sense, it does exert a less pervasive control over economic activity and can in this sense be considered more permissive of economic modernization.

in the strength of social constraints on economic activity within the traditional agricultural sector. There is a striking contrast between the two groups in the influence of purely economic considerations upon economic decisions. The essence of the contrast lies in the fact that at the intermediate level, even within the nonmonetized subsistence sector, economic calculus is to an important extent applied to economic choices. The market philosophy characteristic of what anthropologists often call peasant societies[3] has become quite widespread. Significant numbers of subsistence producers, while illiterate and superstitious, accept as familiar facts of life the importance of organized markets, imported goods, mass communication media, and urban ways of life. This characteristic of the peasant outlook is stressed by the well-known anthropologist Sol Tax, who describes as follows a village in the subsistence sector of Guatemala which he considers to be typical of villages in countries at what we call the intermediate stage of development: "In most 'primitive' societies about which anthropologists write, people behave in our terms irrationally, since they try by devices strange to us to maximize different, hence curious, satisfactions. This happens not to be the case in the part of Guatemala about which I write, where the social institutions and cosmology . . . are as separated from the processes of making a living as are our own."[4]

Not only is the broad outlook of the peasant producers of these countries more conducive to economic development than is the case for the lowest sample, but in addition, the institutional barriers to the commercialization of agriculture are in general significantly smaller. Communal ownership of land is almost nonexistent, and a predominance of peasant owner-operated farms characterizes the agricultural economy in most of the countries in the group. While tenant subsistence farming is still important in a number of countries, its relative importance is declining as the commercialization of agriculture proceeds. These patterns of land tenure stand in strong contrast to those that characterize the lowest sample in which tribal ownership of land is still important.

While countries at the intermediate level have, generally speaking, experienced significant social and economic modernization, it should nevertheless be stressed that the extent of their progress is rather lim-

---

[3] See Robert Redfield, *The Primitive World and its Transformations* (Ithaca, N.Y.: Great Seal Books, 1957), pp. 31ff.

[4] Sol Tax, *Penny Capitalism: A Guatemalan Indian Economy* (Chicago: University of Chicago Press, 1953), p. ix.

ited. Economically, the degree of industrialization in these countries still remains modest; the extent of import substitution, for example, is as yet small, and modern large-scale technology is generally limited to only a few classes of products. Physical overhead capital tends to be concentrated primarily in urban areas. Financial institutions generally extend little long-term credit to agriculture and they still play a limited role in mobilizing savings. With respect to social modernization, in absolute terms, literacy rates are still low, the size of the middle class is not considerable, and social dualism is quite marked. In addition, the actual pattern of social advance has typically been extremely uneven.

The unevenness of social change within countries at this level, which is clearly evident in the variations for individual countries in scores on specific indices of social development, is a salient general characteristic of the group. By contrast, most countries in the highest and lowest groups score consistently with respect to almost all social indicators. In addition, the precise pattern of social imbalance among countries at the intermediate level varies considerably from country to country. For example, some Middle Eastern countries (Iraq, Iran, Jordan) are rather advanced in the size of their indigenous middle classes while lagging greatly with respect to literacy rates. Other countries such as Thailand, Honduras, and Burma, where literacy rates are quite high, have middle classes that are still almost completely composed of expatriate groups. And the white settler countries in the sample, while relatively advanced along many lines of social development, have strong cultural and ethnic barriers to social mobility. Only at the extremes of the intermediate sample do we find a few countries scoring consistently high or low with respect to all social indicators.

This unevenness in social change at the intermediate level is in line with the views of those sociologists who consider the process of development of a society to be inherently one of unbalanced growth. In their view the mechanism of social change is one by which unbalanced advance generates social tensions that in turn lead to further structural change.[5] The association of social tension with unbalanced social de-

---

[5] Theories of conflict, cultural lag, and anomie, as well as Marxian theory, are all theories of unbalanced social dynamics. See, for example, Ralf Dahrendorf, "Toward a Theory of Social Conflict," in *Social Change,* ed. Amitai and Eva Etzioni (New York: Basic Books, 1964), pp. 98–111; W. F. Ogburn, *Social Change* (New York: Dell Publishing Co., 1966); R. K. Merton, *Social Theory and Social Structure* (rev. ed.; Glencoe, Ill.: The Free Press, 1957); Frederick Engels, *Anti-Dühring* (London: Lawrence and Wishart, 1936), pp. 294–312.

velopment is quite evident among countries in this group. Indeed, countries at the intermediate level compose the overwhelming majority of those in the full sample of seventy-four receiving high scores on the index of social tension. In some countries, such as the white settler countries of Africa and Latin American countries having distinct Indian sectors, a high level of social tension is associated with extreme racial or cultural barriers to mobility. In other countries, particularly in the Middle East and South Asia, serious social strains often arise from internal religious animosities or linguistic differences.

In most of the countries in the intermediate sample, the rapid and unbalanced social transformations have been coupled with considerable, or even extreme, political instability. The frequent toppling of governments has usually been accompanied by significant domestic violence in which military coups have often played an important role. Some coups have been designed to unseat traditional hereditary rulers, others to replace "inefficient" civilian governments, and still others to extend the influence of a foreign power. Overt social tensions, having their origin in cultural, ethnic, and religious differences, have been another important source of political instability among the countries in this group.

Not only are the governments of most countries in this group politically insecure, but they are also characterized by considerable ineffectiveness of political leadership. An important impediment to the establishment of functionally effective national governments at this level of development is the extent to which political and cultural integration is still lacking. A substantial majority of them has poorly integrated political systems and populations that exhibit weak senses of national unity; in fact, not a single intermediate-level country is characterized by both a strong degree of national integration and a well-developed sense of national unity. An additional contributor to ineffective government among most of these countries is the marked inadequacy of their government administrative apparatuses. The average score for this group with respect to degree of administrative efficiency is not significantly higher than that for the lowest group of countries. In the economic realm the countries in this group score, on the average, only slightly higher than do countries in the lowest sample with respect to the extent of their leadership's commitment to economic development.

Given the prevalence of social tension, political instability, and the underdevelopment of the government apparatus, perhaps it is not surprising that relatively few countries in the intermediate group have es-

208

tablished effective representative political institutions. Centralized political decision-making tends to characterize their political processes, and serious restrictions upon the freedom of political opposition and press are common. Nevertheless, a majority of countries in the intermediate sample has had, since 1957, more than one political party operating for at least a few years. Even where several political parties have been operating, however, their grass roots base has been very weak, with the result that from an over-all point of view only a handful of countries in this group has even moderately effective democratic institutions.

Our survey of the characteristics of the countries in the intermediate group of less-developed nations suggests that the keynote of their recent history is widespread change of a social, political, and economic nature. The extent of industrialization and the development of economic institutions are noticeably greater here than among countries in the lowest group. The social transformations conducive to the spread of markets and to the modernization of values and outlook have also progressed considerably farther. However, the social advances have generally proceeded at extremely uneven rates and have been accompanied by severe social tension and marked political instability. In addition, modern mechanisms for cultural and political integration have not yet sufficiently developed to provide an alternative basis for a cohesive society and polity. Thus, culturally, socially, technologically, and economically these countries are typified by the intermingling of modern, transitional, and traditional elements. Rapid transformations mark their recent history yet have not proceeded either far enough or with sufficient balance to lead, on the average, to effective social, economic, and political performance.

THE RESULTS

As might be expected from the preceding description of countries in this group, the results of the factor analyses for nations at the intermediate level of development are not as clear-cut and unithematic as are the results for countries at the lowest and highest levels of socioeconomic development. The lack of a well-defined pattern for the intermediate countries is evidenced by a lower degree of explanatory power in the factor analyses than is found in the results for the other two groups and by a lesser degree of consistency among the several factor analyses.

In spite of this difficulty, there are still a few conclusions that can be drawn concerning the forces influencing the growth process in countries at the intermediate stage of development. First of all, economic policies, in particular those that govern the rate of industrialization, the expansion of financial capacity, and the rate of investment in physical overhead capital now constitute the most important influences on the process of economic growth. Secondly, the systematic role of purely social bottlenecks has greatly declined; this can be inferred even though, for reasons inherent in the character of the path of social change in countries at this particular stage of development, the factor analyses underestimate the importance of the social forces. Finally, the mild association that was found for nations at the lowest level of development between more authoritarian forms of government and better economic performance still persists into the intermediate group of countries; however, for the latter there is some evidence that the relationship is even weaker than it was for the lowest group.

In the sections that follow, we shall discuss these conclusions in detail and shall attempt to offer an explanation for the difficulty of deriving stronger conclusions of general applicability for the growth of societies in the intermediate stage of socioeconomic development.

The Important Economic Forces

The clearest picture of the impact of economic forces on the countries in the intermediate group can be obtained from an examination of Table VI–3. It can be seen from this table that the nature of the process responsible for increases in rates of economic growth is different in character from that characterizing the lowest group. The forces most conducive to economic performance at this level are no longer related purely to the dualistic development of a single foreign-trade-oriented modern sector based on the exploitation of natural resource endowments; rather, the important economic forces at this level are associated with the process of industrialization. The most important factor that emerges in the economic analysis of Table VI–3 (Factor III) combines the indicator of the level of modernization of industry with indices of those aspects of economic structure which govern the extent to which industrialization can in fact take place. These are the level of effectiveness of financial institutions, the gross investment rate, the degree of improvement in physical overhead capital, and the abundance of nat-

TABLE VI-1: Rotated Factor Matrix for Change in Per Capita GNP (1950/51–1963/64) Together with Thirty-six Political, Social, and Economic Variables [a] (Intermediate Sample)

Political, Social, and Economic Indicators	Rotated Factor Loadings					h_i^2 (R^2)
	F_1	F_2	F_3	F_4	F_5	
Rate of Growth of Real Per Capita GNP: 1950/51–1963/64	.21	.26	.15	−.05	.59	.484
Size of the Traditional Agricultural Sector	−.61	.30	.25	−.06	−.26	.597
Extent of Dualism	.67	−.02	−.24	−.32	.41	.785
Extent of Mass Communication	.60	−.36	.07	.08	−.42	.668
Gross Investment Rate	.53	.02	.06	−.05	−.07	.287
Level of Modernization of Industry	.58	−.05	.44	−.28	.30	.695
Level of Modernization of Techniques in Agriculture	.81	−.25	−.22	.12	.13	.789
Character of Agricultural Organization	.70	.13	−.07	−.26	−.06	.588
Level of Effectiveness of the Tax System	.71	−.19	−.01	.03	.08	.550
Level of Adequacy of Physical Overhead Capital	.82	.03	.05	−.18	.23	.754
Strength of Democratic Institutions	.12	−.75	−.09	−.49	.06	.826
Degree of Freedom of Political Opposition and Press	.22	−.79	−.15	.05	−.08	.702
Predominant Basis of the Political Party System	.02	−.85	.24	−.01	−.11	.794
Degree of Competitiveness of Political Parties	.31	−.85	.19	.08	−.15	.890
Strength of the Labor Movement	.09	−.47 [b]	.06	−.29	−.51	.578
Extent of Centralization of Political Power	.12	.74	.15	.11	−.02	.601
Extent of Literacy	.17	−.56	−.51	.05	−.01	.609
Character of Basic Social Organization	−.57	−.58	−.22	.30	−.14	.828
Degree of Social Tension	.12	.06	.64	.30	.21	.562
Importance of the Indigenous Middle Class	.04	.04	−.70	.04	.22	.549
Extent of Social Mobility	.33	−.03	−.80	.02	−.08	.762
Rate of Improvement in Human Resources	.26	.00	.68	−.22	.43	.765

TABLE VI-1 (Continued)

Political, Social, and Economic Indicators	Rotated Factor Loadings					h_i^2 (R^2)
	F_1	F_2	F_3	F_4	F_5	
Abundance of Natural Resources	.29	.02	**.78**	.05	-.14	.717
Extent of Political Stability	.07	-.01	-.56	-**.77**	.00	.908
Extent of Leadership Commitment to Economic Development	.05	.21	-.09	-**.83**	.03	.743
Degree of Modernization of Outlook	.39	-.47	.09	-**.66**	-.05	.814
Degree of Administrative Efficiency	.52	-.12	-.17	-**.68**	.12	.794
Political Strength of the Military	-.14	.31	.26	**.52**	.36	.586
Degree of National Integration and Sense of National Unity	.14	.38	-.47	**.55**	-.22	.738
Degree of Cultural and Ethnic Homogeneity	.10	.54	-.17	**.58**	.04	.668
Structure of Foreign Trade	.29	.13	.22	**.49**	.39	.544
Change in Degree of Industrialization since 1950	.01	-.18	-.50	.10	**.71**	.797
Level of Effectiveness of Financial Institutions	.57	.04	-.12	-.40	**.61**	.872
Degree of Improvement in Financial Institutions since 1950	.04	-.22	-.08	.08	**.81**	.713
Degree of Improvement in Physical Overhead Capital since 1950	.13	.17	.27	-.15	**.65**	.566
Degree of Improvement in Agricultural Productivity since 1950	.31	.11	-.44	-.18	**.64**	.747
Degree of Improvement in the Tax System since 1950	-.06	.16	-.43	.03	**.60**	.580

[a] Bold figures indicate the factor to which each variable is assigned. Variables omitted because of insignificant correlations: crude fertility rate and political strength of the traditional elite. Variable omitted because of low/high loadings: extent of urbanization. Percentage of over-all variance explained by factors: 68.8. Percentage of variance explained by last factor included: 7.7.

[b] A variable having loadings on two factors which are not significantly different is assigned to that factor to which it is judged to have the closest affinity.

212

TABLE VI-2: Rotated Factor Matrix for Change in Per Capita GNP (1950/51–1963/64) Together with Twenty-one Political and Social Variables [a] (Intermediate Sample)

Political and Social Indicators	Rotated Factor Loadings				h_i^2
	F_1	F_2	F_3	F_4	(R^2)
Rate of Growth of Real Per Capita GNP: 1950/51–1963/64..........	-.15	.03	.11	.68	.493
Strength of Democratic Institutions..........	**.66**	-.59	-.06	-.06	.793
Degree of Freedom of Political Opposition and Press..........	**.83**	-.07	-.16	-.09	.721
Predominant Basis of the Political Party System..........	**.79**	-.14	.27	-.25	.781
Degree of Competitiveness of Political Parties..........	**.92**	-.06	.13	-.07	.870
Strength of the Labor Movement..........	**.45**	-.38	.03	-.36	.471
Degree of Centralization of Political Power..........	**-.53**	.27	.00	.41	.520
Extent of Mass Communication..........	**.63**	.00	-.13	.14	.428
Extent of Political Stability..........	-.09	**.79**	-.53	.09	.918
Extent of Leadership Commitment to Economic Development..........	-.33	**-.81**	.02	.21	.817
Degree of Modernization of Outlook..........	.52	**-.69**	.03	.23	.802
Degree of Administrative Efficiency..........	.17	**-.71**	-.21	.40	.737
Political Strength of the Military..........	-.30	**.59**	.33	.17	.578
Degree of Cultural and Ethnic Homogeneity..........	-.37	**.65**	-.30	.17	.676
Degree of National Integration and Sense of National Unity..........	-.20	**.57**	-.55	.07	.677
Degree of Social Tension..........	.06	.33	**.68**	.28	.660
Importance of the Indigenous Middle Class..........	-.03	.03	**.69**	.17	.503
Extent of Social Mobility..........	.14	-.04	**-.88**	.07	.798
Extent of Literacy..........	.53	-.08	**.54**	-.20	.620
Size of the Traditional Agricultural Sector..........	-.52	-.01	.22	**.51** [b]	.579
Extent of Dualism..........	.23	-.31	-.26	**.75**	.780
Character of Basic Social Organization..........	.29	.17	-.06	**.79**	.749

[a] Bold figures indicate the factor to which each variable is assigned. Variables omitted because of insignificant correlations: crude fertility rate and political strength of the traditional elite. Variables omitted because of low high loadings: extent of urbanization. Percentage of over-all variance explained by the factors: 68.0. Percentage of variance explained by last factor included: 9.6.

[b] A variable having loadings on two factors which are not significantly different is assigned to that factor to which it is judged to have the closest affinity.

213

TABLE VI–3: Rotated Factor Matrix for Change in Per Capita GNP (1950/51–1963/64) Together with Sixteen Economic Variables [a] (Intermediate Sample)

Economic Indicators	Rotated Factor Loadings			h_i^2
	F_1	F_2	F_3	(R^2)
Rate of Growth of Real Per Capita GNP: 1950/51–1963/64	−.02	−.39	.57	.483
Size of the Traditional Agricultural Sector	**.76**	.33	.09	.690
Extent of Dualism	**−.77**	−.40	.21	.790
Character of Agricultural Organization	**−.79**	.07	.16	.656
Level of Modernization of Techniques in Agriculture	**−.85**	−.13	−.01	.744
Level of Effectiveness of the Tax System	**−.73**	.06	.18	.569
Level of Adequacy of Physical Overhead Capital	**−.75**	−.09	.41	.738
Change in Degree of Industrialization since 1950	−.10	**−.84**	−.01	.718
Degree of Improvement in Financial Institutions since 1950	−.06	**−.76**	.14	.602
Degree of Improvement in the Tax System since 1950	.10	**−.76**	.11	.605
Degree of Improvement in Agricultural Productivity since 1950	−.42	**−.78**	.04	.793
Rate of Improvement in Human Resources	−.47	**−.68**	−.16	.712
Level of Modernization of Industry	−.39	−.01	**.72**	.664
Level of Effectiveness of Financial Institutions	−.47	−.53	**.60**	.860
Gross Investment Rate	−.25	.14	**.58**	.422
Degree of Improvement in Physical Overhead Capital since 1950	.12	−.43	**.77**	.799
Abundance of Natural Resources	.01	.52	**.69**	.740

[a] Bold figures indicate the factor to which each variable is assigned. Variables omitted because of insignificant correlations: none. Variable omitted because of low high loadings: structure of foreign trade. Percentage of over-all variance explained by factors: 68.1. Percentage of variance explained by last factor included: 13.2.

ural resources. Effective financial mechanisms for mobilizing private savings and transmitting them to the expanding sectors of the economy are, of course, an essential aspect of the process of industrialization. The importance of increasing the proportion of total resources devoted to investment is well known and constitutes a *sine qua non* of the initiation of sustained economic growth. The expansion of investment in physical overhead capital can act as a source of external economies, both pecuniary and technological, that greatly facilitate the industrialization process. Finally, the association of natural resource abundance with industrialization and growth indicates the importance of primary agricultural and extractive endowments in the early stages of the development

214

TABLE VI-4: Rotated Factor Matrix for Change in Per Capita GNP (1950/51–1963/64) Together with Twenty-five Social and Economic Variables [a] (Intermediate Sample)

Social and Economic Indicators	Rotated Factor Loadings				h_a^2 (R²)
	F_1	F_2	F_3	F_4	
Rate of Growth of Real Per Capita GNP: 1950/51–1963/64.	-.14	.10	-.68	-.15	.512
Size of the Traditional Agricultural Sector.	.58	-.44	.02	-.16	.557
Extent of Dualism.	.68	.43	-.30	.23	.791
Character of Agricultural Organization.	-.76	.02	-.02	.18	.601
Level of Modernization of Techniques in Agriculture.	-.79	.31	.07	.08	.733
Gross Investment Rate.	.48	-.12	-.14	-.07	.267
Level of Adequacy of Physical Overhead Capital.	-.80	.09	-.30	.15	.763
Level of Effectiveness of the Tax System.	-.77	.05	.01	-.07	.599
Character of Basic Social Organization.	.57	.20	.56	.21	.719
Importance of the Indigenous Middle Class.	-.02	.71	.01	-.27	.576
Extent of Social Mobility.	-.34	.66	.34	-.05	.659
Extent of Literacy.	-.19	.50	.44	.30	.573
Change in Degree of Industrialization since 1950.	.05	.82	-.27	-.02	.741
Degree of Improvement in Agricultural Productivity since 1950.	-.28	.72	-.39	.10	.762
Degree of Improvement in the Tax System since 1950.	.07	.60	-.42	-.36	.668
Rate of Improvement in Human Resources.	-.29	.81	-.08	.17	.766
Abundance of Natural Resources.	-.19	-.70	-.26	.22	.647
Level of Modernization of Industry.	-.48	-.17	.56	.45	.775
Level of Effectiveness of Financial Institutions.	-.53	.39	.62	.17	.844
Degree of Improvement in Financial Institutions since 1950.	.08	.55	-.56	.09	.630
Degree of Improvement in Physical Overhead Capital since 1950.	.01	.10	.78	.14	.638
Structure of Foreign Trade.	-.34	-.06	.57	.14	.463
Degree of National Integration and Sense of National Unity.	-.19	.18	.31	.81	.816
Degree of Cultural and Ethnic Homogeneity.	-.09	.03	-.07	-.84	.719
Degree of Modernization of Outlook.	-.42	-.03	-.09	.62	.571
Extent of Urbanization.	-.34	.06	.09	.68	.581

[a] Bold figures indicate the factor to which each variable is assigned. Variables omitted because of insignificant correlations: extent of mass communication, degree of social tension, and crude fertility rate. Variables omitted because of low high loadings: none. Percentage of over-all variance explained by factors: 65.3. Percentage of variance explained by last factor included: 9.0.

of an indigenous industrial base.[6] Together, the economic influences that make possible successful industrialization account for 33 per cent of intercountry variations in the short-term economic performance of countries at the intermediate level of development. While this degree of explanation is not striking in absolute terms, it forms 68 per cent of the explanation of economic growth rates offered by the economic factor analysis. The analogous economic factor in the combined and socioeconomic analyses accounts for 71 and 90 per cent, respectively, of the total variance in growth rates of per capita GNP which is explained by all the factors.

The contrast between the economic forces that emerge as most important for the intermediate sample and for the low sample is underlined by test runs made for the two groups. It will be recalled that the omission of indicators of dynamic economic improvements and of the level of effectiveness of tax systems and financial institutions actually raised the explanatory power of the economic analysis for the low sample. In contrast, in test runs for the intermediate group, the degree of improvement in physical overhead capital contributed significantly to the explanation of variations in economic growth rates while the level of effectiveness of financial institutions emerged as a crucial aspect of economic structure systematically governing the short-run economic progress.[7] As discussed in Chapter II, the indicator that describes finan-

---

[6] In both the combined and socioeconomic analyses (Tables VI–1 and VI–4) there is an unexpected negative association of natural resource abundance with the importance of the indigenous middle class and the extent of social mobility. An examination of the simple correlation matrix indicates that natural resource abundance has only two significant correlations: it has a correlation of 0.59 with the level of modernization of industry, which accounts for its association in the important factor in the economic analysis; its other significant correlation is a negative one (-0.67) with the importance of the indigenous middle class. This latter association is largely accounted for by the fact that the sample includes seven countries with relatively high scores on natural resource abundance and low scores on the importance of the indigenous middle class in which expatriate exploitation of abundant natural resources, either historically or recently, has played an important role in raising the country to its present level of development.

[7] The omission from the economic analysis of the entire set of dynamic improvements summarized in Factor II, Table VI–3, raises the communality with respect to rates of growth of per capita GNP to 69.4 per cent and regroups the remaining indicators so that the only important factor is composed of the level of effectiveness of financial institutions and the degree of improvement in physical overhead capital which together explain 68.7 per cent of intercountry variations in short-term economic performance.

216

cial institutions is a broad measure of their success in attracting indigenous private savings and in financing investment. Therefore, the importance of this variable in explaining economic growth rates at the intermediate level implies that differences among these countries in short-run economic performance are most closely associated with variations in the capacity to mobilize domestic savings and in the effectiveness of institutional mechanisms for channeling savings into the expansion of industry and agriculture. This finding is consistent with the view that, as the average underdeveloped country progresses economically, its rate of economic growth tends to be constrained successively by several sets of limiting factors: first, those associated with restricted absorptive capacity; then, those associated with inadequate capacity for mobilizing savings; and, finally, those associated with the inability to rapidly replace imports with domestic production.[8] The results for our intermediate sample suggest that these countries have reached a level of socioeconomic development at which specific skill and other resource bottlenecks to the process of industrialization are overshadowed by constraints on the mobilization of domestic savings. Thus, generally speaking, the countries that perform well at this level are those in which the process of industrialization is least constrained by inadequate institutional mechanisms for financing the expansion of industry and agriculture or by insufficient investment in the improvements in the physical overhead capital necessary for further growth.

The Social Forces

Before we turn to an examination of the importance of social forces to the process of economic growth in countries of the intermediate group let us first discuss two peculiarities of the results of the factor analyses. These are (1) the association of the character of basic social organization showing an unexpected negative sign with rates of growth of per capita GNP and the extent of dualism (Factor IV of Table VI–2 and Factor I of Table VI–4)[9] and (2) the association of greater

[8] See H. B. Chenery and A. M. Strout, "Foreign Assistance and Economic Development," *American Economic Review,* Vol. 56 (September, 1966), pp. 680–733.

[9] In Table VI–1 the character of basic social organization has significant loadings in two factors: it associates in Factor I in the same manner as in the socioeconomic and sociopolitical results; in Factor II, it has a slightly higher loading and associates positively with the indicators of the extent of participant democracy

sociocultural and political integration with less modernization of outlook and governments which are less effective politically and economically (Factor IV of Table VI–1, Factor II of Table VI–2, and Factor IV of Table IV–4). Both peculiarities appear to be connected with the geographic and historical heterogeneity of the intermediate sample.

Let us consider the first of these features of the results. Basic social organization is a relatively slow-changing characteristic of social structure which tends to vary more between the major regions of the world than it does within them. Consequently, in view of the marked diversity in the regional composition of the intermediate sample, the results with respect to social organization cannot be interpreted as an indication of the typical pattern of change in an average country of the group. Rather, they must be understood in the context of the specific geographic make-up of the sample. On the one hand, the sample includes a number of low-level Latin American countries with low growth rates, in which the immediate family group predominates outside minority Indian communities. On the other hand, it also includes several rapidly growing African countries in which tribal organization is the dominant social form. The result of this combination which is evident in the factor analyses is the association of smaller family organization with lower economic growth rates.[10] The negative association between social organization and dualism which also can be seen in the results can be explained in a similar manner.[11] If we exclude social organization from

---

and the extent of literacy. This is because the character of basic social organization has a simple correlation of 0.42 with the extent of literacy and of −0.58 with the extent of centralization of political power. The association of the smaller family units characteristic or urbanization and industrialization with higher literacy rates is what one would expect.

[10] In the scoring of countries with respect to the character of basic social organization, countries in which the dominant form of social organization is the immediate family received high scores, countries in which the dominant forms are the clan and the extended family received intermediate scores, and countries in which the dominant form is the tribe received low scores.

[11] It will be recalled that an increase in score with respect to the extent of dualism at the intermediate level represents a movement from marked socioeconomic and cultural cleavages between distinct modern and traditional sectors toward a society in which modern and traditional forms are more closely intermingled throughout the nation. In most of the Latin American countries in the sample, a long-term phenomenon of marked socioeconomic dualism and slow economic progress over the past few decades are notable features; at the same time, the most common social form outside the Indian sectors is the small family. In

the sociopolitical analysis, the size of the traditional sector and the extent of dualism combine alone in the important social factor and account for an even greater proportion of intercountry variations in economic performance than when social organization is included (55 per cent compared with 44 per cent).

The second peculiarity of the intermediate results is the negative relationship between the degree of national integration and of cultural and ethnic homogeneity, on the one hand, and, on the other, the degree of modernization of outlook, the extent of political stability, the extent of leadership commitment to economic development, and the degree of administrative efficiency (Factor IV of Table VI–1 and Factor II of Table VI–2).[12] This feature of the results is also connected with the varied character of the sample. In particular, among the countries in the intermediate group are several heterogeneous societies, such as India and the Philippines, whose relatively long exposure to Western influences has created at least as much receptivity to economic and political change as is found in some of the more homogeneous and integrated nations in the sample (for example, Jordan and Syria). As can be seen in the three sets of results which incorporate social indicators, the factors that include cultural and ethnic homogeneity, national integration, and the degree of modernization of outlook are not significant in explaining economic performance in the short run.

We now turn to a general evaluation of the impact of social influences upon short-run economic growth as it emerges from the factor analyses for the intermediate group. A cursory examination of the results suggests that most of the forces summarized by our indicators of social structure have little systematic effect upon the development process. Only in the sociopolitical analysis do we find any indication that social forces have a significant influence on economic growth. In this set of results, the only important factor is Factor IV (Table VI–2), which includes the indicators of the size of the traditional agricultural sector and

---

contrast, the higher-level African countries, while still characterized generally by the importance of tribal values, have expanded so rapidly during most of the period since 1950 that the intermingling of modern and nonmodern economic activities has procceded farther than in the low-level Latin American countries having distinct Indian sectors.

[12] An examination of the correlation matrix indicates that it is the significant negative correlation between the degree of cultural and ethnic homogeneity and the degree of modernization of outlook (−0.54) which is responsible for the pattern observed.

219

the extent of dualism. However, it is evident from the socioeconomic and combined analyses (Tables VI–3 and VI–1 respectively) that these social indicators are in fact merely surrogates for the purely economic forces that, whenever they are explicitly included in the analysis, pick up the apparent explanatory power of these indicators.

Even though it is evident from the analyses incorporating economic indicators that the size of the traditional sector and the extent of dualism are not systematically important in themselves, it is an inconsistency in the results that these variables which act as proxies for the important economic indicators do not merge with them in the combined and socioeconomic analyses. The reason for the inconsistency appears to be that the extent of dualism is significantly correlated both with the level of effectiveness of financial institutions (a crucial influence at this level) and with basic elements of socioeconomic structure which are not systematically important for this group of countries.[13] As a result, whenever a direct measure of financial institutions is included, the extent of dualism is drawn into the factor summarizing the several other aspects of socioeconomic structure to which it is also closely related (Factor I of Table VI–1 and Factor I of Table VI–4). Only when no direct representation of financial capacity is incorporated as in the sociopolitical analysis, does the indicator of the extent of dualism associate in the important factor, acting as a proxy for the effectiveness of mechanisms for mobilizing savings and financing investment (Factor IV of Table VI–2).

There is thus no real evidence in our factor analyses of a direct systematic impact of changes in social structure upon rates of economic growth in countries at the intermediate stage of socioeconomic development. We cannot accept this result at face value, however, as it is clear that a statistical analysis of countries as diverse in the details of their social development as are the intermediate-level nations must inevitably underestimate the importance of social processes. Among these countries, patterns of social progress are so varied that the binding social constraints differ radically from country to country. Under these

[13] The following are selected significant simple correlations between the extent of dualism and other social and economic indices: 0.77 with the level of effectiveness of financial institutions; 0.67 with the level of modernization of techniques in agriculture; 0.65 with the level of adequacy of physical overhead capital; 0.61 with the size of the traditional agricultural sector; and 0.59 with the character of agricultural organization.

circumstances there is no set of social bottlenecks which is common to a majority of these societies; therefore, no systematic association between economic growth and any group of social phenomena can be expected to emerge from a purely statistical analysis.

That this should be the case is suggested by the typology of countries at the intermediate level. As discussed at the beginning of this chapter, unevenness of social change within individual countries is one of the salient characteristics of countries in the group. Just how uneven and varied these nations are in their respective patterns of social development can be appreciated by an examination of Table VI–5 in which each country in the sample has been ranked with respect to each of our indices of social structure. As a result the correlations between pairs of indices of social structure are markedly lower for this group of countries than they are for either of the other two groups. More specifically, of the 78 simple correlation coefficients among measures of social structure, the number of statistically significant ones for the countries at this level is only 5; the corresponding numbers for countries at the highest and lowest levels are 32 and 15, respectively. Because the wide intercountry differences in patterns of social progress shown in this table preclude the emergence of a clear systematic relationship between specific social forces and economic evolution, any statistical analysis of these effects must, of necessity, underestimate the true weight of social bottlenecks to development for countries at this level. Unfortunately, it is impossible to assess quantitatively the extent to which social influences have been understated in our factor analyses because of the absence of a consistent pattern of social change. However, we believe that the underestimate is significant.

Even though we are reasonably confident that the statistical underestimate of the importance of social forces at this level of development is large, we also have reason to believe that the actual role of social processes in economic development is less crucial for countries at this level than it is at the earlier stage of development. The first argument is rooted in our discussion above of the comparative influence of social forces at the lowest and intermediate levels of socioeconomic attainment. We recall that at the lowest stage of development the social barriers to growth are so strong that the breakdown of the tribal social structure is a *sine qua non* for economic progress and for the diffusion of market organization and attitudes into the subsistence sector. By contrast, while family and clan relationships and subsistence production

221

TABLE VI–5: Ranking of Twenty-one Countries in Intermediate Sample with Respect to Social Indices

Country	Social Indicators									
	Size of the Traditional Agricultural Sector	Extent of Dualism	Extent of Urbanization	Importance of the In-digenous Middle Class	Extent of Social Mobility	Extent of Literacy	Extent of Mass Communication	Degree of National Integration and Sense of National Unity	Degree of Cultural and Ethnic Homogeneity	Degree of Moderniza-tion of Outlook
Algeria	11	12.5	9.5	20	19.5	15.5	8	14.5	8.5	9.5
Bolivia	16.5	19.5	5.5	21	15	9	8	20.5	20.5	9.5
Burma	16.5	19.5	20	18	15	6	18	14.5	13	18
Ceylon	2	6.5	18	1	2.5	4.5	8	2.5	8.5	9.5
Ecuador	5.5	6.5	7	6	6.5	4.5	3	6.5	8.5	13.5
Ghana	5.5	6.5	16	13.5	6.5	15.5	8	6.5	15	5.5
Guatemala	9.5	5.5	16	6	19.5	11	8	14.5	16.5	9.5
Honduras	5.5	19.5	16	18	15	7.5	8	6.5	3	13.5
India	9.5	6.5	13	6	19.5	15.5	18	19	18.5	2.5
Indonesia	16.5	19.5	13	18	15	15.5	18	6.5	8.5	18
Iran	16.5	15.5	9.5	11.5	11	19.5	8	14.5	13	18
Iraq	16.5	15.5	9.5	11.5	11	21	18	14.5	8.5	18
Jordan	5.5	6.5	20	6	6.5	15.5	14	2.5	3	18
Pakistan	16.5	6.5	20	6	15	19.5	21	9.5	13	9.5
Philippines	5.5	6.5	1.5	6	2.5	1	14	9.5	18.5	2.5
Rhodesia	16.5	6.5	5.5	15.5	19.5	11	8	14.5	8.5	2.5
South Africa	1	1	3	15.5	11	7.5	1.5	20.5	20.5	2.5
Surinam	16.5	12.5	1.5	6	1	2.5	1.5	14.5	16.5	9.5
Syria	5.5	6.5	4	6	6.5	11	14	2.5	3	18
Thailand	16.5	6.5	13	13.5	6.5	2.5	18	14.5	3	18
Tunisia	16.5	15.5	9.5	6	6.5	15.5	8	2.5	3	5.5

remain significant within countries in the intermediate group, exposure to cities and markets has been sufficient by now to produce a widespread awareness within the subsistence sector of purely economic considerations and some degree of acceptance of purely economic criteria for economic activity.

There is another source of reduced influence of social forces on the development process for countries at this level. The very strong influence that characterizes the social development of these nations tends, in and of itself, to reduce the likelihood that an environment favorable to economic growth can be produced through specific social improvements. One would expect this to be the case for two reasons. First of all, just as in the process of economic change, there must be important complementarities in the process of social change. The effectiveness of a single improvement or of only a few improvements, *ceteris paribus,* is likely to be considerably less than a simultaneous advance on many social fronts. For example, marked improvements in primary and secondary education without a corresponding expansion of opportunities for social and economic upward mobility are likely to have much less effect upon economic growth than would concurrent increases of lesser magnitude in both education and opportunity. By the same token, a given degree of urbanization in the presence of widespread economic and social dualism is considerably less conducive to economic development than would be the same degree of urbanization accompanied by greater social and economic integration.

Secondly, unevenness in social development contributed greatly to the rise in social tension so characteristic of countries in this group. The existence of a high level of social tensions within these societies, by negating to some extent the affirmative effects on growth which might otherwise result from appropriate changes in social structure, contributes to the inability of piecemeal social improvements to be translated into economic growth. This phenomenon is illustrated by the pattern of associations within the social tension factor (Factor III of Table VI–1 and Factor III of Table VI–2) in which the normally positive relationship between economic growth and increases in the size of the middle class, the degree of social mobility, and the spread of literacy has become a slightly negative association for this group of countries. The reason that social tension is not itself an important contributor to the explanation of intercountry differences in rates of economic growth (Factor III of Table VI–1 and Factor III of Table VI–2 contribute less

223

than 3 per cent to the explanation of short-term growth rates) is that it really reflects the workings of two opposing forces. On the one hand, social tension is an indirect positive measure of the pace and extent of social progress in the intermediate group of countries; as such, it is positively correlated with economic growth. On the other hand, overt social tension, *ceteris paribus,* acts to slow down growth by inducing political instability, disaffection, and anomie, all of which are, of course, negatively associated with economic performance. Since social tension as an index and social tension as a force tend to counteract each other, it is not surprising that the relationship between the degree of social tension and a nation's success in raising economic growth rates is not especially strong.

Our interpretation of the role of social forces in the growth process of countries at the intermediate level of development is sufficiently complex to merit a summary. We found no single systematic social bottleneck hindering the economic development of these countries. However, this did not lead us to conclude that social impediments are unimportant for countries at this level, since the great diversity in patterns of social change so characteristic of these countries leads, in the factor analyses, to an underestimate of the importance of social forces in the process of economic growth. We believe that the extent of this statistical underestimation is quite significant but that, nevertheless, the finding that social influences have a lesser statistical weight for countries in this sample, as compared with their weight in the lowest sample, represents to some extent a genuine phenomenon. Thus, our conclusion with respect to social factors in the economic development of countries at the intermediate level is that individual social bottlenecks, which differ from country to country, exercise an important influence on the growth of countries at this stage. The quantitative magnitude of the impact of social influences, however, is undoubtedly less than for countries at the lowest level.

THE POLITICAL FORCES

Just as for countries at the lowest level of development, we find for the intermediate group a mild positive association between more autocratic forms of government and better short-run economic performance. The relevant factor (Factor II of Table VI–1 and Factor I of Table VI–2) accounts for from 2 to 5 per cent of the intercountry variance in rates of growth. The observed relationship is consistent with the suggestion of Organski in his *Stages of Political Development*[14] that in countries at this and earlier stages of socioeconomic development, where the primary business of the polity is that of national integration, more centralized authoritarian forms of government are functionally better adapted to performing the political tasks facing the nation.

We also find that there is essentially no systematic relationship for countries at this level of development between the quality of the leadership in the economic sphere and actual rates of economic growth. In particular, in both the sociopolitical results (Table VI–2) and the combined results (Table VI–1), the factor describing the characteristics of leadership (Factors II and IV respectively) has negligible weight in accounting for intercountry differences in growth rates. This finding also supports Organski, who argues that by and large, governments at this stage of development do not view economic modernization as their primary task. Our results with respect to the role of leadership for this group of nations are in strong contrast to those for countries at higher levels of socioeconomic development, for which, as we shall see later, affirmative government economic leadership is crucial in determining economic performance.

The fact that most governments at this stage of development do not mobilize effectively for economic modernization is due in great part to the very marked political instability of their regimes. (See Factor IV of Table VI–1 and Factor II of Table VI–2.) A leadership that is constantly engaged in a fight for short-run survival finds it extremely difficult to think in the longer-run terms necessary for effective economic planning. Furthermore, there is a vicious circle between political instability and the inability to mobilize effectively for economic growth. Not only does the ever-present prospect of a coup d'état severely impair the capacity of the government to exercise effective economic leadership but the failure of those in power to produce tangible benefits contributes to political discontent and thus to greater political instability.

It is interesting to inquire into the major causes of the political instability that tends to impede economic progress in countries at this level. Our results indicate that approximately 90 per cent of the variance in political instability in these countries can be attributed to two distinct factors. In the majority of these nations, political instability is associated

[14] Chapter I.

225

with military coups and reflects primarily discontent at the top. This type of instability accounts for about 60 per cent of the over-all **variance** in political stability. (See the loadings of the political stability indicator on Factor II of Table VI–2 and Factor IV of Table VI–1.) In the remaining countries, political instability appears to have deeper grass roots characteristics; it is closely associated with the social tensions that arise mainly because of the limited opportunities offered by the social structure for upward mobility into middle class status (see the relationships represented in Factor III of Table VI–1 and Factor III of Table VI–2). This aspect of political instability is indicated by the loading of political stability on the social tension factor[15] which accounts for close to 30 per cent of the intercountry variance in over-all political stability. In any case, a comparison of our results for this group of countries with the results at the next higher level of development (see Chapter VII) suggest that whatever the origin of political instability, it must be overcome before a country can mobilize effectively for economic development.

Comparison of the Short-run and Long-run Analyses

Just as for the countries at the lowest level of socioeconomic development, one can perform a long-run factor analysis for the intermediate nations analogous to the combined short-run study summarized in Table VI–1. The results of this long-run analysis, in which per capita GNP is treated as the dependent variable, are given in Table VI–6 and appear at first glance to contradict the short-run results. In the long-run study a weight of approximately 60 per cent is found for the factor representing the absolute levels of socioeconomic development (Factor I, Table VI–6),[16] while in the short-run analysis the identical factor (Factor I, Table VI–1) explains less than 5 per cent of intercountry differences in rates of economic growth. There really is no essential conflict in the results, however. In the short-run analysis most of the explanation of differences in rates of economic growth is picked up by a dynamic fac-

[15] Factor III of Table VI–1 and Factor III of Table VI–2.
[16] Experimentation with the omission of the social variables included in this factor indicate that it is the economic rather than the social indicators in this factor which are responsible for its explanatory power. When the indicators of the size of the traditional agricultural sector, the extent of dualism, and the extent of mass communication are omitted, the loading of Factor I of Table VI–6 is reduced by less than 0.01.

226

TABLE VI-6: Rotated Factor Matrix for Per Capita GNP in 1961 Together with Thirty-six Political, Social, and Economic Variables [a] (Intermediate Sample)

Political, Social, and Economic Indicators	Rotated Factor Loadings					h_i^2
	F_1	F_2	F_3	F_4	F_5	(R^2)
Per Capita GNP in 1961	.79	-.08	-.14	-.01	-.19	.685
Size of the Traditional Agricultural Sector	-.60	.28	-.15	-.05	-.38	.603
Extent of Dualism	.64	.00	.11	-.35	.48	.784
Extent of Mass Communication	.66	-.36	.08	.10	-.43	.758
Gross Investment Rate	.53	.03	.00	-.07	-.09	.297
Level of Modernization of Industry	.59	-.04	-.52	-.27	.19	.723
Level of Modernization of Techniques in Agriculture	.81	-.23	.19	.11	.23	.807
Character of Agricultural Organization	.70	.13	.08	-.29	-.02	.589
Level of Effectiveness of the Tax System	.65	-.17	.01	.00	.15	.480
Level of Adequacy of Physical Overhead Capital	.79	.03	-.13	-.20	.26	.742
Strength of Democratic Institutions	.12	.77	.04	-.46	.10	.834
Degree of Freedom of Political Opposition and Press	.22	.79	.17	.07	.02	.709
Predominant Basis of the Political Party System	.02	.86	-.19	.04	-.14	.788
Degree of Competitiveness of Political Parties	.34	.86	-.12	.12	-.17	.908
Strength of the Labor Movement	.07	.51	.03	-.27	-.42	.511
Degree of Centralization of Political Power	.15	.75	-.11	.10	-.12	.616
Extent of Literacy	.16	-.56	.52	.05	.14	.633
Character of Basic Social Organization	-.54	-.57	.24	.33	-.06	.797
Degree of Cultural and Ethnic Homogeneity	.07	.55	.19	.54	.09	.644
Degree of Social Tension	.13	.07	.67	.32	.05	.580
Degree of National Integration and Sense of National Unity	.09	.40	.53	.49	-.05	.684
Importance of the Indigenous Middle Class	.02	.06	.62	-.01	.41	.555

227

TABLE VI-6 (Continued)

Political, Social, and Economic Indicators	Rotated Factor Loadings					h_i^2 (R^2)
	F_1	F_2	F_3	F_4	F_5	
Extent of Social Mobility	.33	-.02	**.81**	-.01	.13	.785
Abundance of Natural Resources	.33	.02	**-.69**	.09	-.36	.725
Extent of Political Stability	.05	-.04	.52	**-.79**	.11	.916
Extent of Leadership Commitment to Economic Development	.03	.18	.04	**-.84**	.04	.737
Degree of Modernization of Outlook	.37	-.50	-.10	**-.64**	-.03	.808
Degree of Administrative Efficiency	.47	-.13	.11	**-.70**	.20	.786
Political Strength of the Military	-.13	.35	-.32	**.53**	.26	.588
Structure of Foreign Trade	.24	.12	-.37	**-.50**	.36	.585
Change in Degree of Industrialization since 1950	.01	-.13	.28	.09	**.83**	.789
Level of Effectiveness of Financial Institutions	.55	.06	-.04	-.42	**.60**	.847
Degree of Improvement in Financial Institutions since 1950	.03	-.18	-.16	.08	**.83**	.754
Degree of Improvement in Physical Overhead Capital since 1950	.14	.20	-.40	-.15	**.49**	.482
Degree of Improvement in Agricultural Productivity since 1950	.28	.15	.22	-.21	**.75**	.754
Degree of Improvement in the Tax System since 1950	-.11	.19	.25	-.01	**.71**	.615
Rate of Improvement in Human Resources	.25	.03	.51	-.25	**.61**	.753

[a] Bold figures indicate the factor to which each variable is assigned. Variables omitted because of insignificant correlations: crude fertility rate and political strength of the traditional elite. Variable omitted because of low high loading: extent of urbanization. Percentage of over-all variance explained by factors: 69.3. Percentage of variance explained by last factor included: 7.7.

tor that is composed of all our indicators of rates of improvement in economic performance as well as our indicator of the level of effectiveness of financial institutions. This latter variable is also dynamic in nature since it is an index of the economy's effectiveness in mobilizing domestic savings and in channeling them into the expansion of industry and agriculture. If we were dealing with a linear system, we would expect to find an analogous degree of correlation of the integrated values of the several indicators with the integrated value of the economic rate of growth, i.e., a correlation of the levels of infrastructure, industrial development, etc., with the level of per capita GNP. Therefore, we see that the relatively heavy weight of our indicators of levels of development in the long-run analysis is perfectly consistent with the relatively heavy weight of our indicators of rates of economic change in the short-run analysis.

From a mathematical point of view, if levels of individual variables turn out to be important in explaining rates of growth, this would indicate that the relationship between growth rates and the rates of change of those characteristics whose levels are statistically important must be nonlinear; such nonlinearities reflect either retardation or acceleration effects. Economically speaking, if the level of some indicator of structure is observed to retard rates of change, it may be interpreted to constitute a bottleneck. Similarly, if it acts to accelerate rates of change, it can be interpreted to engender external and/or internal economies. In the results of our factor analyses, therefore, the unimportance of levels in explaining rates of change in our short-run analyses and the unimportance of rates of change in explaining levels in our long-run analysis both imply that the economic development of countries at the intermediate level is governed by neither strong systematic bottlenecks nor strong systematic external or internal economies,[17] i.e., that these economies are essentially linear. In view of the acknowledged importance of external economies to the process of effective economic development, their absence in countries at this level is consistent with the observed lack of capacity for self-sustained growth among nations in the intermediate stages of socioeconomic development.

---

[17] This is not to say, of course, that strong specific bottlenecks or economies, varying in nature from country to country, may not be important in explaining the economic performance of individual countries. Bottlenecks and economies that are specific in nature would not be reflected in the statistical results since both the short-run and long-run functions represent a statistical average of nations.

SUMMARY

Our analysis of the forces influencing development in countries at the intermediate level of socioeconomic development has been complicated by the great diversity of patterns of change among the transitional societies in this group. As a result of this extreme heterogeneity, the statistical reliability and consistency of the results for this sample are considerably less than they are for either of the other two samples.

It would appear that many of the countries in this group are engaged in creating the economic and social prerequisites for economic development. Economically, the most important systematic influences are those governing the process of industrialization—in particular, the capacity of financial institutions to mobilize domestic savings and to channel them into the expansion of industry and agriculture and the expansion of the physical overhead capital required for further growth. With respect to social influences, we have been unable to identify any systematic forces at work. It is nevertheless our judgment that in each of the countries in this group there exist one or more social bottlenecks that impede economic growth. However, we find good reason to believe that the importance of these bottlenecks is rather less than it is for countries at the lowest stage of socioeconomic development. Politically, the government of a typical nation at this level still does not play an especially effective role in stimulating economic modernization. Furthermore, while the mild, positive association that we found for countries at the lowest level, between more autocratic forms of government and more rapid economic growth, still persists at this level, neither the precise form of the political system nor the leadership's attitude toward development appears to be an important systematic determinant of economic performance for these countries.

VII

THE SHORT-RUN ANALYSIS:
COUNTRIES AT A "HIGH"
LEVEL OF SOCIOECONOMIC
DEVELOPMENT

In Chapters V and VI we examined the patterns of social, political, and economic change which characterize the lowest and intermediate groups of underdeveloped countries. We found that the relative importance of subsets of economic and noneconomic variables in "explaining" short-run dynamic economic performance changes systematically as countries move from lower to higher levels of development. We now shift the focus of our interest to the highest group of underdeveloped countries in order to investigate further the interaction of the various social, political, and economic influences that govern the progress of a typical country moving toward economic maturity.

TYPOLOGY OF COUNTRIES AT A "HIGH" LEVEL OF DEVELOPMENT

The twenty-five nations at the highest of the three levels of socioeconomic development included in our study comprise the most advanced countries of the underdeveloped regions of the world. The majority of them, unlike most of those at lower levels of development, have had a century or more of independent nationhood and are well ahead of most low-income societies in social achievements, industrialization, and the development of economic and political institutions. Yet their transition to maturity is far from complete. The robust ideological and aspirational influences produced by urbanization and industrialization still contend seriously with traditional socioeconomic patterns of thought and action. The drive of leaderships toward modernity is strong and effective in many of the countries in this group, although in others the leaders fail to act as effective catalytic agents in the development process. Finally, a dominant characteristic of this highest group of underdeveloped countries is the presence of strong forces of economic and political change.

An intricate and complex variety of culture, socioeconomic structure,

231

and political systems characterizes this sample of countries, as it did the intermediate sample, although the predominance of Latin American polities gives some regional focus to its makeup.[1] At the lower end of the spectrum are a number of countries (El Salvador, Peru, Colombia, the United Arab Republic) that show significant lags in selected, though varying, aspects of their social and economic development. At the higher end of the spectrum are several countries (Argentina, Israel, Japan, Uruguay) that rank at the top of our full sample with respect to most indicators of socioeconomic and political structure.[2] Sixteen Latin American nations are included in the sample: Argentina, Brazil, Chile, Colombia, Costa Rica, Dominican Republic, El Salvador, Jamaica, Mexico, Nicaragua, Panama, Paraguay, Peru, Trinidad, Uruguay, and Venezuela. The sample also includes the six Mediterranean countries of Greece, Turkey, Cyprus, Lebanon, Israel, the United Arab Republic, and three Far Eastern countries (Japan, South Korea, and Taiwan).

Broadly speaking, the contrast between the highest and intermediate samples in average levels of social and economic achievement is even more marked than the contrast between the intermediate and low groups of countries. It will be recalled that the typical country in the intermediate group still has about 50 per cent of its population largely outside the market sector and suffers from considerable lack of economic and social integration. In contrast, the representative country in the highest group has the overwhelming majority of its population significantly involved in the market economy; marked dichotomies in the socioeconomic sphere have for the most part disappeared and the cultural and national integration of the population has proceeded quite far.

Social development in most countries in the highest group has affected the great majority of the population. The transformation of basic social organization has generally proceeded to the point where the immediate family and close relations form the primary kinship unit rather than the extended family or clan. Under the impact of urbanization and westernization the spiritual ties of the village and the hegemony of the

---

[1] However, the criteria used in dividing the full sample into groups representing different levels of socioeconomic development have resulted in the exclusion from the "high" group of most Latin American countries having large Indian sectors.

[2] It will be recalled that the choice of underdeveloped countries for the full sample was based on their status with respect to social and economic structure and development as of 1950. Some countries that are included, such as Israel, Japan, and possibly Venezuela, have progressed sufficiently since that date to be dropped from the current list of underdeveloped nations.

traditional agrarian land-owning elite have been weakened or destroyed. In almost all countries at this level, an expanding literate urban middle class composed of businessmen, industrialists, specialized bureaucrats, and their salaried employees has become an important element in the society, involving more than 20 per cent of the active male population in almost half of the countries. Since literacy rates, on the average, approach 65 per cent and school enrollment ratios are close to 50 per cent, the barriers to social mobility due to illiteracy and ignorance have been much reduced. Marked social stratification, often based on racial or religious differences, persists, but prohibitive sociocultural impediments are now uncommon.

In all the countries in the highest group, urbanization, with its concomitants of rising aspirations, greater mobility, and increased communication, has produced significant changes in national life. On the average, about 30 per cent of the population resides in urban aggregations of over 20,000 people. The outlook of these urban dwellers toward commercial activity, sophisticated consumer goods, and Western standards of living is significantly modernized. Interest in Western products and ideas has also spread far into the countryside where some support for programs of economic and political modernization is also found. The spread of ideas and aspirations from the cities into rural areas has been promoted through the contacts that newly migrated urban workers keep with their rural homes and through the extensive reach of modern mass communication media. Radios in use typically number about 90 per 1,000 and newspapers in circulation about 80 per 1,000 population.

The rapid pace of urbanization, the inadequacy of urban work opportunities and services, and, in some countries, the persistence of religious and ethnic differences have produced a certain degree of social unrest; on the whole, however, overt social tensions from cultural and ethnic cleavages as well as from other sources tend to be considerably less important than among countries at lower levels of development.

Not only has the average country in the highest sample progressed relatively far with respect to social development, but the typical pattern of social advance is relatively balanced compared with the marked unevenness in social progress characteristic of the intermediate level of development. This is evidenced by individual country scores on social indicators and by the correlations between social indices. Only a handful of countries in the sample have marked variations in scores for the social indicators. Furthermore, as mentioned earlier, for countries at the present level of development there are 32 significant[3] correlations between pairs of social variables as compared with only 5 at the intermediate level. Thus, the countries at the highest of our three levels of socioeconomic development have attained, on the average, a new and higher level of equilibrium in social structure which differentiates them from the typical country in the intermediate group where the level of social development is still rather low and the pace of advance uneven.

The contrast between the intermediate and "high" samples in average degree of social development is paralleled by an equally striking contrast in the typical extent of development of economic structure and institutions. The typical country in the highest group has built up an industrial complex that produces a significant range of products for the domestic market. The use of modern equipment and techniques of production has also become considerably more common, although not yet widespread, in both the industrial and agricultural sectors. In addition, inadequacies in physical overhead capital no longer constitute a serious bottleneck to development in most countries in the sample. The economic institutions of these countries are also fairly advanced. Financial systems are, on the average, able to attract a significant, though of course still small, volume of indigenous private savings and to provide at least some medium- and long-term credit to both industry and agriculture. Tax systems are also more effective with governments generally able to raise revenues comprising at least 15 per cent of the GNP and to raise 10–20 per cent of these in the form of direct income taxes. Serious difficulties in the collection of taxes are usually limited to the collection of income and related taxes.

The political institutions of the countries in the highest group are, on the whole, considerably more effective, articulate, democratic, and stable than those of countries at lower levels of development. In the majority of countries in the group, two or more political parties with a predominantly ideological or personalistic orientation have been operating in recent years. Some of these countries have quite broadly based, relatively impersonal political institutions in which political parties effectively articulate the economic and ideological interests of the populace. In other high-level countries there is a tendency for political parties having reasonably meaningful programs to replace those having a purely personalistic orientation. This trend has been strengthened by

---

[3] At the 1 per cent level.

the growth of the middle classes and by the rising influence of labor movements seeking political expression of their interests. It should be noted, nevertheless, that the grass roots impact of these party systems is still fairly restricted by Western standards, and considerable centralization of political power persists even where several political parties operate. Furthermore, in addition to countries with some form of representative political system, the sample includes both a number of polities with low scores on most indices of the extent of democracy and some in which the exercise of freedom of political opposition has been only intermittent.

The political systems of the countries in this group are in general fairly stable and their government bureaucracies are at least moderately effective. While close to half of them have experienced either a military coup or some other form of abrupt change in government since 1950, these events have not usually been accompanied by much domestic violence and have often been followed by significant periods of relative stability.

The government typical of the countries in this sample has an administrative bureaucracy based on some form of permanent civil service and government leaders have a definite, though not necessarily effective, commitment to promoting economic development. The specific nature of governmental leadership varies tremendously from country to country. The military, for example, has played an influential political role in recent years in about half the countries of the sample, while it has had relatively little influence in the remaining countries. Similarly, the sample is divided fairly evenly between countries characterized by extensive direct government activity in the economic realm and countries characterized by a limited direct role of the government in economic activity. The picture with respect to leadership commitment to economic development is also quite varied: about one-third of the countries in the sample have reasonably effective leadership commitment to economic development; somewhat less than one-third have governments whose measures to promote economic development tend to be ineffectual; and the remaining countries have little or no formal government commitment to development.

Thus, in the social, economic, and political realms the countries at the highest of our three levels of development are, on the whole, significantly more advanced than countries at lower levels of development. The expansion of the market economy, urbanization, and sociocultural integration and the spread of modern ideas and means of communication have proceeded to the point where no segment of their populations remains untouched. The growth of political institutions in the majority of these countries has been characterized by significantly greater articulation of special interests and ideologies as well as by wider popular participation than was typical of countries in the lower-level samples. Finally, the degree of industrialization and the extent of development of economic institutions have progressed considerably beyond the levels that prevail among countries at the two lower levels of socioeconomic development. Partially as a result, social tensions have abated and political stability has increased.

The pace of change characteristic of the countries in the highest group, particularly in the economic area, is striking. It will be remembered that countries at the intermediate level of development were typically undergoing extensive, albeit unbalanced, social transformations together with a rapid growth of the market sector. At the present higher level of development, the pace of changes in social structure appears to have slowed down. By contrast, however, the pace of industrialization and progress in building economic institutions has generally increased. The great majority of highest-level countries has experienced significant or at least moderate improvement in all aspects of economic structure and institutions since 1950. Indeed, in only one of them have real annual rates of change in income originating in the industrial sector averaged less than 3 per cent during the past decade. An overwhelming proportion of them have experienced considerable expansion in the use of modern industrial and agricultural technology. Tax systems and financial institutions have also improved noticeably in a majority of the "high"-level countries. In addition, both the stock of physical overhead capital and the human resource base have increased significantly or, at the very least, moderately in the great preponderance of countries in the sample. Finally, the higher level of economic dynamism among these countries is emphasized by the fact that the majority of them have gross investment rates of more than 16 per cent. These transformations in economic structure and institutions are reflected in the higher rates of growth of per capita GNP typical of the countries in this group. Seventeen of the twenty-five countries averaged rates of increase in income per capita of more than 2 per cent during the period 1950/51–1963/64; half of these approached or exceeded per capita growth rates of 3 per cent per annum.

236

In summary, our typology of underdeveloped nations at the highest level of socioeconomic development suggests several dominant characteristics of the representative "high"-level country which differentiate it significantly from typical countries at lower levels of development. First of all, average achievements in both social and economic realms mark a substantial advance over the average intermediate-level country. Second, the pattern of social progress is characterized by considerable balance among the various aspects of social structure, in contrast to the unevenness of social development typical of lower-level countries. In the third place, it is only in the highest group of underdeveloped countries that we find a tendency toward more democratic, more stable, and relatively more integrated polities. Fourth, the present group of countries is marked by a clear preponderance of societies characterized by rapid transformations of all aspects of economic structure and institutions. Finally, the growth of markets and associated social changes are no longer the focal points of development; rather, the more sophisticated economic and political transformations characteristic of urban industrialized societies prevail.

THE STATISTICAL RESULTS

The results of our investigation of the forces conditioning short-run economic performance for the group of underdeveloped countries at the upper end of the scale of socioeconomic development are perhaps the most interesting of all. It will be recalled that in the results for the lowest income group the social variables were overwhelmingly important in "explaining" growth rates, and the effectiveness of changes in political and economic institutions in improving economic performance was severely limited by the inhibiting nature of the social environment. The analysis of performance in countries of the intermediate group indicated that the social bottlenecks to development were significantly less important than those among countries at the lowest level and that the influence of purely economic forces on the growth process was considerably greater. For the highest of the three groups, we find that social forces no longer constitute a systematic controlling influence, while economic improvements and the strength of fiscal and financial institutions have an almost overriding effect on economic development. The extent to which economic change can take place is significantly conditioned, however, by a single political characteristic, the extent of leadership commitment to economic development. Other political influences, such

237

as the strength of democratic institutions and the role of the military, are relatively unimportant in explaining variations in short-run growth rates. It is rather the absence of national mobilization for development which in general constitutes the prime political obstacle to development.

The Social Forces

Before discussing in greater depth the political and economic aspects of the growth process in countries of the "high" group, we turn to the evidence that social bottlenecks are no longer significant at this level of development. As we discussed in the previous chapter, the intermediate group of countries was characterized by marked imbalance within individual countries in the rate of social development. In addition, correlations within the group among various indices of social development were in general rather low, and the dominant bottleneck tended to vary from country to country. Consequently, the finding for the intermediate group that a particular social index was not significantly associated with economic performance could be interpreted as a reflection of either true unimportance or poor correlation. By contrast, the level of social development within countries in the "high" group is considerably more even, and individual countries tend to rank consistently high or low with respect to most indices of social progress. Since social variables within this group are thus strongly intercorrelated, any systematic social bottlenecks to growth would be revealed in the factor analyses in the form of statistically significant associations between social indices and economic performance. Since the relationships between social development and rates of economic growth are in fact not statistically significant in the results for the present group, we conclude that sociostructural bottlenecks to growth are indeed genuinely unimportant at this level of development.

The negligible influence of social structure upon variations in economic performance within this group of nations is evident from the factor analyses presented in Tables VII–1 through VII–4. Not only are the social structural forces dominated by a combination of political and economic properties of the economy (Table VII–1), but they are overwhelmed in the sociopolitical results (Table VII–2) by a single political influence and in the socioeconomic results (Table VII–4) by economic characteristics alone.[4]

[4] Table VII–3 presents a factor analysis of economic attributes only.

238

TABLE VII-1: Rotated Factor Matrix for Change in Per Capita GNP (1950/51–1963/64) Together with Thirty-six Political, Social, and Economic Variables ᵃ (High Sample)

Political, Social, and Economic Indicators	Rotated Factor Loadings				h_i^2 (R^2)
	F_1	F_2	F_3	F_4	
Rate of Growth of Real Per Capita GNP: 1950/51–1963/64	-.15	.88	.03	.04	.791
Size of Traditional Agricultural Sector	.86	.09	-.12	-.21	.812
Extent of Dualism	-.90	.04	.11	-.18	.857
Importance of the Indigenous Middle Class	-.80	.20	.22	-.01	.732
Extent of Social Mobility	-.70	.27	.27	.23	.689
Extent of Literacy	-.62	-.16	.06	.35	.528
Extent of Mass Communication	-.72	.03	-.23	.33	.681
Degree of Modernization of Outlook	-.68	.20	.47	.09	.738
Crude Fertility Rate	.82	.13	.02	.03	.692
Strength of Democratic Institutions	-.76	-.01	.13	.47	.820
Strength of the Labor Movement	-.70	.01	.22	.55	.837
Political Strength of the Military	.67	-.09	-.07	-.36	.587
Political Strength of the Traditional Elite	.51	-.35	-.30	.27	.543
Degree of Administrative Efficiency	-.59	.44	.53	.18	.843
Level of Modernization of Techniques in Agriculture	-.84	.27	.10	.04	.781
Character of Agricultural Organization	-.53	.40	.48	.17	.698
Level of Modernization of Industry	-.61	.36	.26	.35	.687
Level of Adequacy of Physical Overhead Capital	-.83	.23	.12	.11	.770
Rate of Improvement in Human Resources	-.59	.19	.08	-.07	.399
Extent of Leadership Commitment to Economic Development	-.31	.66	.34	.17	.672
Gross Investment Rate	-.43	.59	.03	.35	.661

TABLE VII-1 (Continued)

Political, Social, and Economic Indicators	Rotated Factor Loadings				h_i^2 (R^2)
	F_1	F_2	F_3	F_4	
Level of Effectiveness of the Tax System..............	-.46	**.60**	-.15	.20	.625
Level of Effectiveness of Financial Institutions.........	-.56	**.59**	.21	.36	.835
Degree of Improvement in Agricultural Productivity since 1950.	.06	**.75**	.25	.14	.643
Change in Degree of Industrialization since 1950......	.21	**.70**	.27	.00	.604
Degree of Improvement in the Tax System since 1950.....	-.12	**.64**	-.30	-.23	.562
Degree of Improvement in Financial Institutions since 1950.	-.03	**.81**	-.16	-.16	.717
Degree of National Integration and Sense of National Unity.	-.26	.09	**.74**	.01	.632
Degree of Cultural and Ethnic Homogeneity............	-.07	-.33	**.54**	-.33	.512
Degree of Social Tension............................	-.01	.00	**.83**	.01	.696
Extent of Political Stability........................	-.31	.22	**.71**	.11	.659
Degree of Freedom of Political Opposition and Press....	-.59	.03	-.29	**.68**	.885
Predominant Basis of the Political Party System.......	-.21	.40	.25	**.67**	.709
Degree of Competitiveness of Political Parties........	-.17	.13	-.41	**.56**	.528
Extent of Centralization of Political Power...........	.65	-.08	.03	**-.67**	.881
Character of Basic Social Organization...............	-.27	-.34	.05	**.70**	.672
Abundance of Natural Resources......................	.18	.07	.04	**.70**	.533

[a] Bold figures indicate the factor to which each variable is assigned. Variables omitted because of insignificant correlations: structure of foreign trade and improvement in physical overhead capital since 1950. Variable omitted because of low high loading: extent of urbanization. Percentage of over-all variance explained by factors: 68.9. Percentage of variance explained by last factor included: 6.7.

TABLE VII-2: Rotated Factor Matrix for Change in Per Capita GNP (1950/51–1963/64) Together with Twenty-three Political and Social Variables [a] (High Sample)

Political and Social Indicators	Rotated Factor Loadings				h_i^2 (R^2)
	F_1	F_2	F_3	F_4	
Rate of Growth of Real Per Capita GNP: 1950/51–1963/64	.05	−.06	**.77**	−.05	.607
Size of the Traditional Agricultural Sector	**−.90**	−.07	−.15	.12	.860
Extent of Dualism	**.77**	.17	.01	−.33	.731
Character of Basic Social Organization	**.63**	−.11	.13	.29	.515
Importance of the Indigenous Middle Class	**.59**	−.04	.15	−.54	.665
Extent of Social Mobility	**.56**	−.32	.14	−.54	.721
Extent of Literacy	**.66**	−.28	−.24	−.25	.634
Extent of Mass Communication	**.69**	−.44	−.08	−.12	.691
Degree of Modernization of Outlook	**.60**	.16	.40	−.46	.761
Crude Fertility Rate	**−.82**	−.09	.12	.22	.735
Strength of Democratic Institutions	**.85**	−.24	.23	−.17	.869
Degree of Freedom of Political Opposition and Press	**.73**	−.57	.13	.13	.897
Strength of the Labor Movement	**.77**	−.18	.35	−.15	.768
Extent of Centralization of Political Power	**−.77**	.42	−.30	.03	.865
Political Strength of the Military	**−.69**	.22	−.28	.14	.621
Predominant Basis of the Political Party System	.18	**.71**	.29	−.44	.813
Degree of Competitiveness of Political Parties	.17	**.84**	−.05	.12	.750
Extent of Leadership Commitment to Economic Development	.17	.02	**.81**	−.35	.812
Degree of National Integration and Sense of National Unity	.06	.00	.11	**.89**	.814
Degree of Cultural and Ethnic Homogeneity	−.03	.26	−.54	**.64**	.772
Extent of Urbanization	.16	−.24	.14	**.70**	.602
Degree of Social Tension	−.03	−.40	−.17	**.53**	.473
Extent of Political Stability	.30	.29	.49	**.50**	.655
Degree of Administrative Efficiency	.41	−.11	.52	**.65**	.873

[a] Bold figures indicate the factor to which each variable is assigned. Variables omitted because of insignificant correlations: none. Variable omitted because of low high loading: political strength of the traditional elite. Percentage of over-all variance explained by factors: 72.9. Percentage of variance explained by last factor included: 7.1.

TABLE VII–3: Rotated Factor Matrix for Change in Per Capita GNP (1950/51-1963/64) Together with Fourteen Economic Variables [a] (High Sample)

Economic Indicators	Rotated Factor Loadings		h_i^2
	F_1	F_2	(R^2)
Rate of Growth in Real Per Capita GNP: 1950/51–1963/64.	−.27	.88	.851
Size of the Traditional Agricultural Sector	**.90**	.19	.842
Extent of Dualism	**−.86**	−.05	.734
Character of Agricultural Organization	**−.68**	.35	.584
Gross Investment Rate	**−.59**	.54	.645
Level of Modernization of Techniques in Agriculture	**−.92**	.14	.870
Level of Modernization of Industry	**−.75**	.26	.627
Level of Effectiveness of Financial Institutions	**−.71**	.52	.780
Level of Adequacy of Physical Overhead Capital	**−.91**	.09	.841
Rate of Improvement in Human Resources	**−.56**	.12	.329
Degree of Improvement in Agricultural Productivity since 1950	−.09	**.80**	.642
Change in Degree of Industrialization since 1950	.06	**.76**	.577
Degree of Improvement in the Tax System since 1950	−.07	**.55**	.310
Degree of Improvement in Financial Institutions since 1950	−.06	**.83**	.691
Level of Effectiveness of the Tax System	−.48	**.53**	.507

[a] Bold figures indicate the factor to which each variable has been assigned. Variables omitted because of insignificant correlations: degree of improvement in physical overhead capital since 1950, structure of foreign trade, and abundance of natural resources. Variables omitted because of low high loadings: none. Percentage of over-all variance explained by factors: 65.5. Percentage of variance explained by last factor included: 19.5.

The significance of these results can readily be seen from their relevance to a problem that has perplexed social scientists dealing with economic development in general and with the development of countries at the present level of development in particular. The dilemma is well expressed in the 1961 report of the United Nations Expert Working Group on Social Aspects of Economic Development in Latin America:

In considering the processes of economic and social development, the working group agreed that, within the framework of the task entrusted to it, an important distinction should be made between various types of 'social aspects' of economic development.

On the one hand, economic development almost inevitably brings certain social changes. Where these changes are uneven—a matter to be deplored— an insufficiently rapid economic tempo or a serious lack of uniformity in the economic development process itself may be responsible. A shift of emphasis in the economic programme might then produce the desired social changes.

TABLE VII–4: Rotated Factor Matrix for Change in Per Capita GNP (1950/51–1963/64) Together with Twenty-four Social and Economic Variables [a] (High Sample)

Social and Economic Indicators	Rotated Factor Loadings			h_i^2
	F_1	F_2	F_3	(R^2)
Rate of Growth in Real Per Capita GNP: 1950/51–1963/64	−.21	.90	.19	.886
Size of the Traditional Agricultural Sector	.91	.12	−.10	.844
Extent of Dualism	−.82	.01	−.17	.708
Importance of the Indigenous Middle Class	−.79	.15	−.35	.774
Extent of Social Mobility	−.74	.22	−.32	.699
Extent of Literacy	−.65	−.21	−.13	.485
Extent of Mass Communication	−.70	−.01	−.07	.493
Degree of Modernization of Outlook	−.77	.18	−.19	.660
Crude Fertility Rate	.78	.16	.15	.655
Level of Modernization of Techniques in Agriculture	−.88	.24	.00	.828
Character of Agricultural Organization	−.66	.40	−.05	.593
Level of Modernization of Industry	−.73	.30	−.16	.645
Level of Effectiveness of Financial Institutions	−.69	.58	−.02	.816
Level of Adequacy of Physical Overhead Capital	−.85	.20	−.06	.763
Gross Investment Rate	−.57	.58	.14	.682
Degree of Improvement in Agricultural Productivity since 1950	−.04	.78	−.01	.607
Change in Degree of Industrialization since 1950	.13	.71	−.30	.619
Degree of Improvement in Financial Institutions since 1950	−.01	.82	.11	.690
Degree of Improvement in the Tax System since 1950	.00	.60	−.15	.388
Level of Effectiveness of the Tax System	−.45	.54	−.23	.537
Degree of National Integration and Sense of National Unity	−.30	.06	−.74	.641
Degree of Cultural and Ethnic Homogeneity	.03	−.32	−.73	.633
Character of Basic Social Organization	−.51	−.32	.51	.626
Extent of Urbanization	−.38	.23	−.63	.602
Rate of Improvement in Human Resources	−.50	.12	−.59	.612

[a] Bold figures indicate the factor to which each variable is assigned. Variables omitted because of insignificant correlations: structure of foreign trade, abundance of natural resources, degree of improvement in physical overhead capital since 1950, and degree of social tension. Variables omitted because of low high loadings: none. Percentage of over-all variance explained by factors: 65.9. Percentage of variance explained by last factor included: 9.3.

On the other hand, economic development might be hampered by obstacles of a social or socio-psychological nature. If so, the economist would in a sense be helpless unless social scientists developed techniques to diagnose, overcome or circumvent such social obstacles.

Lack of detailed information prevented a definite conclusion from being reached as to the relative importance of the two types of "social aspects of economic development."[5]

The present factor analyses suggest strongly that the second of these views—that social obstacles are important in accounting for poor economic performance—is not valid for countries at the present level of development unless social obstacles are interpreted to refer to the absence or weakness of sociopsychological motivations favorable to development. The application of the sociostructural view of economic stagnation to these countries is clearly inappropriate. Indeed, contrary to the position of those who emphasize the need for social reform as a prerequisite for the economic growth of countries at the present level, our results suggest that for this group of countries most of the sociostructural requirements for economic development are already present. It should be stressed, of course, that while social reforms thus do not appear to constitute a *sine qua non* for the acceleration of the economic growth of these countries, further improvements in social conditions may nevertheless be desirable from a welfare or humanitarian point of view.

The unimportance of social structure in explaining growth performance in the high-level countries by no means implies that the motivational aspects of social conduct are insignificant. After all, such economic characteristics as the patterns of investment and savings, the capacity to improve tax collections, and the technical dynamism of the economy reflect the entire range of forces in the culture and are, therefore, strongly conditioned by prevailing social motivations and attitudes. However, the sociopsychological forces are probably reflected indirectly in our results through the indicators of economic performance rather than through the sociostructural ones.[6] The societies in the present group are in general sufficiently integrated, literate, urbanized, and educated and the potentially dynamic strata of the population are sufficiently large so that these aspects of social development no longer constitute significant barriers to the creation of cultural attitudes favorable

[5] Egbert De Vries and J. M. Echavarría (eds.), *Social Aspects of Economic Development in Latin America* (Paris: UNESCO, 1963), I, 386–87.

[6] The motivational aspects of social behavior do not appear explicitly in our model except insofar as they are reflected in our indicator of modernization of outlook. In particular, we have not been able to construct even moderately reliable measures of those sociopsychological attributes that one would expect a priori to influence economic performance significantly: for example, the extent of achievement motivation and the strength of social approval of business activity.

to economic dynamism. Therefore, the sociostructural bottlenecks to growth are no longer important, either in and of themselves or as determinants of the national economic psychology.

Political Forces

At the "high" level of socioeconomic development, differences among countries in the character of the political party system and in the strength of national participant political institutions are not significantly associated with variations in national capacity to mobilize resources for economic growth. Indeed, in no instance does any factor incorporating these characteristics account for more than 3 per cent of intercountry differences in short-run rates of economic growth.[7] This result differs somewhat from the finding for countries at lower levels of development of a weak tendency for more autocratic, more centralized forms of government to associate with faster short-run economic performance. At the present level of development, economic modernization appears to be compatible with a wide variety of political systems ranging from participant democracy to pure dictatorship. In other words, it is clear that in countries in the "high" group, no particular type of political system is necessary for effective short-run economic growth.

By contrast with the unimportance to economic growth of the nature of the political system, the type of political leadership emerges in the results of the factor analyses for this group of countries as a significant force in short-run economic performance. For nations at the "high" level of development, the political variable that is influential in the short run describes the extent of leadership commitment to economic development and thus reflects the ability of the government to mobilize effectively the resources of the country for economic modernization.

While this result is perhaps to be expected, what is surprising is the large percentage of intercountry differences in rates of economic growth explained by this political variable and the significant correlation be-

---

[7] It is a peculiarity of the combined results that the abundance of natural resources is included in the factor describing characteristics of political systems (Factor IV of Table VII–1). This is because the only significant correlation of the abundance of natural resources with other indices is that with the predominant basis of the political party system (0.48). It is intuitively clear that this is a chance association to which no substantive importance should be given. The indicator of the abundance of natural resources is omitted from both the economic and socioeconomic analyses on the basis of low correlations.

tween the latter and those economic indices that appear in the dominant explanatory factor whenever economic quantities are included.

When only social and political variables are used in the analysis, the extent of mobilization of national efforts for economic growth is represented by a single factor (Factor III in Table VII–2) composed of only the indicator of leadership commitment to economic development. This factor alone accounts for close to 60 per cent of cross-country differences in growth rates.

It would appear that this political factor is to an important extent a proxy for the economic measures taken to improve economic performance, a thought that is suggested by an examination of the results of the purely economic factor analysis of Table VII–3 and the combined factor analysis of Table VII–1. When the economic, social, and political variables are included, the leadership commitment variable merges with the indices of change in the economic realm to form a single factor; furthermore, the over-all percentage explanation attributable to the combined economic and political factor (Factor II, Table VII–1) is the same as that attributable to its purely economic equivalent (Factor II, Table VII–3). This degree of explanation (77 per cent) is considerably larger than when only political characteristics are included.

In view of the importance of a single political variable representing the intensity of leadership commitment to economic development, it is useful at this point to review the underlying basis for the classification of countries with respect to this characteristic. The definition of the variable is based on judgments regarding the extent of concerted efforts to promote economic growth made by the leaders of national official and semiofficial agencies involved in the central guidance of the economy, for example, ministries of finance, planning agencies, and publicly or privately owned central banks. Important elements in the classification are the scope of purposive attempts by these leaders to alter institutional arrangements which clearly block development goals, as well as the existence of an over-all national plan with mechanisms for its execution. In scoring individual countries an effort was made to avoid confusion between verbal commitments to development and actual efforts to achieve growth. An attempt was also made to avoid, insofar as possible, the artificially high correlation between leadership commitment and growth rates which results if a purely economic indicator of national growth performance is used as a yardstick of leadership commitment. That this latter goal was achieved, at least in part, is evident

246

from the fact that we did not find a strong association between leadership commitment to development and rates of economic growth at the lower levels of socioeconomic development, and that the simple correlation between the leadership indicator and the rate of growth of per capita income for the "high" group of countries was only 0.59.

Since the observed relationship between the leadership commitment and growth rates thus seems real rather than an effect induced by our method of classification, it might be worthwhile to explore this phenomenon further. Some of the interesting questions are: Why is the relationship significant for countries at the present level of development? Why is it not evident at a lower level? Should governments be encouraged to exercise leadership in the economic sphere?

Let us begin with the first two questions. Basically, it would appear that before political change can have a significant impact in promoting economic growth or economic forces can induce political transformations, mechanisms for transferring change originating in either the economic or the political sphere must exist; and for several reasons these mechanisms require a minimum level of socioeconomic development. First of all, until countries reach a stage at which socioeconomic bottlenecks to economic growth become relatively unimportant, it is not possible, in the short run, for a change in the orientation of political leadership to translate itself effectively into a process of economic growth. Secondly, certain levels of literacy, mass communication, and urbanization must be attained before political mechanisms for the articulation and aggregation of economic interests can develop sufficiently to alter the political climate to one that is more conducive to economic development. Thirdly, while aspirations for improvements in material welfare exist at earlier stages of development, the body of modernizing agents, private or governmental, is too small to enable these aspirations in the short run to penetrate the existing economic and social barriers to sustained growth. Only when the major socioeconomic bottlenecks have been overcome, as in the "high" group, do we find a body of private or public decision-makers which is sufficiently large and sufficiently powerful relative to the strength of the socioeconomic barriers to enable a motivated drive for development to stimulate more or less simultaneous economic and political change. Finally, before an economy reaches a certain level of market-oriented specialization and interdependence, it is social forces rather than changes in the national political framework which are the key influences inhibiting the necessary expansion of market organization and attitudes.

In principle, the balance evident in the "high" group between political inclinations toward economic progress and an economic climate conducive to growth can be brought about by either political pressures or economic influences. However, we believe that the typical process is one of mutual adaptation in which neither political nor economic change can far outpace the other. If economic growth begins as a result of some exogenous economic impetus such as favorable export markets or the influx of foreign aid, the process tends to generate the political changes necessary to sustain cumulative growth, or else the pace of economic development tends to be slowed down eventually by the recalcitrant nature of the political environment. Similarly, if an abrupt change in the government favorable to economic development does not succeed in inducing sufficient growth, this political failure tends to result either in making the innovating regime more conservative or in the replacement of the regime with another more traditionalist government. Countries in this group offer many concrete instances of both processes.

Viewed broadly, our results for countries at the "high" level of development do not provide support for the views held by advocates of complete government laissez-faire or for the views of those who recommend a major, direct government role in economic activity.[8] Rather, they tend to support those writers who emphasize the importance of the motivational and leadership aspects of government. What appears to be necessary at this stage of development, regardless of the relative size of the government and the private sectors, is the effectiveness of government initiative in over-all economic planning and coordination and in the reform of economic institutions.

The economic case for government leadership in promoting economic development rests partly on the failure of the market mechanism to induce sufficiently rapid structural change and partly on the related need for a "big push." The big push is essential, not only to overcome the effects of the Malthusian trap, but also to take advantage of the external economies associated with simultaneous complementary investments. A minimum critical effort is also required in order to reap the benefits of

[8] The simple correlation between short-term rates of economic growth and an indicator of the extent of *direct* government economic activity which did not meet our rather rigorous standards for inclusion in the analysis (see Chapter II) was not significant (-0.19).

the economies of scale associated with modern efficient capital-intensive technology. It seems unlikely that either of these advantages can be successfully obtained without concerted government intervention to allocate more or less optimally the sectoral pattern of investment and to improve the financial position of the nation. Similarly, financial improvements, whether in the form of increasing foreign borrowing or reforming the tax collection system or strengthening financial mechanisms for extending credit to private investors, require government initiative.

The political case for government intervention is based on the need for strong government measures in order to implement certain structural reforms of a political nature which would not come about spontaneously. For example, curtailment of the economic power of the landowners is a structural political reform that is often necessary to achieve appropriate economic technological dynamism in response to market incentives. Then too, public measures to control inflation may be necessary to avoid the distortions in the pattern of investment which characteristically accompany rapidly rising prices. Moreover, changes in governmental bureaucratic and administrative practices, particularly with respect to tax collection and the control of foreign trade, are frequently desirable conditions for the pursuit of development goals.[9]

The sociopsychological case for active government leadership in countries at this stage of development rests mainly upon the crucial importance of the motivational aspects of economic growth. Effective government direction may be significant in mobilizing the national drive to develop. This key role of national psychological commitment in countries of this group has been stressed by many observers. Thus, Rosenstein-Rodan has argued that in addition to the economic indivisibilities which necessitate a "big push" for the initiation of development, there exists a parallel psychological indivisibility with respect to the development drive which requires development efforts on a wide front to create an "atmosphere" conducive to sustained growth.[10]

---

[9] We do not believe a point that has frequently been made in arguing for an active role of government to be valid: that the relative scarcity of private entrepreneurship calls for the substitution of public for private decision-makers for the direction of the development effort. We do not believe this argument to be valid because a shortage of private entrepreneurs would seem to imply a corresponding shortage of high caliber decision-makers in public life.

[10] Rosenstein-Rodan, "Notes on the Theory of the 'Big Push,'" p. 66.

249

One can argue, of course, that the prime requirement for effective private sector performance in these countries is not an active government development drive but rather public measures designed to establish a stable and permissive political environment. The reasoning goes that the conditions which permit effective economic leadership by government are to some extent the very ones that favor economic activity in the private sector. The crucial political forces, in this view, are the lessening of direct political hostility toward domestic entrepreneurial groups and foreign investment and the reduction of continued political instability and government irresponsibility in the economic field rather than the government economic policies that these political improvements make more effective. That a permissive political environment is in general not all that is necessary for growth, however, is suggested by the significant correlation we find for countries at this level between the rate of transformation of economic institutions and structure and the extent to which political leadership is concerned with the implementation of measures for economic development. This correlation can be explained most easily by the hypothesis that an actively affirmative government role, as opposed to mere passive permissiveness, can hasten and smooth the transition of the economy from stagnation to maturity.

One further thought concerning political forces at the "high" level of development relates to the implications of the factor analyses for various approaches to the nature of political development and the interaction between political and economic development. One approach to political development defines it as the process of increasing the strength of national participant political institutions,[11] a definition that associates the notion of political development with an increase in public participation in the process of governmental decision-making. An alternative approach is to define political development as the increasing capacity of the government to organize the nation for the pursuit of the goals chosen by the leadership.[12] While these two definitions are sometimes combined, it is clear from our factor analysis, as well as from casual observation, that they are essentially unrelated. Since our results show a significant correlation between short-run economic growth and leadership effectiveness rather than between short-run growth and participant institutions, it would appear that, if a causal role is to be attached

[11] See, for example, Lerner, *The Passing of Traditional Society,* Chapter 2.
[12] See, for instance, Organski, *The Stages of Political Development,* Chapter 1.

to "political development," the term must be understood in the second sense.

The first definition of political development is not, of course, totally irrelevant. In the long-run factor analysis for the nations at the "high" level of development, a relationship between growth and political participation does indeed appear, as will be discussed below. This suggests that political development in the sense of more participant political mechanisms is a by-product of social and economic development and therefore that the definition of political development as the increasing strength of national participant political institutions is perfectly acceptable as a descriptive or derivative term.

The Economic Variables

The nature of the governmental policies conducive to the creation of a climate favorable to economic growth can be further appreciated through an examination of Table VII–3. The overwhelmingly important economic factor, accounting for 77 per cent of cross-country variations in per capita growth rates, includes all of our indicators of economic change within countries, plus the total investment rate. These indices summarize those aspects of the economy most often cited as constituting the necessary internal measures for more efficacious development performance: the degree of increased effectiveness of financial institutions, the extent of improvement in tax systems, the degree of improvement in agricultural productivity, and the change in the degree of industrialization. In addition, the size of the over-all investment effort has a significant positive loading in this factor. While the importance of these measures has been stressed by development economists for all stages of growth, our results indicate that it is at the "high" level that such improvements make a significant contribution to the increase in growth rates in the short run.

The need for steady increases in the ability of domestic financial institutions to attract savings and to provide loans for economic expansion outside the traditional areas of trade and urban commerce becomes particularly important in countries in which the major socio-structural bottlenecks to growth have been overcome. Since the direct economic tool for raising growth rates is an increase in the proportion of over-all resources devoted to investment, specialized institutions for savings and investment, which free individual sectors from constraints set by their respective savings capacities, obviously have an important role to play. At this level of development, as at the intermediate level, the effectiveness of financial institutions is influential not only in relieving constraints on savings and investment but also as a mechanism for achieving greater economic integration.

Fiscal reform is also important. The list of contributions that improvements in tax systems can make to the acceleration of the development process is quite impressive. Four of them stand out above the rest. First, taxation is a strong instrument for the control of the inflationary tendencies and balance-of-payments disequilibrium inherent in rapid development. Secondly, through taxes, command over resources can be transferred in a noninflationary manner from the private to the public sector. Thirdly, taxes constitute one of the major government instruments for creating the incentives necessary to induce desired reallocations of private investment. And finally, taxes offer a mechanism for the large-scale income redistribution that may be required at this level of development for widening the domestic market, as well as for the achievement of social equity goals. The importance of tax reform at this stage of development may be attributed in part to the fact that extensive programs for the modernization of fiscal systems cannot be carried out effectively before countries have reached a level of socioeconomic development at which their administrative capacity is reasonably advanced and their economy is significantly monetized. Furthermore, the revision of the tax structure takes on particular prominence in our analysis as an indirect indicator of the extent of government commitment to development, since it is the only economic measure included over which the government exercises exclusive control.

Our results for countries at this stage of development also accentuate the importance of simultaneous expansion of the industrial and agricultural sectors. We say "simultaneous" because both industrialization and improvements in agricultural productivity appear in the same dominant factor, which implies that, on the average, they are complements rather than substitutes for each other. While at the intermediate level, industrialization was the overwhelmingly important process, at this level the balanced growth of both industry and agriculture emerges as a crucial condition for successful economic growth.

The returns to investment in agriculture are particularly large for underdeveloped countries at the "high" stage of development. The critical role of agricultural technology arises from the fact that these countries can no longer rely solely upon import substitution and the expansion of exports of primary products as their main strategy for overcoming balance-of-payments problems and for industrialization. As underlined by the Secretariat of the Alliance for Progress, countries at this level rather "must simultaneously look inward to the modernization of agriculture not merely to . . . [supply] food for a rapidly expanding population but also as a source of industrial raw materials, diversified export commodities and as markets for the products of Latin American industry."[13]

An examination of our results on the role of investment at the "high" level of socioeconomic development indicates that in these countries the magnitude of the total resources devoted to investment is an important influence on short-run economic growth. However, the results also indicate that the allocation and efficient use of available investment funds have become fully as important as the size of the investment effort per se. This is suggested by the fact that in the "high" results the influence of the investment rate is diluted by such dynamic effects as the changes in financial and fiscal structures and the increases in agricultural productivity and industrialization.

It is interesting that certain often-cited impediments to the economic growth of the Latin American countries in this group are conspicuously absent from the list of important economic influences. Land reform, for example, does not appear as a prerequisite for increases in the rates of growth of economies at this level. This can be seen from the fact that our indicator of the extent of progress in land reform (the "character of agriculture") appears in the insignificant factor in the purely economic analysis. This finding may not be as surprising as it first appears since, from an economic point of view, it is the increase in agricultural productivity which is important. In the absence of concurrent measures to increase agricultural credit, improve marketing techniques, and expand irrigation and agricultural extension programs, one would not expect the correlation between land reform and short-run improvements in agricultural productivity to be very high.

Similarly, changes in the distribution of income, except insofar as they occur in response to fiscal reform, do not appear to constitute a

[13] Inter-American Economic and Social Council, Organization of American States, *The Alliance for Progress: Its Third Year 1963–1964,* third report on the progress of economic and social development in Latin America and prospects for the future (Washington, D.C.: Pan American Union, 1965), p. 5.

prerequisite for short-run economic growth at the "high" level of development. This conclusion follows, although not rigorously, from the fact that in the purely economic factor analysis a very high fraction of the total intercountry differences in economic growth rates (85 per cent) can be explained without direct reference to income redistribution.

One can also conclude that, on the average, improvements in physical overhead capital exercise little influence on economic growth at this level. The poor correlation for these countries between changes in physical overhead capital and our other indices of economic structure and performance[14] implies that their transport and power networks, while far below those of the developed countries in all respects, do not constitute major bottlenecks to either industrial expansion or over-all economic growth.

Finally, the structural characteristics of the foreign trade sector, in particular the degree of diversification of exports, are also inconsequential in determining the economy's short-run rate of growth. What is probably more significant than decreasing the economy's dependence on foreign trade is improving its ability to respond flexibly to shocks arising from the foreign sector and achieving equilibrium in its balance of payments. Our analysis suggests that greater diversification of exports plays only a minor role in this adaptation process in the short run since the correlations between our indicator of foreign trade structure and all the other indices of economic structure and performance are below the level of statistical significance.

Comparison of the Short-Run and Long-Run Analyses

When the long-run combined analysis for countries at the "high" level of development (Table VII–5) is compared with the corresponding short-run analysis (Table VII–1), several differences stand out. First of all, as was the case at the intermediate level, the weight accorded in the long-run analysis to the factor that includes measures of the level of socioeconomic development (Factor I, Table VII–5) is significantly greater than the weight accorded to the same factor in the corresponding short-run analysis.[15] The major weight in the short-run

[14] It will be recalled that the indicator of degree of improvement in physical overhead capital was omitted from the factor analyses for the "high" group because of insignificant correlations.

[15] Some of this weight, however, is probably due to the fact that measures of the extent of democracy are also included in the factor representing level of development. Further discussion of this point follows below.

254

TABLE VII-5: Rotated Factor Matrix for Per Capita GNP in 1961 Together with Thirty-six Political, Social, and Economic Variables [a] (High Sample)

Political, Social, and Economic Indicators	Rotated Factor Loadings				h_i^2 (R^2)
	F_1	F_2	F_3	F_4	
Per Capita GNP in 1961	-.82	.10	-.08	.28	.768
Size of the Traditional Agricultural Sector	.89	.12	-.14	-.13	.838
Extent of Dualism	-.88	.05	.15	-.25	.859
Importance of the Indigenous Middle Class	-.77	.24	.23	-.05	.715
Extent of Social Mobility	-.68	.30	.29	.18	.674
Extent of Literacy	-.61	-.16	.06	.27	.482
Extent of Mass Communication	-.74	.03	-.22	.27	.661
Degree of Modernization of Outlook	-.69	.20	.49	.06	.758
Crude Fertility Rate	.83	.11	-.02	.11	.720
Strength of Democratic Institutions	-.81	-.05	.15	.41	.845
Extent of Centralization of Political Power	.70	-.03	.01	-.62	.874
Strength of the Labor Movement	-.72	-.04	.23	.48	.811
Political Strength of the Military	.70	-.06	-.09	-.31	.597
Political Strength of the Traditional Elite	.48	-.39	-.33	.29	.571
Degree of Administrative Efficiency	-.58	.41	.55	.16	.835
Level of Modernization of Techniques in Agriculture	-.85	.26	.14	.00	.811
Character of Agricultural Organization	-.53	.36	.50	.16	.685
Level of Modernization of Industry	-.61	.37	.29	.32	.691
Level of Adequacy of Physical Overhead Capital	-.84	.23	.16	.06	.794
Rate of Improvement in Human Resources	-.57	.27	.09	-.11	.418
Extent of Leadership Commitment to Economic Development	.31	.63	.36	.18	.656

TABLE VII-5 (Continued)

Political, Social, and Economic Indicators	Rotated Factor Loadings				h_i^2 (R^2)
	F_1	F_2	F_3	F_4	
Gross Investment Rate	-.46	**.57**	.06	.37	.673
Level of Effectiveness of the Tax System	-.45	**.62**	-.12	.19	.643
Level of Effectiveness of Financial Institutions	-.57	**.55** [b]	.25	.35	.819
Degree of Improvement in Agricultural Productivity since 1950	.07	**.67**	.29	.20	.572
Change in Degree of Industrialization since 1950	.22	**.69**	.30	.06	.612
Degree of Improvement in the Tax System since 1950	-.11	**.71**	-.28	-.20	.637
Degree of Improvement in Financial Institutions since 1950	-.02	**.79**	-.13	-.10	.658
Degree of Social Tension	-.03	.04	**-.83**	.01	.689
Extent of Political Stability	-.30	.14	**.73**	.10	.655
Degree of National Integration and Sense of National Unity	-.23	.14	**.73**	-.00	.615
Degree of Cultural and Ethnic Homogeneity	-.02	-.28	**.53**	-.36	.485
Degree of Freedom of Political Opposition and Press	-.66	.01	-.27	**.62** [b]	.892
Predominant Basis of Political Party System	-.23	.38	.26	**.67**	.722
Degree of Competitiveness of Political Parties	-.19	.15	-.42	**.55**	.536
Character of Basic Social Organization	-.35	-.41	.04	**.66**	.729
Abundance of Natural Resources	.12	.08	.02	**.71**	.526

[a] Bold figures indicate the factor to which each variable is assigned. Variables omitted because of insignificant correlations: degree of improvement in physical overhead capital since 1950 and structure of foreign trade. Variable omitted because of low high loading: extent of urbanization. Percentage of over-all variance explained by factors: 69.0. Percentage of variance explained by last factor included: 6.7.

[b] A variable having loadings on two factors which are not significantly different is assigned to that factor to which it is judged to have the closest affinity.

256

results is accorded to dynamic influences that in the long-run analysis are relatively unimportant. As explained in the previous chapter, these observations are perfectly consistent with each other in light of the assumption that the economic system behaves like a linear system.

The only major difference between the short- and long-run results lies in the political implications of the two factor analyses. Since in both the short-run and long-run combined analyses the factors including indicators of the nature of the political system also included indices of the level of socioeconomic development, test runs were made in order to determine the importance of characteristics of the political system in the process of economic growth. A test run omitting measures of the level of social and economic development confirmed the essential independence of the nature of the political system and short-run economic performance (Factor I of Table VII–6 accounts for less than 4 per cent of intercountry variations in short-run growth rates). In contrast, when the equivalent long-run combined analysis excluding indicators of the level of development was performed, the factor representing the extent of democracy (Factor I of Table VII–7), explained 77 per cent of the variance in levels of per capita GNP. However, other test runs indicated that this degree of explanation cannot be attributed in its entirety to measures of the strength of participant institutions and that characteristics of the political system act to some extent as proxies for the social and economic achievements with which they are most closely associated.[16] Although the factor analyses did not yield an unambiguous estimate of the importance of the character of the political system, they nevertheless indicated the existence of a significant positive relationship between intercountry variations in the strength of participant political institutions and differences among countries in both economic and social achievements in the long run. Were this not the case, it would have proved possible in test runs to separate the political indicators in Factor I of the long-run combined analysis (Table VII–5) from the economic and social variables associated in the same factor. This result stands in sharp contrast to the comparative insignificance of the relationship be-

[16] When indicators of socioeconomic development were retained and the political variables associated with them were omitted from the long-run analysis of Table VII–5 the factor representing the level of socioeconomic attainment accounted for 69 per cent of differences in levels of per capita GNP, and a separate political factor including the indicators of the degree of competitiveness of political parties and the predominant basis of the political party system explained about 6 per cent of variations in average income.

TABLE VII-6: Rotated Factor Matrix for Change in Per Capita GNP (1950/51–1963/64) Together with Fifteen Political, Social, and Economic Variables [a] (High Sample)

Political, Social, and Economic Indicators	Rotated Factor Loadings				h_i^2 (R^2)
	F_1	F_2	F_3	F_4	
Rate of Growth of Real Per Capita GNP: 1950/51–1963/64	.19	−.92	−.07	−.14	.909
Strength of Democratic Institutions	.91	−.01	.14	.03	.679
Degree of Freedom of Political Opposition and Press	.85	−.01	−.18	.33	.692
Degree of Centralization of Political Power	−.93	.05	.02	−.15	.765
Strength of the Labor Movement	.93	.03	.12	−.13	.890
Extent of Leadership Commitment to Economic Development	.43	−.62	.16	−.37	.857
Change in Degree of Industrialization since 1950	−.20	−.73	.34	.15	.865
Degree of Improvement in Financial Institutions since 1950	−.11	−.86	−.19	.01	.823
Degree of Improvement in the Tax System since 1950	−.01	−.58	−.26	.18	.852
Degree of Improvement in Agricultural Productivity since 1950	.08	−.79	.22	−.02	.786
Degree of Social Tension	−.03	.05	−.73	.38	.731
Extent of Political Stability	.37	−.29	.56	−.49	.895
Degree of National Integration and Sense of National Unity	.20	−.07	.80	−.03	.443
Degree of Cultural and Ethnic Homogeneity	−.28	.29	.76	.13	.711
Predominant Basis of the Political Party System	.51	−.39	.41	.49 [b]	.780
Degree of Competitiveness of Political Parties	.39	−.07	−.18	.81	.671

[a] Bold figures indicate the factor to which each variable is assigned. Variables omitted because of insignificant correlations: structure of foreign trade and degree of improvement in physical overhead capital since 1950. Variable omitted because of low high loading: extent of urbanization. Variables omitted for purpose of test (see text): size of the traditional agricultural sector, extent of dualism, importance of the indigenous middle class, extent of social mobility, extent of literacy, extent of mass communication, degree of modernization of outlook, crude fertility rate, political strength of the military, political strength of the traditional elite, degree of administrative efficiency, level of modernization of techniques in agriculture, character of agricultural organization, level of modernization of industry, level of adequacy of physical overhead capital, rate of improvement in human resources, level of effectiveness of the tax system, level of effectiveness of financial institutions, gross investment rate, character of basic social organization, and abundance of natural resources. Percentage of over-all variance explained by factors: 77.2. Percentage of variance explained by last factor included: 8.1.

[b] A variable having loadings on two factors which are not significantly different is assigned to that factor to which it is judged to have the closest affinity.

TABLE VII-7: Rotated Factor Matrix for Per Capita GNP in 1961 Together with Fifteen Political, Social, and Economic Variables [a] (High Sample)

Political, Social, and Economic Indicators	Rotated Factor Loadings				h_i^2
	F_1	F_2	F_3	F_4	(R^2)
Per Capita GNP in 1961..............	.88	−.06	−.10	.05	.782
Strength of Democratic Institutions....	**.89**	.19	.03	−.16	.859
Degree of Freedom of Political Opposition and Press.................	**.83**	−.19	.02	−.39	.871
Degree of Centralization of Political Power...........................	**−.90**	−.02	.00	.26	.879
Strength of the Labor Movement......	**.92**	.20	.05	.01	.892
Degree of Social Tension.............	.01	**−.80**	.03	−.20	.683
Extent of Political Stability...........	.35	**.70**	−.24	.28	.748
Degree of National Integration and Sense of National Unity............	.17	**.77**	−.08	−.08	.634
Degree of Cultural and Ethnic Homogeneity....................	−.32	**.68**	.35	−.21	.736
Extent of Leadership Commitment to Economic Development............	.47	.27	**−.66**	.31	.827
Change in Degree of Industrialization since 1950......................	−.24	.34	**−.70**	−.23	.711
Degree of Improvement in Financial Institutions since 1950.............	−.05	−.15	**−.84**	.03	.730
Degree of Improvement in the Tax System since 1950.................	.02	−.31	**−.67**	−.07	.543
Degree of Improvement in Agricultural Productivity since 1950.............	.05	.28	**−.72**	−.12	.621
Predominant Basis of the Political Party System....................	.42	.35	−.37	**−.64**	.847
Degree of Competitiveness of Political Parties.........................	.33	−.32	−.06	**−.79**	.841

[a] Bold figures indicate the factor to which each variable is assigned. Variables omitted because of insignificant correlations: structure of foreign trade and degree of improvement in physical overhead capital since 1950. Variable omitted because of low high loading: extent of urbanization. Variables omitted for purpose of test (see text): the same as in Table VII-6. Percentage of over-all variance explained by factors: 76.3. Percentage of variance explained by last factor included: 8.4.

tween the same characteristics of the political system and short-run economic growth.

How can this seeming paradox be explained? In order to resolve the apparent inconsistency between our short-run and long-run results for the "high" group, one must appeal to the following propositions:

1. Increases in the strength of democratic influences are not a cause of economic growth at this level. They are a result (direct or indirect)

259

of economic growth, social and economic transformations interact to induce political change, or political influences and economic growth are both consequences of some common set of social forces active in the society.

2. There is a threshold below which economic and social forces cannot effectively change the political system of a country. This threshold lies generally within the range represented by nations at the "high" level of development.

Let us examine the first of these hypotheses. If the extent of democracy were to have a causal impact upon growth, one would expect to find evidence that at some stage of development it is a prerequisite for successful economic performance in the short run as well as in the long run. The results of the factor analyses indicate that, on the contrary, the influence of participant political institutions is not significant in the short run at any of the three levels of development considered in this study. It is thus clear that with respect to type of political system, causality does not run from political structure to the economic sphere.

We are left with several alternative hypotheses concerning the long-run interaction of political systems and economic performance: causality may run from the economic to the political; causality may run from the social to both the political and the economic; or social and economic forces may interact in a manner that strengthens participant political systems. Blanksten, for example, argues that it is economic transformations which alter the nature and relative political influence of groups in the society.[17] In contrast, Daniel Lerner takes the view that it is social changes, such as increases in urbanization, literacy, and mass communication, which promote the development of participant political institutions.[18] Others, such as Millikan and Blackmer, take a more eclectic approach which emphasizes the continuous interaction of long-run economic, social, and political change.[19] There is a final hypothesis that is also consistent with the results of our factor analyses: that economic growth and the evolution of participant political systems are the outcome of common underlying sociopsychological transformations that are not, however, represented in the indicators included in our analysis. Examples of social forces of this type are the spread of rationalist

[17] "Transference of Social and Political Loyalties," p. 191.
[18] *The Passing of Traditional Society*, Chapter 2.
[19] *The Emerging Nations*, p. 46.

thought patterns and the generation of the capacity of individuals to adapt to continual economic and social change, both of which are conducive to the development of participant democracy as well as to successful economic performance.

Regardless of whether the long-run association between political democracy and economic growth can be imputed to economic determinism or exists because of common forces acting within both spheres, an additional thought must be introduced to explain the apparent paradox of the absence of a significant short-run association at this level and the absence of a long-run association at earlier levels of development. The fact that the paradox cannot be resolved within the framework of a linear theory can be seen readily. Time lags, for example, in a uniformly developing system would merely relate present growth to a past condition that is changing at the same rate as the analogous current quantity (by the linearity hypothesis). And, in a strictly linear theory, the difference between the long-run period of the order of fifty years and the short-run term of the order of fifteen years would be expected to leave essentially unaffected the percentage of the variance explained by a given factor. The striking difference between the explanatory power of democratic institutions in the long run and in the short run suggests that strong nonlinearities are clearly at the root of the paradox.

We are therefore led to postulate the existence of significant nonlinearities, in the form of either threshold or acceleration effects, in the impact of social or economic forces on the form of government. The existence of a threshold common to all countries and lying more or less within the range of variation represented by the present group of countries is strongly suggested by an examination of Figure VII–1 in which country scores on the factor representing the extent of democracy are plotted against the level of per capita GNP. The presence of such a threshold at which social and economic forces become effective in inducing political change appears plausible on a priori grounds as well. It is reasonable to assume that before fully participant nationwide democratic institutions can evolve, certain levels of mass communication, urbanization, and literacy, for example, must be achieved and rationalist positivist attitudes must be sufficiently diffused throughout the society. This view is consistent with Daniel Lerner's position that modernization consists of a sequence of phases in which first, urbanization, second, the growth of literacy, and third, the spread of mass media inter-

FIGURE VII–1: Scatter Diagram Relating Per Capita GNP and Country Scores
on Factor Representing the Extent of Democracy [a]

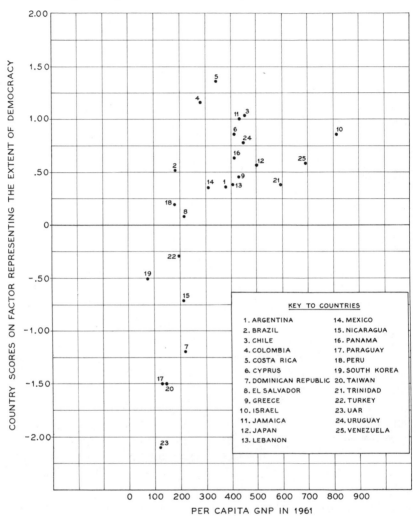

[a] The factor scores plotted on the diagram are from a factor analysis of per capita GNP together with social and political indicators for a sample of seventy-four countries. The factor upon which the scores are based includes the indicators of the strength of democratic institutions, the degree of freedom of political opposition and press, the extent of centralization of political power, the predominant basis of the political party system, the degree of competitiveness of political parties, the strength of the labor movement, and the political strength of the military. The source for the estimates of per capita GNP is the Agency for International Development, Statistics and Reports Division, "84 Underdeveloped Countries—Two Thirds World Population Grouped According to Estimated Annual Per Capita Income (U.S. Dollar Equivalents), 1961" (Washington, D.C., April, 1963).

act to eventually produce a democratic political system.[20] In general, it would appear from our examination of the political implications of our long-run results for the "high" group that the typical country at this stage has reached a critical minimum level of economic and social development at which further socioeconomic change either induces or interacts with the evolution of more effective participant political institutions.

SUMMARY

The results of the factor analyses for the "high" group of countries are quite encouraging. They suggest, first of all, that the structural social bottlenecks to economic growth have been overcome and that the political preconditions for effective government leadership in the economic sphere have been achieved. More specifically, the countries in this group have attained a sufficient degree of economic and sociopolitical integration and sufficient levels of education, mass communication, and urbanization so that these features of their societies no longer pose significant barriers to the acceleration of rates of economic growth. The crucial determinants of short-run economic performance at this level of development are the effectiveness of economic institutions and the extent of national mobilization for development. In short, our results for this group of countries suggest fairly strongly that since the typical country at this level has overcome the significant sociostructural bottlenecks to further growth, a well-planned development program with effective political measures for its execution can result in the initiation of sustained economic growth. The specific economic policies of importance are suggested by those aspects of the economy which are summarized in the dominant economic factor of the factor analyses for the "high" level: in particular, those designed to improve financial institutions and tax systems, accelerate industrialization and promote the spread of improved techniques, and finally, increase both the size and the quality of the investment effort. These policies, while also relevant to the development programs of countries at the low and intermediate levels, are particularly effective in improving the economic performance of countries that have achieved the level of development characteristic of the "high" group.

[20] *The Passing of Traditional Society,* Chapter 2.

CHAPTER $$\text{VIII}$$ IMPLICATIONS FOR THE
PROCESS OF ECONOMIC
DEVELOPMENT

In this chapter, the principal implications of our analysis for the theory of development and for development policy are summarized and the conclusions drawn in earlier chapters are consolidated. First we sketch the outlines of a broad view of the entire process of economic development, making use of the regularities that emerged from our results for countries at the several levels of socioeconomic development. Then we turn to the policy implications of our investigation.

The over-all analysis of the growth process which we present in this chapter may seem to suggest that development proceeds continuously and uniformly from tribal conditions to the fully developed status. Such a view, of course, is neither correct nor intended in any strict sense. In particular, it is obvious that an individual country need not go through all of the several stages described with respect to each aspect of socioeconomic change. Indeed, the details of the growth process of individual nations may vary greatly from the average pattern discernible in the statistical analysis with respect to the specific time sequence of change. Furthermore, it should be emphasized that the breaking up of the analysis into several clearly defined levels of socioeconomic development, an approach that is necessary for statistical purposes, appears to imply much sharper distinctions between successive levels or stages than are actually found. In fact, countries at the end points of our samples are truly marginal between two groups; transitions between successive stages are in reality much smoother than the literal interpretation of our results would suggest. Finally, the inferences concerning the nature of the development process which we are about to draw also suffer from the well-known difficulties involved in deducing temporally valid conclusions from cross-sectional statistical results. In particular, since cross-sectional studies have no specific time dimension, our analysis, in and of itself, does not indicate anything concerning the extent of the time lapse necessary to effect a transition from one level of development to another; nor, indeed, does it indicate whether such transitions will, in fact, take place. Strictly speaking, from the statistical analysis, one cannot even infer a time direction for these changes without appealing to historical evidence concerning the irreversible nature of many of the most important social transformations involved.

In spite of these difficulties, however, we feel that the consistency of our results, both internally and with the broad outlines of history, gives sufficient evidence to justify an attempt to produce a coherent, albeit oversimplified, picture of the process of development. In formulating this structure, we depend heavily on our three short-run analyses as well as upon differences in the economic, social, and political characteristics which typify countries in each of these groups. In order to formulate this synthesis, we must view an average country in each group as being representative of a particular stage of the process that a typical underdeveloped nation goes through in progressing from its current level of socioeconomic development to a state of self-sustained growth. We do this, even though we are aware that, strictly speaking, there is a logical jump involved in this procedure. A more complete validation of this process must await the application of similar analyses to historical data for currently developed nations.[1]

The policy discussions that follow our formulation of a broad schema of development are based primarily on the individual factor analyses for the several groups of countries rather than on the over-all patterns discussed in the first part of the chapter. In order to preserve continuity in exposition throughout the chapter, the empirical evidence essential to the credibility of the argument is not presented. It should be noted, however, that there is strong support in Chapters V–VII for the conclusions given in this final chapter.

THE PROCESS OF ECONOMIC DEVELOPMENT

In the long transition during which a society evolves from tribalism to self-sustained economic growth, the closely woven political, social, and economic strands of the social fabric change their pattern and their relationships. Our research suggests that one may look at the entire process of national modernization as the progressive differentiation of the social, economic, and political spheres from each other and the development of specialized institutions and attitudes within each sphere.

---

[1] The present authors have initiated research in this direction.

More specifically, the process of economic development in underdeveloped countries consists basically of the separation of the economic sphere, first, from the complex of social organization and the norms that govern it, and, subsequently and to a lesser extent, from the political environment by which it is constrained. During this process of successive differentiation, the economic aspects of the society become increasingly more important and more explicit until, at the fully developed stage, economic considerations become a powerful force in shaping national behavior. This is the essence of the picture of economic development which emerges from the data and the statistical analyses of the preceding chapters.

To better understand this broad picture of the development process, let us first consider countries at the level of socioeconomic development corresponding to that of sub-Saharan Africa. Here the primary obstacles to economic growth arise from the all-encompassing nature of the tribal social structure. In order to break down traditional social constraints on economic activity, extratribal forces are required. Our results suggest that the primary motivations for the process of breakdown are provided by an economic force—the expansion of the market economy. Typically, a small foreign or expatriate market sector provides a set of economic incentives that continually erode the structure of tribal society. The gradual penetration of economic ideas into the subsistence sector sooner or later weakens the dominance of tribal structure and values sufficiently to permit a significant enlargement of the sphere within which economic considerations govern economic activity. It is thus a social transformation—the gradual erosion of the economic content of tribal social organization—which becomes the principal mechanism for market expansion. The extent to which the tribal hold is loosened determines in turn the rate at which purely economic advances can be made. Throughout this socioeconomic process, political forces appear to play only a minor role.

The intermediate level of development is characterized by a much greater degree of differentiation of the economic sphere from the social. Among countries at this level, the diffusion of economic concepts has extended throughout the society to the point where market attitudes and values color the outlook toward economic activity of even those who participate only peripherally in market transactions. At this stage, the most effective direct economic processes tend to be associated with the buildup of an industrial and financial base and with massive accumulations of physical overhead capital. The modest improvements in tax institutions, in the productivity of industry and agriculture, and in the human resource base which characterize this level of development still appear to have a rather limited effect upon short-run economic performance.

With respect to the social sphere the dominant theme is one of extreme disequilibrium and disruption. By and large, there has been rapid social change, but progress has been strikingly uneven. As a result, while the previous equilibrium of the social structure has been demolished, the typical society at this level has been unable to find a new state of equilibrium. A major consequence of this unbalanced pattern of social development is extreme social tension reflected in a persistent lack of national integration, intermittent outbreaks of violence, and marked political instability. Since the precise pattern of the social imbalance varies from nation to nation, the social bottlenecks to economic development to which it gives rise vary from country to country; hence, no systematic social obstacles to economic growth appear in our statistical analyses.

As regards the political sphere, neither the form of the political system nor the extent of the leadership commitment to economic development assumes any greater systematic association with economic performance at the intermediate level of socioeconomic development than at the earlier stage. Their unimportance appears to be due largely to political instability and to the other political consequences of rapid social change and imbalance.

Only at the subsequent "high" level of development is it possible for economic development to proceed in earnest. The more progressive countries at this level are typically engaged in the final transition to fully developed status. The severe social tensions of the intermediate level have generally been greatly eased, in most instances by widespread social progress that has tended to restore balance in the social sphere. With the emergence of a new equilibrium in the social structure, national integration and a sense of national unity have crystallized and are in the process of replacing the ethnic and cultural identifications of the majority of the population. As a consequence of these social processes, important prerequisites for effective political change have also been met. A modest degree of bureaucratic efficiency and a fair extent of political stability are characteristic of the nations at this level. Generally, the economic groundwork for development has also been laid; in particular, there now exist a pervasive market system, moderately effective economic institutions, and a fairly adequate level of physical overhead capital. Given these achievements, the rate of economic progress will be conditioned henceforth primarily by improvements in economic institutions and by the political climate of the nation.

Our results for countries at the highest of the three levels of development suggest strongly that the primary economic considerations at this level are the size of the investment effort, the rationality with which investment funds are distributed, and the extent to which the politico-economic environment tends to promote simultaneous advances along many fronts. Thus, the quality and the effectiveness of development planning become crucial at this stage, as does the sincerity of the over-all national commitment to economic development. In general, therefore, the principal obstacles to sustained economic progress have become those political conditions that seriously hamper the adoption or execution of rational economic policies. In countries at this level the extent of leadership commitment to development and the breadth of the national drive for development assume primary importance in the mobilization of efforts to achieve developed status.

In the preceding paragraphs we have discussed the broad view of the lengthy process of transition from economic stagnation to self-sustained growth suggested by our statistical analysis. Let us now consider this schema from another viewpoint. The earliest process in economic development appears to center around the beginnings of the differentiation of the economic sphere from the social. At the same time, the first faint stirrings of a separate political sphere can be discerned. As a society travels along the road of socioeconomic development, the processes of differentiation of the economic and the political realms from the social nexus continue at an accelerated pace, with the economic and the political growing (relatively) at the expense of the social. By the time a nation has reached the "high" stage of development, there is almost as much separation of economic considerations from the social context as there is in a fully developed economy, and the separation of the political from the social is well under way. The political and the economic areas are still, however, fairly strongly interlaced.

One may surmise that full development, the final stage of the process, involves a significant degree of differentiation of the economic from the political sphere as well. We hasten to point out that by this differentiation of the economic from the political we do not mean to imply that in developed economies political units do not engage in economic activity or in the regulation of economic activity nor that economic organs do not have political functions. Indeed, the sheer quantitative magnitude of governmental economic impact may increase. Our meaning is rather that when governmental structures in developed economies take economic decisions (whether regulatory or with respect to direct participation in economic activity) they tend to a greater degree to apply economic reasoning and criteria to these decisions. Similarly, when governments engage in political activity they tend to apply primarily political criteria. This final feature of our conceptual view of the development process is suggested by an extrapolation of the trends evident in our results for underdeveloped countries. It is also suggested by a comparison of underdeveloped countries with developed nations. With respect to the latter, casual empiricism suggests that in Western polities and currently in much of communist Europe, political structures tend to adapt and conform more or less to the demands of the economic sector in such a manner that political organs accord economic considerations heavy weight in their economic activities in order to be effective politically. This final process of partial differentiation of the political sphere from the economic sphere probably occurs through political reactions to the rising strength of economic forces.

Before this differentiation can take place, however, economic forces must become sufficiently strong. Historically, in Western Europe and in the United States, the economic sector turned out to be vigorous enough to lead the way to development and differentiation. In the case of some of the more rapidly developing countries of the "high" group, as well as of most of the communist countries and of nineteenth-century Japan, the strengthening of the economic sector is the result of a conscious decision by the political leadership to make economic growth a central political goal and to assume the role of prime mover in efforts toward economic modernization. In the latter case, therefore, the final trend toward separation of the economic realm from the political is, paradoxically, preceded by a temporary fusion of the political and economic spheres, during which there is often an almost complete blurring of the boundary lines between political and economic decisions. However, the fact that some degree of differentiation of the economic sphere from the political is characteristic of full development is suggested by the much greater degree of application of economic criteria to government economic decision-making[2] and of purely political criteria to political decision-making. Furthermore, in some of the communist countries, particularly in Yugoslavia and the U.S.S.R., where the government economic role is all-pervasive, there has also been a trend toward increasing separation of the economic realm from political control as evidenced by the tendency toward greater managerial autonomy and the "Liebermanization," or the Titoist equivalent, of these socialist economies. It would seem, then, that whatever the political route to development, the eventual result is a tendency for the political and economic spheres to drift apart as the economy and the polity mature.

DEVELOPMENT POLICIES

The schema of economic development just described, or, more accurately, the factor analyses upon which it is based, contribute substantially to a clear set of policy guidelines regarding development priorities for countries at each of the three levels of socioeconomic development. In the section that follows, we draw upon both our statistical results and the differences between levels of development in typical country characteristics in order to determine, for the average country at each level, which policy measures contribute most to promoting economic development. Before proceeding with the discussion, it should be emphasized that we are interested in the relative rather than the absolute importance of different measures for promoting growth at each level of development. We do not suggest, for example, that at the lowest level of development the full range of policy instruments may not have some absolute importance in raising growth rates; nor do we mean to imply that measures omitted from our discussion should be abandoned. Rather, we are interested in ranking various policies, for each level of development, according to the contribution they make to improving economic growth rates. Furthermore, the policy mix described for countries at each level is most appropriate for countries in the middle of each group with respect to their socioeconomic status. As a country moves toward

---

[2] We recognize, of course, that even in a country as developed as the United States, political considerations impinge considerably upon government economic decisions. At the same time, however, the extent to which U.S. public economic agencies such as the Bureau of the Budget, the Federal Reserve Board, and the Tennessee Valley Authority apply economic rather than political criteria to their economic decisions is strikingly greater than is the case with their counterparts in the more advanced of contemporary less-developed countries.

an end point of a given group, the appropriate mix is a combination of policies appropriate for its own group and those suitable for the next highest (or lowest) group.

For nations at the lowest level, our analysis suggests that the primary emphasis of development policy should be on measures to expand the market economy by decreasing the size of the subsistence sector and to increase the dualism of the economy by expanding the modern sector. On the one hand, mechanisms are required that stimulate members of the subsistence sector to participate in the market economy by exposing them to an array of low-priced goods that can be purchased only with cash. On the other hand, steps should be taken to facilitate directly the spread of cash production by creating a network of roads and a system of marketing boards or other middlemen to help distribute goods to the market. Finally, efforts must be made to raise the rate of investment in order to finance programs for economic modernization as well as to create the human resource base necessary to implement them.

For countries at the intermediate level of development, important goals of economic policy should be the promotion of increased industrialization together with the expansion of the physical overhead capital and the improvement of financial capacity necessary to realize these aims. Important as these economic measures are, however, they may be less important than the establishment of a social structure that is sufficiently stable to permit the continued growth of the economy. This means that the extreme social tensions characteristic of the intermediate-level countries must be reduced before significant economic progress can be made. Since a major cause of social tension is social imbalance, the emphasis in social progress must be on a pattern of advances which tends to correct the current unevenness in the development of social structure. The appropriate specific measures vary from country to country; for example, while some countries urgently need improved social mobility accompanied by ready access to the middle class, in others the main requirement is for increased literacy. In all the countries at the intermediate level of development, however, a reduction in the extent and intensity of social tension is necessary to create conditions under which economic policy will be effective.

The crucial policy decisions in the political sphere among countries at the intermediate level are those that contribute to the creation of more effective government. Political stability, the modernization of the

272

bureaucracy, and the creation of a greater sense of national unity should thus be the chief political goals for this group of countries.

For the "high" group of countries the prescription for economic development is one that sounds familiar to economists. In these countries the essential social conditions for the transition to fully developed status have on the whole been met and political systems are relatively mature. Consequently, the paramount requirement for the nations in this group is that they commit themselves to the task of economic modernization. This prescription follows from the significant correlation we observe in our analysis between effective political mobilization for economic development and actual economic performance. At this level of development, therefore, the necessary and sufficient condition for the successful transition of a typical country into a state of self-sustained economic growth is a determined and extensive drive for economic development supported by a reasonably competent committed leadership.

IMPLICATIONS FOR FOREIGN ASSISTANCE

To a large extent the priorities suggested in the previous section for countries representative of the several stages of socioeconomic development serve also to indicate the types of foreign assistance likely to be most productive in individual countries. At the lowest level, for example, aid should primarily take the form of technical assistance and capital projects specifically designed to increase the size of the modern sector and to increase the production and facilitate the distribution of cash crops. Foreign assistance to countries at the intermediate level should include major capital project aid for industrialization and the expansion of transportation and power networks and technical assistance to improve financial institutions. It should also include programs, specially adapted to the individual country, to alleviate social unrest and political instability. Among the instruments used for the latter purpose might be technical assistance to improve social conditions or budget support and assistance to public administration. Finally, at the highest level, foreign aid in the form of program assistance becomes appropriate. Technical assistance to these countries should emphasize the building of economic institutions, the transfer of modern technology, and help with development planning. As mentioned above, of course, there is no sharp discontinuity between the policies appropriate for each level of development. There is, rather, as one moves along the spectrum of socioeconomic development, a continuous change in priorities for foreign aid which is defined by the three sets of prescriptions given above.

Donor nations, in providing assistance, face an additional choice in composing their foreign aid budgets: how to allocate a given aid budget among various underdeveloped countries. Clearly, there are many political considerations involved that are basically outside the scope of this study. Within the present framework, however, our analysis offers some guidelines for policy decisions, although the recommendations are unique only in the context of a given set of national goals.

The first point that emerges from our analysis is that the immediate economic productivity of foreign aid, measured in terms of improvements in the rate of growth of per capita GNP, is likely to be highest in the countries at the "high" level. Our statistical studies demonstrate convincingly the validity of the often-repeated maxim that nations which have already surmounted the major social and political roadblocks to economic progress are in the best position in the short run to translate economic aid directly and effectively into economic improvement. Furthermore, our analysis indicates that aid to this group of countries should be dispensed primarily on the basis of an objective evaluation of the quality of development planning, the strength of the leadership commitment to economic development, and the recent rate of improvement in economic performance across a broad spectrum of economic institutions.

A second criterion for the distribution of aid funds, which is especially appropriate for allocation decisions affecting any group of candidate nations at approximately the same level of development, relates to the internal political situation of the prospective recipient. Our analysis shows that it is neither the type of political system nor the political orientation of the government which is important to short-run economic performance. The key political criterion in terms of which a country's capacity to develop economically should be judged is the potential of its government to effectively execute progressive economic programs.

Both the economic and political considerations discussed in this section thus suggest that the lion's share of aid funds should be given to nations at the "high" stage of development where both the short-run economic productivity of aid and the extent of political mobilization for economic development are typically the greatest. However, if one regards internal political turmoil as a potential threat to world peace, this conclusion must be modified. The transitional countries at the intermediate level, with their serious social stresses and their persistent political instability, are candidates for civil war and/or communist subversion, either of which can lead to open East-West confrontation. One possible aim of Western foreign aid policy, therefore, might well be to reduce the number of countries in the transitional stage. This criterion is equivalent, in an average sense, to reducing the time spent by a typical country in that stage. Over the time horizon of a decade or so, however, it is likely that the number of countries at the intermediate level of development can be reduced most rapidly by concentrating foreign assistance on the best prospects for transition into the next stage rather than by spreading aid more or less evenly over the entire range of transitional countries. The position that countries at the intermediate level should not be neglected in the allocation of aid funds is reinforced by the potential positive influence of foreign assistance in inducing socioeconomic and political improvements that otherwise might not be undertaken. Thus, our analysis suggests two complementary criteria for choosing among intermediate-level countries. The economic productivity of aid to individual countries should be judged largely on the basis of the nation's absorptive capacity, as indicated by the size of the modern sector and the adequacy of its financial base. Concurrently, the candidacy of a recipient country should be evaluated in terms of a "potential political effectiveness" criterion analogous to the one described in the previous paragraph. With respect to the latter, those countries should be preferred in which the likelihood is greatest that foreign assistance will contribute to inducement of effective political mobilization for economic development.

We come now to countries at the lowest level of socioeconomic development. Taking both economic and political considerations into account, it would appear that, cruel as it may seem, the allocation of a major part of foreign assistance funds to countries in this group is, from the point of view of the donor nation, likely to be premature. The social transformations required for economic effectiveness and the political integration of countries at this stage usually have not proceeded far enough to produce economic or political rewards commensurate with those obtainable elsewhere. Nevertheless, while large sums of assistance to these countries out of a limited foreign aid budget are not appropriate, limited project assistance and substantial technical assistance may of course serve important purposes.

A final significant aspect of the impact of foreign assistance, from the point of view of a Western donor nation, is its long-run effect in encouraging the emergence of democratic forms of government in developing nations. It will be recalled that there is very little short-run association between the form of government and economic growth for countries at any of the three levels of development. Our results for countries at the "high" level, however, show a significant positive association between long-run economic performance and the establishment of representative political institutions. It follows from these findings that the success of foreign aid in inducing the growth of democratic forms of government cannot be judged by a recipient nation's progress toward democracy over a period as short as one generation. Indeed, the time scale required to establish reasonably representative and participant political institutions through economic progress is so extended that a donor nation should not consider foreign assistance as a tool for strengthening democracy unless it is willing to adopt a very long view and to ignore relatively short-run (five- to fifteen-year) fluctuations. At the same time, the positive, net long-run relationship between growth and representative government, which is evident in our results, is sufficiently strong to support the expectation that a far-sighted program of aid can lead eventually to significant rewards for the Western donor nation in the sense that, *certeris paribus,* a larger proportion of the world's population will eventually be governed in accordance with participant democratic ideals.

EPILOGUE FOR THE SKEPTIC
BY F. L. ADELMAN

THE FABRIC OF SOCIETY

The fabric of society,
I say in all sobriety,
Has a pattern and a texture and design.

The warp of the social tapestry,
The weave of the nation's polity,
And the economic woof do intertwine.

When threads one tries to separate,
To characterize and differentiate,
The strands become entangled in a froth.

This intersocietal napery
Is made into a drapery
Of pure, untrammeled, integrated cloth!

APPENDIX

CORRELATION MATRICES FOR SOCIAL,
POLITICAL, & ECONOMIC INDICATORS

LIST OF INDICATORS

1. Rate of Growth of Real Per Capita GNP: 1950/51–1963/64
2. Size of the Traditional Agricultural Sector
3. Extent of Dualism
4. Degree of Modernization of Outlook
5. Importance of the Indigenous Middle Class
6. Extent of Social Mobility
7. Extent of Literacy
8. Extent of Mass Communication
9. Degree of Social Tension
10. Degree of National Integration and Sense of National Unity
11. Degree of Cultural and Ethnic Homogeneity
12. Crude Fertility Rate
13. Degree of Administrative Efficiency
14. Extent of Centralization of Political Power
15. Strength of Democratic Institutions
16. Degree of Freedom of Political Opposition and Press
17. Predominant Basis of the Political Party System
18. Degree of Competitiveness of Political Parties
19. Extent of Political Stability
20. Extent of Leadership Commitment to Economic Development
21. Strength of the Labor Movement
22. Political Strength of the Traditional Elite
23. Political Strength of the Military
24. Level of Effectiveness of the Tax System
25. Level of Adequacy of Physical Overhead Capital
26. Level of Modernization of Industry

279

27. Level of Effectiveness of Financial Institutions
28. Level of Modernization of Techniques in Agriculture
29. Gross Investment Rate
30. Degree of Improvement in the Tax System since 1950
31. Change in Degree of Industrialization since 1950
32. Degree of Improvement in Financial Institutions since 1950
33. Degree of Improvement in Agricultural Productivity since 1950
34. Degree of Improvement in Physical Overhead Capital since 1950
35. Rate of Improvement in Human Resources
36. Structure of Foreign Trade
37. Abundance of Natural Resources
38. Character of Agricultural Organization
39. Extent of Urbanization
40. Per Capita GNP in 1961
41. Character of Basic Social Organization

TABLE A–1: Correlation Matrix for Social, Political, and Economic Indicators (Full Sample)

CORRELATION COEFFICIENTS

```
ROW  1
 1.00000  -0.57203   0.65561   0.53774   0.52307   0.49979   0.44652   0.49961  -0.01C55   0.40216
 0.25865  -0.30829   0.39698   0.13656   0.26717   0.13789   0.20791   0.15766   0.17557   0.34685
 0.09291  -0.03651   0.13212   0.52575   0.57055   0.58586   0.69575   0.55477   0.63052   0.45504
 0.58327   0.69190   0.61089   0.44116   0.52250   0.32410   0.25267   0.58984   0.46134   C.52319
 0.36480

ROW  2
-0.57203   1.00000  -0.87910  -0.82348  -0.77404  -0.80255  -0.79434  -0.81792   0.12278  -0.70633
-0.45663   0.54750  -0.467C1   0.08432  -0.59830  -0.47392  -0.48340  -0.44302  -0.11208  -0.24236
-0.54143   0.17937  -0.065C7  -0.67934  -0.86504  -0.79265  -0.77511  -0.88167  -0.62792  -0.37184
-0.55617  -0.55928  -0.46139  -0.15710  -0.80162  -0.23634  -0.27582  -0.79244  -0.76856  -0.77730
-0.77919

ROW  3
 0.65561  -0.87910   1.00000   0.82460   0.80814   0.80147   0.76811   0.81389  -0.13615   0.63780
 0.37493  -0.60903   0.60689  -0.C1160   0.59436   0.41478   0.40181   0.37858   0.20725   0.29440
 0.48325  -0.23302   0.01594   0.72272   0.87495   0.81310   0.81880   0.86101   0.64606   0.44769
 0.58324   0.59920   0.50799   0.28822   0.80131   0.41689   0.24508   0.78289   0.73816   0.73385
 0.65370

ROW  4
 0.53774  -0.82348   0.82460   1.C0000   0.71871   0.74705   0.69951   0.71973  -0.23369   0.60945
 0.24425  -0.50127   0.64672  -0.15100   0.69390   0.46700   0.54939   0.48454   0.28564   0.41420
 0.62069  -0.30450  -0.09867   0.65703   0.81452   0.79874   0.77040   0.80259   0.63326   0.29400
 0.47036   0.49303   0.41710   0.19019   0.66793   0.43885   0.29708   0.77371   0.72580   0.69823
 0.64585

ROW  5
 0.52307  -0.77404   0.80814   0.71871   1.00000   0.86177   0.71712   0.72721  -0.23653   0.73332
 0.40912  -0.53169   0.53070  -0.08445   0.52883   0.43953   0.42582   0.31910   0.21887   0.28295
 0.43686  -0.25734   0.00817   0.61683   0.75464   0.67956   0.73987   0.77046   0.59487   0.49234
 0.65026   0.57776   0.53740   0.22474   0.77468   0.25353   0.10047   0.68320   0.66312   0.63014
 0.68895

ROW  6
 0.49979  -0.80255   0.80147   0.74705   0.86177   1.00000   0.85812   0.79184  -0.34016   0.78588
 0.47310  -0.55084   0.53586  -0.12113   0.58845   0.47030   0.50259   0.39768   0.26751   0.26510
 0.49436  -0.32915  -0.C6810   0.65634   0.79760   0.76142   0.74981   0.81515   0.67289   0.41226
 0.61180   0.46343   0.49759   0.20721   0.81616   0.19403   0.19592   0.77636   0.74128   0.69879
 0.74370

ROW  7
 0.44652  -0.79434   0.76811   0.69951   0.71712   0.85812   1.00000   0.81218  -0.28139   0.68630
 0.45806  -0.58457   0.44887  -0.14883   0.62962   0.51604   0.56223   0.49350   0.16015   0.13662
 0.48839  -0.10807   0.01794   0.67402   0.72597   0.69642   0.65517   0.77563   0.59583   0.28245
 0.54809   0.44939   0.38213   0.13034   0.80323   0.20271   0.19949   0.70507   0.74983   0.67424
 0.82172

ROW  8
 0.49961  -0.81792   0.81389   0.71973   0.72721   0.79184   0.81218   1.00000  -0.17962   0.72079
 0.45501  -0.58688   0.46018  -0.05367   0.56424   0.51690   0.56701   0.47882   0.13959   0.16643
 0.54414  -0.12315  -0.02376   0.66165   0.84783   0.79272   0.68297   0.80402   0.63327   0.34470
 0.46272   0.48235   0.35928   0.15548   0.78807   0.27594   0.41757   0.70524   0.79585   0.78925
 0.75403

ROW  9
-0.01099   0.12278  -0.13615  -0.23369  -0.23653  -0.34016  -0.28139  -0.17962   1.00000  -0.32407
-0.26800   0.16923  -0.25198  -0.06602  -0.23346  -0.13356  -0.08220   0.09726  -0.66098  -0.25005
-0.13436   0.13831   0.18251  -0.08336  -0.11289  -0.15327  -0.13103  -0.12727  -0.11770  -0.10755
-0.17227   0.02111  -0.16094  -0.08745  -0.22910  -0.05743   0.06860  -0.28431  -0.18731  -0.14430
-0.22799

ROW 10
 0.40216  -0.70633   0.63780   0.60945   0.73332   0.78588   0.68630   0.72079  -0.32407   1.00000
 0.74243  -0.50609   0.36157   0.04559   0.35946   0.25161   0.41186   0.18546   0.15512   0.18906
 0.32901  -0.18696   0.17874   0.54416   0.71688   0.64119   0.56156   0.72026   0.45838   0.36578
 0.50851   0.40262   0.38062   0.09006   0.72970   0.18097   0.20791   0.65793   0.68484   0.66598
 0.70441

ROW 11
 0.25865  -0.45663   0.37493   0.24425   0.40912   0.47310   0.45806   0.45501  -0.26800   0.74243
 1.00000  -0.41003   0.05367   0.16823   0.06801   0.04040   0.08951  -0.06043  -0.0190C  -0.12348
-0.02559   0.04819   0.29622   0.28683   0.43310   0.34459   0.27310   0.43957   0.22361   0.25541
 0.34105   0.26836   0.13357   0.C8709   0.48109   0.09148   0.04849   0.32604   0.44290   0.29824
 0.44317

ROW 12
-0.30829   0.54750  -0.60903  -0.50127  -0.53169  -0.55084  -0.58457  -0.58688   0.16923  -0.50609
-0.41003   1.00000  -0.35335   0.05302  -0.39970  -0.52248  -0.41418  -0.29502  -0.14245  -0.16997
-0.39418   0.06679   0.05302  -0.39970  -0.59631  -0.54344  -0.48193  -0.62187  -0.35851  -0.23038
-0.30668  -0.30184  -0.20044  -0.06858  -0.60118  -0.35532  -0.07934  -0.39102  -0.49207  -0.56806
-0.43398

ROW 13
 0.39698  -0.46701   0.60689   0.64672   0.53070   0.53586   0.44887   0.46018  -0.25198   0.36157
 0.05367  -0.35335   1.00000  -0.15429   0.64608   0.50398   0.40120   0.41658   0.37843   0.51326
 0.56948  -0.44011  -0.32380   0.57581   0.60287   0.57705   0.66477   0.5996C   0.51725   0.29068
 0.35539   0.29166   0.49441   0.21790   0.46333   0.44412   0.19843   0.58103   0.42794   0.49043
 0.25626

ROW 14
 0.13656   0.08432  -0.C1160  -0.15100  -0.08445  -0.12113  -0.14883  -0.05367  -0.06602   0.04559
 0.16823  -0.00366  -0.15429   1.00000  -0.39555  -0.41412  -0.35367  -0.33986  -0.00892  -0.10158
-0.32141   0.17018   0.38358  -0.10344  -0.09020  -0.04148  -0.08877  -0.12070  -0.02574   0.02005
 0.03189   0.04553   0.05037   0.10934   0.01894   0.11288   0.07434  -0.06343   0.00899  -0.14726
-0.16558

ROW 15
 0.26717  -0.59830   0.59436   0.69390   0.52883   0.58845   0.62962   0.56424  -0.23346   0.35946
 0.06801  -0.52248   0.64608  -0.39555   1.00000   0.81722   0.61875   0.62390   0.31451   0.28969
 0.72110  -0.27940  -0.41526   0.47723   0.61693   0.57927   0.60080   0.65595   0.41128   0.15361
 0.28668   0.23026   0.27424   0.07501   0.47103   0.26576   0.16558   0.56404   0.52572   0.63235
 0.52178
```

```
ROW 16
 0.13789   -0.47392    0.41478    0.46700    0.43953    0.47030    0.51604    0.51690   -0.13356    0.25161
 0.04040   -0.41818    0.50398   -0.41412    0.81722    1.00000    0.65496    0.73161    0.12754    0.09395
 0.63250   -0.15931   -0.40637    0.45778    0.46666    0.43235    0.41331    0.54223    0.35781    0.14099
 0.22493    0.14333    0.14501    0.03996    0.35537    0.07894    0.23757    0.34897    0.35300    C.50672
 0.42640

ROW 17
 0.20791   -0.48340    0.40181    0.54939    0.42582    0.50259    0.56223    0.56701   -0.C822C    0.41186
 0.08951   -0.29502    0.40120   -0.35367    0.61875    0.65496    1.00000    0.75512    0.08107    0.13987
 0.56267   -0.10454   -0.22893    0.50135    0.49214    0.55590    0.44835    0.50511    0.45641    0.19492
 0.32404    0.25555    0.22427    0.11023    0.38489    0.07040    0.35083    0.43145    0.47451    0.42963
 0.56549

ROW 18
 0.15766   -0.44302    0.37858    0.48454    0.31910    0.39768    0.49350    0.47882    0.09726    0.18546
-0.06043   -0.14245    0.41658   -0.33986    0.62390    0.73161    0.75512    1.00000   -0.14191   -0.04735
 0.50510   -0.01501   -0.16146    0.47377    0.40664    0.41958    0.36424    0.44996    0.33606    0.06606
 0.22726    0.13476    C.10009    0.10982    0.25526    0.05771    0.30078    0.33588    0.37947    0.37843
 0.43658

ROW 19
 0.17557   -0.11208    0.20725    0.28564    0.21887    0.26751    0.16015    0.13959   -0.66098    0.15512
-0.01900   -0.17788    0.37843   -0.C0892    0.31451    0.12754    0.08107   -0.14191    1.00000    0.50968
 0.20155   -0.20533   -0.44154    0.10617    0.15675    0.17160    0.22594    0.15673    0.21439    0.12111
 0.15678    0.02844    0.29437    0.11941    0.18487    0.17417   -0.00681   -0.32094    0.10155    0.19953
-0.00551

ROW 20
 0.34685   -0.24236    0.29440    0.41420    0.28295    0.26510    0.13662    0.16643   -0.25005    0.18906
-0.12348   -0.16997    0.51326   -0.10158    0.29869    0.09395    0.13987   -0.04735    0.50968    1.00000
 0.29139   -0.48969   -0.22026    0.45460    0.31595    0.31863    0.49895    0.32431    0.40093    0.36540
 0.26171    0.23961    0.4CC93    0.17033    0.26500    0.31216    0.14089    0.42284    0.25281    0.34340
 0.10608

ROW 21
 0.09291   -0.54143    0.48325    0.62069    0.43686    0.49436    0.48839    0.54414   -0.13436    0.32901
-0.02559   -0.39418    0.56548   -0.32141    0.72110    0.63250    0.56267    0.50510    0.20155    0.29139
 1.00000   -0.35247   -0.42230    0.41574    0.57119    0.58150    0.46752    0.56305    0.39222    0.05052
 0.13983    0.13084    0.17832   -0.02089    0.35157    0.15908    0.34972    0.50996    0.44333    0.57392
 0.43752

ROW 22
-0.03651    0.17937   -0.23302   -0.30450   -0.25734   -0.32915   -0.10807   -0.12315    0.13831   -0.18696
 0.04819    0.06679   -0.44C11    0.17018   -0.27940   -0.15931   -0.10454   -0.01501   -0.20533   -0.48969
-0.35247    1.00000    0.34869   -0.20568   -0.27015   -0.23403   -0.24639   -0.26044   -0.19521   -0.30406
-0.06380   -0.03312   -0.16535    0.05481   -0.23613   -0.16146    0.04766   -0.32068   -0.12927   -0.16923
-0.11902

ROW 23
 0.13212   -0.06507    0.01594   -0.C9867    0.00817   -0.06810    0.01794   -0.02376    0.18251    0.17874
 0.29622    0.05302   -0.32380    0.38558   -0.41926   -0.40637   -0.22893   -0.16146   -0.44154   -0.22026
-0.42230    0.34869    1.00000    0.00846   -0.06504   -0.07399    0.00879    0.01504   -0.11248    0.04288
 0.28709    0.21819    0.07301    C.09766    0.07810    0.07628   -0.00657    0.00558    0.09474   -0.16844
 0.19038

ROW 24
 0.52575   -0.67934    0.72272    0.65703    0.61683    0.65634    0.67402    0.66165   -0.08336    0.54416
 0.28683   -0.39970    0.57581   -0.10344    0.47723    0.45778    0.50135    0.47377    0.10617    0.45460
 0.41574   -0.20568    0.00846    1.C0000    0.72846    0.67146    0.75916    0.72518    0.6765E    0.50987
 0.55778    0.49800    0.46C88    0.25542    0.65519    0.32745    0.33085    0.68192    0.60755    0.61470
 0.52243

ROW 25
 0.57055   -0.86504    0.87495    0.81452    0.75464    0.79760    0.72597    0.84783   -0.11289    0.71688
 0.43310   -0.59631    0.60287   -0.C9020    0.61693    0.46666    0.49214    0.40664    0.15675    0.31595
 0.57119   -0.27015   -0.06504    0.72846    1.00000    0.86824    0.82547    0.88884    0.68070    0.41826
 0.52211    0.53265    0.48141    0.16517    0.78144    0.38371    0.32959    0.79460    0.77102    0.80158
 0.64726

ROW 26
 0.58586   -0.79265    0.81310    0.79874    0.67956    0.76142    0.69642    0.79272   -0.15327    0.64119
 0.34459   -0.54344    0.57705   -0.04148    0.57927    0.43235    0.55590    0.41958    0.17160    0.31863
 0.58150   -0.23403   -0.07399    0.67146    0.86824    1.00000    0.80128    0.79415    0.68839    0.35054
 0.55228    0.55930    0.45920    0.30129    0.75706    0.37077    0.49760    0.73836    0.75535    0.73895
 0.60549

ROW 27
 0.69575   -0.77511    0.81880    0.77040    0.73987    0.74981    0.65517    0.68297   -0.13103    0.56156
 0.27310   -0.48193    0.66477   -0.C8877    0.60080    0.41331    0.44835    0.36424    0.22594    0.49895
 0.46752   -0.24639    0.00879    0.75916    0.82547    0.80128    1.00000    0.79594    0.7608C    0.51753
 0.66173    0.61255    0.65881    0.37556    0.70669    0.35299    0.28303    0.7608C    0.72824    0.71199
 0.55445

ROW 28
 0.55477   -0.88167    0.86101    0.80259    0.77046    0.81515    0.77563    0.80402   -0.12727    0.72026
 0.43957   -0.62187    0.5956C   -0.12070    0.65595    0.54223    0.50511    0.44996    0.15673    0.32431
 0.56305   -0.26044    0.01504    0.72518    0.88884    0.79415    0.79594    1.00000    0.64590    0.38220
 0.55556    0.54599    0.48424    0.15482    0.77238    0.39221   -0.24467    0.78493    0.72943    0.77746
 0.69313

ROW 29
 0.63052   -0.62792    0.64606    0.63326    0.59487    0.67289    0.59983    0.63327   -0.1177C    0.45838
 0.22361   -0.35851    0.51725   -0.02574    0.44128    0.35781    0.45641    0.33606    0.21439    C.40093
 0.39222   -0.19521   -0.11248    0.67658    0.68070    0.68839    0.76484    0.64590    1.00000    0.33660
 0.49237    0.43845    0.41847    0.27646    0.56457    0.19133    0.34477    0.65965    0.58C05    0.69087
 0.50316

ROW 30
 0.45504   -0.37184    0.44769    0.29400    0.49234    0.41226    0.28245    0.34470   -0.10755    0.36578
 0.25541   -0.23038    0.2906E    0.02005    0.15361    0.14099    0.19492    0.06606    0.12111    0.36540
 0.05052   -0.30406    0.04288    0.50987    0.41826    0.35054    0.51753    0.3822C    0.3366C    1.00000
 0.58508    0.59078    0.47677    0.25336    0.49278    0.33137    0.06846    0.32620    0.35557    0.22911
 0.28031

ROW 31
 0.58327   -0.55617    0.58324    0.47036    0.65026    0.61180    0.54809    0.46272   -0.17227    C.50851
 0.34105   -0.30668    0.35539    0.C3189    0.28668    0.22493    0.32404    0.22726    0.15678    0.26171
 0.13983   -0.06380    0.287C9    0.55778    0.52211    0.55228    0.66173    0.55556    0.49237    0.585C8
 1.00000    0.73054    0.63008    0.34052    0.67585    0.23806    0.18003    0.50173    0.5332C    0.31501
 0.52883

ROW 32
 0.69190   -0.55928    0.5952C    0.49303    0.57776    0.46343    0.44939    0.48235    0.02111    0.40262
 0.26836   -0.30184    0.29166    0.04553    0.23026    0.14333    0.25555    0.13476    0.02844    0.23961
 0.13084   -0.03312    0.21819    0.49800    0.53265    0.55930    0.61255    0.54599    0.43845    C.59078
 0.73054    1.00000    0.65931    0.34903    0.58535    0.34040    0.17508    0.48523    0.47182    0.39709
 0.45103
```

282

```
ROW 33
  0.61089   -0.46139    0.50799    0.41710    0.53740    0.49759    0.38213    0.35928   -0.16094    0.38062
  0.13357   -0.20044    0.49441    0.05037    0.27424    0.14501    0.22427    0.10009    0.29437    0.40093
  0.17832   -0.16935    0.07301    0.46088    0.48141    0.45920    0.65881    0.48424    0.41847    0.47677
  0.63008    0.65931    1.00000    0.40733    0.52203    0.28477    0.02690    0.58688    0.38329    0.32107
  0.27713

ROW 34
  0.44116   -0.15710    0.28822    0.19019    0.22474    0.20721    0.13034    0.15548    0.08745    0.09006
  0.08709   -0.06858    0.21790    0.10934    0.07501    0.03996    0.11023    0.10982    0.11941    0.17033
 -0.02089    0.05481    0.09766    0.25542    0.16517    0.30129    0.37556    0.15482    0.27646    0.25336
  0.34052    0.34903    0.40733    1.00000    0.20757    0.15667    0.29714    0.20408    0.22790    0.13996
  0.01850

ROW 35
  0.52250   -0.80162    0.80131    0.66793    0.77468    0.81616    0.80323    0.78807   -0.22910    0.72970
  0.48109   -0.60118    0.46333    0.01894    0.47103    0.35537    0.38489    0.25526    0.18487    0.26500
  0.35157   -0.23613    0.07810    0.65519    0.78144    0.75706    0.70669    0.77238    0.56457    0.49278
  0.67585    0.58535    0.52203    0.20757    1.00000    0.29016    0.21199    0.67602    0.78401    0.64672
  0.67758

ROW 36
  0.32410   -0.23634    0.41689    0.43885    0.25353    0.19403    0.20271    0.27594   -0.05743    0.18097
  0.09148   -0.35532    0.44412    0.11288    0.26576    0.07894    0.07040    0.05771    0.17417    0.31216
  0.15908   -0.16146    0.07628    0.32745    0.38371    0.37077    0.35299    0.39221    0.19133    0.33137
  0.23806    0.34040    0.28477    0.15667    0.29016    1.00000    0.13567    0.34846    0.30459    0.15902
  0.04890

ROW 37
  0.25267   -0.27582    0.24508    0.29708    0.10047    0.19592    0.19949    0.41757    0.06860    0.20791
  0.04849   -0.07934    0.19843    0.07434    0.16558    0.23757    0.35083    0.30078   -0.00681    0.14089
  0.34972    0.04766   -0.00657    0.33085    0.32959    0.49760    0.28303    0.24467    0.34477    0.06846
  0.18003    0.17508    0.02690    0.29714    0.21199    0.13967    1.00000    0.27560    0.38396    0.31650
  0.25373

ROW 38
  0.58984   -0.79244    0.78289    0.77371    0.68320    0.77636    0.70507    0.70524   -0.28431    0.65793
  0.32604   -0.39102    0.58103   -0.06343    0.56404    0.34897    0.43145    0.33588    0.32094    0.42284
  0.50996   -0.32068    0.00558    0.68192    0.79460    0.73836    0.76080    0.78493    0.65965    0.32620
  0.50173    0.48523    0.58688    0.20408    0.67602    0.34846    0.27560    1.00000    0.68843    0.70221
  0.62982

ROW 39
  0.46134   -0.76856    0.73816    0.72580    0.66312    0.74128    0.74983    0.79585   -0.18731    0.68484
  0.44290   -0.49207    0.42794    0.00899    0.52572    0.35300    0.47451    0.37947    0.10155    0.25281
  0.44333   -0.12927    0.09474    0.60755    0.77102    0.75539    0.72824    0.72943    0.58005    0.35597
  0.53320    0.47182    0.38329    0.22790    0.78401    0.30459   -0.38396    0.68843    1.00000    0.66261
  0.70400

ROW 40
  0.52319   -0.77730    0.73385    0.69823    0.63014    0.69879    0.67424    0.78925   -0.14430    0.56598
  0.29824   -0.56806    0.49043   -0.14726    0.63235    0.50672    0.42963    0.37843    0.19953    0.34340
  0.57392   -0.16923   -0.16844    0.61470    0.80158    0.73895    0.71199    0.77746    0.69087    0.22911
  0.31501    0.39709    0.32107    0.13996    0.64672    0.15902    0.31650    0.70221    0.66261    1.00000
  0.60667

ROW 41
  0.36480   -0.77919    0.65370    0.64585    0.68895    0.74370    0.82172    0.75403   -0.22795    0.70441
  0.44317   -0.43398    0.25626   -0.16558    0.52178    0.42640    0.56549    0.43658   -0.00551    0.10608
  0.43752   -0.11902    0.19038    0.52243    0.64726    0.60549    0.55445    0.69313    0.50316    0.28031
  0.52883    0.45103    0.27713    0.01850    0.67758    0.04890    0.25373    0.62982    0.70400    0.60667
  1.00000
```

TABLE A–2: Correlation Matrix for Social, Political, and Economic Indicators (Low Sample)

```
CORRELATION COEFFICIENTS

ROW 1
  1.00000   -0.41102    0.69664    0.56506    0.35987    0.39516    0.24293    0.24146    0.12452    0.03954
 -0.02713   -0.03175    0.27344    0.22498   -0.00556   -0.06404   -0.28379   -0.04376    0.16748   -0.01984
 -0.02184    0.09901   -0.04672    0.19695    0.29283    0.41003    0.37902    0.14602    0.53606    0.26958
  0.33754    0.53074    0.44111    0.41810    0.26695    0.29827    0.34833    0.33599    0.21949    0.59771
 -0.13156

ROW 2
 -0.41102    1.00000   -0.59561   -0.57778   -0.25069   -0.33360   -0.26792   -0.26155   -0.19272   -0.04710
 -0.14879   -0.24283   -0.21221   -0.09340   -0.22061   -0.23479   -0.19809   -0.43097    0.09060    0.01724
 -0.24460   -0.06821    0.07257   -0.42917   -0.56268   -0.61381   -0.63217   -0.42590   -0.18329   -0.38241
 -0.26633   -0.34662   -0.26199   -0.37987   -0.22345    0.04217   -0.29917   -0.32306   -0.57506   -0.44149
 -0.34241

ROW 3
  0.69664   -0.59561    1.00000    0.69494    0.60335    0.51062    0.30747    0.58156    0.12946   -0.09563
 -0.20736    0.05754    0.60083    0.12340    0.33287    0.26112    0.10494    0.36109    0.12715    0.15514
  0.40367   -0.10448   -0.19216    0.60244    0.67851    0.77240    0.77961    0.44458    0.41235    0.58255
  0.44649    0.60164    0.53966    0.51436    0.41655    0.36521    0.55663    0.39862    0.35823    0.64040
  0.08091

ROW 4
  0.56506   -0.57778    0.69494    1.00000    0.52594    0.65326    0.29529    0.08924    0.37495   -0.27673
 -0.36867    0.34522    0.51928   -0.01828    0.33912    0.22403    0.16005    0.44533   -0.01225    0.21157
  0.38826   -0.24810   -0.21179    0.55257    0.44047    0.44484    0.60608    0.37367    0.41706    0.39463
  0.35696    0.40008    0.43656    0.35291   -0.03020    0.47004    0.33027    0.35744    0.15042    0.27146
  0.00765
```

283

```
ROW  5
  0.35987   -0.25069    0.60335    0.52594    1.00000    0.73633    0.16534    0.13610    0.10417   -0.18135
 -0.24437    0.06729    0.61389   -0.23045    0.50223    0.43066    0.27054    0.37369    0.05672    0.36827
  0.41003   -0.28362   -0.27441    0.56926    0.32385    0.36878    0.59592    0.38198    0.22652    0.47569
  0.51679    0.52499    0.70052    0.40780    0.06702    0.13739    0.07317    0.36406    0.03533    0.11742
  0.06256

ROW  6
  0.39516   -0.33360    0.51062    0.65326    0.73633    1.00000    0.41041    0.09960    0.08135   -0.16396
 -0.14037    0.26521    0.55960   -0.20794    0.58581    0.51953    0.34929    0.51416    0.09190    0.27721
  0.47952   -0.35107   -0.49778    0.65720    0.36186    0.35726    0.43718    0.35465    0.46420    0.38556
  0.45190    0.30270    0.42261    0.40622    0.09809    0.24069    0.23622    0.46365    0.08460    0.12871
  0.15205

ROW  7
  0.24293   -0.26792    0.30747    0.29529    0.16534    0.41041    1.00000    0.29578    0.32529    0.16408
  0.14187    0.09553    0.40163   -0.02476    0.44822    0.22870    0.29090    0.41420   -0.22440   -0.12242
  0.28523   -0.00647   -0.05528    0.42480    0.39731    0.27087    0.35483    0.55300    0.30631    0.11822
  0.13082    0.08284    0.15537    0.25064    0.38885    0.34714    0.17932    0.40722    0.44943    0.19742
  0.35960

ROW  8
  0.24146   -0.26155    0.58156    0.08924    0.13610    0.09960    0.29578    1.00000   -0.02689    0.31639
  0.13733   -0.28246    0.28039    0.07168    0.24972    0.30880    0.22346    0.16243    0.11778    0.01680
  0.36833   -0.06424   -0.25152    0.30945    0.75289    0.60657    0.32289    0.36882    0.08675    0.54106
  0.11829    0.28903    0.07090    0.29376    0.73390    0.34052    0.56065    0.09611    0.47976    0.60864
  0.13920

ROW  9
  0.12452   -0.19272    0.12946    0.37495    0.10417    0.08135    0.32529   -0.02689    1.00000   -0.03628
 -0.13623    0.07887    0.15985   -0.30927    0.06387   -0.03319    0.16442    0.35861   -0.64583   -0.23829
  0.10647   -0.06919    0.22316   -0.05919    0.13405   -0.02487    0.25223    0.20959   -0.02647   -0.20527
 -0.00450   -0.02551    0.03625    0.20109   -0.20265    0.15865   -0.21116    0.03101    0.20453   -0.08628
  0.21721

ROW 10
  0.03954   -0.04710   -0.09563   -0.27673   -0.18135   -0.16396    0.16408    0.31639   -0.03628    1.00000
  0.72219   -0.47801   -0.31906    0.12549   -0.07374   -0.12241    0.01833   -0.18401   -0.07879   -0.25268
 -0.30950    0.25594    0.33797    0.00556    0.23462    0.05136   -0.16046    0.25651   -0.36863    0.28191
  0.22479    0.24517   -0.02514   -0.10586    0.57635   -0.04645   -0.03724   -0.11008    0.25163    0.08802
  0.43692

ROW 11
 -0.02713   -0.14879   -0.20736   -0.36867   -0.24437   -0.14037    0.14187    0.13733   -0.13623    0.72219
  1.00000   -0.34829   -0.34491    0.03046   -0.11374   -0.13917   -0.13120   -0.27069   -0.06901   -0.26457
 -0.41221    0.29836    0.23185   -0.12293    0.11062    0.00057   -0.12488    0.11759   -0.17988    0.04674
  0.06971    0.10488   -0.22637   -0.02579    0.33403   -0.22726   -0.12297   -0.24645    0.32969    0.10467
  0.27758

ROW 12
 -0.03175   -0.24283    0.05754    0.34522    0.06729    0.26521    0.09553   -0.28246    0.07887   -0.47801
 -0.34829    1.00000    0.00108   -0.37617   -0.02807   -0.04318    0.07544    0.17501   -0.10119    0.11435
  0.14793   -0.20575   -0.23197    0.20670   -0.04697   -0.02862    0.18880    0.01894    0.07389    0.03920
  0.01409    0.05659   -0.02429   -0.02599   -0.08869   -0.19810   -0.06285    0.29040    0.07480   -0.11427
  0.15274

ROW 13
  0.27344   -0.21221    0.60083    0.51928    0.61389    0.55960    0.40163    0.28039    0.15985   -0.31906
 -0.34491    0.00108    1.00000   -0.00028    0.58824    0.52610    0.17505    0.56388   -0.15410    0.18358
  0.64391   -0.41134   -0.27901    0.47842    0.37072    0.42006    0.53329    0.55041    0.22380    0.18927
  0.17996    0.22063    0.52847    0.25418    0.09253    0.56589    0.33585    0.25980    0.03217    0.11795
 -0.04895

ROW 14
  0.22498   -0.09340    0.12340   -0.01828   -0.23045   -0.20794   -0.02476    0.07168   -0.30927    0.12549
  0.03046   -0.37617   -0.00028    1.00000   -0.13757   -0.27157   -0.23733   -0.25023    0.34075    0.09691
 -0.04974    0.17945    0.20928    0.12278    0.03488    0.20258    0.12521   -0.00050    0.26902    0.10588
  0.13565    0.00442    0.19250    0.07894    0.20421    0.16531    0.30776    0.02628    0.13772    0.22722
 -0.06945

ROW 15
 -0.00556   -0.22061    0.33287    0.33912    0.50223    0.58581    0.44822    0.24972    0.06387   -0.07374
 -0.11374   -0.02807    0.58824   -0.13757    1.00000    0.86445    0.53684    0.78083    0.03149    0.15613
  0.66675   -0.33678   -0.45024    0.41253    0.35281    0.34260    0.29042    0.49146    0.02298    0.18620
  0.28451   -0.06746    0.16015    0.34041    0.12888    0.34676    0.30131    0.27895    0.13633    0.00539
  0.08613

ROW 16
 -0.06404   -0.23479    0.26112    0.22403    0.43066    0.51953    0.22870    0.30880   -0.03319   -0.12241
 -0.13917   -0.04318    0.52610   -0.27157    0.86445    1.00000    0.55041    0.74768    0.07937    0.14603
  0.66940   -0.43665   -0.57396    0.26719    0.31400    0.31901    0.17010    0.43048   -0.02965    0.15492
  0.17579   -0.13683    0.11301    0.28774    0.09657    0.20823    0.29144    0.14602    0.04627   -0.04175
 -0.05028

ROW 17
 -0.28379   -0.19809    0.10494    0.16005    0.27054    0.34929    0.29090    0.22346    0.16442    0.01833
 -0.13120    0.07544    0.17505   -0.23733    0.53684    0.55041    1.00000    0.69901   -0.15012   -0.05626
  0.56894   -0.26032   -0.47467    0.25945    0.31857    0.08653    0.36455    0.05729    0.23409
  0.03784   -0.19924   -0.08034    0.03017    0.05318   -0.03703    0.09618    0.04824    0.14648   -0.02701
  0.29895

ROW 18
 -0.04376   -0.43097    0.36109    0.44533    0.37369    0.51416    0.41420    0.16243    0.35861   -0.18401
 -0.27069    0.17501    0.56388   -0.25023    0.78083    0.74768    0.69901    1.00000   -0.33822   -0.06623
  0.64914   -0.30421   -0.37087    0.36424    0.38755    0.42735    0.34168    0.45657    0.04002    0.05550
  0.10292   -0.19882    0.07637    0.21649   -0.03497    0.18360    0.18034    0.22964    0.17162   -0.02791
  0.31843

ROW 19
  0.16748    0.09060    0.12715   -0.01225    0.05672    0.09190   -0.22440    0.11778   -0.64583   -0.07879
 -0.06901   -0.10119   -0.15410    0.34075    0.03149    0.07937   -0.15012   -0.33822    1.00000    0.44722
 -0.02086   -0.10820   -0.37869    0.14376   -0.10358    0.07169   -0.09488   -0.13052    0.21828    0.30185
  0.20587    0.23333    0.04025    0.18781    0.11087    0.07104    0.43440    0.17153   -0.14640    0.16714
 -0.43547

ROW 20
 -0.01984    0.01724    0.15514    0.21157    0.36827    0.27721   -0.12242    0.01680   -0.23829   -0.25268
 -0.26457    0.11435    0.18358    0.09691    0.15613    0.14603   -0.05626   -0.06623    0.44722    1.00000
  0.00835   -0.57216   -0.22889    0.45319   -0.01204   -0.17503    0.22303    0.14002    0.11578    0.42113
  0.11992    0.21238    0.43900    0.22861   -0.10406    0.17543    0.01702    0.32215   -0.15333   -0.07832
 -0.10679

ROW 21
 -0.02184   -0.24460    0.40367    0.38826    0.41003    0.47952    0.28523    0.36833    0.10647   -0.30950
 -0.41221    0.14793    0.64391   -0.04974    0.66675    0.66940    0.56894    0.64914   -0.02086    0.00835
  1.00000   -0.33580   -0.47400    0.40794    0.40707    0.52953    0.32287    0.42499    0.10952    0.24230
  0.23336   -0.00468    0.16746    0.25997    0.18529    0.31821    0.50513    0.33375    0.19129    0.13028
 -0.04960
```

ROW 22
```
6.09901   -0.06821   -0.10448   -0.24810   -0.28362   -0.35107   -0.00647   -0.06424   -0.06919    0.25594
0.29836   -0.20575   -0.41134    0.17945   -0.33678   -0.43665   -0.26032   -0.30421   -0.10820   -0.57216
-0.33580   1.00000    0.53359   -0.19417    0.03044    0.04898   -0.0625C   -0.25561    0.10507   -0.25852
0.05741    0.06184   -0.18166    0.10345    0.09637   -0.15077    0.03737   -0.05238    0.20506    0.16287
0.17072
```

ROW 23
```
-0.04672    0.07257   -0.19216   -0.21179   -0.27441   -0.49778   -0.05528   -0.25152    0.22316    0.33797
0.23185   -0.23197   -0.27901    0.20928   -0.45024   -0.57396   -0.47467   -0.37087   -0.37869   -0.22889
-0.47400    0.53359    1.00000   -0.13918   -0.19620   -0.21263    0.06037   -0.08265   -0.29629   -0.15324
0.15067    0.13907    0.19149   -0.05950    0.03864   -0.16466   -0.30558   -0.04164    0.05248   -0.13162
0.25664
```

ROW 24
```
0.19695   -0.42917    0.60244    0.55257    0.56926    0.65720    0.42480    0.30945   -0.05919    0.00556
-0.12393    0.20670    0.47842    0.12278    0.41253    0.26719    0.25945    0.36424    0.14376    0.45319
0.40794   -0.19417   -0.13918    1.00000    0.55175    0.40968    0.67929    0.52518    0.27865    0.65279
0.45353    0.41691    0.51458    0.40926    0.35262    0.26154    0.34031    0.51700    0.28282    0.15553
0.39418
```

ROW 25
```
0.29283   -0.56268    0.67851    0.44047    0.32385    0.36186    0.39731    0.75289    0.13405    0.23462
0.11062   -0.04697    0.37072    0.03488    0.35281    0.31400    0.31857    0.38755   -0.10358   -0.01204
0.40707    0.03044   -0.19620    0.55175    1.00000    0.73178    0.64441    0.43788    0.25193    0.58722
0.35964    0.37083    0.21252    0.29822    0.56897    0.39216    0.45506    0.25326    0.62205    0.60149
0.31488
```

ROW 26
```
0.41003   -0.61381    0.77240    0.44484    0.36878    0.35726    0.27087    0.60657   -0.02487    0.05136
0.00057   -0.02862    0.42006    0.20258    0.34260    0.31901    0.36152    0.42735    0.07169   -0.17503
0.52953    0.04898   -0.21263    0.40968    0.73178    1.00000    0.60179    0.31503    0.31407    0.51498
0.46608    0.37587    0.26780    0.24724    0.50286    0.13744    0.57329    0.27642    0.50362    0.69940
0.15929
```

ROW 27
```
0.37902   -0.63217    0.77961    0.60608    0.59592    0.43718    0.35483    0.32289    0.25223   -0.16046
-0.12488    0.18880    0.53329    0.12521    0.29042    0.17010    0.08653    0.34168   -0.09488    0.22303
0.32287   -0.06250    0.06037    0.67929    0.64441    0.60179    1.00000    0.47236    0.30805    0.53917
0.51594    0.51928    0.63917    0.51222    0.30165    0.16095    0.21950    0.34359    0.47596    0.36768
0.25169
```

ROW 28
```
0.14602   -0.42590    0.44458    0.37367    0.38198    0.35465    0.55300    0.36882    0.20959    0.25651
0.11759    0.01894    0.55041   -0.00050    0.49146    0.43048    0.36455    0.45657   -0.13052    0.14002
0.42499   -0.25561   -0.08265    0.52518    0.43788    0.31503    0.47236    1.00000    0.00752    0.41094
0.36522    0.35431    0.43643    0.32604    0.41192    0.39606    0.30395    0.22506    0.22323   -0.04743
0.28158
```

ROW 29
```
0.53606   -0.18329    0.41235    0.41706    0.22652    0.46420    0.30631    0.08675   -0.02647   -0.36863
-0.17988    0.07389    0.22380    0.26902    0.02298   -0.02965    0.05729    0.04002    0.21828    0.11578
0.10952    0.10507   -0.29629    0.27865    0.25193    0.31407    0.30805    0.00752    1.00000    0.08048
0.16350    0.04696    0.17875    0.37737   -0.06032    0.29972    0.3048C    0.24688    0.07048    0.39616
-0.20370
```

ROW 30
```
0.26958   -0.38241    0.58255    0.39463    0.47569    0.38556    0.11822    0.54106   -0.20527    0.28191
0.04674    0.03920    0.18927    0.10588    0.18620    0.19492    0.23409    0.05550    0.30185    0.42113
0.24230   -0.25852   -0.15324    0.65279    0.58722    0.51498    0.53917    0.41094    0.08048    1.00000
0.51040    0.57417    0.56491    0.30287    0.60251    0.10681    0.20308    0.22532    0.23272    0.35515
0.13506
```

ROW 31
```
0.33754   -0.26433    0.44649    0.35696    0.51679    0.45190    0.13082    0.11829   -0.00450    0.22479
0.06970    0.01409    0.17996    0.13565    0.28451    0.17579    0.03784    0.10292    0.20587    0.11992
0.23336    0.05741    0.15067    0.45353    0.35964    0.46608    0.51594    0.36522    0.16350    0.51040
1.00000    0.57011    0.57498    0.40568    0.40294    0.08646    0.25045    0.43657    0.18827    0.13769
0.12531
```

ROW 32
```
0.53074   -0.34662    0.60164    0.40008    0.52499    0.30270    0.08284    0.28903   -0.02551    0.24517
0.10488    0.05659    0.22063    0.00442   -0.06746   -0.13683   -0.19924   -0.19882    0.23333    0.21238
-0.00468    0.06184    0.13907    0.41691    0.37083    0.37587    0.51928    0.35431    0.04696    0.57417
0.57011    1.00000    0.61843    0.29146    0.45753    0.15824    0.32970    0.41389    0.30043    0.4C289
0.16996
```

ROW 33
```
-0.44111   -0.26199    0.53966    0.43656    0.70052    0.42261    0.15537    0.07090    0.03625   -0.02514
-0.22637   -0.02429    0.52847    0.19250    0.16015    0.11301   -0.08034    0.07637    0.04025    0.43900
0.16746   -0.18166    0.19149    0.51458    0.21252    0.26780    0.63917    0.43643    0.17875    0.56491
0.57498    0.61843    1.00000    0.39808    0.23398    0.17616   -0.01149   -0.40759    0.01267    0.08784
0.05429
```

ROW 34
```
0.41810   -0.37987    0.51436    0.35291    0.40780    0.40622    0.25064    0.29376    0.20109   -0.1C586
-0.02579   -0.02599    0.25418    0.07894    0.34041    0.28774    0.03017    0.21649    0.18781    0.22861
0.25997    0.10345   -0.05950    0.40926    0.29822    0.24724    0.51222    0.32604    0.37737    0.30287
0.40568    0.29146    0.39808    1.00000    0.19154    0.23196    0.28094    0.32035    0.29465    0.13125
-0.01586
```

ROW 35
```
0.26695   -0.22345    0.41655   -0.03020    0.06702    0.09809    0.38885    0.73390   -0.20265    0.57635
0.33403   -0.08869    0.09253    0.20421    0.12888    0.09657    0.05318   -0.03497    0.11087   -0.1C406
0.18529    0.09637    0.03864    0.35262    0.56897    0.50286    0.30165    0.41192   -0.06032    0.6C251
0.40294    0.45753    0.23398    0.19154    1.00000    0.08723    0.41181    0.21300    0.53712    0.44856
0.38031
```

ROW 36
```
0.29827    0.04217    0.36521    0.47004    0.13739    0.24069    0.34714    0.34052    0.15865   -0.04645
-0.22726   -0.19810    0.56589    0.16531    0.34676    0.20823   -0.03703    0.18360    0.07104    0.17543
0.31821   -0.15077   -0.16466    0.26154    0.39216    0.13744    0.16095    0.39606    0.29972    0.11681
0.08646    0.15824    0.17616    0.23196    0.08723    1.00000    0.47894    0.14955   -0.C1113    0.13432
-0.25896
```

ROW 37
```
0.34833   -0.29917    0.55663    0.33027    0.07317    0.23622    0.17932    0.56065   -0.21116   -0.03724
-0.12297   -0.06285    0.33585    0.30776    0.30131    0.29144    0.09618    0.18034    0.43440    0.01702
0.50513    0.03737   -0.30558    0.34031    0.45506    0.57329    0.21950    0.30395    0.30480    0.02308
0.25045    0.32970   -0.01149    0.28094    0.41181    0.47894    1.00000    0.36019    0.35020    0.52544
-0.04254
```

ROW 38
```
0.33599   -0.32306    0.39862    0.35744    0.36406    0.46365    0.40722    0.09611    0.03101   -0.11008
-0.24645    0.29040    0.25980    0.02628    0.27895    0.14602    0.04824    0.22964    0.17153    0.32215
0.33475   -0.05238   -0.04164    0.51700    0.25326    0.27642    0.34359    0.22506    0.24688    0.22532
0.43657    0.41389    0.40759    0.32035    0.21300    0.14955    0.36019    1.00000    0.33960    0.31860
0.25053
```

285

```
ROW 39
 0.21949   -0.57506    0.35823    0.15042    0.03533    0.08460    0.44943    0.47976    0.20453    0.25163
 0.32969    0.07480    0.03217    0.13772    0.13633    0.04627    0.14648    0.17162   -0.14640   -0.15333
 0.19129    0.20506    0.05248    0.28282    0.62205    0.50362    0.47596    0.22323    0.07048    0.23272
 0.18827    0.30043    0.01267    0.29465    0.53712   -0.01113    0.35020    0.33960    1.00000    0.54403
 0.50015

ROW 40
 0.59771   -0.44149    0.64040    0.27146    0.11742    0.12871    0.19742    0.60864   -0.08628    0.08802
 0.10467   -0.11427    0.11795    0.22722    0.00539   -0.04175   -0.02701   -0.02791    0.16714   -0.07832
 0.13028    0.16287   -0.13162    0.15553    0.60149    0.69940    0.36768   -0.04743    0.39616    0.35515
 0.13769    0.40289    0.08784    0.13125    0.44856    0.13432    0.52544    0.31860    0.54403    1.00000
 0.01412

ROW 41
-0.13156   -0.34241    0.08091    0.00765    0.06256    0.15205    0.35960    0.13920    0.21721    0.43692
 0.27758    0.15274   -0.04895   -0.06945    0.08613   -0.05028    0.29895    0.31843   -0.43547   -0.10679
-0.04960    0.17072    0.25664    0.39418    0.31488    0.15929    0.25169    0.28158   -0.20370    0.13506
 0.12531    0.16996    0.05429   -0.01586    0.38031   -0.25896   -0.04254    0.25053    0.50015    0.01412
 1.00000
```

TABLE A–3:   Correlation Matrix for Social, Political, and Economic Indicators (Intermediate Sample)

```
CORRELATION COEFFICIENTS

ROW  1
 1.00000   -0.14258    0.30870    0.00472    0.05097   -0.06193   -0.09036   -0.12247    0.14124   -0.10931
 0.14803   -0.01527    0.11123    0.28610   -0.10310   -0.20471   -0.17535   -0.06625    0.12016    0.15556
-0.59031    0.38073    0.28923    0.14150    0.19528    0.23553    0.55949    0.12761    0.13106    0.27410
 0.23392    0.30387    0.28129    0.62655    0.12973    0.19515    0.09616    0.17506   -0.18225    0.24100
-0.44972

ROW  2
-0.14258    1.00000   -0.60759   -0.35434   -0.20966   -0.25191   -0.24808   -0.37366   -0.07677   -0.09260
 0.10621    0.13044   -0.26272    0.27210   -0.22659   -0.32203   -0.16075   -0.27527   -0.11145   -0.02087
-0.14508   -0.14284    0.09786   -0.44273   -0.46576   -0.26370   -0.34391   -0.72565    0.01166   -0.16123
-0.26685   -0.40715   -0.60608   -0.03928   -0.52217   -0.15105    0.06374   -0.62339   -0.15141   -0.39347
 0.10931

ROW  3
 0.30870   -0.60759    1.00000    0.47430    0.28554    0.32616    0.24905    0.16776   -0.02225   -0.10970
-0.13897   -0.32871    0.58345    0.01322    0.35069    0.14711   -0.12911    0.07460    0.40456    0.31368
-0.12180    0.15504   -0.08951    0.53251    0.64775    0.41004    0.77682    0.66598    0.21524    0.14528
 0.29403    0.34723    0.64747    0.32302    0.60279    0.47145   -0.20364    0.58754    0.30603    0.42250
-0.48082

ROW  4
 0.00472   -0.35434    0.47430    1.00000   -0.00233   -0.01894    0.17879    0.35823   -0.19800   -0.38228
-0.53512   -0.24708    0.65116   -0.29707    0.75413    0.43937    0.40434    0.50774    0.47336    0.35859
 0.52558    0.02739   -0.54108    0.30585    0.38913    0.50034    0.40455    0.32158    0.13486   -0.19756
-0.13643    0.15478    0.07492    0.00562    0.07807    0.48530    0.04153    0.36382    0.42122    0.29137
-0.22103

ROW  5
 0.05097   -0.20966    0.28554   -0.00233    1.00000    0.57614    0.06082   -0.07074   -0.27791    0.40635
 0.11067   -0.21500    0.14977    0.04686    0.05343    0.14779   -0.15878   -0.14106    0.34354   -0.06223
-0.15765    0.00955   -0.26001   -0.05907    0.07866   -0.19004    0.27190    0.14564    0.09453    0.41861
 0.50196    0.31139    0.38232    0.04662    0.50448   -0.16840   -0.66572   -0.13007   -0.07677   -0.12740
-0.05989

ROW  6
-0.06193   -0.25191    0.32616   -0.01894    0.57614    1.00000    0.58011    0.28016   -0.44181    0.35625
 0.06650   -0.25340    0.21929   -0.05791    0.11918    0.16874   -0.14321    0.02070    0.48878   -0.03183
 0.01388   -0.18271   -0.46282    0.10050    0.23616   -0.06571    0.31379    0.37892    0.25224    0.24802
 0.40925   -0.04574    0.42345   -0.03987    0.62794   -0.34803   -0.36993    0.18959    0.36166    0.17121
-0.01788

ROW  7
-0.09036   -0.24808    0.24905    0.17879    0.06082    0.58011    1.00000    0.26080   -0.49722   -0.01387
-0.08222   -0.32595    0.17985   -0.48035    0.49120    0.49344    0.27873    0.46312    0.31761   -0.13303
 0.18259    0.12820   -0.21996    0.30468    0.06985   -0.12702    0.14950    0.37847    0.02987    0.06643
 0.34336    0.09932    0.19113   -0.12535    0.35693   -0.19325   -0.28193    0.11409    0.39618    0.04388
 0.41965

ROW  8
-0.12247   -0.37366    0.16776    0.35823   -0.07074    0.28016    0.26080    1.00000   -0.09578   -0.04534
-0.14597    0.07444    0.13620   -0.05582    0.21640    0.33529    0.40532    0.64275    0.04516   -0.14791
 0.34585    0.28231   -0.38896    0.22672    0.30208    0.32071    0.04508    0.47558    0.45091   -0.37340
-0.21058   -0.13388   -0.12156   -0.13489   -0.12679   -0.17284    0.41821    0.35247    0.49436    0.74415
-0.02828

ROW  9
 0.14124   -0.07677   -0.02225   -0.19800   -0.27791   -0.44181   -0.49722   -0.09578    1.00000   -0.10116
-0.05556    0.13951   -0.26404    0.02147   -0.25284   -0.15354    0.12678    0.05219   -0.64015   -0.18872
-0.04733    0.12006    0.25578    0.14331    0.21164    0.22126   -0.00895    0.03371   -0.00278   -0.17273
-0.15302    0.06729   -0.05998    0.27637   -0.34451   -0.00514    0.43293   -0.06666   -0.36580    0.11029
-0.28911

ROW 10
-0.10931   -0.09260   -0.10970   -0.38228    0.40635    0.35625   -0.01387   -0.04534   -0.10116    1.00000
 0.71329    0.05992   -0.22897    0.24258   -0.47163   -0.10610   -0.37426   -0.27438   -0.14641   -0.31993
-0.16281    0.00789    0.14513    0.09673   -0.05329   -0.36365   -0.21016    0.16272   -0.03658    0.22413
 0.02026   -0.10239    0.03984   -0.31241    0.02354   -0.21190   -0.31206   -0.03709   -0.34022   -0.21726
-0.10611
```

286

```
ROW 11
  0.14803     0.10621    -0.13897    -0.53512     0.11067     0.06650    -0.08222    -0.14597    -0.05556     0.71329
  1.00000    -0.08985    -0.25366     0.46575    -0.60248    -0.23488    -0.48313    -0.42459    -0.32743    -0.34293
 -0.34520     0.19483     0.41372     0.04623    -0.02961    -0.19763    -0.09403     0.10823     0.04816     0.39242
  0.03165     0.07786    -0.03111    -0.05829    -0.09363     0.05814    -0.09096    -0.14912    -0.33237    -0.13224
 -0.18441

ROW 12
 -0.01527     0.13044    -0.32871    -0.24708    -0.21500    -0.25340    -0.32595     0.07444     0.13951     0.05992
 -0.08985     1.00000    -0.25289     0.00318    -0.31081    -0.43441    -0.14077    -0.03054    -0.17541    -0.01942
 -0.26374    -0.22649     0.27539    -0.08140    -0.35546    -0.18114    -0.25899    -0.36346     0.15270    -0.17916
 -0.15949    -0.24561    -0.21306     0.01547    -0.36824    -0.29385     0.20505     0.18615    -0.21789     0.02918
  0.22852

ROW 13
  0.11123    -0.26272     0.58345     0.65116     0.14977     0.21929     0.17985     0.13620    -0.26404    -0.22897
 -0.25366    -0.25289     1.00000    -0.12395     0.51989     0.30004     0.11372     0.17797     0.64095     0.64008
  0.19881    -0.28320    -0.39258     0.57682     0.54214     0.37649     0.71729     0.38930     0.47672     0.20088
  0.20657     0.06439     0.31291     0.14079     0.38107     0.57937    -0.06981     0.49722     0.32877     0.25189
 -0.39020

ROW 14
  0.28610     0.27210     0.01322    -0.29707     0.04686    -0.05791    -0.48035    -0.05582     0.02147     0.24258
  0.46575     0.00318    -0.12395     1.00000    -0.49610    -0.37253    -0.57009    -0.50223    -0.15548    -0.09217
 -0.37179     0.16199     0.31551    -0.24407     0.04071     0.12490     0.04692    -0.11876     0.03606    -0.11339
 -0.24451    -0.09463     0.03643     0.24118    -0.10189     0.09060     0.13847     0.06522    -0.07417     0.19425
 -0.58236

ROW 15
 -0.10310    -0.22659     0.35069     0.75413     0.05343     0.11918     0.49120     0.21640    -0.25284    -0.47163
 -0.60248    -0.31081     0.51989    -0.49610     1.00000     0.74016     0.53681     0.63467     0.40873     0.17068
  0.43884     0.01246    -0.46311     0.15702     0.16243     0.24619     0.29383     0.31988    -0.01198    -0.18242
  0.08199     0.15812     0.07830     0.02969     0.22834     0.25856    -0.16251     0.05037     0.51458     0.18758
  0.19224

ROW 16
 -0.20471    -0.32203     0.14711     0.43937     0.14779     0.16874     0.49344     0.33529    -0.15354    -0.10610
 -0.23488    -0.43441     0.30004    -0.37253     0.74016     1.00000     0.69223     0.72832     0.02925    -0.23653
  0.38830     0.21320    -0.26680     0.28244     0.08020     0.01675     0.06145     0.47646    -0.06067    -0.13217
  0.08981     0.09186    -0.09946    -0.20663     0.14449    -0.00567    -0.14125    -0.07136     0.30298     0.20434
  0.31673

ROW 17
 -0.17535    -0.16075    -0.12911     0.40434    -0.15878    -0.14321     0.27873     0.40532     0.12678    -0.37426
 -0.48313    -0.14077     0.11372    -0.57009     0.53681     0.69223     1.00000     0.83090    -0.06202    -0.14625
  0.39390     0.23525    -0.34184     0.20412    -0.04564     0.04166    -0.08887     0.06903     0.18051    -0.14764
 -0.04090     0.05331    -0.29893    -0.14500    -0.25481    -0.13576     0.22964    -0.18817     0.08060     0.05897
  0.38043

ROW 18
 -0.06625    -0.27527     0.07460     0.50774    -0.14106     0.02070     0.46312     0.64275     0.05219    -0.27438
 -0.42459    -0.03054     0.17797    -0.50223     0.63467     0.72832     0.83090     1.00000    -0.07000    -0.23321
  0.36715     0.39443    -0.24586     0.38814     0.14319     0.19493     0.05686     0.37797     0.26483    -0.36275
 -0.00394     0.05772    -0.26185    -0.11176    -0.23053    -0.12144     0.23924     0.03733     0.29951     0.40312
  0.30422

ROW 19
  0.12016    -0.11145     0.40456     0.47336     0.34354     0.48878     0.31761     0.04516    -0.64015    -0.14641
 -0.32743    -0.17541     0.64095    -0.15548     0.40873     0.02925    -0.06202    -0.07000     1.00000     0.72701
  0.09607    -0.31441    -0.57491     0.03115     0.07415    -0.03846     0.45764     0.05469     0.13289     0.24743
  0.20260    -0.04267     0.36705     0.04676     0.49802     0.19924    -0.39593     0.28773     0.26635     0.01620
 -0.14075

ROW 20
  0.15556    -0.02087     0.31368     0.35859    -0.06223    -0.03183    -0.13303    -0.14791    -0.18872    -0.31993
 -0.34293    -0.01942     0.64008    -0.09217     0.17068    -0.23653    -0.14625    -0.23321     0.72701     1.00000
  0.06903    -0.38958    -0.25271     0.14828     0.17383     0.04051     0.37628     0.00159     0.04640     0.09889
  0.02727    -0.14208     0.24078     0.00651     0.23828     0.49520    -0.12114     0.34877    -0.00828     0.05937
 -0.33749

ROW 21
 -0.59031    -0.14508    -0.12180     0.52558    -0.15765     0.01388     0.18259     0.34585    -0.04733    -0.16281
 -0.34520    -0.26374     0.19881    -0.37179     0.43884     0.38830     0.39390     0.36715     0.09607     0.06903
  1.00000    -0.22911    -0.64018     0.00168     0.12292     0.12723    -0.26680     0.10989    -0.16703    -0.38843
 -0.34072    -0.10803    -0.17719    -0.40051    -0.19003     0.01976     0.09069     0.06337     0.26284     0.05095
  0.10608

ROW 22
  0.38073    -0.14284     0.15504     0.02739     0.00955    -0.18271     0.12820     0.28231     0.12006     0.00789
  0.19483    -0.22649    -0.28320     0.16199     0.01246     0.21320     0.23525     0.39443    -0.31441    -0.38958
 -0.22911     1.00000     0.37459     0.06709     0.01791     0.11496     0.06936     0.26723    -0.09004    -0.11909
  0.12691     0.44638    -0.04439     0.17146    -0.23730     0.05358     0.11154    -0.22758    -0.05670     0.27482
 -0.01476

ROW 23
  0.28923     0.09786    -0.08951    -0.54108    -0.26001    -0.46282    -0.21996    -0.38896     0.25578     0.14513
  0.41372     0.27539    -0.39258     0.31551    -0.46311    -0.26680    -0.34184    -0.24586    -0.57491    -0.25271
 -0.64018     0.37459     1.00000     0.10357    -0.18050    -0.17195    -0.12838    -0.03175    -0.23425     0.00891
  0.15144     0.16517    -0.03263     0.06893    -0.14958     0.10353     0.01395    -0.04920    -0.40274    -0.07391
  0.08815

ROW 24
  0.14150    -0.44273     0.53251     0.30585    -0.05907     0.10050     0.30468     0.22672     0.14331     0.09673
  0.04623    -0.08140     0.57682    -0.24407     0.15702     0.28244     0.20412     0.38814     0.03115     0.14828
  0.00168     0.06709     0.10357     1.00000     0.56822     0.18558     0.49027     0.59516     0.50333     0.07102
  0.18127     0.03146     0.11964    -0.04223     0.11092     0.28637     0.05316     0.56550    -0.01926     0.27053
 -0.23481

ROW 25
  0.19528    -0.46576     0.64775     0.38913     0.07866     0.23616     0.06985     0.30208     0.21164    -0.05329
 -0.02961    -0.35546     0.54214     0.04071     0.16243     0.08020    -0.04564     0.14319     0.07415     0.17383
  0.12292     0.01791    -0.18050     0.56822     1.00000     0.72929     0.59755     0.66287     0.34071     0.03639
  0.17543     0.23949     0.44666     0.16064     0.35607     0.48427     0.21506     0.49863     0.36209     0.47302
 -0.64751

ROW 26
 -0.23553    -0.26370     0.41004     0.50034    -0.19004    -0.06571    -0.12702     0.32071     0.22126    -0.36365
 -0.19763    -0.18114     0.37649     0.12490     0.24619     0.01675     0.04166     0.19493    -0.03846     0.04051
  0.12723     0.11496    -0.17195     0.18558     0.72929     1.00000     0.54679     0.35315     0.30493    -0.03957
  0.02257     0.31198     0.27627     0.45533    -0.12645     0.52855     0.58750     0.32623     0.58999     0.50281
 -0.53591

ROW 27
  0.55949    -0.34391     0.77682     0.40455     0.27190     0.31379     0.14950     0.04508    -0.00895    -0.21016
 -0.09403    -0.25899     0.71729     0.04692     0.29383     0.06145    -0.08887     0.05686     0.45764     0.37628
 -0.26680     0.06936    -0.12838     0.49027     0.59755     0.54679     1.00000     0.44752     0.50187     0.43017
  0.50095     0.39901     0.57626     0.62258     0.51922     0.48587    -0.00190     0.41277     0.28078     0.35794
 -0.52867
```

```
ROW 28
  0.12761   -0.72565    0.66598    0.32158    0.14564    0.37892    0.37847    0.47558    0.03371    0.16272
  0.10823   -0.36346    0.38930   -0.11876    0.31988    0.47646    0.06903    0.37797    0.05469    0.00159
  0.10989    0.26723   -0.03175    0.59516    0.66287    0.35315    0.44752    1.00000    0.16649   -0.01205
  0.23388    0.20311    0.37400   -0.07549    0.45031    0.29712   -0.03144    0.47554    0.34584    0.66033
 -0.24904

ROW 29
  0.13106    0.01166    0.21524    0.13486    0.09453    0.25224    0.02987    0.45091   -0.00278   -0.03658
  0.04816    0.15270    0.47672    0.03606   -0.01198    0.06067    0.18051    0.26483    0.13289    0.04640
 -0.16703   -0.09004   -0.23425    0.50333    0.34071    0.30493    0.50187    0.16649    1.00000    0.20118
  0.07518   -0.18681   -0.13454    0.25650   -0.03039   -0.01097    0.35922    0.27447    0.24470    0.38289
 -0.23700

ROW 30
  0.27410   -0.16123    0.14528   -0.19756    0.41861    0.24802    0.06643   -0.37340   -0.17273    0.22413
  0.39242   -0.17916    0.20088   -0.11339   -0.18242   -0.13217   -0.14764   -0.36275    0.24743    0.09889
 -0.38843   -0.11909    0.00891    0.07102    0.03639   -0.03957    0.43017   -0.01205    0.20118    1.00000
  0.64515    0.49598    0.47891    0.29749    0.47018    0.20725   -0.28625   -0.11453   -0.21160   -0.38228
 -0.01612

ROW 31
  0.23392   -0.26685    0.29403   -0.13643    0.50196    0.40925    0.34336   -0.21058   -0.15302    0.02026
  0.03165   -0.15949    0.20657   -0.24451    0.08199    0.08981   -0.04090   -0.00394    0.20260    0.02727
 -0.34072    0.12691    0.15144    0.18127    0.17543    0.02257    0.50095    0.23388    0.07518    0.64515
  1.00000    0.66200    0.61425    0.23168    0.59503    0.06680   -0.41014   -0.07423   -0.02046   -0.09618
  0.18228

ROW 32
  0.30387   -0.40715    0.34723    0.15478    0.31139   -0.04574    0.09932   -0.13388    0.06729   -0.10239
  0.07786   -0.24561    0.06439   -0.09463    0.15812    0.09186    0.05331    0.05772   -0.04267   -0.14208
 -0.10803    0.44638    0.16517    0.03146    0.23949    0.31198    0.39901    0.20311   -0.18681    0.49598
  0.66200    1.00000    0.60392    0.36719    0.28433    0.37409   -0.21818   -0.09878   -0.07645   -0.08473
 -0.02169

ROW 33
  0.28129   -0.60608    0.64747    0.07492    0.38232    0.42345    0.19113   -0.12156   -0.05998    0.03984
 -0.03111   -0.21306    0.31291    0.03643    0.07830   -0.09946   -0.29893   -0.26185    0.36705    0.24078
 -0.17719   -0.04439   -0.03263    0.11964    0.44666    0.27627    0.57626    0.37400   -0.13454    0.47891
  0.61425    0.60392    1.00000    0.39858    0.78183    0.28482   -0.28521    0.40379    0.14423    0.05802
 -0.30223

ROW 34
  0.62655   -0.03928    0.32302    0.00562    0.04662   -0.03987   -0.12535   -0.13489    0.27637   -0.31241
 -0.05829    0.01547    0.14079    0.24118    0.02969   -0.20663   -0.14500   -0.11176    0.04676    0.00651
 -0.40051    0.17146    0.06893   -0.04223    0.16064    0.45533    0.62258   -0.07549    0.25650    0.29749
  0.23168    0.36719    0.39858    1.00000    0.16077    0.14399    0.30972    0.07854    0.17588    0.13530
 -0.37536

ROW 35
  0.12973   -0.52217    0.60279    0.07807    0.50448    0.62794    0.35693   -0.12679   -0.34451    0.02354
 -0.09363   -0.36824    0.38107   -0.10189    0.22834    0.14449   -0.25481   -0.23053    0.49802    0.23828
 -0.19003   -0.23730   -0.14958    0.11092    0.35607    0.12645    0.51922    0.45031   -0.03039    0.47018
  0.59503    0.28433    0.78183    0.16077    1.00000    0.14319   -0.44053    0.34741    0.35496    0.09025
 -0.07774

ROW 36
  0.19515   -0.15105    0.47145    0.48530   -0.16840   -0.34803   -0.19325   -0.17284   -0.00514   -0.21190
  0.05814   -0.29385    0.57937    0.09060    0.25856   -0.00567   -0.13576   -0.12144    0.19924    0.49520
  0.01976    0.05358    0.10353    0.28637    0.48427    0.52855    0.48587    0.29712   -0.01097    0.20725
  0.06680    0.37409    0.28482    0.14399    0.14319    1.00000    0.05320    0.20864    0.12345    0.09819
 -0.48652

ROW 37
  0.09616    0.06374   -0.20364    0.04153   -0.66572   -0.36993   -0.28193    0.41821    0.43293   -0.31206
 -0.09096    0.20505   -0.06981    0.13847   -0.16251   -0.14125    0.22964    0.23924   -0.39593   -0.12114
  0.09069    0.11154    0.01395    0.05316    0.21506    0.58750   -0.00190   -0.03144    0.35922   -0.28625
 -0.41014   -0.21818   -0.28521    0.30972   -0.44053    0.05320    1.00000    0.15508    0.31315    0.41863
 -0.24033

ROW 38
  0.17506   -0.62339    0.58754    0.36382   -0.13007    0.18959    0.11409    0.35247   -0.06666   -0.03709
 -0.14912    0.18615    0.49722    0.06522    0.05037   -0.07136   -0.18817    0.03733    0.28773    0.34877
  0.06337   -0.22758   -0.04920    0.56550    0.49863    0.32623    0.41277    0.47554   -0.27447   -0.11453
 -0.07423   -0.09878    0.40379    0.07854    0.34741    0.20864    0.15508    1.00000    0.26324    0.49842
 -0.37674

ROW 39
 -0.18225   -0.15141    0.30603    0.42122   -0.07677    0.36166    0.39618    0.49436   -0.36580   -0.34022
 -0.33237   -0.21789    0.32877   -0.07417    0.51458    0.30298    0.08060    0.29951    0.26635   -0.00828
  0.26284   -0.05670   -0.40274   -0.01926    0.36209    0.58999    0.28078    0.34584    0.24470   -0.21160
 -0.02046   -0.07645    0.14423    0.17588    0.35496    0.12345    0.31315    0.26324    1.00000    0.49534
 -0.00828

ROW 40
  0.24100   -0.39347    0.42250    0.29137   -0.12740    0.17121    0.04388    0.74415    0.11029   -0.21726
 -0.13224    0.02918    0.25189    0.19425    0.18758    0.20434    0.05897    0.40312    0.01620    0.05937
  0.05095    0.27482   -0.07391    0.27053    0.47302    0.50281    0.35794    0.66033    0.38289   -0.38228
 -0.09618   -0.08473    0.05802    0.13530    0.09025    0.09819    0.41863    0.49842    0.49534    1.00000
 -0.31631

ROW 41
 -0.44972    0.10931   -0.48082   -0.22103   -0.05989   -0.01788    0.41965   -0.02828   -0.28911   -0.10611
 -0.18441    0.22852   -0.39020   -0.58236    0.19224    0.31673    0.38043    0.30422   -0.14075   -0.33749
  0.10608   -0.01476    0.08815   -0.23481   -0.64751   -0.53591   -0.52867   -0.24904   -0.23700   -0.01612
  0.18228   -0.02169   -0.30223   -0.37536   -0.07774   -0.48652   -0.24033   -0.37674   -0.00828   -0.31631
  1.00000
```

288

TABLE A–4: Correlation Matrix for Social, Political, and Economic Indicators ("High" Sample)

CORRELATION COEFFICIENTS

```
ROW  1
 1.00000   -0.14879    0.25588    0.29653    0.19926    0.24208   -0.05308    0.12787   -0.04403   -0.05224
-0.30224   -0.05422    0.47415   -0.22714    0.20730    0.16070    0.32220    0.02274    0.41157    0.58659
 0.13918   -0.28948   -0.27250    0.48570    0.35929    0.35373    0.61113    0.42590    0.60237    0.42605
 0.59428    0.81585    0.77881    0.31408    0.09736    0.21320   -0.07354    0.50869    0.11111    0.29377
-0.09835

ROW  2
-0.14879    1.00000   -0.74221   -0.74120   -0.62769   -0.54808   -0.50078   -0.55422    0.07953   -0.20802
-0.01969    0.69754   -0.52961    0.70030   -0.82468   -0.61735   -0.16858   -0.16610   -0.39621   -0.31882
-0.80039    0.41120    0.56811   -0.26564   -0.77771   -0.52347   -0.55253   -0.82510   -0.46573    0.10313
 0.18648    0.06807    0.05356    0.21657   -0.40064   -0.02781    0.04930   -0.53142   -0.24425   -0.80783
-0.53397

ROW  3
 0.25588   -0.74221    1.00000    0.67169    0.70417    0.65244    0.52779    0.48536   -0.07564    0.22794
 0.21790   -0.81044    0.53404   -0.49231    0.62240    0.36474    0.14344    0.02137    0.39165    0.25656
 0.50186   -0.46837   -0.53265    0.39435    0.73717    0.53461    0.47447    0.82244    0.34215    0.11910
-0.05924    0.07840    0.00328    0.C1927    0.47563    0.32000   -0.32287    0.56352    0.31170    0.56889
 0.15676

ROW  4
 0.29653   -0.74120    0.67169    1.00000   ,0.69257    0.66371    0.20554    0.25407   -0.36005    0.51303
 0.15031   -0.50925    0.70294   -0.58130    0.61633    0.31462    0.29493    0.01762    0.51833    0.57578
 0.64951   -0.67311   -0.48877    0.33483    0.76724    0.65007    0.66331    0.79401    0.47585    0.11077
 0.12516    0.05518    0.14439    0.08397    0.37564    0.25479    0.11321    0.70514    0.45315    0.58666
 0.33840

ROW  5
 0.1992C   -0.62769    0.70417    0.69257    1.00000    0.66557    0.44890    0.60853   -0.09440    0.52989
 0.08545   -0.58913    0.58528   -0.51736    0.53368    0.34938    0.31458    0.00721    0.40593    0.48771
 0.58504   -0.47476   -0.42639    0.49867    0.74492    0.62573    0.64300    0.76750    0.42812    0.19628
-0.02881    0.12244    0.13978    0.10418    0.54223    0.43217    0.02322    0.62921    0.63908    0.65299
 0.09839

ROW  6
 0.24208   -0.54808    0.65244    0.66371    0.66557    1.00000    0.56575    0.46320   -0.21324    0.48281
 0.15692   -0.51961    0.65970   -0.62340    0.66137    0.48180    0.60976    0.31783    0.29475    0.38212
 0.58626   -0.60542   -0.52861    0.48054    0.60023    0.78203    0.67946    0.63314    0.5301C    0.19206
 0.19137    0.16965    0.17215    0.24085    0.52575    0.17678    0.07912    0.65600    0.43830    0.49898
 0.19389

ROW  7
-0.05308   -0.50078    0.52779    0.20554    0.44890    0.56575    1.00000    0.67561   -0.18052    0.13112
 0.16222   -0.58913    0.31268   -0.45889    0.57599    0.56591    0.44488    0.29121    0.27873    0.05622
 0.46690    0.00945   -0.55326    0.40902    0.29820    0.49886    0.27440    0.32370    0.33638   -0.20538
-0.12302   -0.10664   -0.05786    0.02801    0.56236    0.00098    0.00133    0.34412    0.19400    0.52951
 0.35705

ROW  8
 0.12787   -0.55422    0.48536    0.25407    0.60853    0.46320    0.67561    1.00000    0.20476    0.06918
-0.07140   -0.64499    0.39481   -0.64615    0.62963    0.73240    0.40555    0.36988    0.19118    0.09336
 0.55477   -0.04213   -0.62402    0.46098    0.57758    0.50393    0.44738    0.48883    0.38751    0.02821
-0.14075    0.07207    0.07544   -0.10597    0.63718    0.13430    0.11882    0.28125    0.35388    0.68229
 0.22543

ROW  9
-0.04403    0.07953   -0.07564   -0.36005   -0.09440   -0.21324   -0.18052    0.20476    1.00000   -0.45710
-0.41591    0.06415   -0.37245   -0.04499   -0.14001    0.19583   -0.11437    0.33923   -0.55315   -0.30617
-0.13959    0.26476    0.09515    0.04601    0.03672   -0.15613   -0.20260    0.02530   -0.01155    0.17834
-0.29556    0.15747   -0.18256    0.00143   -0.06892   -0.14221    0.10218   -0.42810   -0.16423    0.08979
-0.07937

ROW 10
-0.05224   -0.20802    0.22794    0.51303    0.52989    0.48281    0.13112    0.06918   -0.45710    1.00000
 0.50693   -0.15233    0.68294   -0.13555    0.26707   -0.03775    0.44071   -0.14047    0.46596    0.42373
 0.32086   -0.43224   -0.21209    0.16277    0.38112    0.41063    0.33093    0.29140    0.10163    0.02279
 0.15382   -0.08437    0.17440    0.16040    0.42007    0.08920    0.17394    0.41738    0.63554    0.14718
-0.06572

ROW 11
-0.30224   -0.01969    0.21790    0.15031    0.08545    0.15692    0.16222   -0.07140   -0.41591    0.50693
 1.00000   -0.11589    0.13100    0.22850   -0.03678   -0.27450   -0.00309   -0.23422    0.16191   -0.28715
-0.18040   -0.08777    0.08188   -0.15457   -0.02402   -0.09545   -0.21416   -0.10188   -0.31045   -0.28111
 0.11015   -0.25913   -0.10933    0.13893    0.29936    0.03677   -0.16321    0.03657    0.20259   -0.23457
-0.21621

ROW 12
-0.05422    0.69754   -0.81044   -0.50925   -0.62080   -0.51961   -0.58913   -0.64499    0.06415   -0.15233
-0.11589    1.00000   -0.40105    0.54613   -0.62952   -0.47628   -0.12330   -0.02380   -0.26107   -0.20404
-0.49908    0.25750    0.46075   -0.34069   -0.55924   -0.45087   -0.41241   -0.68275   -0.22808   -b.04475
 0.10659    0.04030    0.15961    0.03004   -0.53574   -0.31332    0.12065   -0.31561   -0.37821   -0.57339
-0.30045

ROW 13
 0.47415   -0.52961    0.53404    0.70294    0.58528    0.65970    0.31268    0.39481   -0.37245    0.68294
 0.13100   -0.40105    1.00000   -0.50353    0.62822    0.36861    0.56441    0.09184    0.70729    0.67570
 0.60911   -0.54506   -0.64277    0.43826    0.70790    0.67573    0.69140    0.65073    0.56953    0.20931
 0.31480    0.23856    0.40178    0.06963    0.53923    0.07460    0.05887    0.68957    0.53693    0.53948
 0.08797

ROW 14
-0.22714    0.70030   -0.49231   -0.58130   -0.51736   -0.62340   -0.45889   -0.64615   -0.04499   -0.13555
 0.22850    0.54613   -0.50353    1.00000   -0.84957   -0.84845   -0.52297   -0.45294   -0.23356   -0.36915
-0.81826    0.19053    0.67318   -0.45157   -0.64025   -0.58997   -0.70435   -0.62173   -0.53904   -0.01832
 0.06310    0.06776   -0.10052    0.06594   -0.22150    0.07400   -0.35539   -0.45500   -0.35774   -0.71688
-0.65636

ROW 15
 0.20730   -0.82468    0.62240    0.61633    0.53368    0.66137    0.57599    0.62963   -0.14001    0.26707
-0.03678   -0.62952    0.62822   -0.84957    1.00000    0.80234    0.48130    0.30862    0.40006    0.32719
 0.81908   -0.34622   -0.76171    0.32169    0.71177    0.53399    0.64801    0.69682    0.48252    0.03474
-0.15204   -0.04081    0.09382   -0.28720    0.29647    0.01850    0.05110    0.62455    0.36308    0.73954
 0.63428
```

ROW 16
```
  0.16070    -0.61735     0.36474     0.31462     0.34938     0.48180     0.56591     0.73240     0.19583    -0.03775
 -0.27450    -0.47628     0.36861    -0.84845     0.80234     1.00000     0.49736     0.57893     0.05348     0.17353
  0.66613    -0.03165    -0.69730     0.47234     0.54884     0.48270     0.54240     0.50777     0.51457     0.04879
 -0.11811     0.01492    -0.00991    -0.21612     0.29605    -0.21839     0.32442     0.29621     0.19725     0.70366
  0.60411
```

ROW 17
```
  0.32220    -0.16858     0.14344     0.29493     0.31458     0.60976     0.44488     0.40555    -0.11437     0.44071
 -0.00309    -0.12330     0.56441    -0.52297     0.48130     0.49736     1.00000     0.51453     0.31762     0.33593
  0.45262    -0.09405    -0.04495     0.45528     0.36077     0.64070     0.58210     0.29453     0.46063     0.10167
  0.34900     0.19955     0.48042     0.29204     0.35417     0.00007     0.48212     0.49046     0.43745     0.31219
  0.26327
```

ROW 18
```
  0.02274    -0.16610     0.02137     0.01762     0.00721     0.31783     0.29121     0.36988     0.33923    -0.14047
 -0.23422    -0.02380     0.09184    -0.45294     0.30862     0.57893     0.51453     1.00000    -0.27817    -0.08760
  0.25484     0.11960    -0.19295     0.32475     0.15960     0.22384     0.21352     0.09342     0.25341     0.24369
  0.02345    -0.03223     0.05819     0.06427     0.25046    -0.19808     0.32580     0.09546     0.07091     0.28385
  0.20001
```

ROW 19
```
  0.41157    -0.39621     0.39165     0.51833     0.40593     0.29475     0.27873     0.19118    -0.55315     0.46596
  0.16191    -0.26107     0.70729    -0.23356     0.40006     0.05348     0.31762    -0.27817     1.00000     0.50355
  0.43922    -0.17030    -0.38920     0.10379     0.39689     0.44848     0.43017     0.45385     0.37432    -0.17358
  0.25249     0.07316     0.44820     0.00553     0.22996     0.23545    -0.05242     0.65550     0.29944     0.25345
  0.10226
```

ROW 20
```
  0.58659    -0.31882     0.25656     0.57578     0.48771     0.38212     0.05622     0.09336    -0.30617     0.42373
 -0.28715    -0.20404     0.67570    -0.36915     0.32719     0.17353     0.33593    -0.08760     0.50355     1.00000
  0.47175    -0.50701    -0.34430     0.63829     0.44097     0.52614     0.69506     0.48781     0.61031     0.45540
  0.40344     0.36930     0.40345     0.22013     0.23698     0.18134     0.24311     0.51151     0.50415     0.45971
  0.09925
```

ROW 21
```
  0.13918    -0.80039     0.50186     0.64951     0.58504     0.58626     0.46690     0.55477    -0.13959     0.32086
 -0.18040    -0.49908     0.60911    -0.81826     0.81908     0.66613     0.45262     0.25484     0.43922     0.47175
  1.00000    -0.37420    -0.60146     0.33415     0.70263     0.66179     0.66807     0.66131     0.48487    -0.09168
 -0.18536    -0.14178     0.06866    -0.13140     0.25892    -0.07204     0.25151     0.54712     0.29149     0.74845
  0.59732
```

ROW 22
```
 -0.28948     0.41120    -0.46837    -0.67311    -0.47476    -0.60542     0.00945    -0.04213     0.26476    -0.43224
 -0.08777     0.25750    -0.54506     0.19053    -0.34622    -0.03165    -0.09405     0.11960    -0.17030    -0.50701
 -0.37420     1.00000     0.33818    -0.27587    -0.60294    -0.49973    -0.46778    -0.51014    -0.31367    -0.43058
 -0.10375    -0.30744    -0.11680    -0.02123    -0.32265    -0.26012     0.14105    -0.53976    -0.20620    -0.31493
  0.04676
```

ROW 23
```
 -0.27250     0.56811    -0.53265    -0.48877    -0.42639    -0.52861    -0.55326    -0.62402     0.09515    -0.22199
  0.08188     0.46075    -0.64277     0.67318    -0.76171    -0.69730    -0.40499    -0.19295    -0.38920    -0.34430
 -0.60146     0.33818     1.00000    -0.44680    -0.66061    -0.59663    -0.44387    -0.51276    -0.44817    -0.06007
  0.17748    -0.07960    -0.12903     0.22249    -0.43257     0.07203    -0.04634    -0.46175    -0.19902    -0.64401
 -0.40525
```

ROW 24
```
  0.48570    -0.26564     0.39435     0.33483     0.49867     0.48054     0.40902     0.46098     0.04601     0.16277
 -0.15457    -0.34069     0.43826    -0.45157     0.32169     0.47234     0.45528     0.32475     0.10375     0.63829
  0.33415    -0.27587    -0.44680     1.00000     0.42385     0.55473     0.61458     0.40823     0.58233     0.54373
  0.34966     0.35127     0.30239     0.32239     0.54159     0.14648     0.23307     0.28035     0.50836     0.49279
 -0.05130
```

ROW 25
```
  0.35929    -0.77771     0.73717     0.76724     0.74492     0.60023     0.29820     0.57758     0.03672     0.38112
 -0.02402    -0.55924     0.70790    -0.64025     0.71177     0.54884     0.36077     0.15960     0.39689     0.44097
  0.70263    -0.60294    -0.66061     0.42385     1.00000     0.65382     0.68833     0.87438     0.53487     0.18853
 -0.06585     0.16420     0.20106    -0.16486     0.46642     0.14451     0.01302     0.66014     0.36137     0.71044
  0.25904
```

ROW 26
```
  0.35373    -0.52347     0.53461     0.65007     0.62573     0.78203     0.49884     0.50393    -0.15613     0.41063
 -0.09545    -0.45087     0.67573    -0.58997     0.53399     0.48270     0.64070     0.22384     0.44848     0.52614
  0.68179    -0.49973    -0.59663     0.54473     0.65382     1.00000     0.64074     0.67104     0.55728     0.07225
  0.26247     0.24773     0.22580     0.22119     0.58440     0.20056     0.32183     0.54488     0.30741     0.49835
  0.21045
```

ROW 27
```
  0.61113    -0.55253     0.47447     0.66331     0.64300     0.67946     0.27440     0.44738    -0.20260     0.33093
 -0.21416    -0.41241     0.69140    -0.70435     0.64801     0.54240     0.58210     0.21352     0.43017     0.69506
  0.66807    -0.46778    -0.44387     0.61458     0.68833     0.64074     1.00000     0.71384     0.78825     0.29500
  0.36086     0.32818     0.53117     0.13228     0.30146     0.15510     0.13547     0.70753     0.54062     0.61967
  0.23558
```

ROW 28
```
  0.42590    -0.82510     0.82244     0.79401     0.76750     0.63314     0.32370     0.48883     0.02530     0.29140
 -0.10188    -0.68275     0.65073    -0.62173     0.69682     0.50777     0.29453     0.09342     0.45385     0.48781
  0.66131    -0.51014    -0.51276     0.40823     0.87438     0.67104     0.71384     1.00000     0.58728     0.18017
  0.07011     0.25084     0.15122    -0.03906     0.41133     0.29856    -0.07089     0.64739     0.41568     0.70911
  0.27865
```

ROW 29
```
  0.60237    -0.46573     0.34219     0.47589     0.42812     0.53010     0.33638     0.38751    -0.01155     0.10163
 -0.31045    -0.22808     0.56953    -0.53904     0.48252     0.51457     0.46063     0.25341     0.37432     0.61031
  0.48487    -0.31367    -0.44817     0.58233     0.53487     0.55728     0.78825     0.58728     1.00000     0.17684
  0.36094     0.43203     0.45289     0.15570     0.34803    -0.06216     0.10806     0.54270     0.30375     0.59530
  0.19089
```

ROW 30
```
  0.42605     0.10313     0.11910     0.11077     0.19628     0.19206    -0.20538     0.02821     0.17834     0.02279
 -0.28111    -0.04475     0.20931    -0.01832     0.03474     0.04879     0.10167     0.24369    -0.17358     0.45540
 -0.09168    -0.43058    -0.06007     0.54373     0.18853     0.07225     0.29500     0.18017     0.17684     1.00000
  0.27648     0.46665     0.20819     0.07635     0.14890     0.43804    -0.03286     0.20590     0.37417     0.08294
 -0.34051
```

ROW 31
```
  0.59428     0.18648    -0.05924     0.12516    -0.02881     0.19137    -0.12302    -0.14075    -0.29556     0.15382
  0.11015     0.10659     0.31480     0.06310    -0.15204    -0.11811     0.34900     0.02345     0.25249     0.40344
 -0.18536    -0.10375     0.17748     0.34966    -0.06585     0.26247     0.36086     0.07011     0.36094     0.27648
  1.00000     0.52556     0.46884     0.41922     0.20536     0.20873     0.17165     0.15360     0.26577    -0.18156
 -0.33283
```

ROW 32
```
  0.81585     0.06807     0.07840     0.05518     0.12244     0.16965    -0.10664     0.07207     0.15747    -0.08437
 -0.25913     0.04030     0.23856     0.06776    -0.04081     0.01492     0.19955    -0.03223     0.07316     0.36930
 -0.14178    -0.30744    -0.07660     0.35127     0.16420     0.24773     0.32818     0.25084     0.43203     0.46665
  0.52556     1.00000     0.59044     0.42853     0.16293     0.23045    -0.07159     0.27467    -0.01594     0.16343
 -0.25171
```

```
ROW 33
  0.77881    0.05356    0.00328    0.14439    0.13978    0.17215   -0.05786    0.07544   -0.18256    0.17440
 -0.10933    0.15961    0.40178   -0.10052    0.09382   -0.00991    0.48042    0.05819    0.44820    0.40345
  0.06866   -0.11680   -0.12903    0.30239    0.20106    0.22580    0.53117    0.15122    0.45289    0.20819
  0.46884    0.59044    1.00000    0.37416    0.08875    0.15901   -0.03879    0.51812    0.17433    0.07416
 -0.19316

ROW 34
  0.31408    0.21657    0.01927    0.08397    0.10418    0.24085    0.02801   -0.10597    0.00143    0.16040
  0.13893    0.03004    0.06963    0.06594   -0.28720   -0.21612    0.29204    0.06427    0.00553    0.22013
 -0.13140   -0.02123    0.22249    0.32239   -0.16486    0.22119    0.13228   -0.03906    0.15570    0.07635
  0.41922    0.42853    0.37416    1.00000    0.18911    0.01421    0.26344    0.03756    0.10465   -0.01769
 -0.20236

ROW 35
  0.09736   -0.40064    0.47563    0.37564    0.54223    0.52575    0.56236    0.63718   -0.06892    0.42007
  0.29936   -0.53574    0.53923   -0.22150    0.29647    0.29605    0.35417    0.25046    0.22996    0.23698
  0.25892   -0.32265   -0.43257    0.54159    0.46642    0.58440    0.30146    0.41133    0.34803    0.14890
  0.20536    0.16293    0.08875    0.18911    1.00000    0.19873    0.01676    0.20288    0.45670    0.42738
 -0.22000

ROW 36
  0.21320   -0.02781    0.32000    0.25479    0.43217    0.17678    0.00098    0.13430   -0.14221    0.08920
  0.03677   -0.31332    0.07460    0.07400    0.01850   -0.21839    0.00007   -0.19808    0.23545    0.18134
 -0.07204   -0.26012    0.07203    0.14648    0.14451    0.20056    0.15510    0.29856   -0.06216    0.43804
  0.20873    0.23045    0.15901    0.01421    0.19873    1.00000   -0.18589    0.33674    0.40804   -0.09088
 -0.27383

ROW 37
 -0.07354    0.04930   -0.32287    0.11321    0.02322    0.07912    0.00133    0.11882    0.10218    0.17394
 -0.16321    0.12065    0.05887   -0.35539    0.05110    0.32442    0.48212    0.32580   -0.05242    0.24311
  0.25151    0.14105   -0.04634    0.23307    0.01302    0.32183    0.13547   -0.07089    0.10806   -0.03286
  0.17165   -0.07159   -0.03879    0.26344    0.01676   -0.18589    1.00000   -0.06052    0.13863    0.07118
  0.40166

ROW 38
  0.50869   -0.53142    0.56352    0.70514    0.62921    0.65600    0.34412    0.28125   -0.42810    0.41738
  0.03657   -0.31561    0.68957   -0.45500    0.62455    0.29621    0.49046    0.09546    0.65550    0.51151
  0.54712   -0.53976   -0.46175    0.28035    0.66014    0.54488    0.70753    0.64735    0.54270    0.20590
  0.15360    0.27467    0.51812    0.03756    0.20288    0.33674   -0.06052    1.00000    0.31228    0.45891
  0.26186

ROW 39
  0.11111   -0.24425    0.31170    0.45315    0.63908    0.43830    0.19400    0.35388   -0.16423    0.63554
  0.20259   -0.37821    0.53693   -0.35774    0.36308    0.19725    0.43745    0.07091    0.29944    0.50415
  0.29149   -0.20620   -0.19902    0.50836    0.36137    0.30741    0.54062    0.41568    0.30375    0.37417
  0.26577   -0.01594    0.17433    0.10465    0.45670    0.40804    0.13863    0.31228    1.00000    0.34090
 -0.07774

ROW 40
  0.29377   -0.80783    0.56889    0.58666    0.65299    0.49898    0.52951    0.68229    0.08979    0.14718
 -0.23457   -0.57339    0.53948   -0.71688    0.73954    0.70366    0.31219    0.28385    0.25345    0.45971
  0.74845   -0.31493   -0.64401    0.49279    0.71044    0.49835    0.61967    0.70911    0.59530    0.08294
 -0.18156    0.16343    0.07416   -0.01769    0.42738   -0.09088    0.07118    0.45891    0.34090    1.00000
  0.50306

ROW 41
 -0.09835   -0.53397    0.15676    0.33840    0.09839    0.19389    0.35705    0.22543   -0.07937   -0.06572
 -0.21621   -0.30045    0.08797   -0.65636    0.63428    0.60411    0.26327    0.20001    0.10226    0.09925
  0.59732    0.04676   -0.40525   -0.05130    0.25904    0.21045    0.23558    0.27865    0.19089   -0.34051
 -0.33283   -0.25171   -0.19316   -0.20236   -0.22000   -0.27383    0.40166    0.26186   -0.07774    0.50306
  1.00000
```

SELECTED BIBLIOGRAPHY

The following bibliography contains books and articles of general interest which the authors have found particularly useful in studying the process of economic development. For specialized treatment of particular aspects of development, see the footnote references on social, political, and economic indicators in Chapter II.

General

Asher, R. E., *et al*. *Development of the Emerging Countries: An Agenda for Research*. Washington, D.C.: The Brookings Institution, 1962.

Geertz, Clifford (ed.). *Old Societies and New States*. New York: The Free Press of Glencoe, 1963.

Gerschenkron, Alexander. *Economic Backwardness in Historical Perspective: A Book of Essays*. Cambridge, Mass.: The Belknap Press, 1962.

Ginsburg, Norton (ed.). *Essays on Geography and Economic Development*. Chicago: The University of Chicago Press, 1960.

Halpern, Manfred. *The Politics of Social Change in the Middle East and North Africa*. Princeton: Princeton University Press, 1963.

Hoselitz, B. F. (ed.). *The Progress of Underdeveloped Areas*. Chicago: The University of Chicago Press, 1952.

Kerr, Clark, Dunlop, J. T., Harbison, F. H., and Myers, C. A. *Industrialism and Industrial Man*. Cambridge, Mass.: Harvard University Press, 1960.

Lerner, Daniel, with Pevsner, L. W. *The Passing of Traditional Society*. Glencoe, Ill.: The Free Press, 1958.

Mair, Lucy. *New Nations*. Chicago: The University of Chicago Press, 1963.

Millikan, Max F., and Blackmer, Donald L. M. (eds.). *The Emerging Nations*. Boston: Little, Brown and Co., 1961.

Novack, David E., and Lekachman, Robert (eds.). *Development and Society*. New York: St. Martin's Press, 1964.

Polanyi, Karl. *The Great Transformation*. Boston: Beacon Press, 1957.

Russett, Bruce M., *et al*. *World Handbook of Political and Social Indicators*. New Haven, Conn.: Yale University Press, 1964.

Economic Influences

Agarwala, A. N., and Singh, S. P. (eds.). *The Economics of Underdevelopment*. New York: Oxford University Press, 1958.
Chenery, H. B. "Patterns of Industrial Growth," *American Economic Review,* Vol. 50 (September, 1960), pp. 624–54.
Ellis, Howard S. (ed.), with Wallich, Henry C. *Economic Development of Latin America*. New York: St. Martin's Press, 1963.
Fei, John C. H., and Ranis, Gustav. *Development of the Labor Surplus Economy*. Homewood, Ill.: Richard D. Irwin, 1964.
Higgins, Benjamin. *Economic Development*. New York: W. W. Norton & Co., 1959.
Hirschman, A. O. *The Strategy of Economic Development*. New Haven, Conn.: Yale University Press, 1958.
Kuznets, Simon. "Quantitative Aspects of the Economic Growth of Nations: I. Levels and Variability of Rates of Growth," *Economic Development and Cultural Change,* Vol. 5 (October, 1956), pp. 5–94.
Leibenstein, Harvey. *Economic Backwardness and Economic Growth*. New York: John Wiley & Sons, 1957.
Lewis, W. Arthur. "Economic Development with Unlimited Supplies of Labor," *Manchester School of Economic and Social Studies,* Vol. 22 (May, 1954), pp. 139–191.
―――. *The Theory of Economic Growth*. Homewood, Ill.: Richard D. Irwin, 1955.
―――. "Unlimited Labour: Further Notes," *Manchester School of Economic and Social Studies,* Vol. 26 (January, 1958), pp. 1–32.
Meier, G. M. *Leading Issues in Development Economics*. New York: Oxford University Press, 1964.
Myint, Hla. *The Economics of the Developing Countries*. New York: Praeger, 1965.
Myrdal, Gunnar. *Economic Theory and the Under-developed Regions*. London: Gerald Duckworth, 1957.
Nurkse, Ragnar. *Problems of Capital Formation in Underdeveloped Countries*. New York: Oxford University Press, 1953.
Ranis, Gustav, and Fei, J. C. H. "A Theory of Economic Development," *American Economic Review,* Vol. 51 (September, 1961), pp. 533–65.
Rosenstein-Rodan, P. N. "International Aid for Underdeveloped Coun-

tries," *Review of Economics and Statistics,* Vol. 43 (May, 1961), pp. 107–38.

Rostow, W. W. *The Process of Economic Growth.* 2nd ed. New York: W. W. Norton & Co., 1962.

————. *The Stages of Economic Growth.* New York: Cambridge University Press, 1962.

————. "The Take-Off into Self-Sustained Growth," *Economic Journal,* Vol. 66 (March, 1956), pp. 25–48.

Schumpeter, Joseph A. *The Theory of Economic Development.* Cambridge, Mass.: Harvard University Press, 1934.

Smith, Adam. *An Enquiry into the Causes of the Wealth of Nations.* New York: Random House, 1927.

Social and Cultural Influences

Braibanti, Ralph, and Spengler, Joseph J. (eds.). *Tradition, Values, and Socio-Economic Development.* Durham, N.C.: Duke University Press, 1961.

De Vries, Egbert, and Echavarría, J. M. (eds.). *Social Aspects of Economic Development in Latin America.* 2 vols. Paris: UNESCO, 1963.

Durkheim, Emil. *The Division of Labor in Society.* Glencoe, Ill.: The Free Press, 1949.

Firth, Raymond, and Yamey, B. S. (eds.). *Capital, Saving and Credit in Peasant Societies.* Chicago: Aldine Publishing Co., 1964.

Galenson, Walter, and Pyatt, Graham. *The Quality of Labour and Economic Development in Certain Countries.* Geneva: International Labour Office, 1964.

Hagen, Everett. *On a Theory of Social Change.* Homewood, Ill.: The Dorsey Press, 1962.

Harbison, Frederick, and Myers, C. A. *Education, Manpower and Economic Growth.* New York: McGraw-Hill, 1964.

Hoselitz, B. F. "Non-Economic Barriers to Economic Development," *Economic Development and Cultural Change,* Vol. 1, No. 1 (1952), pp. 8–21.

————. *Sociological Aspects of Economic Growth.* Glencoe, Ill.: The Free Press, 1960.

Hoselitz, B. F., and Moore, W. E. (eds.). *Industrialization and Society.* Paris: UNESCO-Mouton, 1963.

Lerner, Daniel. "Communication Systems and Social Systems: A Statistical Exploration," *Behavioral Science,* II (October, 1957), 266–75.

McClelland, David C. *The Achieving Society.* Princeton: D. Van Nostrand, 1961.

Moore, Wilbert E. *Industrialization and Labor: Social Aspects of Economic Development.* Ithaca, N.Y.: Cornell University Press, 1951.

——. *Social Change.* Englewood Cliffs, N.J.: Prentice-Hall, 1963.

Moore, Wilbert E., and Feldman, Arnold S. (eds.). *Labor Commitment and Social Change in Developing Areas.* New York: Social Science Research Council, 1960.

Parsons, Talcott. *The Social System.* Glencoe, Ill.: The Free Press, 1951.

Parsons, Talcott, and Smelser, Neil J. *Economy and Society.* New York: The Free Press of Glencoe, 1965.

Redfield, Robert. *Peasant Society and Culture.* Chicago: The University of Chicago Press, 1956.

Schramm, Wilbur. *Mass Media and National Development.* Stanford, Calif.: Stanford University Press, 1964.

Smelser, Neil J. *Social Change in the Industrial Revolution.* Chicago: The University of Chicago Press, 1959.

——. *The Sociology of Economic Life.* Englewood Cliffs, N.J.: Prentice-Hall, 1963.

Southall, Aidan (ed.). *Social Change in Modern Africa.* London: Oxford University Press, 1961.

Spengler, Joseph J. "Sociological Value Theory, Economic Analyses, and Economic Policy," *American Economic Review: Papers and Proceedings,* Vol. 43 (May, 1953), pp. 340–49.

United Nations. *Report on the World Social Situation, with Reference to the Problem of Balanced Social and Economic Development.* New York, 1961.

UNESCO. *Social Implications of Industrialization and Urbanization in Africa South of the Sahara.* Paris, 1956.

Weber, Max. *The Theory of Social and Economic Organization.* Translated by A. M. Henderson and Talcott Parsons. Glencoe, Ill.: The Free Press, 1957.

Wolf, Charles. "Institutions and Economic Development," *American Economic Review,* Vol. 45 (December, 1955), pp. 867–83.

Political Influences

Almond, G. A., and Coleman, J. S. (eds.). *The Politics of the Developing Areas.* Princeton: Princeton University Press, 1960.

Apter, D. E. *The Politics of Modernization.* Chicago: The University of Chicago Press, 1965.

Banks, Arthur, and Textor, Robert. *A Cross-Polity Survey.* Cambridge, Mass.: M.I.T. Press, 1964.

Baran, P. A. *The Political Economy of Growth.* New York: Monthly Review Press, 1957.

Coleman, J. S. (ed.). *Education and Political Development.* Princeton: Princeton University Press, 1965.

De Schweinitz, Karl, Jr. *Industrialization and Democracy.* New York: The Free Press of Glencoe, 1964.

Deutsch, K. W. *Nationalism and Social Communication.* New York: John Wiley & Sons, 1953.

La Palombara, Joseph G. (ed.). *Bureaucracy and Political Development.* Princeton: Princeton University Press, 1963.

Lieuwen, Edwin. *Arms and Politics in Latin America.* Revised edition. New York: Praeger, 1961.

Lipset, S. M. "Some Social Requisites of Democracy: Economic Development and Political Legitimacy," *American Political Science Review,* Vol. 53 (March, 1959), pp. 69–105.

Organski, A. F. K. *The Stages of Political Development.* New York: Alfred A. Knopf, 1965.

Pennock, J. Roland (ed.). *Self-Government in Modernizing Nations.* Englewood Cliffs, N.J.: Prentice-Hall, 1964.

Pye, L. W. (ed.). *Communications and Political Development.* Princeton: Princeton University Press, 1963.

Shils, E. A. *Political Development in the New States.* The Hague: Mouton, 1962.

Staley, Eugene. *The Future of Underdeveloped Countries.* New York: Harper & Brothers, for the Council on Foreign Relations, 1961.

AUTHOR INDEX

SUBJECT INDEX

301

Designed by Gerard A. Valerio

Composed in Times Roman by Monotype Composition Co.

Printed offset by Universal Lithographers, Inc.,
on 60 lb. Perkins and Squier R

Bound by Maple Press Co. in G.S.B. s/535 #10 maroon